Gendering Party Politics

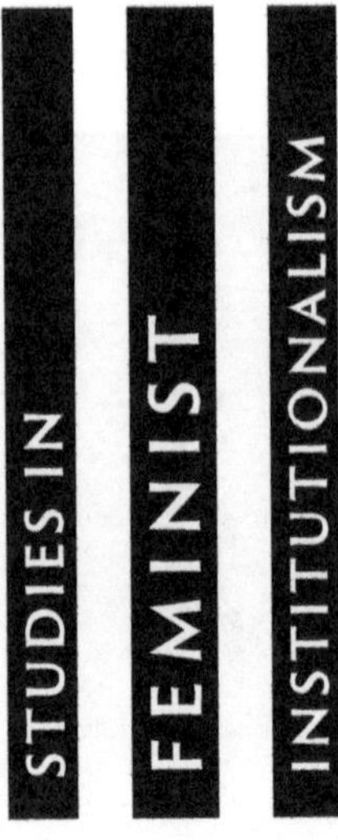

Series Editors

Between Rights and Rightfulness: Regulating Gender and Violence in the Pacific Islands
Nicole George

Defending the Status Quo: On Adaptive Resistance to Electoral Gender Quotas
Cecilia Josefsson

Gendering Party Politics: Feminist Institutionalist Perspectives
Edited by Meryl Kenny and Elin Bjarnegård

The Face of the Nation: Gendered Institutions in International Affairs
Elise Stephenson

Gendering Party Politics

Feminist Institutionalist Perspectives

Edited by

MERYL KENNY
AND
ELIN BJARNEGÅRD

OXFORD
UNIVERSITY PRESS

Oxford University Press is a department of the University of Oxford.
It furthers the University's objective of excellence in research, scholarship,
and education by publishing worldwide. Oxford is a registered trade mark of
Oxford University Press in the UK and in certain other countries.

Published in the United States of America by Oxford University Press
198 Madison Avenue, New York, NY 10016, United States of America.

CIP data is on file at the Library of Congress.

ISBN 9780197793992
ISBN 9780197793985 (hbk.)

DOI: 10.1093/oso/9780197793985.001.0001

Paperback printed by Integrated Books International, United States of America
Hardback printed by Lightning Source, Inc., United States of America

The manufacturer's authorized representative in the EU for product safety is
Oxford University Press España S.A., Parque Empresarial San Fernando de Henares,
Avenida de Castilla, 2 – 28830 Madrid (www.oup.es/en or product.safety@oup.com).
OUP España S.A. also acts as importer into Spain of products made by the manufacturer.

Contents

List of Contributors

Ọmọ́máyọ̀wá O. Àbàtì is a senior research officer in the Department of Government at the University of Essex, United Kingdom. His research focuses on the comparative politics of democratic inclusion for groups like youth, women, and persons with disabilities in institutions like parliament, parties, and government across all governance levels. He is also involved in research about the intersection of multilingualism, conflict and conflict resolution in Africa.

Mayowa M. Adeniji holds a bachelor's degree in political science from Obafemi Awolowo University and recently completed his master's degree at Redeemer's University, Ede. His research interests include public policy, representation, and democratic governance.

Petra Ahrens is Academy of Finland Research Fellow at Tampere University, Finland. Her research focuses on gender policies and politics in the European Union and its institutions, gender equality in Germany, gender-sensitive parliaments, and transnational civil society. Alongside articles, she authored *Actors, Institutions, and the Making of EU Gender Equality Programs* (Palgrave, 2018); coauthored *Gender Equality in Politics* (Springer, 2020); and coedited *Gendering the European Parliament* (Rowman & Littlefield/ECPR Press, 2019).

Karen Beckwith is the Flora Stone Mather Professor in the Department of Political Science at Case Western Reserve University. Her research focuses on the comparative politics of gender, political movements (with particular interests in women's movements), and gendered processes of cabinet formation and party leadership contests. Her work has been published in the *European Journal of Political Research, Journal of Politics, Perspectives on Politics,* and *Politics & Gender,* among others. Her most recent book is *Cabinets, Ministers, and Gender,* with Claire Annesley and Susan Franceschet (Oxford University Press, 2019).

Elin Bjarnegård is Professor of Political Science at Uppsala University, Sweden, and co-director of the Feminism and Institutionalism International Network (FIIN). Her research focuses on gender, masculinities, corruption, political parties, and conflict and has been published in journals such as *American Political Science Review, Party Politics, Journal of Democracy, Politics & Gender,* and *Journal of Peace Research.* She is the author of *Gender, Informal Institutions and Political Recruitment* (Palgrave, 2013) and an editor of *Gender and Violence Against Political Actors* (Temple University Press, 2023).

Sarah Childs is Professor of Politics and Gender at the University of Edinburgh, Scotland, UK. Coauthor of the award-winning book *Feminist Democratic Representation* (2020, with Karen Celis), she is also an impactful academic, collaborating with international organizations and parliaments on gender and diversity sensitivity and guidelines.

Kimberly Cowell-Meyers is Associate Professor of Government, director of the School of Public Affairs Honors Program, and affiliated faculty with the Women & Politics Institute at American University. Her work focuses on how representative democracy functions—specifically, on how political parties, social movements, and legislatures structure and channel different political identities.

Louise K. Davidson-Schmich is Professor of Political Science at the University of Miami, US, and editor of *German Politics*. She is the author of *Gender Quotas and Democratic Participation* (University of Michigan Press, 2016) and *Becoming Party Politicians* (University of Notre Dame Press, 2006). Davidson-Schmich also edited *Gender, Intersections and Institutions* (University of Michigan Press, 2017).

Malu A.C. Gatto is Associate Professor of Latin American Politics at University College London (UCL). She is the author of *Resistance to Gender Quotas in Latin America* (Oxford University Press, 2025). Her work explores questions about the gendered dynamics of political behavior, representation, and policy-making and has been published at *Comparative Political Studies*, the *British Journal of Political Science*, *Party Politics*, *Democratization*, and *Politics & Gender*, among others. She has been a Visiting Fellow at the Kellogg Institute for International Studies at the University of Notre Dame, a Global Fellow at the Woodrow Wilson Center for International Scholars, and a postdoctoral researcher at the University of Zurich.

Carmen Geha is a scholar-activist and a social entrepreneur specializing in gender-inclusive policies. She is an Associate Fellow at Chatham House, and a Research Fellow and Associate Faculty member at the Barcelona Institute for International Studies (IBEI). She has held visiting positions at Pompeu Fabra University as a Maria Zambrano scholar, at Harvard University as a Fulbright scholar, at Brown University, and at the Institute for Advanced Study. Until 2022, she was Associate Professor at the American University of Beirut.

Michal Grahn is Associate Professor and Associate Senior Lecturer at the Department of Government, Uppsala University. His research interests include party politics, gender- and LGBTQ+ politics, as well as political participation and behavior. His recent work can be found in the *Journal of European Public Policy*, *European Journal of Political Research*, and *Political Research Quarterly*, among other outlets.

Cecilia Josefsson is Associate Professor in the Department of Government at Uppsala University. Her research focuses on political institutions and representation from a gender perspective in a wide variety of contexts, including sub-Saharan Africa, Latin America, and Scandinavia. Her publications have appeared in *Comparative Political Studies*, *Perspectives on Politics*, *Politics & Gender*, *International Political Science Review*, and *Politics, Groups, and Identities*. She is the author of *Defending the Status Quo: On Adaptive Resistance to Electoral Gender Quotas* (OUP 2024)

Johanna Kantola is Professor of European Societies and their Politics in the Centre for European Studies, University of Helsinki. She was Director of the Consolidator Grant project EUGenDem—funded 2018–2023 by the European Research Council (ERC)—which studied the gendered practices and policies of European Parliament's political groups. She is Distinguished Visiting Professor of Gender and EU Studies in the University of Tübingen, Germany (2022–2025). She is the author and editor of several books on gender and politics, and her work has been published in leading journals of the field, including *American Political Science Review*, *European Journal of Political Research*, *Journal of Common Market Studies*, *Social Politics*, and *Politics & Gender*, among others.

Meryl Kenny is Professor of Gender and Politics at the University of Edinburgh and co-director of the Feminism and Institutionalism International Network (FIIN). Her research focuses on feminist institutionalism, parties and political recruitment, and territorial politics, and has been published in the *European Journal of Political Research*, *Politics & Gender*, *Political Studies*, *European Journal of Politics & Gender*, and *Government & Opposition*, among others. She is the author of *Gender and Political Recruitment* (Palgrave, 2013).

Karina Kosiara-Pedersen is Associate Professor in Political Science at the University of Copenhagen. Her research focuses on political parties as channels of activism as well as on candidate recruitment, vote structuring, and representation.

Sabine Lang is Professor of International and European Politics at the Henry M. Jackson School of International Studies, University of Washington, US. Her research focuses on comparative and European gender politics with an emphasis on political representation, quotas, NGOs, and civil society. Together with Petra Meier and Birgit Sauer, she coedited *Party Politics and the Implementation of Gender Quotas: Resisting Institutions* (Palgrave, 2023).

Joni Lovenduski is Professor Emerita at Birkbeck College London and Visiting Professor and Global Institute for Women's Leadership Advisory Council Member at King's College London. Her research focuses on gender, political representation, and political institutions. Her books include *Gendering Politics, Feminising Political Science* (ECPR Press, 2015), *State Feminism and Political Representation* (Cambridge University Press, 2005), *Feminizing Politics* (Polity, 2005), *Contemporary Feminist Politics* (Oxford University Press, 1993, with Vicky Randall), *Political Recruitment: Gender, Race and Class in the British Parliament* (Cambridge University Press, 1995, with Pippa Norris), as well as *Gender and Party Politics* (Sage, 1993, with Pippa Norris). Lovenduski is a fellow of the British Academy and a member of the American Academy of Arts and Science. She is the recipient of the Gender and Politics Award of the ECPR Standing Group on Gender and Politics, the UK PSA's Sir Isaiah Berlin Lifetime Achievement Prize, the ECPR Lifetime Achievement Award, and the IPSA Mattei Dogan Foundation Award. She was awarded an Honorary Doctorate in Social Sciences by Edinburgh University in 2017.

Petra Meier is Professor of Politics at the Faculty of Social Sciences, University of Antwerp, Belgium. Her research focuses on the (in)formal institutions (re)producing gender (in)equality in politics and policies. She has extensively worked on electoral systems, gender quotas, and the politics of representation. Her recent work focuses on how all of these factors play out in multi-level settings, and on anti-gender and anti-feminist tendencies across Europe.

Pippa Norris is the Paul F. McGuire Lecturer in Comparative Politics at the John F. Kennedy School of Government, Harvard University; founding director of the Electoral Integrity Project; and vice president of the World Values Survey. Her research compares public opinion and elections, political institutions and cultures, gender politics, and political communications in many countries worldwide. Major career honors include, among others, the Johan Skytte Prize in Political Science, IPSA's Karl Deutsch Award, APSA's Charles Merriam Award, Warren E. Millar Award, and Samuel Eldersveld Award, as well as the PSA's Sir Isaiah Berlin prize.

Proma Raychaudhury is Assistant Professor of Politics at Krea University, India. She completed her PhD in Gender and Political Parties in India at the School of Law and Government at Dublin City University under the EU Marie Curie ETN Global India Fellowship. Her research interests involve gender and politics, feminist institutionalism, populism, and right-wing politics.

Zahra Runderkamp obtained her PhD in Political Science from the University of Amsterdam. Her research focuses on the political representation of women and ethnic minorities, as well as their portrayal in the media, in the Netherlands.

Birgit Sauer is Professor Emerita of Political Science at the Department of Political Science, University of Vienna, Austria. Her research field includes political quotas in Austria, emotion and politics, feminist state and democracy theory, as well as gender and right-wing populism.

Tània Verge is Professor of Politics and Gender in the Department of Political and Social Sciences, Universitat Pompeu Fabra, Barcelona, where she directed the Equality Unit (2014–2021). Between 2021 and 2024, she was the Minister of Equality and Feminisms in the Government of Catalonia, a cabinet portfolio created for the first time in May 2021. Her research has focused on gender power relations in political parties and parliaments and on the adoption and implementation of equality policies. She has advised several Catalan and international institutions on equality policies.

Kristin N. Wylie is Professor of Political Science and Minor Coordinator of Latin American, Latinx, and Caribbean Studies at James Madison University. Her research focuses on gender, political parties, and representation in the Americas and has been published in *Party Politics, Politics & Gender, Politics, Groups, & Identities, Opinião Pública, International Feminist Journal of Politics, European Journal of Politics & Gender, Journal of Politics in Latin America*, and *Journal of Black Studies.* Her first book, *Party Institutionalization and Women's Representation in Democratic Brazil* (Cambridge University Press, 2018), was awarded the 2019 Alan Rosenthal Prize by the American Political Science Association's Legislative Studies Section.

Acknowledgments

This book has been a long time in the making—reflecting an ongoing academic and personal friendship over many years. We met at the first European Conference on Politics and Gender in Belfast in 2009, as PhD students working on the gendered and institutional dynamics of political recruitment in very different contexts (Thailand and Scotland). Colleagues in the Feminism and Institutionalism International Network (FIIN) made sure that we connected with each other, and our shared interests turned us into research collaborators—reconnecting over various projects, coauthored papers, and workshops in the United Kingdom, Sweden, and beyond over the last 15 years. While in many ways this book is a culmination of this partnership, we also hope it is a "beginning"—opening up new questions, collaborations, and directions for research.

The idea for this book builds on a series of conversations over a long period of time but draws especially on an European Consortium of Political Research (ECPR) Joint Sessions Workshop in Edinburgh, and a panel at the European Conference of Politics and Gender in Ljubljana, both in 2022. We first want to thank all our chapter authors for their contributions to those wider debates and to this volume. We also thank our FIIN co-directors and network coordinator, past and present—Fiona Mackay, Louise Chappell, Georgina Waylen, Mona Lena Krook, Proma Raychaudhury, Claire Annesley, Josefina Erikson, and Cecilia Josefsson—for their support. We are further grateful to Angela Chnapko at Oxford University Press for her enthusiastic support and patience, and to the anonymous reviewers for their helpful comments.

Meryl Kenny acknowledges the support of the Uppsala Forum, which allowed her to complete portions of this book as a visiting fellow in the Department of Government at Uppsala University, aided by the collegiality and good humor of Uppsala colleagues and regular sixth-floor fika breaks. Her daughter Kiva has also been a persistent cheerleader of the project, excited by the prospect that mum and her pal Elin are writing a book about something "interesting" ("parties are fun!").

Elin Bjarnegård acknowledges the support of funding from the Swedish Research Council (#2915-03488), which enabled her stay in Edinburgh as a short–term visiting fellow in 2019, to plan this book project. She is also grateful for research funding from Forte (#2019-00986), which made it possible to co–organize the ECPR Joint Sessions workshop that led up to this book.

Finally, and foremost, we wish to acknowledge our intellectual, professional, and personal debts to Joni Lovenduski and Pippa Norris, whose work, both individually and collaboratively, inspired us to start this project—and, indeed, to study gender and politics in the first place. We would like to dedicate this book to them.

INTRODUCTION

1
Gender, Parties, and Institutions

Elin Bjarnegård and Meryl Kenny

Political parties are gendered organizations. Historically (and often still) dominated by men from majority groups, they have been shaped by traditional and often unacknowledged understandings of gender relations that generally disadvantage women, and that are embedded into party organizations, rules, and practices—both formal and informal (Lovenduski 2005, 58). Parties are therefore a crucial site of gendered power relations. We cannot understand the persistence of men's political over-representation and the corresponding under-representation and marginalization of women in politics without focusing on the inner lives and external activities of political parties. Gender, in turn, is also crucial to wider questions of why and how (and whether) parties adapt and change, and what their role is in representative democracy.

In investigating the interplay between gender and party politics, scholars have increasingly drawn on the concepts, tools, and methods of feminist institutionalism (FI). FI provides a framework for describing how political institutions are gendered in design, function, and operation (Waylen 2017). These gendered characteristics are often internalized by political actors and seen as synonymous with "politics" by external observers and scholars. FI has provided a language and framework for studying how the formal and informal rules and practices of political parties are gendered in favor of masculine norms (Mackay and Waylen 2014; Murray and Bjarnegård 2023).

What do FI perspectives tell us about party politics? This book offers a thorough response by reformulating and developing established concepts in FI and party research and adding new ones; offering a substantial methodological "toolkit" of approaches and methods; expanding the reach and scope of party research through new cases; and engaging with wider questions of relevance and real-world impact. In this introductory chapter, we outline the feminist institutionalist challenge to the field, addressing not

Elin Bjarnegård and Meryl Kenny, *Gender, Parties, and Institutions*. In: *Gendering Party Politics*.
Edited by: Meryl Kenny and Elin Bjarnegård, Oxford University Press. © Oxford University Press (2025).
DOI: 10.1093/oso/9780197793985.003.0001

only the who, what, where, and how of party politics research, but also the why. We explore the interactive and two-way relationship between gender and party politics; outline the key dimensions of an FI approach to studying party politics; and make the case for why it matters, including beyond the academy. The chapter concludes with an outline of the structure of the volume and its subsequent chapters, which together comprise a rich and wide-ranging research agenda, providing a more comprehensive understanding of the relationship between gender and political parties, and the institutional dynamics of power, continuity, and change.

A Feminist Institutionalist Turn

As Joni Lovenduski (2011, vii), one of the founding figures of both gender party and FI research, argues, "Good feminist social science is simply good social science; it is no more or less than good practice." When women as actors and issues related to gender equality are left out of party research, the picture becomes distorted. For example, one of the most significant changes that political parties have adapted to in the past three decades is the *feminization of politics*—that is, the political integration of women and women's policy concerns (Lovenduski and Norris 1993; Lovenduski 2005; Kittilson 2006). Bolstered by the call for women's increased political inclusion in the 1995 Beijing Platform for Action, parties around the world experienced increased pressure to diversify. The increase in women's numerical (or descriptive) representation worldwide has been supported by, and is largely due to, the most far-reaching electoral reform of our times—the introduction of different forms of political gender quotas in more than 130 countries (Hughes et al. 2019). A gender equality reform has therefore been an important source of party change that has transformed the social and political context in which parties and legislatures operate. Yet, these major trends are often overlooked—or left to the sidelines—of mainstream party research (Kenny et al. 2022).

Efforts by feminists to "gender" party research have focused not only on integrating women as actors and gender equality concerns, but also on incorporating a more complex conception of gender into party frameworks and analysis. Here, gender can be seen as "a constitutive element of social differences based upon perceived differences" between women and men that is also a "primary means of signifying relationships of power"

(Scott 1986, 1070). From an analytical perspective, gender can therefore be seen as a useful "category" to examine and identify the socially constructed institutional roles, identities, and practices conceived of as "masculine" or "feminine" in particular contexts (Beckwith 2005, 131). But it can also be understood as a feature of institutions and social structures—in other words, as a "process" through which structures and policies may have a differential impact upon (different groups of) women and men, while also providing different opportunities to those seeking favorable gendered outcomes (Beckwith 2005, 132).

Gender party research has therefore gradually shifted from studying "women *in*" to "gender *and*" political parties, exploring the ways in which party organizations are stratified by gender and productive of power inequalities (Lovenduski 2005; Kittilson 2013). In this view, parties are seen as both *gendered* and *gendering*, while also capable of being *re-gendered* in more equal directions (cf. Beckwith 2005; Webb and Childs 2011; Celis et al. 2016). While political parties were notably once described as the "missing variable" in women and politics research (Baer 1993), research in this area is now flourishing—reflected, for example, in recent special issues on gender and internal party regulation (van Biezen and Rashkova 2013), the regendering of party politics (Celis et al. 2016), political recruitment (Kenny and Verge 2015; 2016), political ambition (Piscopo and Kenny 2020), conservative parties (Celis and Childs 2018), women's parties (Cowell-Meyers et al. 2020), and populist parties (Kantola and Lombardo 2021a), among others. These more recent research agendas have been greatly shaped by foundational work in the field—particularly by the classic edited volume *Gender and Party Politics* (Lovenduski and Norris 1993) and by *Political Recruitment: Gender, Race and Class in the British Parliament* (Norris and Lovenduski 1995). Crucially, this early work already emphasized the interplay between gender and parties, the diversity among women and women's interests, and the importance of understanding parties within their wider institutional contexts.

Building upon this foundation, gender and party scholars have increasingly drawn upon FI, a now well-established institutionalist perspective focused on the interplay between gender and the operation and effect of political institutions (Mackay et al. 2010; Krook and Mackay 2011; Grahn 2024). FI integrates new institutionalist insights with gender politics research to pinpoint how institutional rules are biased (Kenny 2014; Lowndes 2020), center power in explanations of how institutions work

(Bjarnegård 2013; Erikson 2017), and explain outcomes and stasis/change (Waylen 2007; Thomson 2019). FI has therefore been a useful tool to begin excavating the ways in which gender shapes the structures, practices, and rules (both formal and informal) of party politics, and its intersection with other structures of power, and with institutions inside and outside the political realm. For example, in investigating the ways in which "gender makes parties" (Kenny and Verge 2016), gender and party scholars highlight the gendered dimensions of party rules, and their interplay with wider social structures (see also Kenny et al. 2022). Such social structures include patterns of gender socialization that result in men seeing other men as more likable and reliable peers when recruiting candidates (Bjarnegård 2013; Tremblay and Pelletier 2001; Murray 2014), organizational arrangements within parties and parliaments that do not take care responsibilities into account (Franceschet 2005; Verge and de la Fuente 2014; Campbell and Childs 2014), and prevailing "ideal" types of good party leaders or officers that are biased toward stereotypically masculine traits (Lovenduski 2005; Waylen 2021; Devroe and Van Trappen 2022).

Simultaneously, gender and party scholars highlight the ways in which "parties make gender," (re)producing gender power relations through practices that discriminate against women, either directly or indirectly. This gendered 'disposition' is reflected, for example, in patterns of horizontal and vertical segregation in the distribution of party roles, mandates, and functions (Kittilson 2006; Verge and de la Fuente 2014; Smrek 2022); indirect and direct discrimination in the candidate selection process (Lovenduski 2005; Murray 2010; Verge 2015); and slow responses to adopting and implementing effective anti-harassment measures within party organizations or parliaments (Collier and Raney 2018; Krook 2018; Verge 2022). Gender, then, is also a primary means through which party change and reform can be resisted, with the "stickiness" of informal rules often facilitating the redeployment of "old ways of doing things" by party actors (Bjarnegård and Kenny 2016, 387).

While not all the work reviewed in this chapter is explicitly labeled as FI, the influence of institutional perspectives in gender politics scholarship has strongly shaped the perspectives taken and the type of knowledge produced. The field of FI has rapidly expanded in recent years, leading to an increasing diversity of analytical and methodological approaches (Bogaards 2022; Grahn 2024), which are at the same time still centered around a common set of preoccupations.

Formal and Informal Institutions

Turning first to the object of institutional explanation and definitions of institutions (cf. Schmidt 2010), one important distinction picked up by and elaborated on in FI studies of political parties is between formal and informal institutions. This includes gendered rules that accord different roles and opportunities to women and men within parties, as well as "apparently gender-neutral rules" that nonetheless produce gendered effects due to their interaction with wider social norms (Gains and Lowndes 2014, 536; see also Verge and Claveria 2018; Bjarnegård and Zetterberg 2019; Lowndes 2020). As much as a distinction, however, it can be seen as an explicit acknowledgment that the political game in many parties and political settings cannot be fully understood by reading formal, written rules and regulations. This may be particularly important for deciphering the gendered codes in parties, and the ways in which these include or exclude particular groups of actors.

Political parties need to be studied beyond their formal rulebooks. Often, political parties operate according to regularized practices, norms, expectations, or conventions that are obvious only to insiders, and attainable only by experience or exclusive invitation (Hinojosa 2012; Bjarnegård 2013; Bjarnegård and Kenny 2015, 2016). While formal party rules are "detailed, explicit, standardized, implemented by party officials, and authorized in party documents" (Norris 1997, 202), informal procedures may be institutionalized although they are not reflected in party documents, and are "created, communicated and enforced outside of officially sanctioned channels" (Helmke and Levitsky 2004, 727). Parties often have a set of standard operating practices and norms that remain stable over time, reflecting social norms, logics of appropriateness, and "the way things are done around here" (Chappell 2006; Lowndes 2014; Bjarnegård and Zetterberg 2016a; Waylen 2017).

Research on political parties demonstrates that formal and informal rules are both important, not least through the way they interact and shape unique configurations of gendered party rules over time (Bjarnegård and Kenny 2017). For a long time, informal institutions were primarily pointed to as detrimental for inclusion (Bjarnegård 2013; Kenny 2013; Bjarnegård and Kenny 2015). Gradually, a more nuanced view, focusing on the content of rules—whether formal or informal—has gained ground (Waylen 2017; Bjarnegård and Zetterberg 2019). Informal rules can override formal rules, making change difficult, but they can also substitute or challenge formal rules, enabling change (Cheng and Tavits 2011; Piscopo 2016; Wang and Muriaas 2019; Gatto and Wylie 2022). Political parties can also create or revise formal rules in an attempt to deal with gendered challenges and problems. As we have set out elsewhere (Bjarnegård and Kenny 2016), understanding the mix of formal and informal elements in a particular institutional context is an empirical question. The argument is not that scholars should abandon the analysis of formal rules to focus on the informal or prejudge how they operate—rather, it is more helpful to map different constellations of (in)formality and institutionalization over time, and their general and gendered effects.

Power and Resistance

While power is generally underplayed in the new institutionalist literature, it is central to FI explanations of how institutions work (Kenny 2007). For gender party scholars, party politics is fundamentally a site of power relations. Whereas the wider party politics field has come under critique for its perceived abandonment of "bigger picture" debates (Gauja and Kosiara-Pedersen 2021), feminist scholars of political parties have never lost sight of these broader questions about power, representation, and democracy (Kenny et al. 2022). They also increasingly recognize that although a gendered lens is sorely needed, it is not sufficient. Power is unevenly distributed, not just by gender, but also by other dimensions of exclusion and marginalization, such as class, ethnicity, age, sexuality, and ableism (for example, see Krook and Nugent 2016; Childs and Hughes 2018; Evans and Reher 2024). Political parties and parliaments are not just dominated by men, they are dominated by majority elite men. Women are a diverse group of people with different interests, and substantive representation also requires diversity among women.

From an FI perspective, power often begets power (cf. Thelen 2004, 216)—and is protected by those who have it, not least in organizations such as political parties, which are often conservative when it comes to change (Panebianco 1988). Historically founded by and for men from majority groups, political parties generally reinforce the dominant positions of their creators, both nominally and substantively. Ongoing contestation and power struggles can provide openings for women and other under-represented groups to disrupt and challenge unequal power relations, including through their embodied presence and through more gradual and incremental change that takes place under the radar. But these moments can also open opportunities for those who wish to maintain the status quo to actively resist change (Josefsson 2024). In politics, institutional "losers" do not just walk away; they (or their institutional successors) often live to fight another day (Schickler 2001; Kenny 2013). Therefore, explaining resistance to gendered change requires a deeper investigation of power struggles within parties, the logic underpinning the status quo, and the rationale of actors who stand to gain from preventing change to take place (Bjarnegård 2018a; Staab and Waylen 2020; Murray and Bjarnegård 2023).

Continuity and Change

While much of the debate in the wider new institutionalist literature is around static versus more dynamic conceptions of change, FI approaches to change are purposeful (see Bogaards 2022). That is to say, the "feminist" commitment in FI requires not only the intellectual investigation of inequalities, but also an active commitment to change them (Kenny et al. 2022). Accompanying this commitment is a recognition that research should make a wider contribution beyond the academy, reflected in the crucial role of gender politics scholars as change actors, working with and advising parties, parliaments, and governments around the world (Campbell and Childs 2013; Childs and Dahlerup 2018; Dahlerup and Leyenaar 2013).

Political parties—and political party research—have undergone substantial changes in the twenty-first century, evidenced in new actors, new issues, and new types of parties. FI research clearly demonstrates that "newness" is not synonymous with change. Even in the face of formal political change, informal institutions can be sticky, and what is "new" is always nested in previous understandings and agreements (Beckwith 2007; Mackay 2014). In seeking to explain why parties change, gender party scholars focus both on women's mobilization within parties and on the gendered dynamics of the opportunity structures within and outside of parties (Lovenduski and Norris 1993; Kittilson 2006). In doing so, they draw attention to both external change drivers and to the "inner lives" of parties, with party responses to reform pressures seen as shaped by their histories, organizational arrangements, and internal (gendered) power relations (Kenny and Verge 2013; Kenny et al. 2022). These insights are of relevance not just to the study of gender equality issues, but also to the wider questions of why parties adapt and change (or stay the same).

The FI understanding of parties as gendered organizations also shifts the focus of reform strategies—put simply, it is parties, not individual women, that need to change to ensure equal representation (Piscopo 2019; Piscopo and Kenny 2020). In other words, parties, as key vehicles for democratic equality and inclusion, must take responsibility for redressing gendered and intersectional inequalities. Gender quotas are one important aspect of party-focused and institutionally focused reform strategies, but they do not guarantee the integration of women and their concerns within parties, or that party rules and organizational arrangements are hospitable to women and other under-represented groups more broadly (Verge 2020). The re-gendering of party rules, practices, and cultures should therefore be a central focus of change efforts—with increasing recognition not only from academics, but also international organizations, that work to ensure equal representation must begin in political parties (e.g., Organization for Security and Co-operation in Europe (OSCE) 2014, 2016).

A Research Agenda

It is our hope that this book will speak to broader audiences, both within and beyond the gender politics field. This book moves beyond the (still important) goal of investigating specific substantive areas of gender and party politics to also consider how the "big questions" of party politics scholarship are gendered, and with what effect. In doing so, it bridges the intersection of the fields of gender politics and party politics scholarship, which have tended to talk past, rather than to, each other (Kenny et al. 2022). We hope that the book will be an accessible resource that will help party politics research better account for the realities and institutional complexities of gender as a category and as a process. In doing so, we propose an engagement with the established and emerging concepts and frameworks in FI and party politics scholarship to strengthen our collective tools for analysis. The book showcases how these tools can be applied to different cases and to various aspects of political party functions, using a diversity of methodological approaches. Overall, the collective theory-building enterprise of this book takes forward the broad questions at the heart of the study of political parties: who, what, where, how, and why (Bjarnegård and Kenny 2017; Kenny et al. 2022).

Who and what do we study? In the contributions in this book, gender inequalities in party politics are still in focus, but no longer with a sole focus on women—examining parties themselves as gendered institutions, and the ways in which interactions between different identity categories shape political behavior, processes, and outcomes. The book clearly showcases how FI has facilitated the study of gender by its focus on formal and informal rules, pointing to the importance of changes in formal rules as well as incremental shifts in informal institutions, and the ways in which these interact with each other to open up or limit possibilities for reform and transformation.

Where do we study party politics? The book demonstrates the global scope of this research agenda, and many individual chapters also forward the comparative agenda, demonstrating how an institutionalist perspective and language facilitates comparison across seemingly different cases. The question of "where" is not limited to geographical scope. Party scholarship is also concerned with parties operating in various types of party systems and regimes, and gender party scholarship is no different. Autocracies have been active adopters of gender quotas, and gender has become an important goal, target, or tool for dominant parties of non-democratic regimes (Bjarnegård and Zetterberg 2022). This variety of empirical contexts is also evident in this book, as FI perspectives are applied to different types of regimes in different parts of the world.

How do we study party politics? The chapters of this book all contribute to moving the research agenda forward, retaining a commitment to methodological pluralism, ranging from interpretivist approaches to quantitative methods. Deploying a wide range of methods is crucial for capturing the complex interplay between formal and informal institutions.

Why does it matter? Here, the contributions to the volume make the case for the "re-gendering" of political parties, raising important normative questions about how and to what extent parties act as vehicles for equality and inclusion, as well as considering possible strategies for change, and the role of gender party scholars themselves as change actors.

Putting these questions together, this book is divided into three parts, focused on concepts (Part One), methods and cases (Part Two), and change (Part Three). Each part is prefaced by a brief theoretical discussion, followed by an overview of the chapters.

Part One focuses on *concepts*, with contributions either gendering classic concepts and frameworks in the party field and/or developing new ones. As already highlighted, any discussion of the "who" and the "what" of party scholarship looks different through a gender lens. While by no means covering all relevant concepts in the party politics field, this part demonstrates the added value of integrating women as actors and more complex understandings of gender into the "mainstream" of party politics research, while also highlighting the progress and potential of FI concept development.

Part Two on *methods and cases* brings together the "who" and the "what" with the "where" and the "how." It focuses on contemporary and new areas of research and debate, demonstrating the broad application of FI frameworks for understanding the importance of and interplay between the formal and the informal, extending the FI and party politics methodological toolkit, and investigating how the gendered "rules of the game" play out within and across different party types and political systems.

While change is a central preoccupation of the volume as a whole, Part Three focuses centrally on the "why," evaluating opportunities for and obstacles to *transforming political parties* from a feminist perspective. With FI scholars driven by the "feminist imperative" (Campbell and Childs 2013) to both change and study party politics, this final part particularly focuses on the impact of gender party research, the role of feminist academics as potential change actors, and the wider implications for understandings of institutional change.

This collective research endeavor is placed in context in a concluding discussion between the editors (Elin Bjarnegård and Meryl Kenny) and two pioneers in the gender party field: Joni Lovenduski and Pippa Norris. We bring Lovenduski and Norris back together to reflect on the origins of the field, the direction it has since taken, and the value added by FI perspectives to gender party research. At the time of writing, there has been no systematic comparative edited volume on gender and party politics since the publication of the influential book *Gender and Party Politics* (Lovenduski and Norris 1993) and the definitive study of political recruitment focusing on the UK parliament (Norris and Lovenduski 1995).

This book thus represents a long-overdue update of the field. It also serves as a form of what Sarah Ahmed calls "feminist bricks" and "feminist memory"—an acknowledgment of "our debt to those who came before; those who helped us find our way when the way was obscured because we deviated from the paths we were told to follow" (2017, 15–16). We therefore leave the last words of this volume to Joni and Pippa.

PART I
CONCEPTS

Gender politics scholarship often begins by critiquing the self-evident "truths" and assumptions embedded in the "mainstream" of political science, including exposing the gendered foundations and biases embedded in core concepts of political analysis. Gender party research is no exception—with feminist party scholars highlighting the often-contested nature of key concepts and questions in the party politics field and excavating the ways in which they are shaped by gender (and other intersecting) power dynamics (Kenny et al. 2022). This can involve reformulating old concepts or introducing new ones. The former entails not only integrating new groups or concerns not covered by or ignored in standard understandings of existing concepts, but also integrating a more complex notion of gender into concept analysis (Goertz and Mazur 2008, 6–7). The ultimate goal of this "gendering" is good social science (cf. Lovenduski 2011). From a feminist institutionalist (FI) perspective, any good party politics scholar should recognize the importance of gender relations (and their intersection with other structures of power) in their analyses.

Chapters in this part of the volume take different approaches to concept critique and (re) formulation—with some authors "gendering" classic concepts in the party politics field and others introducing new concepts or taking forward emerging ones. Petra Meier, Sabine Lang, and Birgit Sauer advance an FI reading of the core concept of *intra-party democracy*, drawing on comparative research of gender quota implementation in European political parties to unpick the tensions between party- and system-level democracy in relation to gender equality. A fully engendered understanding of intra-party democracy, they argue, would necessarily integrate gender equality at the core of formal and informal institutions, with gender quotas as one possible route to ensure gender equality as an outcome, but also as a founding principle of society more broadly. Louise K. Davidson-Schmich similarly draws on gender party research to interrogate the relationship between gender and *political ambition*, pointing to the ways in which parties shape what having and expressing political ambition means, with gendered consequences. While political ambition is conventionally understood as the function of the opportunities open to an individual, Davidson-Schmich demonstrates that these opportunities are not equally open to all, mapping the ways in which parties' formal and informal institutions curtail nascent, expressive, and progressive ambition of women—particularly women of color. Zahra Runderkamp and Meryl Kenny subsequently shift the focus from gendered pathways into political office to ask when, why, and how women politicians leave. Bringing together insights from FI and gendered workplace approaches, they make the case for an institutionally focused approach to understanding political *dropout*, disentangling the contextual and gendered dynamics of the "leaky pipeline" of politics.

FI approaches to the study of gender and parties highlight the need to consider how institutions and actors interact in dense institutional environments, opening up or foreclosing possibilities for change (Krook 2009; Kenny 2013; Josefsson 2020). In this vein, Karen Beckwith takes forward the theorization of *newness*, a prominent concept in FI studies of political institutions (Beckwith 2007; Mackay 2014), to examine the intersection of the "new" and the "old" in advanced democracies that have experienced change and/or stasis in their party systems. While Beckwith highlights the opportunities that new institutions and new actors may present for change, Cecilia Josefsson asks the important question of why gender equitable policies sometimes fail, introducing a new framework for studying party *resistance*. Focusing on gender quotas, Josefsson argues that resistance to these measures has different "roots," which vary across different types of political parties, with resultant implications for change strategies.

2
Between Party Democracy and Parity Democracy

Petra Meier, Sabine Lang, and Birgit Sauer

This chapter takes forward a feminist reading of intra-party democracy. It focuses on the potential frictions between intra-party democracy and principles of gender equality. Historically across Europe, parties have mostly been masculinist organizations as they are nested within societal norms, including the predominant gender regime. As parties reflect societal gender(ed) norms, they also reproduce them in various ways. As a consequence, intra-party democracy frequently pits overall party goals, such as vote winning and power seeking, against goals of inclusion and equality. This chapter aims to dissect how party democracy and parity democracy intersect. We rely on the concept of parity democracy as it underlines that it does not suffice to simply add a principle of gender equality to the norms, values, rules, and processes prevailing within institutions. The latter require a fundamental rethinking and reconceptualization. Doing so, we are aware of the fact that wc limit our focus to gender. Nonetheless, we consider it central to any discussion about intra-party democracy to address the multiple and often intersecting power inequalities reproduced by political parties. We think that there is scope to build on our argument for gender equality as a founding principle taking precedence over intra-party democracy to address other power inequalities reproduced by political parties, and we hope that our chapter serves as a stepping stone for that work.

Gender equality is a central concept for gender scholars, including those investigating party politics, as their research focuses on the drivers of gender—and other—inequalities and how to overcome them. The same cannot be said of the mainstream party literature, much of which (still) ignores gender and party politics research, as well as the gendered organization and functioning of parties (Bjarnegård and Kenny, this volume). The

Petra Meier, Sabine Lang, and Birgit Sauer, *Between Party Democracy and Parity Democracy*. In: *Gendering Party Politics*. Edited by: Meryl Kenny and Elin Bjarnegård, Oxford University Press. © Oxford University Press (2025). DOI: 10.1093/oso/9780197793985.003.0002 concept of intra-party democracy, on the contrary, is a central preoccupation in the party politics literature, as it is considered to be a crucial feature for parties to better connect with members and citizens in (increasingly) volatile political times. Gender scholars also see intra-party democracy's relevance, but connect it to the concept of gender equality, as we will discuss in the next section. This chapter focuses on intra-party democracy and the role of parties within the wider context or political system, not on the relations among parties or internal party dynamics (complementing Josefsson in this volume, who primarily addresses the latter). However, as we will contend, it is important to understand parties' internal power dynamics in order to assess parties within their wider context.

We build our argument on empirical findings from a coordinated study on how parties implement gender quotas across Europe—their own voluntary party quotas and/or legislative quotas imposed by law (Lang, Meier, and Sauer 2023).[1] Our contributors investigated systemic, inter- and intra-party power dynamics when faced with implementing quotas in 17 European countries. The data provide insights in how parties negotiate, support, contest, and resist quotas, highlighting what is put in practice and who the main actors of implementation are. In doing so, we assessed cultural, institutional, and political factors that impact parties' interest and ability to implement gender quotas from a feminist institutionalist perspective, focusing on formal and informal institutions within parties as well as broader political and societal contexts, such as the prevailing gender regime (Lang, Meier, and Sauer 2023). Our chapter showcases a particular aspect of the path dependency of political parties as institutions and the stickiness of their masculinist traditions. From a point of view of intra-party democracy, the issue with gender quotas tends to be presented as whether such—or similar—measures can be imposed upon parties, not how they are implemented. However, their implementation nicely illustrates intra- and inter-party power dynamics, and, of relevance for this chapter, the tension between parties and parity democracy. Indeed, as we will argue in this chapter, the tension we observe manifests mainly between gender equality and existing gendered power hierarchies within parties, more than between parity democracy and intra-party democracy.

Our argument evolves in three sections. First, we discuss the relationship between intra-party democracy and gender quotas, particularly how gender quotas are perceived in that context. Second, we explore the relationship between intra-party democracy and parity democracy, demonstrating how the implementation of gender quotas relies on a culture of gender equality. In the final section, we reflect on how party and parity democracy intersect and to what extent parties (can) act as vehicles for democratic equality and inclusion.

Intra-Party Democracy and Gender Quotas: The Logic of Process and the Logic of Outcome

Political parties, while crucial players in representative democracies, are not inherently democratic organizations. Many have roots in top-down organizational cultures with oligarchic tendencies, often depending on when, why, and how they were founded. Intra-party democracy, a topic increasingly attracting interest as parties seek sources of legitimation, refers to the extent to which parties' internal organization meets democratic standards. According to Cross and Katz (2013, 6), intra-party democracy is about the distribution of power and influence within a party. A crucial element in this respect is the extent to which members have a say in important party decisions, such as appointing the party leader(s) and selecting candidates for elections (Hazan and Rahat 2010; Rahat 2013). Intra-party democracy can take many forms, and each involves winners and losers, as different interests can be served by different variants of intra-party democracy. Carty (2013), for instance, analyzing different party models, argues that most are not well equipped for intra-party democracy. The prevailing "simplified models of the core elite-member relationships have yet to find a way to account for the subtle complexities of these processes" (Carty 2013, 26). Interestingly, much of this literature focuses on (the relationships between) elites and party members, or even voters with an eye on their respective power and influence, and not so much on the functioning of parties as organizations that exhibit particular modes of governance.

Literature on party governance, thus, tends to focus on formal rules and procedures. In this context, Katz (2013) raises the question whether making the governance of parties more democratic would be essential for the democratization of the political system in which these parties operate. If we start from the premise of parity democracy that democracies can only be democratic if they are gender-equal, then our answer to Katz's question is a resounding "yes": Yes, the governance of parties needs to be democratic for democracy to materialize, and it needs to be democratic in the sense of putting gender equality center stage. Meryl Kenny and her colleagues, in their recent critique of Anika Gauja and Karina Kosiara-Pedersen's assessment of the field of party politics, have observed that much of mainstream party research has "abandoned the 'big questions' ... around power, democracy and representation" (Kenny et al. 2022, 281). A feminist political science lens, by contrast, homes in exactly on these big questions.

Gender quotas are a tool used to increase gender equality, with the latter seen as a democratic value and/or as a means to enhance democracy. While their primary purpose is to promote descriptive gender equality, bringing women into politics (as candidates and, if elected, politicians) and, eventually, the party (successful women politicians becoming important players within parties), this may spill over into more substantive gender equality. There has been an ever-growing interest in gender quotas since the 1980s (Krook 2006). Building on the path-breaking work of Lovenduski and Norris (1993) and Kittilson (2006, 2013), much of this literature acknowledges that parties are important actors and gatekeepers when it comes to the recruitment, selection, and election of women, as Bjarnegård and Kenny set out in this volume, but also when it comes to the role gender quotas play in these processes. More particularly, with respect to gender quotas, factors such as party ideology (Murray 2010), or the extent of centralization, factionalization, and formalization in the nomination process (Baldez 2007; Bjarnegård and Zetterberg 2016b; Hinojosa 2012; Kenny and Verge 2013) are at play in the process of adopting and implementing gender quotas. Critical institutionalist research on Spain and Portugal highlights how the implementation of gender quotas did not by definition alter intra-party gendered power relations as the latter can obstruct formal rule change (Verge and De La Fuente 2014; Verge and Espírito-Santo 2016). In contrast, some Latin American countries have become trailblazers in recognizing gender equality as a foundational principle—equally important to, and shaping and shaped by, intra-party democracy (Piscopo and Vàzchez Correa 2024). Piscopo (2016) shows for the Mexican case how cross-party alliances and networks of women activists and state authorities successfully countered parties' strategies to implement gender quotas in only a minimalist way. As a result of these mobilizations, a landmark ruling by the federal electoral court in 2011 required all Mexican parties to implement a 40 percent gender quota without exception, forcing parties to close loopholes and revise election procedures that favored men. A constitutional revision in 2014 guaranteed gender parity for both federal and state legislatures (Piscopo 2017; Piscopo and Vàzchez Correa 2024).

Childs (2013a), in an attempt to bridge the gender and party politics literature with intra-party democracy literature, develops an interesting argument on gender quotas and other measures to enhance the position of women within parties and politics. Indeed, intra-party democracy as traditionally understood might not be compatible with gender quotas, with the party center intervening to get more women selected, or with a gender balance among candidates. Specifically, it hampers the decision-making power of members in selecting candidates in more decentralized processes as put forward by intra-party democracy. Similarly, the involvement of a party's women's section in party politics might not be compatible with a traditional understanding of intra-party democracy, as it stands for top-down decision-making. But, as Childs argues, intra-party democracy from a gender perspective would require that women gain power relative to men, and that they do so within parties relative to where that power lies. This is what Childs calls a fully engendered understanding of intra-party democracy (Childs 2013a, 93). In sum, electing more women shifts power from men to women and makes the party more democratic in that sense. And this may lead to women gaining power where it lies, in political decision-making in the party, in parliament, and beyond. Looking at the presumed trade-off from this perspective, Childs submits that interventions to increase women's descriptive and/or substantive representation may re-balance the distribution of power between men and women in parties, thus institutionalizing women's power as compared to that of men. Thus, gender quotas, or rather their aim—a more balanced inclusion of women in political representation and decision-making—may constitute an indicator of greater intra-party democracy even if gender quotas do not match with a traditional reading of intra-party democracy.

To support her claim, Childs argues that we can approach the issue of intra-party democracy in terms of a logic of process or a logic of outcome. While gender quotas—and other measures—to increase the presence and power of women as compared to that of men within parties and politics might not be compatible with the logic underlying the *process* of intra-party democracy, this may be the case with the logic feeding an *outcome* that intra-party democracy stands for. It would be, in her words, an engendered intra-party democracy outcome (Childs 2013a, 93). She recognizes that such an understanding of intra-party democracy—actually the whole debate of the position of women as compared to men within parties and politics at large—is often considered to be something other than an issue independent of intra-party democracy. But she argues in favor of making a normative choice for a gendered conception of intra-party democracy. Controlling candidate recruitment and selection processes so as to ensure that enough women candidates have the potential to get elected should be understood as enhancing intra-party democracy, not hampering it. As a consequence, understanding quotas

> as an anti-democratic effort ... fails to recognize the intersection of party and system-level [intra-party democracy]. A strong case can and should be made that women's parliamentary representation may require a limit on (traditionally understood) IPD [intra-party democracy] for the good of system-level democracy. Without so acting, parties will be anti-democratic in the sense of excluding or descriptively under-representing half the population in its parliamentary representation.
>
> (Childs 2013a, 99)

Our next section takes Childs's argument forward and puts it in conversation with recent empirical work on gender quotas.

Intra-Party Democracy and Parity Democracy: The Logic of Founding Principles

Connecting intra-party democracy to system-level democracy relates to the debate that Cross and Katz (2013, 5) advance in the introduction to their volume on the challenges of intra-party democracy, namely to what extent parties within democracies must respect certain (democratic) principles themselves given their role in realizing democracy at the system level. Parties are traditionally (seen as) voluntary—but, above all, private—organizations. Over time, often in the wake of public funding, their legal regulation became customary (van Biezen and Piccio 2013). Such legal regulation applies to their activities, behavior, and internal organizational structure, and is supported by supranational and international organizations such as the Council of Europe, International Institute for Democracy and Electoral Assistance (IDEA), or Inter-Parliamentary Union (IPU). In this respect, parties, especially if publicly funded, are nested within wider context-related norms and regulatory frameworks, and thus showcase important links between intra-party and system-level democracy. The question in this chapter is, to what extent this relationship also applies—and could or should apply—to gender norms.

Around the globe, there are many examples of parties adopting quotas. Often such measures are imposed by law—in some countries they are even enshrined in the constitution. The point here is that gender quotas are imposed upon parties, even though parties often (by way of parliamentary or executive action) participate in the negotiation of those gender quota regulations. Thus, gender quotas are similar to other rules imposed upon parties such as party finance laws (to which the same logic applies that parties are oftentimes involved in their negotiation in parliament or government). The latter and gender quotas are both good examples of rules imposed upon parties that stem from a broader political or societal concern for the respect of certain norms and values. Paraphrasing Gauja's work on party reforms (2017), the implementation of gender quotas can be categorized as a systemic pressure to reform (contrary to micro-level intra-party or meso-level party-system pressures to reform). Such pressure is "emanating from long-term developments but also broader social and cultural shifts that challenge existing conventions, norms and democratic practices" (Gauja 2017, 78), which are themselves often due to a universalization of such trends. According to Gauja, such developments "may arise from changes to public expectations, legitimacy concerns, and more intangible factors such as shifting or developing norms of democratization" (Gauja 2017, 78–79). Gauja highlights issues that are close to parties, such as the individualization of society and the fact that citizens engage in a different way in politics than they did in the past—in sum, issues changing membership rates and roles of party supporters. In contrast, we propose widening the scope and assessing how broader social, political, and cultural shifts relate to intra-party democracy and democracy at a systemic level.

One of the most profound systemic changes is an increasing emphasis on gender equality in many contemporary democracies—and beyond—compared to when the majority of political parties were founded. Gender quotas are the expression of and tool to realize a broader social and cultural shift—namely, gender equality. Linking this back to Childs's plea to consider intra-party democracy not only in terms of a logic of process but also one of outcome, we add a logic of founding principles. This is where parity democracy comes in. Parity democracy was a concept coined in the 1990s mainly by French scholars (*la démocratie paritaire*; Collin 1999; Gaspard 1994; Martin 1998; Mossuz-Lavau 1998). The underlying idea of parity democracy is that gender equality is not a principle to be simply added to current institutions. Institutions of contemporary democracies tend to have been established at—or their roots in—a time when women (and many other social groups) were not recognized as full members of society to the same extent as the often small group of men who were. Therefore, it makes no sense to try and simply add on a principle or policy of gender equality. The basic logic, spirit, and functioning of these institutions are inherently masculinist, making it difficult to change them by intervening in the process, or expecting an outcome to happen without tackling the foundations. Indeed, the idea is that these institutions are often beyond repair and need to be re-evaluated and re-conceived. Hence, the coining of the concept of parity democracy—a democracy defined as gender-equal in its founding principles.

Relating this to contemporary democracies involves situating gender equality as a basic principle of its formal and informal institutions. Parity democracy is in essence a thick democracy, giving normative body to what a democracy stands for or should strive for beyond procedural aspects. This includes all matters related to the working of democracy in its political sense, to the organization and processes of political representation, participation, and decision-making. Approaching intra-party democracy from such a perspective comes close to what Childs calls a fully engendered intra-party democracy, contrary to a definition of intra-party democracy rejecting gender quotas. Indeed, we could coin the latter as a "thin" definition of intra-party democracy, putting procedural aspects center stage, notwithstanding the outcome such procedures would produce from a gender perspective. In such a thin definition of intra-party democracy, gender quotas are seen as hampering the process and are therefore to be rejected, notwithstanding the fact that they would enhance gender equality. In a thick or fully engendered intra-party democracy, gender quotas would be one of the possible routes to not only ensuring gender equality as a potential outcome, but also to embedding it as a founding principle of society.

The importance of underlying principles of gender equality in the political sphere for advancing gender policies has been clearly illustrated by the research, done by us and our colleagues, on the implementation of gender quotas across Europe (Lang, Meier, and Sauer 2023). The findings in part confirm earlier evidence, showcasing how the implementation of gender quotas is strongly related to party ideology and organization, the presence of strong intra-party women's networks, and the electoral system. But they also show that gender attitudes play a central role in shaping gender quota implementation processes, and that they tend to reflect the broader gender regime (Lang, Meier, and Sauer 2023, 20). The prevailing gender regime, including a gendered division of labor, a division between public-political and private-family realms, and related notions of masculinity and femininity (mostly hierarchical and binary) is also reflected in party cultures.

The two Scandinavian countries in our study sample, Denmark (Rolandsen Agustín et al. 2022) and Sweden (Freidenvall 2022), are characterized by an egalitarian gender regime with (informal) social gender equality norms. These form the background for egalitarian attitudes in society and in parties, and thus facilitate the implementation of gender equality in politics; interestingly, in both countries this implementation occurs without legislative or party gender quotas. The equality norm in society puts pressure on all parties to nominate a sufficient number of women, including in top positions. Formal and informal gender equality norms shared by the main party actors and respective selectorates form a solid basis for the implementation of gender equality. Conservative gender regimes, by contrast, correspond with parties being skeptical toward gender quota regulations to achieve gender equality in politics, sticking to traditional and non-egalitarian understandings of gender, and essentialized notions of womanhood. Some societies' attitudes toward politics are biased, as in the cases of Poland (Gaweda 2022) and Serbia (Čičkarić 2022), where the ideal politician is male, men are "winning candidates," and women are seen as a disruptive factor in politics. Party women can become "men's standins," as in the Croatian case (Šinko 2022). In Slovenia (Antić Gaber and Selišnik 2022), women candidates have to have a "pleasant appearance" to be accepted. Even in countries with formally institutionalized but not internalized egalitarian gender regimes, parties often preserve a masculinist organization and culture. Especially in former state socialist countries, such as Slovenia (Antić Gaber and Selišnik 2022) and Serbia (Čičkarić 2022), parties continue the state socialist tradition of male leadership, networks, and privilege, notwithstanding their egalitarian tradition.

Masculinist Party Institutions and the Logic of Gender Equality

The findings of our study showed that parties often reproduce societal gender(ed) norms, and that the main agents responsible for implementing both self-imposed party quotas and legislative quotas are also responsible for blocking successful implementation. Parties rely on passive and implicit modes of resistance to quotas—for instance, creatively utilizing institutional settings of electoral laws, the size of electoral districts, or preferential vote settings to undermine gender quotas. Explicit and active resistance to gender quotas persists as well—for example, through the discrediting of women politicians as "quota women" or coercing elected women into giving up their mandate to make room for a man. There are, however, also challengers to quota-hesitant or -resistant institutions; these challengers insist on putting existing rules and regulations into practice, and promote new and innovative modes of gender quota implementation. In Ireland, for instance, parties set up a committee to develop a candidate selection strategy to implement the legislative gender quotas (Brennan, Buckley, and Galligan 2022).

In many cases, however, the task of implementing gender quotas did not incentivize parties to embark on organizational change: they neither revised their recruitment and selection rules, procedures, or strategies, nor altered their general internal structures. Meeting the gender quota was often left to unofficial recruitment practices employed by the selectorate or delegated to the party's women's branch. Hierarchies dominated by men and male networks or privileges were not touched upon when implementing gender quotas, nor were intra-party gendered divisions of labor. Even in gender equality-oriented party cultures as in the Danish or Swedish examples, masculinist legacies such as the order of succession or seniority still trump gender equality; male networks, especially on local levels with a culture of "strongmen," try to overturn gender-equal list composition by, for instance, insisting on geographical rather than gender representation. Nonetheless, countries with egalitarian gender regimes fare better than conservative gender regimes when it comes to implementing gender quotas or other measures fostering gender equality in politics.

The difficult implementation of gender quotas illustrates the stickiness of masculinist traditions within political parties. Parties reflect wider gender norms. A progressive gender regime and gender equality culture are central to successful gender quota implementation; at the same time, in a progressive gender regime, gender quotas may not be needed to foster gender equality within and by parties. While from a point of view of intra-party democracy, gender quotas tend to be presented as an imposition on parties, their implementation mainly illustrates the tension between party organizations and gender equality. Our findings overwhelmingly show that the resistance to gender quotas mainly targets gender equality more broadly. Actors within and beyond parties in a position to implement gender quotas refuse to do what Childs argues for—namely, to share power with women—unless the main actors subscribe to an egalitarian gender culture. The tension we observe thus is primarily between gender equality and existing gendered power hierarchies and masculinist norms within parties, more than between intra-party democracy and parity democracy.

This does not come as a surprise; feminist institutionalist research underlines that we cannot simply add the principle of gender equality to current formal and informal institutions, and expect those to change organically (Krook and Mackay 2011). The question is, how greater emphasis on gender equality norms in contemporary democracies—of which gender quotas are a symbol—relates to parties, their organization and functioning. Parties, when it comes to aspects of legal regulation applying to their internal organizational structure and behavior, need to comply with a set of basic principles emanating from the current understanding of democracy. There is no reason why this should not go for gender equality. The issue is not one of choosing between intra-party democracy or gender equality. Rather, gender equality, when considered to be important as a principle, takes precedence over party organization, much the same as other legal regulations do. Gender quotas—or other measures to make parties achieve gender equality—are a consequence of these principles.

Conclusion

There is not, and should not be, just one way for parties to organize themselves, but this is not the point of our contribution. Our findings indicate that if gender equality is to become a credible party goal, compliance with gender quotas should not be left to parties alone. There is ample proof of the stickiness of masculinist traditions within political parties, illustrating the path dependency of institutions and reflecting the legacy of traditional gender cultures. Many political parties in our comparative study did not institute any changes in organization or governance after formal quota adoption, and this in turn led to an incomplete and piecemeal implementation of quota regulations. As parties in most contemporary democracies continuously adapt their organizations and procedures to an increasing set of rules, there is no reason why gender equality should not be among them.

What does this mean for a fully engendered understanding of intra-party democracy as put forward by Childs (2013a)? Childs raises the issue that a party is not internally democratic if women lack substantive power and/or are underrepresented at different levels of internal decision-making. Thus, her concept of a fully engendered intra-party democracy goes beyond sound quota implementation. Indeed, while broader principles of gender equality as enshrined in gender quotas (among other things) take precedence in intra-party democracy, they do not by definition lead to a fully engendered intra-party democracy. Achieving a fully engendered intra-party democracy depends on how such gender equality principles are translated into gender quota regulations and other measures, on how carefully these measures are implemented, and on whether and how non-implementation is sanctioned.

More generally, this chapter illustrates how links between intra-party democracy and system-level democracy are key to understanding the internal power dynamics of parties and their role and functioning within gender regimes. Parties are nested within societal norms and reflect and reproduce them. The party literature would benefit from empirically and normatively integrating in their analyses the formal and informal wider gender(ed) norms and rules that affect parties. Conversely, feminist institutionalist research will benefit from further investigating this nestedness of parties as institutions within the broader logic of democracy.

On a final note, we consider it central to any discussion about intra-party democracy to ask how to move beyond gender equality. While a narrow understanding of parity democracy may exclusively focus on men and women, the need for a more inclusive and especially intersectional understanding of equality is obvious. Putting forward the argument that gender equality as a principle takes precedence over intra-party democracy in contexts of inequality, does not imply that only gender equality matters. Indeed, contemporary democracies also put forth other principles of equality, and we need to investigate how a more inclusive and intersectional understanding of equality might infuse party democracy.

Note

1. This study is part of the project "Gender Equality Policy in Practice Network." For more information, visit https://geppn.com.

3
Gender and Political Ambition

Louise K. Davidson-Schmich

Political parties perform a core democratic function: identifying and selecting candidates for elective offices. Without individuals willing to stand for election, representative democracy would not be possible. In addition, when elected representatives are motivated by the prospect of *re*-election, they have incentives to represent the desires of their constituents while in office. Thus, the success of democracy depends on individual political ambition; the broader and more widespread such ambition is among the general population, the more likely parties are to be able to identify talented candidates. Moreover, the larger the number of politically ambitious people seeking (re)election, the more choices of representatives citizens will have, and the easier it will be to hold underperforming representatives accountable by replacing them with alternative candidates.

Scholars studying political ambition—that is, a person's desire to run for elective office or to continue in office once elected—have determined that ambition is a function of the opportunities open to a person (Schlesinger 1966). When individuals are encouraged by gatekeepers to run for office, they are likely to develop political ambitions (Fox and Lawless 2010); conversely, when gatekeepers signal that selection as a candidate is unlikely, political ambition can be stifled (Carroll and Sanbonmatsu 2013, 107). In the words of Tània Verge, "demand makes its own supply" of aspirants for elective offices (2015, 758).

In democracies around the world, parties are important gatekeepers determining who appears on the ballot (Hazan and Rahat 2010). Thus, parties play a crucial role in influencing political ambition. As is the case with the other areas of party politics discussed in this volume, parties' influence on political ambition is gendered. Traditional party practices, both formal and informal, have curtailed women's political ambition, while stoking the ambitions of cisgender, ethnic majority men (Bjarnegård and Kenny 2015).

Louise K. Davidson-Schmich, *Gender and Political Ambition*. In: *Gendering Party Politics*.
Edited by: Meryl Kenny and Elin Bjarnegård, Oxford University Press.
DOI: 10.1093/oso/9780197793985.003.0003

Women of color or those belonging to other disempowered groups face greater hurdles to developing political ambition than women from empowered social categories (Brown and Dowe 2020). As a result, citizens of democracies enjoy fewer, less-representative choices in elections, reducing the quality of democracy and limiting their ability to hold representatives accountable.

This chapter proceeds as follows. The section "Nascent Political Ambition" discusses the gendered relationship between parties and *nascent political ambition*, or a person's abstract desire to hold elective office. The section "Expressive Political Ambition" explores the gendered impact of party politics on *expressive political ambition* or a person's actual attempt to run for elective office. The section "Static/Progressive Political Ambition" briefly turns to the gendered interplay between parties and *static* or *progressive political ambition*, or the desire of an elected office holder to pursue the same (static) or higher level (progressive) elected office in the future (Lawless 2012). In each section, I point to the role of both formal and informal institutions in shaping women's political ambition.

Nascent Political Ambition

Nascent political ambition is the "embryonic or potential interest in office seeking that precedes ... deciding whether to enter a specific political contest" (Lawless 2012, 5). While some people may aspire to be athletes, pilots, or teachers, others may desire to become elected officials. Men citizens more commonly harbor nascent political ambition than women citizens (Pruysers and Blais 2019, 233; Lawless and Fox 2010; Shames 2017; see also Bolin, Backlund, and Jungar 2023; Ammassari, McDonnell, and Valbruzzi 2023). Many drivers of the gendered gap in nascent political ambition are beyond the scope of political parties. For example, genetics may shape nascent political ambition. One study of children raised by an adoptive family rather than by their biological parents found the adopted children twice as likely to run for office if their biological parents had done so (Oskarsson, Dawes, and Lindgren 2018). Similarly, personality traits such as extraversion and openness to new experiences have been found to spur ambition (Kolltveit 2022). Family socialization encourages political ambition too; children whose parents discuss politics at home are more likely to become politically ambitious than those with apolitical parents (Kolltveit 2022).

Gendered socialization teaches even young children that politics is a man's business (Bos et al. 2022), and discourages girls and women from developing the agentic traits and values associated with politics (Conroy and Green 2020). Self-confidence, more common among men, can increase nascent political ambition (Wolak 2020), whereas election-aversion, more frequent among women, dims nascent political ambition (Kanthak and Woon 2015).

As such, it might seem that gender and nascent political ambition are topics unrelated to political parties. Indeed, the scholarly focus on nascent ambition stems from research conducted in the United States, where entrepreneurial candidate selection rules are in place (Piscopo and Kenny 2020). The US system of candidate recruitment relies heavily on self-nominations from politically ambitious individuals in the general population, rendering gender gaps in nascent ambition important in explaining gender gaps in descriptive representation there.

In most long-term democracies, however, candidates do not self-nominate, but rather are selected by political parties (Hazan and Rahat 2010). Surveys across countries indicate that for most political party members, the desire to run for elective office was *not* the primary motivation for joining their party (van Haute and Gauja 2015; Bale, Webb, and Poletti 2020, 79; Heidar and Kosiara-Pedersen 2019). Nascent political ambition has been found to be higher among those who join their political party's youth wing at an early age, but even in youth wings large percentages of young people do not report nascent political ambitions (Bolin, Backlund, and Jungar 2023; Ammassari, McDonnell, and Valbruzzi 2023).

Instead, research on political ambition conducted in systems in which parties select candidates to appear on the ballot indicates that expressive political ambition—actually entering an electoral contest—comes *as a result of* party membership, not prior to it (e.g., Geissel and Hust 2005; Carroll and Sanbonmatsu 2013; Davidson-Schmich 2016). Involvement in a political party demystifies the process of running for and holding elective office and offers insights into the skills and abilities needed to do so. Party membership puts individuals on gatekeepers' radars and increases the likelihood that they will be encouraged and asked to run for elective office more often than non-members; this encouragement is especially important in awakening women's political ambitions (Fox and Lawless 2010). Thus, parties can have an extensive influence on cultivating women's political ambition once they have taken the step to join.

However, there is clear cross-national evidence that women are less likely to join political parties than are men, even though women are equally (or more) willing to vote and engage in other forms of civic participation (Coffé and Bolzendahl 2010; Kjaer and Kosiara-Pedersen 2019). While the gender gap holds across parties, it is larger in parties of the right than parties of the left (Ammassari, McDonnell, and Valbruzzi 2023, van Haute and Gauja 2015, 194).[1]

Thus, one of the largest ways in which political parties—especially parties of the right—shape women's ambition is in deterring them from becoming party members in the first place. As one team of scholars observed, "To make political careers in parliamentary democracies more appealing to women involves, first and foremost, making joining a party more attractive" (Ammassari, McDonnell, and Valbruzzi 2023, 19; see also Thomsen and King 2020). Both formal and informal institutions drive women's hesitancy to join parties. By *formal institutions* I mean those "rules of the game" that are written down in party statutes or available in other "official," publicly-visible places—for example, official qualifications for party membership. *Informal institutions* shape how parties' formal rules and procedures are actually interpreted and implemented. These include both what Helmke and Levitsky refer to as informal "*social* [institutions] (e.g., the handshake, or the rules of dating)" and what they term informal *political* institutions: "rules ... that structure political life—created, communicated, and enforced outside of officially sanctioned channels" (2004, 725–726). For example, a party's budget statute may allow it to give resources to individuals running for office, but informal institutional practices are used to decide which candidates are perceived worthy of actually receiving funding (for example, see Gatto and Wylie 2022).

Formal Institutions, Gender, and Party Membership

A widespread literature suggests that, in addition to "material" incentives such as becoming a professional politician, the main drivers of party membership are "purposive incentives" and "solidarity" (Bale, Webb, and Poletti 2020). Purposive incentives include wanting to support an organization's mission, in this case contributing to a party's overall ideological, policy, and office-seeking goals. However, elite women who would make excellent candidates for elective office have been found less likely than their male counterparts to see partisan politics as being capable of addressing problems they view as important (Shames 2017, 108). In addition, the gender gap in voting, with women preferring parties of the left to parties of the right cross-nationally (Giger 2009), can also partially help explain women's disinterest in joining parties of the right.

Purposive incentives also include people joining a party to show support for its leadership. Some studies indicate that high-profile women candidates and elected officials will serve as role models for other women and girls and inspire them to become politically active, taking steps such as joining a political party (Broockman 2014; but see also Gilardi 2015), which would place them in a position to develop political ambitions. Because left-of-center political parties are more likely to elect women (Weeks et al. 2023) and to have gender quotas for party leaders (Caul 2001), they are also more likely to attract women members via this "role model" mechanism than right-of-center parties.

However, while women's presence in left-of-center political parties is more frequent than in right-of-center parties, in part surely due to their offering women more purposive incentives, gender parity in party membership remains extremely rare, indicating that even formal programmatic and leadership changes would not be enough to solve the problem of men's overrepresentation among party members and, in turn, among those whose political ambitions are likely to be awakened.

Other formal barriers to women joining parties may include the cost of membership, as women have fewer disposable financial resources than men (World Economic Forum 2022), or the requirement of being sponsored by an existing party member. Gendered social networks and male-dominated parties mean women are less likely to have a social connection who could vouch for them (Bjarnegård 2013). However, dues are generally minimal and often assessed on a sliding scale; many parties across the world have unsuccessfully undertaken campaigns to attract women to their ranks, showing a willingness to sponsor them but finding few takers (Piscopo 2019; Davidson-Schmich 2018).

Informal Institutions, Gender, and Party Membership

Instead, the primary drivers of women's disinterest in party membership can be found in parties' informal social and political institutions. Aside from purposive incentives, the other main motivation individuals attribute their party membership to are solidarity incentives, the desire to join a group in which one finds opportunities for pleasurable social interaction and camaraderie (Bale, Webb, and Poletti 2020; Heider and Kosiara-Pedersen 2019; van Haute and Gauja 2015). An extensive literature makes abundantly clear that political parties, regardless of their ideological positions, fail to provide these solidarity incentives for women. As Joni Lovenduski observed, parties are "institutionally sexist" and "require women to behave like the men they seek" to join (2005, 53, 48). As a result, "the ways in which everyday party politics is structured ... push women out" (Verge 2015, 755). Qualitative research from across long-term democracies has identified several informal social aspects of party life that deter women from participating in these grassroots-level party organizations where expressive political ambition can be awakened. The informal social and political institutions most frequently identified include these groups' masculinized ethos, discourse, and time management—in other words, the who, when, where, what, and how of political party life.

Party members commonly report that prior to approaching their party and deciding to join, they discussed the possibility with friends and family who are in the organization (Bale, Webb, and Poletti 2020; Heider and Kosiara-Pedersen 2019). Due to gendered social networks, women may be less likely to have a social connection who could encourage them to join than men (Bjarnegård 2013); they may also learn from others that party life is dominated by men and male norms, making membership an unattractive prospect. The fact that there are more women among left-leaning parties' members may create a more virtuous circle leading to increasing percentages of women members, as young women become more likely to join these organizations (Ammassari, McDonnell, and Valbruzzi 2023, 19; Davidson-Schmich 2016, 92–93). The emergence of social movements such as #MeToo exposing men party elites' misbehavior, and the identification of violence against women in politics as a chronic phenomenon, may act as a further deterrent (Krook 2020; see also Kosiara-Pedersen, this volume). As Piscopo and Kenny (2020, 4) have argued, women's lack of nascent political ambition and willingness to get involved in a party may be a rational decision to opt out given the gendered political opportunity structure.

In addition to the "who" (many men), the informal "when and where" of party organizations also suppress women's participation. Meetings often take place in proverbial "smoke-filled rooms" where women feel uncomfortable, and important decisions are made in informal "meetings after the meeting" from which women are excluded (Davidson-Schmich 2018).

Party gatherings typically occur during evenings and weekends, when women are more likely than men to be tasked with care responsibilities (Verge 2015, 757). If women decide to attend, they find themselves in a double bind, conforming to party norms but violating societal mores by delegating care work (Verge 2015, 755). Party meetings are notoriously lengthy due to self-promotion norms, which require members to assert themselves in conversation; unnecessarily long discussions prolong the time commitment required for membership, creating an additional burden for women who are more likely than men to shoulder a double burden of professional and domestic responsibilities (Verge 2015, 757; Davidson-Schmich 2016). Party membership, and with it the opportunity to develop political ambitions, is simply too time-consuming for many women, especially during their childbearing years (see Àbàtì and Adeniji, this volume).[2]

Moreover, even for women who do have time to devote to party life, the prospect of doing so may be unattractive given informal social institutions such as the "what and how" of party life. For example, parties prize "speaking assertively, displaying authoritative leadership styles or showing overt ambition," but these practices are all incompatible with "appropriate" feminine behavior (Verge 2015, 755). As a result, women may see themselves as unqualified for, or unsuited to, party life—or they may simply find it unattractive. Women become much more interested in political participation when politics is framed as being about communal goals rather than about conflict, self-promotion, and power (Schneider et al. 2016). Women are more likely than men to be motivated to pursue politics in order to address policy concerns, so when parties focus on jockeying for position rather than addressing public problems, women become less interested in taking part (Thomas and Wineinger 2020).

Men members may deploy violence against women in their parties to "keep women in their place" (see also Kosiara-Pedersen, this volume). This can include "semiotic violence" through tactics like ignoring or belittling party women, using sexist "humor" (Krook 2020), employing tactics of "super-surveillance" (Verge and de la Fuente 2014, 72–73), claiming credit for women's ideas, demanding women perform time-consuming service such as taking minutes, or viewing issues of interest to men as more worthy of agenda time than women's concerns. In sum, parties' formal and informal institutions deter women across democracies from entering an arena that could place them in a position to develop expressive political ambition and run for elective office.

Expressive Political Ambition

Not everyone with nascent political ambition who joins a party eventually runs for office (Bernhard, Shames, and Teele 2021), yet party members without nascent political ambition often do stand for election (Kjaer and Kosiara-Pedersen 2019, 312; Davidson-Schmich 2016). Thus, it is important to examine the factors leading "eligibles" or those with the qualifications to run for elective office—in this case party membership—to express political ambition by seeking a spot on the ballot. A gendered expressive ambition gap has been documented among women party members across countries, even when these members hold interest in other forms of political participation such as appointed positions (Kjaer and Kosiara-Pedersen 2019, 312; Bauer and Darkwah 2020; Kolltveit 2022).

While expressive political ambition is generally context-specific for both men and women (Schlesinger 1966), increasing when the chances of receiving a promising ballot nomination increase, women are particularly sensitive to the costs and benefits of running (Fulton et al. 2006)—often concluding that costs outweigh benefits (Shames 2017). One reason is that women's calculations are more likely than men's to be "relationally embedded" (Carroll and Sanbonmatsu 2013): women take caregiving (Davidson-Schmich 2016, 132–137) and their ability to support their family (Bernhard, Shames, and Teele 2021) into consideration before deciding to run. Gender-specific costs can involve the problem of violence (Krook 2020), including physical violence from community members, rape and death threats on social media, or being interrupted by opponents in political debates. Bauer and Darkwah (2020), for example, describe how the common "politics of insult" is manifested across Africa: women candidates' sexuality and marital status are routinely questioned by other party members as well as political opponents, which prevents many women from aspiring to candidacy. Similarly, worldwide many potential women candidates fear sexist press coverage should they choose to run (Shames 2017).

Formal Institutions, Gender, and Expressive Political Ambition

Against this backdrop, parties themselves have further depressed women's political ambition. For example, when no clear criteria for candidate selection are in place, party gatekeepers (those tasked with selecting candidates) tend to turn to their personal networks to identify individuals to place on the ballot. Given male dominance in political parties, this means that parties prefer to select those with what Bjarnegård refers to as "homosocial capital"—trusted places in men's social networks (2013; see also Àbàtì and Adeniji, this volume; Wylie 2018; Mufti and Jalalzai 2021; Hazan and Rahat 2010). This condition dampens women's political ambition through two key mechanisms. First, since women are generally excluded from such networks, they are unlikely to be selected as candidates. Second, because women are less likely to be present in the networks from which politicians are drawn, they are less likely than the men who enjoy membership in these networks to view themselves as "qualified" to run for office, again dampening their expressive ambition (Fox and Lawless 2012).

Thus, if parties adopt more formalized candidate selection procedures that provide more specific information to prospective candidates about the qualifications required to obtain a ballot nomination, parties can potentially awaken women's political ambitions. Women interested in running for office in such settings may have a better chance of fulfilling specific candidate criteria—such as holding a certain position within the party's ranks—than they do of developing homosocial capital (Wylie 2018). In mixed electoral systems, women are more likely to express ambition to be nominated via a party list, where more formal criteria for balancing candidates are present, than via a single-member district, where qualifications are more amorphous (Coffé and Davidson-Schmich 2020).

However, formalized candidate selection procedures can only awaken women's expressive ambitions if the nomination qualifications are actually obtainable for women (Bjarnegård and Zetterberg 2019). As Rainbow Murray observes, "we prioritize the policy areas associated with wealthy men" (2015, 774); if criteria for selection include masculinized expertise such as business or military experience, women are unlikely to see themselves as appropriately qualified and unlikely to express political ambition. Similarly, many parties require what Germans refer to as an "*Ochsentour*"—years of time-consuming service to the party—before being selected as a candidate. Women often do not have time to do this service given their care responsibilities; taking time away from care work means violating social norms of feminine behavior (Verge 2015, 757; Verge and de la Fuente 2014, 71; Davidson-Schmich 2016). In other party contexts, assertive speech and competitive behavior may be included as qualifying characteristics (Verge and de la Fuente 2014, 71). This puts women in a double bind, creating social role incongruity and backlash if women adopt the behaviors that would qualify them for office, but disqualifying them for a ballot nomination if they fail to adopt masculinized behaviors. The more strongly parties emphasize masculine qualities in their candidates, the less qualified women are likely to feel—and the less expressive political ambition they are likely to manifest (Pruysers and Blais 2017).

To remedy this state of affairs, numerous parties and non-governmental organizations have begun programs to train women to run for elective office, believing that such development efforts will help close the gendered expressive ambition gap. Training classes are beneficial in developing high-quality candidates (male or female) and can increase women's self-confidence (Wylie 2018, 106). This is especially true when programmatic political parties offer education to empower women to speak publicly about the party's platform and policies. Such communally-oriented speech is more consistent with feminized norms of behavior than women's self-aggrandizing behavior, rendering it more comfortable for women to engage in and more positively perceived by others (Wylie 2018, 108). A dearth of investment in such training programs has been hypothesized to partially explain a lack of candidate emergence in certain conservative parties (Och 2020).

However, such programs have met with limited success in closing the gendered gap in expressive political ambition (Piscopo 2019, 824; Davidson-Schmich 2018). Framing training programs as necessary for women (but not men) to prepare to run for elective office underscores the already masculinized nature of political office and suggests (to already underconfident women) that women are inherently unsuited to hold such positions. Further, training programs may make women more clearly aware of the structural barriers to elective office, such as high financial costs of running, which cannot be addressed by training workshops (Geha 2019; Piscopo 2019). Thus such "lean in" programs may paradoxically undermine women's expressive ambition.

If they are indeed present, a party's formal candidate selection procedures shape women's expressive ambition not only in terms of the qualities sought in a candidate, but also via the procedures used to select candidates, some of which are more women-friendly than others. For example, many parties employ primaries to select candidates, but this entrepreneurial process requires women themselves to step forward and declare their ambition to best other party members, which can lead to backlash for violating expectations about women's appropriate conduct (Josefsson 2020). It may also be a daunting requirement for women who lack confidence or are election-averse (Kanthak and Woon 2015). Moreover, to successfully contest a primary, candidates require financial resources and support networks within the party, which many women do not have.

When parties employ more centralized candidate selection procedures with transparent (obtainable) criteria for nominees, women are more likely to express political ambition (Coffé and Davidson-Schmich 2020). One of the clearest ways parties can signal to women within their ranks that their aspirations are desired and likely to yield ballot nominations is by adopting candidate gender quotas. Parity quotas, which require including women in winnable ballot positions, can significantly increase women's expressive political ambition (Davidson-Schmich 2016, 207–208). Left-wing parties are more likely to have such quotas than parties of the right (Piscopo 2019, 821), which may help explain why women in left-wing parties have been found to be more politically ambitious than women in more conservative parties (Kjaer and Kosiara-Pedersen 2019; but see also Ammassari, McDonnell, and Valbruzzi 2023). Effectively employed quotas can boost political ambition because they increase women's odds of actually being (s)elected as a candidate if they express ambition. The more chance women have of being selected, the more likely they are to aspire to seek a ballot nomination.

Another mechanism through which formal quotas can increase women's expressive ambition is by leading gatekeepers (in this case party leaders) to try and recruit women to run for office in order to comply with the party's quota. Women who are recruited by party leaders are more likely to express political ambition than unrecruited women (Preece, Stoddard, and Fisher 2016; Wylie 2018; Karpowitz, Monson, and Preece 2017). Encouragement by a political party to run is important in awakening any member's expressive ambition but women are especially sensitive to such cues—and are less likely to receive them than their male peers (Lawless and Fox 2010; Dittmar 2015; Crowder-Mayer 2020). When candidate selection is decentralized, cues from central party leaders that women candidates are welcomed and that equality is taken seriously can go a long way to prompting grassroots gatekeepers to select women candidates, creating more positive political opportunity structures and boosting the chances that women will express political ambition (Karpowitz, Monson, and Preece 2017, 929).

Such expressive ambition is not only dependent on being asked to run, however. Women also must possess the resources needed to actually win an election. A global gender wealth gap means that on average women have fewer financial resources to bring to campaigns (World Economic Forum 2022), and many women cite the cost of campaigning or the need for fundraising as a reason for not running for elective office (Bauer and Darkwah 2020; Dittmar 2015; Shames 2017, 122; see also Och 2020). This wealth gap is even larger for women of color (Wylie 2020). Parties can help overcome this barrier to women's expressive ambition by establishing formal processes through which candidates can receive material assistance from the party to promote their campaigns.

Informal Institutions, Gender, and Expressive Political Ambition

Formal institutions, such as party gender quotas and programs to aid candidates with campaign finance, can therefore be created to narrow the gendered gap in expressive ambition. However, these formal rules must be accompanied by a willingness on the part of party elites to actually employ them to promote equity. Experience shows this is often not the case—and transpires mainly when it is in the interest of powerful male party leaders (Valdini 2019; for a more theoretical treatment of resistance, see Josefsson, this volume).

For example, rather than being inspired to ask women to run for office in order to fill a party quota, men gatekeepers may employ informal institutions to resist sharing power. While formal candidate gender quotas have the potential to send a signal to women that their expressive ambition is desired and will meet with success in achieving a ballot nomination, quotas only stoke expressive ambition when they are actually utilized. Extensive cross-national research shows that quotas are often simply not implemented (e.g., Piscopo 2019; Gatto and Wylie 2022; see also Josefsson, this volume). Parties find loopholes not to run women candidates (Murray 2004), or women are selected as candidates but only as "window dressing" or "sacrificial lambs" holding ballot positions where winning would be impossible (Wylie 2018, 106; see also Martinez i Coma and McDonnell 2023).

Indeed, one cause of the observed gendered political ambition gap is gatekeepers' failure to ask women to run for office (Shames 2017; Fox and

Lawless 2010). Elite cues are a particular barrier for women of color in the United States, who are not only less likely to be asked by party leaders to run, but who are actively discouraged by their parties when they do express ambition (Brown and Dowe 2020; see also Shah, Scott, and Juenke 2019). Moreover, when US women of color are made aware of such negative recruitment, they are even less likely to express ambition (Holman and Schneider 2018), even though they are very communally minded and hope to make a difference in their communities (Shames 2017, 149). Negative recruitment is a problem across the aisle, but, at least in the United States, it is particularly common in the rightist Republican Party (Crowder-Meyer 2013).

Even more dampening to expressive ambition is the use of informal institutions involving sexual violence—for example, "sextortion," when male gatekeepers require sexual favors from women to obtain party leadership positions and ballot nominations (Krook 2020). Men may also simply spread rumors that sextortion has occurred (Verge and de la Fuente 2014, 73; Bauer and Darkwah 2020). Physical, psychological, and economic violence by party "colleagues" to prevent women from expressing political ambition have been reported by women around the world as well (Krook 2020).

Similarly, even in cases where parties have material resources to aid ambitious women's campaigns, women often are not convinced that their parties will grant them the resources they require to successfully campaign and win, further depressing expressive ambition (Butler and Preece 2016; see also Shames 2017). In the United States, Republican women appeared more skeptical on this front than Democratic women (Preece, Stoddard, and Fisher 2016), as were women of color (Shames 2017). Such suspicions may be well-founded. For example, in Brazil, party elites provide female candidates (who were indeed recruited by the party) less advantageous candidate identification numbers, less financial support, and less media access than they provide male candidates of equal quality (Janusz, Barreiro, and Cintron 2022). Parties in the United States similarly undercut ambitious women of color from their own ranks (Brown and Dowe 2020).

In short, informal social and political institutions, communicated outside of officially sanctioned channels by men party leaders around the world, send a clear signal to women that their expressive ambition will be met with indifference or resistance. Against this backdrop, it is surprising that so many brave women *have* expressed political ambition.

Static/Progressive Political Ambition

If women manage to overcome the myriad of obstacles to expressive political ambition and ultimately are elected to public office, what happens next? What role do parties play in shaping women's static and progressive political ambition? That is, do elected women desire to run for re-election or for higher office? Evidence on this subject is limited and contradictory. While some studies find that for those elected women it is a question of *when* to run for higher level office, not *whether* to run (Maestas et al. 2006; Fulton et al. 2006; see also Geissel and Hust 2005), others report that women have less progressive ambition than their male counterparts (Erikson and Josefsson 2025), while still other scholars have determined there is no gender difference in progressive ambition (Galais, Öhberg, and Coller 2016). When it is uncovered, women's lack of such ambition is often attributed to the family-unfriendly nature of parliamentary work and the demands of childcare (Davidson-Schmich 2016, 134–135; Galais, Öhberg, and Coller 2016). An emerging literature on gender-sensitive parliaments has also begun to identify the myriad ways in which legislatures, like political parties themselves, as gendered institutions hostile to women's presence (Erikson and Verge 2022).

While Zahra Runderkamp and Meryl Kenny discuss the "leaky pipeline" in more detail in Chapter 4, here I include a few observations on the formal and informal ways in which parties can awaken or discourage even elected women's political ambition. Certain formal institutions hold the power to awaken women's progressive ambition akin to the way they can promote expressive ambition. For example, effectively implemented quotas for women in legislative leadership or cabinet positions can send a powerful signal to women Members of Parliament (MPs) that their pursuit of a higher position is welcomed and feasible; recruitment efforts by party leaders can send this signal as well (Erikson and Josefsson 2025). Specialist rather than generalist cabinet member selection—like clear-cut qualifications for ballot nominations—can also encourage women's aspirations for cabinet posts (Claveria 2014).

Informal institutions, however, can dull even elite women's static and progressive political ambitions. If party gatekeepers do not seriously approach women about moving up the ranks of elected office (Sweet-Cushman 2020), for example, or wait longer to encourage them than their male colleagues

(Kerevel 2019), women MPs are less likely to aspire to higher positions. Evidence also finds that parties are more likely to punish their women members more than their male members for failing to gain a higher post (Verge and de la Fuente 2014, 73; Kerevel 2019), reducing the likelihood they would desire to risk such a step.

How parties' informal institutions allocate committee and cabinet positions can also shape women's progressive ambitions. Parties often follow a logic of "gender appropriateness" that creates horizontal segregation with women given "softer" portfolios than men, as well as vertical segregation, with women assigned lower ranking positions than men (Verge and de la Fuente 2014, 71). These decisions render women less "qualified" for higher posts than their male colleagues, depressing their progressive ambition. Finally, violence against women MPs is already widespread. If, as is often the case, male members of their own parties perpetrate such violence in an effort to force women out of office or prevent their further rise (Krook 2020), women's desire to remain in office will be stifled.

Conclusion

Democracy, a system of political equality, requires men and women to equally share places in legislatures and political parties across the ideological spectrum. Such equality would not only represent a just allocation of power and provide both symbolic and substantive representation for half the population, but it would also eliminate the political overrepresentation of "mediocre men," a byproduct of the current male dominance in political parties (Besley et al 2017). At the moment, however, the world remains far from this state of affairs. Parties' formal and informal institutions continue to dampen political ambition of women—especially women of color—preserving men's overrepresentation. However, these partisan institutions do hold the potential to awaken the political ambitions of a far broader array of women than they do now. Doing so would provide an important public good (Piscopo 2019, 45).

If more women were to enter parties and rise to top positions of power within these organizations, it might be possible to begin to chip away at the barriers outlined in this chapter. Women's entry into parties has been shown to change these parties' programs to become more women-friendly, creating purposive incentives for joining (Weeks 2022). Female gatekeepers make it more likely that women will be selected as candidates (Crowder-Meyer 2013; Kerevel 2019), raising the odds that women might join parties to support their leaders. Many observers have pointed to the important role that women's auxiliaries of political parties have played in promoting both formal reforms and women's leadership within parties (Wiliarty 2010). Women in leadership positions can change parties' informal social and political institutions (e.g., by holding more efficient meetings during times when childcare is available or excusing a female colleague who cannot participate if her child is sick). Women party leaders may serve as role models for other women within the party, increasing their ambition (Verge and de la Fuente 2014). Women's organizations within parties can promote quotas (Wiliarty 2010) and act as "watchdogs" ensuring that quotas are actually implemented against informal institutional barriers (Davidson-Schmich 2016, 170–172; Verge and Espírito-Santo 2016; Wylie 2018). Women's auxiliaries with powerful positions within a party can awaken women party members' ambition by asking them to run for office and providing them with resources to successfully campaign. They may also be able to convince their male colleagues that other women are assets to the party and winning candidates (Wylie 2018, 105). Women leaders in parties can identify violence against women in their ranks and work to both criminalize this practice and change norms regarding its acceptability.

However, since men currently make up the majority of party members and leaders, it is incumbent upon men—not women—to actually implement changes to parties' formal and informal institutions in order to awaken women's political ambitions. This chapter pinpoints roadblocks to women's ambition, suggesting a range of reforms that could be implemented to close the long-standing gender-ambition gap. To increase women's nascent ambition, parties can alter the informal nature of party life, changing the who, when, where, what, and how of their activities to provide women more solidarity incentives to join; programmatic changes to address women's issue concerns would create greater purposive incentives for party membership. Addressing all types of violence against women party members, candidates, and elected officials would also help parties attract politically ambitious women. Other reforms designed to reduce the cost and increase the benefit of running for elective office could increase women members' expressive ambition. Centralized and formalized candidate selection procedures with obtainable qualifications would attract more women candidates, as would targeted recruitment efforts by party gatekeepers willing to provide resources to make women's candidacies tenable. Finally, gender-sensitive parliaments, quotas for women in executive posts, specialist selection criteria for cabinet members, and a willingness to appoint women to powerful cabinet portfolios could all go a long way to increase elected women's static and progressive ambitions. Reforms such as these could help parties overcome their previous failure to awaken women's political ambitions, improving the quality of democracy everywhere.

Notes

1. In addition to a party's ideological placement, its organizational type (i.e., programmatic, clientelist, etc.) also has a gendered impact. For more on this subject, see Josefsson, this volume.
2. The older a person becomes, the less likely they are to develop political ambitions (Fulton et al. 2006).

4

The Leaky Pipeline of Politics

Zahra Runderkamp and Meryl Kenny

The causes and consequences of women's political under-representation are much studied—reflected in a large and wide-ranging body of scholarship focusing on the factors that facilitate and block women's entry into politics. But questions of when, how, and why women leave politics have been studied far less.

There is reason for worry. Empirical evidence from around the world shows gendered patterns of getting into and out of politics. In many countries, women are less often party members or aspirants (Davidson-Schmich, this volume); they tend to enter politics after their child-bearing years (Joshi and Och 2021; Lazarus et al. 2022); they have shorter parliamentary careers on average (Lawless and Theriault 2005; Allen 2013); and they are more likely to be "pushed toward the exit" by their political party (Vanlangenakker et al. 2013). In other words, the political pipeline is "leaky," with women and many other underrepresented groups progressively lost both as the level of political power rises and over time. This chapter focuses squarely on the questions of how and why women exit politics, and on the role that political parties and institutions play therein.

The chapter outlines the importance of studying the leaky pipeline of political office. It argues that there is much to learn about the daily reality of politics from those who leave, countering a so-called survivorship bias in the study of parties and political institutions. The chapter assesses the existing literature on legislature turnover and (in)voluntary exit, and on the variety of ways in which scholars have studied the question of who stays and who goes in politics (and why). Building on feminist institutionalism (FI) and gendered workplace frameworks, it then makes the case for a gendered and institutionally focused approach to studying the dynamics of dropout. The chapter illustrates the value of this approach through a case study of the Netherlands, drawing on a qualitative study of politicians who have

Zahra Runderkamp and Meryl Kenny, *The Leaky Pipeline of Politics*. In: *Gendering Party Politics*.
Edited by: Meryl Kenny and Elin Bjarnegård, Oxford University Press. © Oxford University Press (2025).
DOI: 10.1093/oso/9780197793985.003.0004

dropped out of politics at the local level (Runderkamp 2024). We conclude by outlining implications for future studies, and end with a call to action, focusing on strategies for change.

The Leaky Pipeline to Political Office

In seeking to answer the question of why some politicians move up the political ladder and others do not, studies have sought to link the process of legislative recruitment with the outcome for the composition of political elites (Norris and Lovenduski 1995). The dominant framework for studying the political pipeline is a multi-step ladder or pyramid that separates between voters, party members, aspirants, candidates, and elected Members of Parliament (MPs) (cf. Norris and Lovenduski 1995; see also Davidson-Schmich, this volume). Eligibles are understood as those of voting age (Stockemer and Sundstrom 2023), a smaller proportion of which will make the decision to join a political party. Aspirants are the group of party members that decide to stand for election, only some of whom will be selected as candidates, and even fewer of whom will be successfully elected as politicians. Every step along the way, some keep going, and some do not (Lovenduski 2016, 521). Supply-side and demand-side factors interact at each stage of this process—with political access controlled by a series of gatekeepers, and with the "narrowest gate" of all guarded by political parties, who in most countries have exclusive control of candidate selection processes (Gallagher and Marsh 1988, 2; Norris and Lovenduski 1995).

While recruitment has been traditionally seen as a multi-step process that loses women at each stage, a study by Kjaer and Kosiara-Pedersen (2019) outlines an alternative "hourglass pattern" of women's representation. Based on the case of Denmark, the authors show that the main bottleneck—or thinnest part of the "hourglass"—for women politics is the transition from being party members to being willing to stand as a candidate. But they also argue that political recruitment scholars cannot assume a "the higher, the fewer" pattern to women's political recruitment. In the Danish case, for example, there is a higher proportion of women among nominated party members than among potential candidates, and women are more likely to get elected than their male counterparts, though numbers are still below gender parity (Kjaer and Kosiara-Pedersen 2019). The authors suggest that this pattern is particularly likely in cases where there are strong norms around gender equality, a pattern which may be particularly pronounced in countries that have adopted gender quota reforms.

In both of these frameworks, however, the political pipeline ends at elections. Norris and Lovenduski's (1995) multi-stage model of recruitment, for example, implies the possibility that the recruitment ladder could be expanded or collapsed, which includes adding more rungs at the top of the ladder as MPs move into government positions (see Lovenduski 2016). Yet Norris and Lovenduski's main focus is on process and outcome in legislative recruitment—that is, on the crucial steps from "lower levels to parliamentary careers" (1995, 1). In the "hourglass pattern," similarly, what happens after election is left out. Meanwhile, the small but growing body of work on women's progressive political ambition—that is, the desire to climb the political ladder further after elections—highlights gendered differences in men's and women's desire to seek higher office (Davidson-Schmich, this volume; see also, for example, Fulton et al. 2006; Schwindt-Bayer 2011; Erikson and Josefsson 2024), but does not usually address the question of why and under what conditions women leave higher positions (for an exception, see Claveria and Verge 2015) or exit politics altogether.

This focus, in turn, has implications for strategies to increase women's representation. Policymakers and non-governmental organizations alike have focused largely on getting more women to "lean in" to candidacy (Piscopo 2019; Piscopo and Kenny 2020)—with many programs existing around the world preparing women to run for office (Davidson-Schmich, this volume; Geha, this volume). This is still important and necessary work, given the identified gender gaps in party membership and aspirants. But in reality, of course, the political pipeline does not end at elections, requiring a deeper investigation of the dynamics of post-election departure.

Who Stays and Who Goes, and Why Does It Matter?

The dynamics of legislative turnover have important consequences for the quality and "health" of representative democracy. On the one hand, politicians leaving office is not necessarily a problem on its own—low turnover rates might, for example, lead to a growing disconnect between politicians and voters, block the entry of new talent, ideas, and experiences, and diminish the legitimacy of political institutions (Matland and Studlar 2004; Byrne and Theakston 2016; Weber et al. 2024). On the other hand, high turnover rates can limit the accumulation of skills and experience by politicians, and, in turn, the effectiveness of legislatures more broadly (Norris 1997; François and Grossman 2015; Byrne and Theakston 2016).

When there are differences in terms of who stays and who leaves among particular groups of politicians, this raises further concerns around representativeness and (in)equality. Addressing unequal power relations within parties and political institutions requires not only that women and other underrepresented groups are present, but that they also gain political power—including through building expertise and networks. If women and other underrepresented groups are exiting early, then, this keeps a particular type of political power—built around knowledge, authority, and seniority—in the hands of men from majority groups (Muriaas and Stavenes 2023), limiting opportunities for substantive impact and potentially curtailing the symbolic effects of political presence on citizen attitudes and political engagement (Vanlangenakker et al. 2013).

Studies have approached the question of who stays and who goes in politics (and why) from a variety of perspectives—focusing on different levels of analysis, which has (at times) resulted in a somewhat scattered body of work. The literature on aggregate turnover rates, for example, largely focuses on politico-institutional and systemic factors at the legislative level. Electoral volatility, the structure of political career opportunities, strong bicameral legislatures, the level of regional autonomy, the size of the legislature, and the electoral system are all factors found to affect turnover rates (e.g., Matland and Studlar 2004; Heinsohn and Freitag 2012; Gouglas et al. 2018).

While macro-level studies can provide interesting insights into change over time, they are less helpful in identifying why and how political careers end (cf. Vanlangenakker et al. 2013). Micro-level studies of turnover, in contrast, focus on individual-level MP data. Often employing surveys, elite interviews, and/or personal visits aimed at former politicians, these studies delve deeper into the reasons why MPs leave—whether voluntarily before or at the end of a parliamentary term or involuntarily through party deselection or electoral defeat (see, for example, Borders and Dockery 1995; Shaffir and Kleinknecht 2005; Allen 2013; Vanlangenakker et al. 2013; Byrne and Theakston 2016). Lack of resources and opportunity costs (such as care responsibilities), career ceilings or ambitions for post-parliamentary careers, and health and age have been identified as potential drivers for MPs' retirement, among others (e.g., Francis and Baker 1986; Weber et al. 2024).

Fewer scholars, however, have paid attention to meso-level (party-level) explanations for (in)voluntary exit, though several authors point to their importance (Slegten and Heyndels 2022; see also François and Grossman 2015; Gouglas et al. 2018). As van de Wardt et al. (2021) argue, the demographics and cultures of political parties play a key role—with underrepresented groups (women, visible minorities, and lower educated MPs, amongst others) more likely to exit (either voluntarily or involuntarily) if the share of their group within the party is low. Vanlangenakker et al. (2013) similarly point to the crucial role of parties in shaping women's exit from politics—with women less likely than men to report that they are leaving politics because they want to retire, and significantly more likely to report that they had been de-selected by their party. Slegten and Heyndels (2022) find that female incumbents are less likely to depart when their local party leader is female; but that incumbents' turnover is also more sensitive to previous electoral performance when they are the same sex as their local party leader.

Together and separately, these different approaches are important additions to our understanding of who stays in politics and who does not. But there is a need to bring these different strands together to evaluate the interplay between personal, party-political, and institutional and contextual factors; and to unpick the who, how, and why of political dropout. This requires researchers to understand and disentangle how power is distributed in parties and political institutions. Studies of women's political tenures, for example, often focus on comparing women's and men's entry points and career length (see, for example, Lawless and Theriault 2005; Joshi and Och 2020; Lazarus et al. 2022). These studies make important contributions to explaining whether and why there is a "leaky pipeline" in politics—with most studies suggesting that women enter politics later and leave earlier than their male counterparts (Lawless and Theriault 2005; Lazarus et al. 2022), though this trend is not always straightforward (Praino and Stockemer 2018; Joshi and Och 2021). These individual-level dynamics, however, must be contextualized within their (gendered) institutional settings.

Muriaas and Stavenes (2023), for example, shift the focus from individual political careers to the gendered composition and institutional dynamics of parliament. They argue that political endurance is (in itself) an important source of parliamentary power, and that understanding these dynamics and measuring political seniority requires an evaluation of not just the share of women who serve by term, but also their share relative to those who have served longer and reached a certain "saturation point" of skills, knowledge, and networks. The question of "short" and "long" careers then is a relative matter, rather than absolute; it requires a contextual approach to understanding power relative to the dominant group, and within parties and political institutions relative to where that power lies (Childs 2013a; see also Meier, Lang, and Sauer, this volume). In the following section, we make the case for considering the dynamics of "dropout" through an FI lens—drawing especially on insights from gendered workplace approaches (cf. Erikson and Josefsson 2022). We focus particularly on the gendered dynamics of "dropout," which we define as politicians standing down for reasons other than non-election (cf. Allen 2013; see also Runderkamp 2024)—thereby narrowing in on the crucial issue of (non-)retention. We then briefly illustrate our argument through a case study of political dropout in the Netherlands.

Dropout from a Feminist Institutionalist Perspective

Questions of how and to what degree a given party and/or parliament's inner workings are gendered are crucial to understanding (in)equalities in the representative process (Erikson and Verge 2022; see also Bjarnegård and Kenny, this volume). The formal and informal rules of political institutions structure the way its inhabitants work and act. Political dropout, then, may say something about a group's satisfaction with political work and their ability to do that work (Bernstein and Wolak 2002). Given that these institutions were founded historically for and by men from majority groups, gender and other structures of power are deeply embedded in the inner workings of parties and political institutions, shaping organizational cultures and "ways of doing things," and distributing power and resources in unequal ways. An FI lens further highlights the ways in which "outside" factors may impact "inside" political work (cf. Runderkamp 2024), pointing to the interplay of seemingly neutral institutional rules with wider social norms like the sexual division of labor and gendered stereotypes (Krook and Mackay 2011; Lowndes 2020; Erikson and Verge 2022). These dynamics create particular challenges for women and other underrepresented groups, and the different circumstances they face in their representative work after being elected may in turn affect their desire to stay in these institutions (Vanlangenakker et al. 2013; van de Wardt 2021; Runderkamp 2024).

To assess these dynamics, we draw on the FI-inspired Gendered Workplace Approach (GWA) (Erikson and Verge 2022; Erikson and Josefsson 2022)—which we argue can help scholars better understand why and under what conditions women exit politics. While studies of parliaments as gendered workplaces usually focus on women in office, we argue that they can also be used to study gendered dropout decisions (Runderkamp 2024). Politicians who drop out are usually outside the reach of the existing empirical focus on interviews or surveys of sitting MPs (Erikson and Josefsson 2022), or even ethnographic and direct observational work in parliaments (Miller 2021). Focusing on those who leave can provide a counter to this "survivorship bias," presenting an often-untapped resource for better understanding the inner workings of parties and political institutions. In turn, the GWA framework can offer insights into the institutional and contextual factors that might shape dropout decisions, including beyond the political (Runderkamp 2024).

GWA distinguishes between five dimensions that comprise the parliamentary workplace—each of which, in combination or alone, can contribute to drop out and should be part of our scrutiny of the leaky pipeline of politics (cf. Erikson and Josefsson 2022; adapted by Runderkamp 2024). *Dimension 1* focuses on the organization of work—this requires researchers to explore the interplay between the personal and the political, as well as how work is regulated—for example, through parental leave or working hours. The "ideal" party member or representative, for example, is often based on a "full-time dedication norm" (Verge and de la Fuente 2014), where it is assumed that others are handling caregiving responsibilities. This norm is reflected in un-family-friendly sitting times and party activities, limited work-family policies, and informal expectations about "working long hours" and "being seen" (Lowndes 2020, 546; Erikson and Verge 2022). This can create additional obstacles and costs for women (especially mothers), where the sexual division of labor and caring responsibilities at home can in turn shape the time and energy women have "left" to spend on their political careers (Runderkamp 2024).

Dimension 2 focuses on how tasks and assignments are determined and allocated within political institutions—for example, in committees, party groups, and leadership bodies. This requires not only mapping numbers, but also gathering evidence on the more informal "status and expectations" associated with particular tasks and positions (Erikson and Josefsson 2022, 29) to establish where power *really* lies. Lawless and Theriault (2005), for example, highlight that women are less willing than men to stay in the US Congress when they hit a "career ceiling"—that is, when they have served for longer periods of time but have not accrued powerful positions (see also Theriault 1998). Lawless and Theriault (2005) argue that this situation relates to women's focus on policy influence as a career goal (versus status): women opt out of the political process once their ability to influence the legislative agenda stalls. Related to this, *Dimension 3* centers on how leadership is appointed and performed—with gendered inequalities in appointments to leadership positions and gendered stereotypes around the "doing" of leadership making it more difficult for women to not only become, but also remain leaders.

Dimension 4 focuses on the institutional infrastructure that supports political work. This includes both "hard" infrastructure—for example, the physical features of political institutions—and the "soft" infrastructure and human support functions that support politicians in their daily work (staffers, civil servants, clerks, etc.) (Erikson and Josefsson 2022). Here, seemingly small issues—the location of women's restrooms, the presence (or not) of recreational spaces, the physical layout of the chamber—can either facilitate or present further obstacles to women's daily work in parliament, making them more or less likely to want to stay.

Finally, *Dimension 5* relates to the interaction between politicians, and the formal and informal rules that "establish the terms for how to behave" (Erikson and Josefsson 2022, 32)—whether in formal spaces like the chamber or committees, or in more informal interactions. Gendered patterns of speech—centered around adversarial, zero-sum styles of debate (see, for example, Lovenduski 2005)—and/or homosocial (Bjarnegård 2013) and homophilic practices (van de Wardt 2021)—whereby those in power prefer to work and network with demographically similar individuals—can mean that women and other underrepresented groups are less likely to "fit" within parties and institutions, and thus are more likely to leave (see also Raychaudhury, this volume). Bullying, micro-aggressions, sexual harassment—compounded by the general lack of robust formal measures adopted by parties and parliaments to act on these issues (see Kosiara-Pedersen, this volume)—may additionally affect women's decisions about whether to run for office again.

The Gendered Dynamics of Dropout in the Netherlands

We briefly illustrate the gendered dynamics of dropout through a case study of the Netherlands, drawing on the findings of Runderkamp's (2024) qualitative analysis of dropout among women politicians at the local level. While collecting data from former politicians is "notoriously difficult and time consuming" (Vanlangenakker et al. 2013, 64), interviews can provide important insights into the contextual conditions of dropout; into the interplay between the formal, informal, personal, and political; and into the "inner workings" of parties and political institutions. Focusing on the local level is of crucial importance to understanding the "leaky pipeline"—as it is a critical pathway into political careers at other levels (Allen 2013; Slegten and Heyndels 2022) and into other roles in local politics (e.g., in Dutch politics, councilors often become mayors, and alder(wo)men).

In the Netherlands, women have been politically underrepresented since they were able to vote and get elected. Currently, women make up 40 percent of the Lower House and 37 percent of the Upper House (Inter-Parliamentary Union 2024), but only around 30 percent of local-level politicians. It is also a context where dropout has been increasingly politicized in public debate as a democratic problem—with successive reports highlighting the worrying trend of Dutch politicians serving shorter terms and of high turnover rates (Remkes 2018; Ministerie van Binnenlandse Zaken en Koninkrijksrelaties 2022). The few studies that do exist on women and dropout in the Dutch context show that women councilors serve for shorter periods and drop out more often than men (Castenmiller et al. 2002; Tjalma-den Oudsten 2006). Women are more likely to be replaced by men (Castenmiller 2015), and are less likely to move up the political ladder (Jansen et al. 2016) or to obtain more attractive positions post-dropout (Claessen et al. 2021).

Runderkamp's (2024) study explores these gendered dynamics through a set of semi-structured interviews with Dutch councilors and alderpersons who had dropped out of politics during the legislative term of 2018–2022. Her study investigated interviewees' lived experiences, their perceptions of dropout, and their reasons for leaving politics. Drawing on the GWA framework, her interviewees highlighted the interplay between the organization of work within political institutions and outside of them as an important factor that pushed them to drop out of politics (Dimension 1). Described by some female former councilors as "playing simultaneous chess" (Runderkamp 2024, 6), many faced not only a "second" shift of care and domestic work at home, but also a "third shift" of paid employment alongside the part-time (and poorly remunerated) political occupation of councilor. Political and party meetings were frequently scheduled in the evenings or on afternoons when children were off from school, with working hours structured around the needs of those without caring responsibilities.

Local councils were perceived as "greedy institutions," with conventions of long hours (well beyond those that were officially stipulated) and prioritization of the political work over other commitments. While this greediness "consumes" both women and men, it creates additional obstacles and costs for women, who are more likely to shoulder the bulk of care and domestic responsibilities and may therefore be less able to live up to the expectations of being a "good worker" (cf. Mackay and Rhodes 2013). These dynamics were compounded by the increasing professionalization and complexity of local government work (Dimension 2), which favors highly educated politicians with particular areas of specialization ("gray men" as one interviewee described them), rather than "lay-people's governance." Even topics deemed "soft" or perceived as feminized—such as youth services—were very complex and required extensive preparation and consultation outside "normal" working hours. Indeed, several interviewees stepped down directly due to stress-related health reasons.

Runderkamp's analysis further highlights that women's leadership is far from normalized in local councils (Dimension 3)—reflected vividly in one municipality where the meeting of party leaders was colloquially called the "wise gentleman's meeting" (Runderkamp 2024, 9). Women's decisions to drop out were further shaped by gender-role incongruity and the high work pressures of leadership, as well as more informal and gendered practices of silencing (with one young woman party leader reporting that none of her interventions had been included in the formal minutes of party leader meetings). These experiences were compounded by inequalities embedded in the political infrastructure of local councils (Dimension 4)—including old town halls that were not accessible to disabled women or had no suitable rooms for breastfeeding. Local party infrastructure offered little support for development or training (for example, on budgeting and finance), disadvantaging political newcomers (including women), who were then more likely to leave as a result ("last in, first out").

Women in local politics also navigated institutional logics of appropriateness, networks, and relationships (Dimension 5) that did not always align comfortably with "new" or more inclusive ways of working. In discussing their reasons for dropping out of politics, women local politicians cited the privileging of adversarial styles of political debate over cooperation and consensus; informal sanctions for "doing things differently"; and experiences of everyday sexism and insecurity. These "do's and don'ts" had been decided on by those who had been present the longest, putting women and other underrepresented groups at a disadvantage, and contributing to a wider sense of "non-belonging" among many women local politicians.

Conclusion

A more equitable politics for women rests not just on being able to enter, but also being able to remain in political institutions. Pathways into and out of politics often differ for men and women, with wider consequences for the representativeness, efficacy, and legitimacy of parties and political institutions. Studies of political recruitment emphasize the importance of understanding individual-level decisions and interactions within their broader institutional and party-political context in order to explain representative outcomes (Norris and Lovenduski 1995; Kenny 2013). This chapter argues for a deeper examination of the interplay between personal, party-political, and institutional factors in order to unpick the who, how, and why of political dropout. Drawing on FI and gendered workplace approaches, it contends that an understanding of the gendered and internal power dynamics of parties and political institutions is highly relevant to the question of who leaves politics - and why. The chapter suggests that the gendered logic of dropout needs to be contextualized within its wider institutional setting.

We highlighted the potential value of this approach in the context of an illustrative case study of Dutch local politicians who dropped out of politics. Qualitative findings highlighted the gendered dynamics of and interplay between different dimensions of working conditions within local councils (both formal and informal), as well as the ways in which institutions and structures "outside" of the political workplace shape and constrain what happens "inside" it. In the Dutch case, women have tried to adapt to institutions and ways of working that are often not designed for them—and that favor experienced and highly educated individuals with time and resources to spare and no caring responsibilities. Gender inequalities in the organization and operation of political work, in turn, produce gendered outcomes, including dropout. Future studies could further explore the institutional and party-political context, as well as politicians' lived experiences of dropout, including intra- and inter-group differences. While we have touched briefly upon age and disability here, other inequalities merit further investigation throughout the political lifecycle, as well as across cases and countries.

Activists, policymakers, and organizations seeking to increase women's representation must also take dropout into account when devising reform strategies. Practitioners and academics can strengthen each other's efforts—for example, building on shared collaborations to gender-sensitize political institutions and parties and improve their working conditions and distribution of political power (see Verge, this volume; Childs, this volume). Without these efforts, a truly gender-equal politics will remain out of reach.

5

Gender, Newness, and Party System Change

Karen Beckwith

Do new institutions open new political opportunities for women?[1] Evidence from a range of scholarship indicates that when new political institutions are established, women often benefit by having their presence increased, as numbers of elected women rise. New institutions may offer particular opportunities for new actors. Newly established institutions (e.g., new parliaments) and new institutional arrangements (e.g., new electoral systems) are likely to introduce unpredictability for political parties and political elites. In conditions of uncertainty, all potential contenders for political office grapple with new circumstances, and previous knowledge and experience may fail to position previously established ("old") political elites for electoral advantage. Those representing new groups, or persons who have not previously held or contested for office—like women—may find themselves, in relative terms, less disadvantaged than was their experience under long-standing institutions (Beckwith 2007; see also Mackay 2014).

This chapter focuses on "newness" regarding how two sets of institutions—electoral systems and political party systems—shape electoral competition. Electoral systems scholarship has identified how the type of electoral system sets the context for party competition and how such competition may, within parties, affect party decisions about candidacies, with profound impacts on women's candidacy opportunities and strategies. There has been little attention, however, to how party systems—generally understood to be distinguished by the number of effective political parties and the level of electoral competition among them—influence women's nomination and election opportunities (but see Valentim and Dimas 2024). Because the electoral system impact is seen as direct and consequential

Karen Beckwith, *Gender, Newness, and Party System Change*. In: *Gendering Party Politics*. Edited by: Meryl Kenny and Elin Bjarnegård, Oxford University Press. © Oxford University Press (2025).
DOI: 10.1093/oso/9780197793985.003.0005

for women's candidacies,[2] few scholars have addressed the indirect impact of electoral systems, mediated by party systems—or the potentially direct impact of party system type—on women's access to national elective office. There is even less scholarship that specifically addresses change in political party systems and the impact of such change on the numbers of female candidates for national office.

There is reason to anticipate that changes in a country's party system, with new political parties and new arrangements of party competition, will offer opportunities for previously excluded or underrepresented groups, such as women. Treating the party system as the institution of interest, this chapter develops a framework for examining the intersection of new institutions and new actors and considers the potential impacts of changes in a party system upon women's access to national legislative seats. The following sections theorize the relationship between electoral systems and party systems (Electoral Systems, Party Systems), what is meant by "newness" (Newness and Party Systems), and how party systems might specifically have an impact on political women (New Party Systems, Gender, and Women's Candidacies). The chapter then considers how party system newness might function, employing brief examples from France, Italy, and the United Kingdom, regarding changes and/or stasis in their party systems (Party Systems and Women's Representation).[3]

Electoral Systems, Party Systems

The extensive scholarship on the relationship between type of electoral system and women's access to candidacies identifies multi-member proportional representation (MMPR) systems as offering greater opportunities for women's candidacies than do single-member plurality (SMP) systems or majority electoral systems. In MMPR systems with multiple nomination slots available, political parties have scope to nominate women, among many nominees, and to place them on party lists that can assure their election or that can render their election highly unlikely. Closed lists, with no preference vote or panachage opportunities, similarly increase party control of election outcomes for their nominees, including women. MMPR systems also arguably more easily accommodate gender quotas for candidacies than do other electoral arrangements. Closed lists, with quota provisions requiring gender equity with zipped lists, further increase the likelihood of the election of women. Note, however, that proportional representation alone does not guarantee women's candidacies; although proportional representation offers parties the opportunity of listing women as candidates, at low cost to the party, political parties may simply choose not to nominate women.

Electoral systems also change, in response to party preferences regarding inter-party competition and with anticipated changed outcomes (see Issever-Ekinci 2023). That is, the structure of the party system is endogenous to electoral system change. For example, France changed its majoritarian electoral system to proportional representation (PR) for the 1986 National Assembly elections, as the Parti Socialiste (PS) anticipated an electoral sweep by parties of the right. Those parties subsequently rescinded the 1985 election law and returned France to its two-stage majoritarian system for the 1988 Assembly elections. Similarly, Italy changed its electoral system in 1992, in the hopes that such changes would decrease the number of parties competing for political office and produce a majority governing party. In each case, change in inter-party competition was at issue; particularly in the Italian case, electoral system changes were intended to produce changes in the party system, to increase government stability and accountability (Morlino 1996).

In short, electoral systems shape candidacy opportunities, opening or foreclosing nomination likelihood. As Chappell (2014, 575) argues, feminist institutionalist analysis can reveal opportunities identified by "institutional outsiders," such as women, who can employ them to advance their goals, including access to office. Where an electoral system—developed across time by male parliamentarians and sustaining incumbency and reselection advantages for male candidates—changes, the party system may also change. In so doing, institutions of political recruitment may be revealed as gendered (Kenny 2013, 5–10), transforming the candidate opportunity structure for women. As political parties recalculate in the context of changed formal rules for nominations and translation of votes into seats, party elites recognize such changes (i.e., "how things are done around here") and adjust their behavior in terms of nomination and campaign strategies (Lowndes 2014, 688). In so doing, a potentially newly gendered party system may emerge, and, with new patterns of competition, opportunities are recognized that can produce new political parties, as established parties collapse or reconfigure themselves.

Newness and Party Systems

As new institutional arrangements in a party system emerge, how does "newness" function? Which components (or combination thereof) of newness produce specific outcomes? Research identifies innovation, flexibility, inexperience, openness, and freedom from convention and conventional practices as aspects of new institutions and new actors. In contrast, absence of change—or continuity of institutions and actors—includes factors of experience, established structures, rules and practices, closedness, inability to adapt to unforeseen challenges (Pierson 2000, 2004), and susceptibility to "surprise" (Kanter 1977, 969). Not all aspects of "new" are carried into newly established institutions; similarly, "old" institutions, persisting, may relinquish some components of the old (Mackay 2014).

Newness in party systems may be evidenced in two ways: (1) as a change in the number of effectively competitive political parties, creating a new arena of competition; and (2) as a change in the types of parties that contend for office, creating a new candidate opportunity structure. As Regalia (2018, 82) notes, the morphology of party systems includes "the number of units making up the system and their relative strengths" and "the dynamics of competition (... how the parties relate to and compete with each other)." In each case, newness in a party system is likely to offer the possibility of gendered changes.

The importance of newness is its introduction of unpredictability in extant power relationships. As public opinion changes, uncertainty is introduced into the party system. Party system change can be ignited by those parties that (1) recognize the change in public opinion and (2) act on the opportunity by offering voters new issue positions. The emergence of a new political party—or a reconfiguration of an established party—can create uncertainty; a shift in support for one party can radically change the competitive balance among parties in a party system. New social movements, with new actors, can also challenge this balance.

This chapter treats the party system as an institution. In summarizing the literature on institutional change, Mahoney and Thelen (2009) find that most scholarship treats individual parties, individual branches of government, or single policies as institutions rather than the complex of strategic interaction in which all single institutional examples are located. As a result, these authors argue, the institutional scholarship focuses on statis and replicability across time, emphasizing "continuity over change" and path dependence (Mahoney and Thelen 2009, 6). In treating the party system as the institution to examine individual party change and women's electoral opportunities within individual parties, this chapter focuses on exogenous shocks and "critical junctures" to analyze individual party response to party system change. Party systems are not self-replicating institutions but are at the mercy of external impacts, including changes in public opinion, key international events, changes in the electorate such as extension or contraction of voter eligibility, changes in election law and election rules, voter behavior, citizen access to voting, and the strategic decision-making of political parties within the system. Individual parties face conditions over which they may have little control when a party system changes, the consequences with which individual parties must contend if they are to persist. As Mahoney and Thelen write (2009, 8), "there is nothing automatic, self-perpetuating, or self-reinforcing about institutional arrangements."

New Party Systems, Gender, and Women's Candidacies

How does newness of parties and party systems change the gendered opportunity structure for female candidates? Note, first, that new opportunities for candidacies that may open for women often open for others or for specific subsets of women (e.g., men who are new actors, women from a privileged class or from specific ethnic groups). Second, the relationship between party systems and candidacies has always been gendered, insofar as the political parties that constitute a party system have been dominated by men, creating both political parties and their systems that are structured to elite men's life experiences and policy preferences.[4] Potential candidates and party elites are therefore seen both as "gendered actors working with rules" (Lowndes 2020, 546) and gendered actors strategizing for access—or blocking or facilitating access—within institutions.

The best opportunities for women's political representation, as new actors, should emerge when new institutions are formed or forming. With the disruption of incumbency and with the termination of institutional facets hostile to newcomers, a new party system should offer openings for new actors to shape the institution in ways that are friendlier to them and more inclusive. New actors will have their best chances of influencing institutional development to their advantage when they anticipate the new institutional openings and are prepared to participate at the outset in shaping institutional alternatives to their advantage (or to forestalling changes that would exclude them from political access). Activist feminists, recognizing opportunity and mobilizing early, have the potential to shape new institutional arrangements before institutional change consolidates to their disadvantage (e.g., see Waylen 2007; Mackay 2014).

New institutions, however, do not guarantee that new actors will prevail; new institutions offer opportunities to everyone, including "old" or established actors. Established actors with appropriate skills, vision, and flexibility in the face of change are likely to be advantaged in the construction of new institutions. Located in pre-existing networks and with access to resources, established actors will be able to take advantage of new institutional arrangements, excluding or diminishing opportunities for new actors. Even where new political parties and/or new internal party arrangements are targeted toward women's issues and female voters, "old" established actors may still predominate among party nominees, given that "[a]ctors carry their existing scripts forward when building [or facing] new institutions" (Mahoney and Thelen 2009, 5). Male political elites, in particular, have the advantage of homosocial capital developed across time, and are located in social networks that may survive major disruptions to the party system (Bjarnegård 2013; see also Àbàtì and Adeniji, this volume). Moreover, new actors may not immediately recognize a changed context and an emergent new party system; if so, new actors will be unable to take advantage of any opportunities for access that a changing party system might offer. It is unlikely, however, that all incumbent actors will anticipate institutional change or be positioned (or willing) to take advantage of the changes to protect their interests or to prevent new actors from shaping new institutions (Lowndes 2014).

Third, "old" institutions, carrying established structures of inclusion and exclusion, present challenges to marginalized or underrepresented political actors, constituting the current, dominant candidate opportunity structure that women face in most political systems when militating for access to nominations (see Josefsson, this volume). Even where women as new actors challenge established party system institutional arrangements, persistence of an established party system may foreclose opportunities for women's access to nominations. Scholarship on the means by which institutions are gendered emphasizes the apparently neutral but thoroughly gendered structural arrangements that embed women's political exclusion (Mackay 2014; Lowndes 2014; Connell 1990). In these cases, the exclusionary components of institutions may persist beyond the presence of established political elites.

Nonetheless, old institutions may offer some limited openings to those previously excluded, where established incumbents are no longer present (or willing) to "work" the exclusionary mechanisms of institutional arrangements. Established incumbents and party elites may see some limited opportunities for their own advancement and accede to challenges by (a few) new actors. As Chappell (2014, 575) observes, "The interaction between 'old' institutional actors with new external 'critical friends,' and vice versa, can also (re)politicize the other, providing essential ideas, resources, and ballast for pursuing new gender agendas." Under such conditions—where low-competition openings emerge (Beckwith 2015), where social movements organize to insist upon inclusion, and where remaining elites come into conflict with each other, creating elite splits that lead to political opportunities for others (Tarrow 2011)—aspiring new actors may find occasional openings that can be exploited to increase their political representational presence. In the absence of changes in the party system, rules benefiting male candidates persist, to the disadvantage of women as new actors seeking nomination.

Moreover, absent women's mobilization or party changes in the rules, women's access to candidacies will continue to be limited (or even diminished). Under these conditions (no institutional change), women's mobilization within and outside parties for gender quotas—combined with internal pressure on parties from individual women seeking nomination—have been necessary. When political, electoral, or party system arrangements persist, but previous political actors have been removed from power, women's candidacy opportunities are likely to improve.

An example of the set of conditions where old actors persisting under unchanged institutional arrangements but pushed by new actors seeking entry is that of political parties that had begun to respond to internal mobilization by women within the party, absent any party system change. A powerful established party that, with difficulty, is willing to nominate more women than had been the party's past practice, has the capacity to elect more women in its party delegation to the national legislature.

Finally, established, entrenched actors in institutions of long standing are likely to foreclose meaningful access for already marginalized actors or for new emerging actors. Old actors, inhabiting already existing institutions built by and for them, will be strongly positioned to maintain and to protect their power and to exclude challengers, and will hold strong veto power over challenges to the party system (see Mahoney and Thelen 2009, 18–22). Absent major institutional change and/or disruption, new actors will confront conditions of inclusion that advantage those already established in power, and they are likely to find access only on established terms, in competition with experienced incumbents. The presence of "old" actors in "old" institutions is likely to present serious, persistent closedness, the "worst opportunity" for new actors, discouraging them from attempts to challenge existing nomination practices. In the absence of party system changes or internal changes within individual political parties, established actors—primarily men—will continue to dominate party nominations and hence election to national legislatures. Absent unforeseen events or major changes in electoral competition among political parties, women are likely to continue to be underrepresented among party candidates and hence among elected legislators.

Party Systems and Women's Representation: Examples from France, Italy, and the United Kingdom

The relationship between party systems and women as a new candidacy group can be illustrated through three brief examples of a subset of the intersections of party systems and women's election to parliaments. These examples illustrate how party systems, varying by newness, may provide electoral entry to women. They also suggest how party systems, in the context of newness, may be re-gendered.

New Party System and New Actors: Party System Change in France

The French political party system changed dramatically in 2017. A new party, République en Marche (REM), emerged to contest the 2017 elections, winning the presidency and an outright majority of National Assembly seats. The two major parties grounding the French party system, representing the center-right (Les Républicains [LR], formerly Union pour un Mouvement Populaire) and the established left (PS) lost many seats: the former lost 82 and the latter 250. Front National, a radical right party seen as violating the historic republican commitments of French political culture, continued to compete as a minor party, unsuccessfully in 2017, winning only eight seats.

The critical elections of 2017 signaled a major change in the French party system, "changing the nature and content of party competition" (Gougou and Persico 2017, 308). Formed in 2016, in 2017 in its first outing, REM won an absolute majority of National Assembly seats (350/577), while the established party blocs faced substantial seat losses, with PS particularly hard hit.[5] The 2017 elections were also remarkable for the high turnover in National Assembly membership: "no less than 60% of the outgoing members who ran again were beaten, and roughly 75% of the elected members of parliament [were] elected for the first time" (Kriesi 2018, 53).

With a new party and a newly configured party system, female candidates fared particularly well in the 2017 elections. A record number of 224 women were elected to the Assembly in 2017 (38.82 percent of deputies),[6] an increase of 69 more women elected since 2012. In addition, 69.2 percent (143) of all elected women were from REM, which had nominated a slight majority of women on its candidate lists. REM, as a new party with no incumbent candidates, opened major nomination opportunities for women.[7]

The 2022 National Assembly election results confirmed the shift in the party system that had begun in 2017. REM—now competing as Ensemble!—prevailed as the party with the highest number of seats, despite failing to win an absolute majority. PS did not submit individual lists, instead joining with other left parties in the alliance Nouvelle union populaire écologique et sociale (NUPES). LR, submitting separate candidate lists, won 61 seats with 6.98 percent of the vote, losing 51 seats since its 2017 results. In contrast, Front National, competing in 2022 as the Rassemblement National (RN), with 17.3 percent of the vote, increased its previous share of Assembly seats by a factor of 11 (from eight to 89 seats); this permitted RN to form a parliamentary group for the first time since 1986 (Lorimer and Herman 2023, 85). Formerly a minor party, RN became the largest opposition party in the Assembly. In this context, Reconquête!—a new radical right party—emerged in 2021, constituting a challenge to RN to its right.

As in 2017, in 2022, a large number of women stood as Assembly candidates which, in percentage terms, was a record high (44.13 percent); "in one third of constituencies the number of women candidates [was] greater than the number of men candidates."[8] Female candidates won 215 Assembly seats in 2022, a slight decline from the 224 women elected in 2017.

It is not clear whether the changes in the French party system have constructed a clear bipolar arrangement (Kriesi 2018, 55) or instead have established a "tripolarized" party system around a new set of issues beyond a traditional left–right cleavage (Lorimer and Herman 2023, 86; Durovic 2023, 625). What is clear is that 2017 "represented an important shift in French politics [and] a paradigmatic shift in ... party competition" (Durovic 2023, 614). With a new party system confirmed by the 2022 Assembly results, opportunities for women's candidacies opened; women ran for office and won seats in the Assembly. Between 2012 and 2017, the percentage of women in the National Assembly jumped by more than 10 percent.

Changes in the party system facilitated these candidacies. In the context of French gender parity requirements for candidate lists (Lépinard 2018), with new parties emerging in the changing party system, compliance issues became key for small parties (or parties with declining support, such as PS), given their dependence on government campaign subsidies. Although several parties declined to nominate gender parity lists in previous elections, their shift to nominating more equitable numbers of women in 2017 and 2022 is indicative of the impact of the reconfigured party system and the uncertainties of a new competitive party context.

Old Party System Opening to New Actors: Italy and the United Kingdom

Activist women seeking access to legislative candidacies have generally faced a closed-candidate opportunity structure, absent institutional transformation. Without a change in the party system, where few women have been able to gain access to nominations, women are not likely to be nominated for seats in parliament. Nonetheless, women, mobilizing for access, can bring pressure on their parties to nominate (more) women for parliamentary seats. Even without a change in the party system, women within parties can argue that their party will benefit electorally if more women are candidates—even if this claim is inaccurate. Two cases are illustrative of the successes that women can have in entering elective offices in established party systems that are unchanged (or as yet unchanged): the Italian Communist Party (1972–1979) and the British Labour Party (1992–1997).

The Italian party system, from the end of World War II until the 1990s, was dominated by two major political parties: the Christian Democratic

Party (DC) and the Italian Communist Party (PCI)[9]. Between 1950 and 1972, neither party had any particular interest in advancing women as candidates or within the party leadership; few women were elected to the Chamber of Deputies from either party, and few electoral changes had been made that could have transformed the party system. Moreover, the postwar feminist movement had not yet developed to the point at which it could make claims within either party. From the end of the war until 1992, with major electoral system reform, the Italian party system was "old"; that is, the party system was well established, with the DC and the PCI jointly holding approximately two-thirds of all Chamber seats through the end of the 1970s.

Nonetheless, the PCI began to shift its attention to women as a potentially mobilizable electoral force, evidenced by discussion at the Thirteenth Party Congress in 1972, with positive consequences for women's candidacies and election. Between 1958 and 1972, less than 10 percent of the PCI's deputies in the Chamber were women. This changed in 1976. Supported by autonomous feminist activists (e.g., in the Unione donne italiane), feminists within the party mobilized to pressure the PCI to recast its understanding of women's role. They organized to urge the party's support for the liberalization of divorce in the 1974 national referendum and, by 1976, for nominating substantially more women for election to the Chamber of Deputies than had previously been the case. In the 1976 Chamber elections, the PCI nominated 155 women in 29 constituencies, of whom 37 were elected (23.9 percent success rate), constituting 16.7 percent of the PCI parliamentary group.[10] In the subsequent 1979 Chamber elections, the PCI nominated fewer women (115), but presented women in all 31 districts in which the PCI nominated candidates. Female candidates were slightly more successful in 1979: 36 women (31.3 percent) won election,[11] constituting 18.8 percent of the PCI parliamentary group.[12] From 1968 to 1972, the number of PCI women elected to the Chamber doubled (from eight to 16) and doubled again in 1976 (37), thereafter confirmed in 1979 (36).

With no change in the party system, a major political party yielded to the influence of potential new actors (women) seeking access to electoral office. The case of the PCI is illustrative of the relationship between party system stasis and women's electoral access. Under circumstances where women mobilized extensively and intensely within a political party of the left, a major party opened slightly to offer nominations to a previously excluded underrepresented group—women—absent any major electoral or party system changes. In a context of no change, an established political party was willing to welcome (some) new actors, under old rules (even if grudgingly), in response to women's concerted efforts to influence the party and to gain access. The PCI, a party of the left, more responsive to women's inclusion, offered the opening.

In the United Kingdom, the Labour Party is a second example of an established political party opening parliamentary electoral opportunities for women, with little change in the party system. The Labour and Conservative Parties dominated the British party system; since 1974, the two parties have routinely captured more than 70 percent of the vote in national parliamentary elections and, although the joint percentage declined between 2005 and 2015,[13] the two parties continue to dominate and define the national British party system.

In 1997, Labour won the parliamentary elections in a landslide: with 43.7 percent of the vote, in a SMP electoral system, Labour won 418 seats, an increase of 146 seats over the party's previous showing in the 1992 elections. Entering government for the first time since 1974, Labour brought into the Commons an historically high number of women (101), constituting 24.16 percent of Labour seats. The nomination of large numbers of women, in seats where Labour was anticipated to win, and changes in Labour's nomination process by creating all-women candidate short lists, provided the context within which an established political party, with male incumbents present, opened opportunities for a previously marginalized group, absent party system changes. Internal actors, primarily men, responded to persistent mobilization for inclusion by Labour women and feminists. As Harriet Harman wrote, "By 1997, we had a fully formed woman-friendly policy agenda, 100 women candidates in seats we were set to win, and women in the shadow cabinet ready to take their place in the cabinet. This had taken more than 20 years to achieve—but it was a massive change."[14] Similar to the case of the PCI, UK Labour, the major left party in the United Kingdom, with no change in the party system, opened in response to the influence of potential new actors (women) seeking access to electoral office.

In both these cases, in relatively short time spans, one major party opened candidate and election opportunities for women. In neither case did a second major political party match the offer of the party of the left. In Italy, in the same time frame, the DC did not change its nomination or election practices regarding women. The DC elected few women to the Chamber between 1953 and 1979, the numbers actually declining in the 1968 elections and thereafter; the mean number of DC *deputate* across five parliamentary elections resulting in DC government (1963–1979) was 8.8. Similarly, in the United Kingdom, as Labour responded positively to activist women's insistence on inclusion as candidates, the Conservative Party continued to nominate few women, electing only 13 to the Commons in 1997 (Childs 2000). The mean number of Conservative women elected across the previous four parliamentary elections that brought the Conservatives into government (1979–1992) was 14.5 (2.23 percent).[15] Such openings were not a result of any party system change, and hence there was no introduction of newness that might have facilitated women's access to national elective office.

Absent any change in the party system, women's access in these cases required new actors to mount concerted challenges for access, under difficult conditions and across time. Nonetheless, as these cases demonstrate, such challengers may be able to create modest opportunities for themselves. Opening the electoral opportunity structure requires concerted mobilization and strategy by new actors for access to candidacies, across multiple years, and the opening may encompass few parties in the party system. Even in the cases of the PCI and Labour, the opening created in these two major left parties did not create a "contagion of the left" that would have inspired the other major parties to increase their numbers of women's candidacies (Duverger 1954, xxvii).

Conclusion

This chapter provides a preliminary mapping of how newness of institutions may create, forestall, or foreclose candidacy opportunities for women. Newness is of crucial importance, given that institutions "reflect the interests of those who devise them" (Geddes 1995, 239, in Mair 1998, 7). Feminist institutionalism reveals their gendered nature. Party systems, at their outset highly gendered institutions, produced highly disproportionate numbers of male candidates in every effectively competitive political party throughout the twentieth century. Closed to new actors, party systems offered few opportunities for access to candidacies, regardless of party type, marginalizing women and hence requiring institutional change and new party system configurations open to new actors. Newness of party systems, including numbers of new electorally effective political parties, creating new levels of electoral competition among parties, offers opportunities to new actors.

Not all changes in party systems are likely to create openings for women. Even as the number of effectively competitive political parties can change, a change in the number of effectively competitive political parties, as gendered institutions, does not necessarily create new opportunities for women's inclusion. New configurations of electoral competition provide no guarantee of women's inclusion on candidate lists if parties do not make strategic calculations concerning potential advantages of nominating women (or if they fail to recognize an opportunity; see Sawyers and Meyer 1999).

Party systems can also transform as a result of a change in the types of parties that can effectively contend for office, creating a new candidate opportunity structure open to women. If new parties are supportive of women's issues, they may be more willing to nominate women for legislative seats; moreover, new parties, in their first electoral foray, have no incumbents—hence, candidate lists are open to new contestants, including women.[16] Parties of the left have generally but not universally been more receptive to women's candidacies than have parties of the right; European left-libertarian parties, at their founding, worked with feminists on policy issues and election campaigns (Kitschelt 1989). Although not discussed in this chapter, from their origins, Green parties have had long-standing commitments to gender parity in party leadership and candidacies (see Ahrens and Kantola, this volume). Green parties have not had major electoral success at the national level (and none have governed alone in Europe), but the emergence of this type of party has provided a context within which activist women can not only be nominated for office but also leverage other parties to include women on their candidate lists.

Finally, this chapter suggests how party systems, in the context of newness, may be re-gendered. By mobilizing, activist women may bring pressure from within a party to increase attention to inequities in women's candidacies for parliament (as well as for intra-party leadership positions). Mobilizing outside of parties, feminist activists may raise policy issues of importance to women that rise to the level of the political agenda, becoming electoral campaign issues as well. These efforts may be less successful or require heightened organizing in contexts where the party system is not new, but where a single party, absent party system change, may nonetheless provide space for women's candidacies. Where a new party system is emerging, however, activist women have their best chances—sans guarantee—for having an impact that increases their opportunities for candidacies and hence for parliamentary representation.

Notes

1. I have many persons to thank for their help with this chapter. Professor Marta Regalia generously shared her data on women's parliamentary candidacies and election to the Italian Chamber of Deputies for this chapter. Professor Rainbow Murray similarly shared data on women's election to the French National Assembly. Art Martinez provided additional data collection assistance. His work was funded by the CWRU Department of Political Science Undergraduate Research and Mentoring Assistantship Program, through the generosity of an anonymous donor. I also thank Dr. Mark A. Eddy, CWRU Research Services Librarian, for data assistance.
2. One electoral system change is the widespread introduction of gender quotas (see Meier, Lang, and Sauer, this volume).
3. This chapter focuses on three European country cases and their party systems. The relationship between party system change and women's political representation could be elaborated in future research, with particular regard to electoral system and party system changes in countries of the Global South and the introduction of gender quotas in those cases (see Högström 2016; Arendt 2018; Hughes et al. 2019; Clayton 2021).
4. This chapter does not discuss the details of accessing party nominations for elected office, but rather focuses on how changes in a party *system* may create or confirm candidate political opportunities (or lack thereof) for women; or how a change in the party system might serve to disrupt the gate-keeping practices of male-dominated parties (see Geha, this volume). For a detailed discussion of how political party elites may employ informal party rules to deter women from running for party nominations, see Davidson-Schmich, this volume.
5. The Republicans (LR, formerly, the Union for a Popular Movement) took 112 seats, down from 194; the Socialist Party (PS) of former president François Hollande won only 30, down from 280.
6. "France: Assemblée Nationale." Parline: Inter-Parliamentary Union, 2017. http://archive.ipu.org/parline-e/reports/2113_E.htm. The previous Assembly, elected in 2012, included 155 women (26.86 percent; "France: Assemblée Nationale." Parline: Inter-Parliamentary Union, 2012. http://archive.ipu.org/parline-e/reports/arc/2113_12.htm).
7. Jemima Kelly, "France Elects Record Number of Women to Parliament," *Reuters*, June 19, 2017, https://www.reuters.com/article/idUSKBN19911E; see also "France: National Assembly." Global Data on National Parliaments: Inter-Parliamentary Union, 2017. https://data.ipu.org/node/61/elections?chamber_id=13396&election_id=27836.
8. Bruno Cautrès, Vincent Martigny, Olivier Rozenberg, and Martial Foucault. "Legislative elections 2022 – a growing share of women MPs?" *Le Monde*, June 11, 2017, https://www.lemonde.fr/en/2022-legislative-elections/article/2022/06/11/legislative-elections-2022-a-growing-share-of-women-mps_5986477_129.html.
9. The DC was dissolved in 1994; the PCI in 1991.
10. Of these, 27 women were elected for the first time.
11. Eight of these women were elected for the first time.
12. For data concerning the PCI and women's nomination and election, see Beckwith 1981, 241–246; see also Regalia 2021.
13. See "UK Election Statistics: 1918–2023: A Century of Elections," UK Parliament: House of Commons Library, August 9, 2023, https://commonslibrary.parliament.uk/research-briefings/cbp-7529.
14. Harriet Harman, "Labour's 1997 Victory Was a Watershed for Women, *The Guardian*, March 10, 2017, https://www.theguardian.com/commentisfree/2017/apr/10/labour-1997-victory-women-101-female-mps. See also Wäckerle 2022.
15. See Wäckerle 2022, 21: "Conservative women are consistently nominated in constituencies they are less likely to win than men." See also Buchanan 2025, 10: Table: "Female MPs Elected at General Elections, by Party."
16. A minor exception is that some candidates nominated by new parties have been incumbents in "old" parties, leaving their former parties to run on the new party's lists.

6

Political Parties and Roots of Resistance to Gender-Equitable Change

Cecilia Josefsson

Political parties play an important role in the struggle for gender-equitable institutional change as they set agendas, shape motives, and constitute the institutional context in which many struggles over change take place. This chapter focuses on how internal party dynamics matter for struggles over gender-equitable institutional change. In particular, the emphasis is on party elites' resistance to gender-equitable formal institutional change—i.e., policies seeking to advance gender equality—and how party dynamics shape the roots and strategies of resistance to such changes.

Focusing on how parties shape resistance is essential to understanding the worldwide variation in gender equality policy. The gender and politics literature, in pursuit of increasing our knowledge about viable strategies to achieve gender-equitable institutional change, has tended to focus on explaining policy success rather than policy failure and shortcomings (Bergqvist, Bjarnegård, and Zetterberg 2013; Verloo 2018, 4). Undoubtedly, women have achieved significant progress and celebrated numerous gender equality victories in recent decades, which naturally has attracted the attention of feminist researchers. However, the emphasis on gendered institutional change, policy success, and feminist strategies for attaining such success also means that our understanding of the factors behind the lack of change, failure, or shortcomings of gender equality policies remains limited.

In this chapter, I focus on resistance—an often-overlooked factor behind the failures and shortcomings of gender-equitable change. In pursuing such change, feminist actors or change agents are involved in a power struggle in which they encounter adversaries who seek to defend the status quo (Celis and Lovenduski 2018). These opponents actively resist policies perceived as threats to the masculine and male-dominated status quo by dismissing,

Cecilia Josefsson, *Political Parties and Roots of Resistance to Gender-Equitable Change*. In: *Gendering Party Politics*. Edited by: Meryl Kenny and Elin Bjarnegård, Oxford University Press. © Oxford University Press (2025). DOI: 10.1093/oso/9780197793985.003.0006 marginalizing, penalizing, redefining, and undermining the policy and those advocating for it. As gender equality issues often do not neatly align with the left–right political dimension around which many party systems are structured (Catalano Weeks 2022), such power struggles between change agents and status quo defenders often occur *inside* political parties. While resistance essentially is about agency, resistance is also constrained and enabled by the gendered institutional context. Here, party ideology and organization provide the scene and the institutional context in which these struggles occur, shaping both strategies and outcomes.

This chapter begins with a conceptualization of resistance to gender-equitable institutional change, followed by a discussion of the role of political parties in such resistance. In the second half of the chapter, I explore how party ideology, institutions, and organizations shape the roots of resistance to gender quotas, one of the most widespread gender-equitable reforms in recent decades that have sought to reform recruitment practices of political parties. I outline distinct roots of resistance to quotas and suggest that these are likely to vary across different types of political parties. Such roots of resistance matter for parties' and party elites' resistance strategies and, ultimately, how resistance can be challenged and overcome.

Resistance to Gender-Equitable Institutional Change

Scholars across various disciplines—including sociology, anthropology, cultural studies, history, and political science—have shown great interest in resistance, covering a diverse range of topics, from political revolutions to hairstyles (Hollander and Einwohner 2004; Weitz 2001). Resistance can be viewed as attempts to achieve progressive change, where marginalized groups challenge dominating structures and elites (Leblanc 1999; Scott 1985; Skocpol 1979), or as privileged groups' efforts to obstruct such changes (Ambrosio 2016; Bourdieu 1984; Lewin 1988). Drawing on research on gender and politics, and gender and organizations (Celis and Lovenduski 2018; Cockburn 1991; Krook 2016; Lombardo and Mergaert 2013; Pincus 2002; Thomson 2018; Verloo 2018), in this chapter, I focus on political parties and party elites' resistance to gender-equitable formal institutional change—i.e., policies that seek to advance women's rights and gender equality. Resistance, as perceived in this manner, primarily aims at safeguarding established structures, institutions, and power hierarchies within a political system. Hence, the analytical attention is directed toward the privileged political elite and the gendered institutions and strategies that uphold the prevailing male-dominated status quo within the political sphere.

While the concept of resistance is widely discussed in the gender and politics literature—often used to elucidate why gender equality policies encounter obstacles in gaining traction, are inadequately formulated, or fail to be implemented effectively—few researchers have explicitly sought to conceptualize the term. Instead, as Bjarnegård (2018a) points out, many scholars tend to lump all impediments to gender equality initiatives or women politicians under the umbrella of resistance. In contrast to this approach, I distinguish between the (gendered) institutional context and active resistance manifested through deliberate efforts to maintain the status quo (see Josefsson 2024). Drawing from extensive research on resistance across various disciplines (see Hollander and Einwohner 2004 for a review), I propose that resistance should be understood as opposition coupled with some form of broadly defined action, encompassing verbal, physical, material, and symbolic expressions. Viewing it in this light, the gendered institutional context—encompassing rules, norms, and practices—may impose constraints on efforts toward gender equality, but the institutions themselves do not resist. Instead, individuals advocating for or against gender-equitable institutional change engage in a power struggle, which is situated in an institutional and ideational context that distributes power unevenly among actors, thereby facilitating or hindering different approaches and strategies (Celis and Lovenduski 2018; Krook 2016). Thus, (gendered) institutional stability and change are perceived as residing in the relationship between strategic action and the institutional context that favors certain strategies, ideas, and actors over others (Hay and Wincott 1998).

The term "resistance" has frequently been employed alongside the concept of "backlash" to describe reactionary responses with the aim to uphold or strengthen gender inequalities (Flood, Dragiewicz, and Pease 2018; Mansbridge and Shames 2008). I argue that resistance and backlash should be conceptually separated. Backlash represents a particular type of reaction that presupposes and is related to prior advancements—such as reactions to women's progress within society more broadly.[1] Moreover, those who use the term "backlash" often seem to imply that the intensity of backlash is exceptional or disproportionate compared to everyday gender discrimination and harassment (Piscopo and Walsh 2020). Resistance, in contrast, is not necessarily linked to past progress and does not inherently involve an exaggerated response, although it may at times. Consequently, while backlash can be viewed as a form of resistance, not all forms of resistance can be categorized as backlash.

Importantly, political elites' resistance strategies aimed at protecting the status quo from challenges posed by gender-equitable policies vary and can take on many different forms. Such strategies are shaped both by the underlying motive behind resistance—what is perceived to require protection—and what is perceived as possible in the specific institutional and ideational context in which actors are located. First, resistance strategies can be passive or active (Pincus 2002). Passive resistance, such as silence and conscious inaction, might suffice when the change threat is low, such as at the beginning of a policy process, or when policy support is low. In contrast, active resistance strategies, such as arguing and voting against a specific policy proposal, are likely more prominent when the policy idea has gained widespread support and become more threatening. Closely related to the distinction between passive and active resistance, resistance strategies may also be hidden or overt. Here, the extent to which resistance to a specific policy is generally perceived as acceptable plays an important role (Josefsson 2024). In a context where open resistance is perceived as being attached to sanctions, such as public blame, resistance is likely more covert. Actors seeking to defend the status quo may appear to support the policy on the surface while simultaneously seeking to undermine its effects through more hidden forms of resistance (e.g., see Johnson 2017; Krook 2016). Finally, resistance strategies may be primarily individual or collective in character. Individual resistance is characterized by independent and uncoordinated acts of opposition. In contrast, collective resistance entails the coordination of resistance strategies among a group of actors, such as a political party.

Political Parties: Shaping Resistance Motives and Strategies

A study of resistance to gender-equitable policy change must put political parties at the center of the analysis. Political parties are central actors shaping policy outcomes in democracies. Party characteristics—such as the party-specific combination of (gendered) rules, norms, and ideas—shape the underlying motives of resistance to gender-equitable change and the resistance strategies available to actors. Thus, if we are interested in what party elites seek to protect and whether they, in fact, can protect it, we must be open to and empirically explore how these simultaneous and interlocking modes of constraints vary across political parties. This implies that a form of resistance perceived viable for elites in one political party will be more difficult to enact for others due to (perceived) sanctions attached to that specific form of resistance.

Several party-specific factors shape both motivations behind resistance to gender-equitable policies and the resistance strategies actors use to stop gender-equitable policy from being adopted and having an effect. One of the most commonly cited explanations behind a party's support or opposition to gender-equitable policies is ideology. A common assumption is that left-wing parties that put a more significant emphasis on social justice are more supportive of gender-equitable policies. In contrast, right-wing parties, which tend to locate the explanation for social inequalities in individual choices, are more prone to resist policies seeking to advance gender equality. Following this, we could assume that resistance toward gender-equitable policies is motivated by a conservative ideology and is more likely to be open, active, and collective in right-wing parties in comparison to left-wing parties.

Yet, recent research shows that support and opposition to gender-equitable policy do not neatly map onto the left–right divide in politics but instead often cut across this dominant political cleavage (Blofield, Ewig, and Piscopo 2017; Catalano Weeks 2022; Erzeel and Celis 2016; Morgan and Hinojosa 2018; O'Brien 2018). First, the labels of "left-wing" and "right-wing" political parties obscure important differences in attitudes to gender equality among conservative, Christian democratic, and radical right populist parties on the one hand and social democratic, green, and communist parties on the other hand. What is more, while class-based gender equality issues—such as parental leave, childcare, and equal employment—are often associated with social democratic parties, gender equality issues relating to women's status—such as domestic violence or reproductive rights—are not necessarily more often promoted by left-wing parties (Annesley, Engeli, and Gains 2015; Blofield, Ewig, and Piscopo 2017). Catalano Weeks (2022) posits that political parties seek to avoid issues demanded by politically marginalized groups that lie outside the main political cleavage shaping competition in a country. In particular, programmatic parties are constrained by their ideological reputation and want to avoid issues that could exacerbate internal tensions and divert attention from their core "owned" issues (Catalano Weeks 2022, 31).

Moreover, the discussion about ideology as an explanation for parties' support or opposition to gender-equitable policies assumes that parties are programmatic: grounded in a particular ideology, with clear and consistent policy agendas and elaborated political platforms. Yet, many political parties, particularly outside of Western Europe, take a more flexible and pragmatic stance toward policy, seeking to appeal to a broad base of voters to win elections. In such non-programmatic parties, resistance to specific policies is likely not motivated and shaped by ideology. Thus, to explain why parties and party elites resist gender-equitable policies, we must look beyond ideology as an all-encompassing explanatory factor.

In addition to ideology, I argue that we need to closely examine (1) why actors resist— what specific aspect(s) of the status quo actors strive to protect—and (2) the constraints and opportunities afforded to political elites wishing to defend the status quo against challenges posed by gender-equitable policies. This implies that we must consider other party characteristics beyond ideology, such as the party's level of institutionalization, its organization and logic, and constraints on elite decision-making. To illustrate the importance of factors beyond ideological differences for resistance to gender-equitable policies, we will now turn to resistance to gender quotas.

Roots of Resistance to Gender Quotas

One of the most important and widespread gender-equitable policies in recent decades has been the adoption of electoral gender quotas in national parliamentary elections. While some quota laws have proved incredibly effective in "fast-tracking" women's numerical representation in elected legislative bodies (Dahlerup and Freidenvall 2005), in other cases, the percentage of women elected has remained stagnant or even decreased under the new reform (Hughes et al. 2019). Despite much international and domestic advocacy, quota policies have failed to be adopted in many countries or been poorly designed and returned fewer women to parliament than their stipulated goal in many other countries. Indeed, men still dominate legislatures in almost all countries in the world (Inter-Parliamentary Union 2024). Despite the importance of the attitudes and behaviors of the actors in charge of adopting and implementing gender quota policies—the male political party elite—few in the now-vast literature on gender quotas have systematically attended to why and how these actors resist the adoption and implementation of gender quotas (for exceptions, see Krook 2016; Verge and Lombardo 2021).

I suggest that resistance to gender quotas has different roots as it aims to protect distinct facets of the status quo. In Table 6.1, I outline four different roots or forms of quota resistance, what they serve to protect, in which type of political parties we can expect them to be most prominent, what specific resistance strategies they are likely to yield, at what point in the policy process they are most likely to occur, and whether they are gendered in form or not—i.e., whether they are directed at excluding women *because they are women*. These motivations are certainly overlapping, and resisting actors might have difficulty distinguishing between different motivational grounds for their resistance. Moreover, the list of different motivations that I suggest is not exhaustive, and there are likely other roots of resistance at play as well. Nevertheless, the different motives behind quota resistance developed here

Table 6.1 Roots of Resistance to Gender Quotas

	What is sought to be protected?	Types of political parties	Forms of resistance strategies	Stage in the policy process	Gendered in form? (i.e., purpose to exclude *women*?)
Power-seeking resistance	One's chances to get (re-)elected	All parties	Covert, individual	Pre-adoption	No
Idea-based resistance	The party's ideological core The party's core "owned" issues	Programmatic parties (right-wing parties + parties with conflicting core "owned" issues)	Open, active, collective	Pre-adoption	No
Patronal resistance	Candidate selection rules from outside interference, party structures from having to include outsiders	Clientelist parties	Covert, passive/active, collective	Entire policy process	No
Patriarchal resistance	Male privilege, masculine institutions	All parties	Covert passive/active, individ-ual/collective	Entire policy process	Yes

are based on a close engagement with the gender quota literature and my own research on resistance to gender quotas in Uruguay—a case displaying extraordinarily strong and persistent resistance to quotas across very different political parties, including both programmatic and clientelist parties, as well as conservative and left-wing parties (see Josefsson 2024).

While some of the resistance types I outline might be generalizable to policies beyond quotas, different gender-equitable policies challenge the status quo in different ways, which have implications for why actors resist these policies (e.g., see Htun and Weldon 2010). Whereas adopting a quota law can bring important benefits for the male political elite (Bush 2011; Krook 2009; Valdini 2019), it is not surprising that political parties and the male political elite resist gender quota policies. A strong candidate quota law has effective sanctions, such as the rejection of electoral ballots, and placement mandates that force parties to put women in winnable positions on ballots. As such, a strong quota law reduces men incumbents' chances of reelection and deeply interferes with political parties' internal candidate selection procedures. Other gender-equitable policies—such as abortion, parental leave, and policies targeting violence against women—also generate resistance among political parties and party elites. Still, such policies might not target the heart of political parties in the same explicit ways as electoral quotas do. Thus, resistance to such policies might have different motivational grounds and be stronger among other actors in society.

Power-Seeking Resistance: Protecting Reelection

A simple and commonly voiced explanation for gender quota resistance is that the policy threatens male political elites' power and chances to get reelected. Legislators are often described as seeking reelection before pursuing other goals, such as influencing or enacting good public policies (Arnold 1990). A strong candidate quota law with effective sanctions and placement mandates can be perceived as a zero-sum game, where women quota beneficiaries win, and men incumbents lose. Thus, seen from this perspective it is rational that men parliamentarians and party elites resist a policy that threatens their survival in office. In line with such a perspective, Gatto (2016) argues that both individual and aggregate levels of political ambition and electoral security matter for the likelihood of quota adoption, but also for the strength of the design of an adopted quota. Thus, incumbent legislators who have the most to lose from the adoption of a strong quota policy—i.e., ambitious male incumbents who are electorally insecure—should be more likely to resist quota adoption, or if non-adoption is not perceived possible, strong quota designs (Gatto 2016). Both electoral insecurity and political ambition vary across contexts and political parties. In countries where formal institutions prohibit immediate reelection, such as in Mexico and Costa Rica, this form of resistance is likely less prominent in comparison to countries where competition, turnover, and electoral insecurity are high but where legislative office is valued. Likewise, political parties have different rules, norms, and practices for selecting candidates—such as different norms relating to seniority and incumbency benefits—which likely affect to what extent quotas are perceived to threaten individual men party elites.

Given that this type of resistance is motivated by protecting one's chances to be elected, the strategies attached to this form of resistance are likely individual in character, such as arguing against the quota in legislative debates. Consequently, strategies that require more collective efforts at the party level further along in the policy process—such as voting against a quota proposal in a party-centered system or subverting the quota in the implementation stage—are less likely to materialize from this root of resistance. Resistance may also be covert—at least its motivating grounds—as opponents will use values and ideology to dress their resistance in more normatively acceptable terms.

While power-seeking most likely is an important root of resistance to gender quotas worldwide and in many different types of political parties, quotas seldom threaten party elites in safe places on candidate lists, but rather men lower down in party hierarchies in unsafe list positions. Still, party elites and entire political parties resist quotas. For instance, Kjerulf Dubrow (2011) found that Polish male Members of Parliament (MPs) placed in lower, insecure positions on candidate lists displayed greater support for quotas in comparison to men placed higher on lists in safer positions. Thus, in most cases, quotas are also resisted for other types of reasons.

Idea-Based Resistance: Protecting Ideas and Core Owned Issues

Another explanation often put forward to explain variation in quota support and opposition across political parties is ideology, or what I label *idea-based resistance*. Right-wing political parties typically attribute social inequalities to individual rather than structural factors. Given this problem formulation, gender quotas are often not seen as an appropriate solution to women's underrepresentation. Instead, solutions that target individual women by seeking to enhance their political ambition and skills, such as training and capacity building for women, are often deemed more suitable. Not surprisingly, conservative parties have been more resistant to adopt voluntary (Davidson-Schmich 2006; O'Brien 2018) and electoral gender quotas (Murray, Krook, and Opello 2012), and MPs in economically liberal and religiously conservative parties are less likely to support quotas (Kjerulf Dubrow 2011). While left-wing parties generally have been more supportive of gender quotas (Caul 2001), large differences are also found in this party family, where far-left or communist parties have been more unwilling to adopt gender quotas (Josefsson 2024; Keith and Verge 2018). For example, the Argentine leftist party Movimiento al Socialismo, the Portuguese Communist Party, and the Uruguayan leftist party Movimiento de Participación Popular all opposed the adoption of electoral quotas. As noted above, political parties are generally reluctant to support policies that risk diverting attention from their core owned policy issues and that risk aggravating internal conflict (Catalano Weeks 2022).

This form of resistance, aimed at protecting the party's core ideas and ideology, is more likely to be found in programmatic parties. It is also more likely to generate resistance strategies that are collective, open, and active, as this type of resistance is likely perceived as more normatively acceptable than other forms of resistance. If resistance to quotas is primarily idea-based, I argue that we can expect the most intense phase of resistance to take place pre-adoption. Political elites and parties that resist quotas on ideological grounds will try to ignore the policy idea in the agenda-setting phase, and argue and vote against it in the decision-making phase. If a quota policy is adopted, idea-based resistance does not necessarily lead to subversion in the implementation stage. Finally, I argue that this type of resistance is not necessarily gendered in form, meaning that it is not primarily aimed at excluding women because they are women. Both men and women are likely to resist quotas on ideological grounds, and parties that resist quotas in this way may simultaneously promote women's political inclusion in other ways.

Yet ideology alone is often insufficient to explain the variation in opposition and support to gender-equitable policies across parties worldwide.

To fully understand why parties and party elites resist the adoption and implementation of legislated gender quotas, we must go beyond explanations at the individual level or ideology.

Patronal Resistance: Protecting Party Structures

Another form of resistance to quotas that has received less attention in the literature is what I label *patronal resistance*. The primary goal of this type of quota resistance is to protect party structures from outside interference and parties' power over candidate selection (see also Meier, Lang, and Sauer, this volume). Strong gender quotas have the potential to change the way parties operate and how they recruit legislative candidates. By forcing party elites to choose better candidates instead of close acquaintances, quota reforms can contribute to disrupting insular male networks and increasing diversity in the legislature (Barnes and Holman 2020; Besley et al. 2017; Murray 2014). It follows that for a party whose entire structure rests on insular male networks, a gender quota reform is indeed threatening.

Here, party elites resist quotas because they want to protect party structures by retaining control of whom to select and reward within this hierarchical structure. Viewed this way, resistance to gender quotas and women's political inclusion is not directed toward women because they are women—it is a byproduct of the need for certain types of candidates that are functional to the party leadership. Such candidates must have valuable resources—*instrumental* resources, such as access and insertion into local political networks, political experience, and campaign finances, but also *expressive* resources, such as trustworthiness and perceived loyalty (Bjarnegård 2018a). Research on homosociality has shown that people are inclined to trust those whom they perceive to be "like themselves" by using similarity as a proxy for reliability (Kanter 1993). Thus, while these resources are not exclusive to men, in a context where the important gatekeepers are men, men candidates are much more likely to have homosocial capital consisting of both instrumental and expressive resources (Bjarnegård 2013, 2018a).

I argue that this type of quota resistance is more common in heavily male-dominated parties and in clientelist parties (as opposed to programmatic parties). Clientelist parties typically have weak organizations and place little emphasis on programs and ideology (Gunther and Diamond 2003). In a clientelist party structure, which is built on loyalty and trust between men leaders at different levels (Bjarnegård 2013; Josefsson 2024), when the possibilities of distributing list places to men allies are circumscribed by the quota, the entire party structure is threatened. In this case, quotas threaten male political elites' power indirectly by threatening to destabilize their political support networks and the bonds of trust that hold them together. As quotas are perceived to challenge the very organization and the core functions of the party, resistance strategies are likely to be collective in character and employed across the entire policy process. In order to preserve party elites' power to uphold clientelist networks and distribute list places to their allies, the primary goal must be to stop the quota from being adopted by arguing and voting against the policy. If quota adoption is perceived inevitable, these actors might seek to weaken the design of the quota or subvert the quota in the implementation stage by using loopholes. While resistance strategies might be open, motives may be dressed in language emphasizing values such as constitutionality and democracy.

Patriarchal Resistance: Protecting Male Dominance

Finally, while women's political exclusion can be understood as a byproduct or an unintended consequence emerging from the protection of party structures, party elites' resistance to gender quotas might also be grounded in sexism and an outright desire to exclude women from political power. What I label *patriarchal resistance* is aimed at preserving male power and a male logic of doing politics and thus aimed at excluding women from politics because they are *women*. In this view, the inclusion of more women in politics is perceived as more threatening than forced inclusion of men outsiders.

Sexism has been described as a deeply ambivalent ideology that includes both benevolent and hostile attitudes (Glick and Fiske 1996, 2001). While hostile sexism is described as "antipathy towards women who are viewed as usurping men's power," benevolent sexism involves a chivalrous view of women as pure and moral, but also weak and passive, deserving men's protection and admiration, as long as they conform to traditional gender stereotypes (Glick and Fiske 2001, 109). Hostile sexist attitudes have been found to correlate with citizens' negative attitudes to gender quotas and women's political inclusion, while benevolent sexist attitudes are associated with higher support of quotas among citizens. According to benevolent sexists, women are in need of help and protection, and as such, they might not have what it takes to succeed in politics without assistance from quotas (Beauregard and Sheppard 2021). While women's inclusion in parties and parliament might be positive according to the benevolent sexist, this is only as long as these women conform to male norms and do not seek to change masculine institutions that uphold male power and privilege.

Yet, research from a wide variety of contexts has shown that women tend to do politics differently, that they have a different legislative style, and that socialization and marginalization of women in parliament incentivize women to collaborate more across party lines (e.g., see Barnes 2016; Kathlene 1994; Lovenduski 2005; Piscopo 2016; Rosenthal 2000). Consequently, in many contexts, women MPs have disrupted gendered and informal rules surrounding decision-making in parliament, which might be deeply disturbing to the male political elite.

What men can do, then, to protect masculine institutions that work to the advantage of men is to resist the adoption of gender quotas, weaken the design of quota policies, and subvert the quota in the implementation phase. What is more, they can use their gatekeeping powers to prevent the election of autonomous women who will challenge rules, norms, and practices that advantage men. Yet, the inclusion of loyal women might still disrupt the male logic of doing things in parliament. Including women at higher rates, although these women are loyal and submissive, is not just like including other men.

Patriarchal resistance that aims at excluding women because they are women in order to protect masculine institutions that work to the advantage of men is likely a root of quota resistance in all types of political parties, including both left-wing, conservative, and clientelist parties. Yet in many contexts, patriarchal resistance is likely dressed in more morally acceptable terms. While this root of quota resistance is likely to be found everywhere, I argue that the scope for threatened party elites to act upon their concerns varies by party type and organization. In organizationally thin, elite-based clientelist parties, party elites likely have greater possibilities to simply exclude women in accordance with their sexist attitudes. In comparison, in organizationally thick, mass-based, and bureaucratized parties in which a larger number of people and even grass-roots have been incorporated into party decision-making and where candidate selection is guided by formal rules, sexist party elites may find it more difficult to exclude women and subvert quota laws (see Gunther and Diamond 2003 for a party typology, and Bjarnegård and Zetterberg 2016a on bureaucratized parties).

Conclusion

This chapter has argued that to understand why gender-equitable policies fail to be adopted, are weakly designed, or are poorly implemented, we need to take resistance among political party elites into account. Policy outcomes must be perceived as the result of power struggles over reform that include both opponents and proponents of change (Celis and Lovenduski 2018). I contend that resistance—conceptualized as opposition in combination with action—ought to be analytically separated from institutional inertia. While gendered rules, norms, and practices indeed contribute to failure and inertia—i.e., why gender-equitable change does not materialize—institutions do not resist. Instead, resisting actors' agency must be perceived as enabled and circumscribed by (gendered) institutions. As both motivations behind resistance—what I label *the roots of resistance*—and status quo defenders' (and change agents') power and room for maneuver vary across different types of political parties, the variation in party-specific institutional contexts is central for understanding broader patterns of resistance against various types of gender-equitable reforms. In this chapter, I have focused on the roots of resistance to gender equality change: essentially, what it is that status quo defenders seek to protect. I have suggested that resistance to gender quotas, one of the most important and widely diffused gender equality reforms in recent decades, is likely rooted in diverse desires to protect very different aspects of the status quo. This has implications for the resistance strategies that are perceived viable and where and what type of resistance is likely to emerge. I suggest that power-seeking and patriarchal resistance is likely to emerge in all parties, while ideological resistance is more prominent in programmatic parties, and patronal resistance is more likely to materialize in clientelist parties.

Many policy struggles are fought inside rather than between political parties. Thus, exploring how party-specific formal and informal institutions condition such power struggles by posing constraints or empowering status quo defenders and change agents is crucial if we are to better understand the failure and success of various types of policy initiatives, including but not limited to gender equality policies. Future research should explore to what extent the reasons to resist quotas presented here apply to different contexts and policy issues. While idea-based and patriarchal resistance are likely to emerge also for other gender-equitable policies, power-seeking and patronal resistance are likely more connected to electoral reforms. Moreover, this chapter has primarily focused on the relationship between different types of parties and the motives behind resistance. Yet, how party-specific constraints condition power struggles over institutional change warrants more scholarly attention.

Note

1. Indeed, in her groundbreaking work on backlash against women in the United States, Susan Faludi (1991, xviii), defines backlash as an "attempt to retract the handful of small and hard-won victories that the feminist movement did manage to win for women."

linked to gender equality policies. Future research should explore the [illegible] extent to which [illegible] and policy issues. [illegible] other gender-equality policies [illegible] connected to electoral [illegible]. [illegible] chapter has primarily focused on the relationship [illegible] of parties [illegible] attention.

[illegible]

PART II
METHODS AND CASES

As the introduction (Chapter 1) to this volume highlights, a central insight of gender party research is the equal weight given to not only formal (written) "rules of the game," such as party constitutions, by-laws, or criteria for candidate selection, but also the informal (non-written) rules and shared understandings of "how things are done around here." From a feminist institutionalist (FI) perspective, revealing the gender and institutional dynamics of the "secret garden" of party politics requires a deeper investigation of the interaction between formal and informal rules, tracing dynamic and changing processes of (in)formalization and institutionalization over time (cf. Bjarnegård and Kenny 2015, 750–751). A key first step is to map what *is* actually written down. Here, Karina Kosiara-Pedersen makes the case for starting with formal party regulations—as the structure within de facto party organization takes place—to understand party change. Focusing on parties' organizational dynamics in the context of #metoo and #enblandtos movements in Denmark, Kosiara-Pedersen brings together theories of party organization and party change, FI, and the rapidly growing body of work on violence against women in politics to explore when and why parties adopt formal regulations around harassment, intimidation, and violence.

In contexts with weak formal rules, however, informal rules may either be congruent with these institutions, or may override or compete with them (cf. Helmke and Levitsky 2004). Ọmọ́máyọ̀wá O. Àbàtì and Mayowa M. Adeniji highlight the ways in which informal candidacy requirements and selection practices have worked to blunt the impact of new formal legislative changes reducing candidacy age, with gendered consequences for the political recruitment of young women. Similarly, Malu A.C. Gatto and Kristin N. Wylie's examination of the Brazilian case provides further evidence of the ways in which (white, male-dominated) party elites can deploy informal institutions to subvert formal reforms aimed at ensuring political inclusion. Yet, these authors also argue that the failure of formal rules can open up spaces for informal institutional innovation "from below." Their analysis of the informal institution of *coletivos* points to one way in which politically marginalized groups can themselves draw on informal institutions to circumnavigate exclusionary formal institutions, albeit within the constraints of their own informality.

Alongside these chapters, subsequent contributions further expand the already substantial collection of FI methods and approaches. Proma Raychaudhury draws on post-structuralist approaches and introduces new concepts of "institutional belonging" and "self-making" to center the ways in which women frame themselves as political actors within party cultures, and in relation to other categories of social identity—including caste, class, and religion. Focusing on the Hindu right-wing Bharatiya Janata Party (BJP) in India, Raychaudhury argues that the gendered institutional culture of the BJP is sustained by an "ideal" model of the self-effacing, deferential, and often defeminized woman party worker. While qualitative methods are particularly useful in accessing the underpinning values and beliefs that shape actors' actions, and actors' interpretations of formal and informal rules, quantitative methods can also allow researchers to identify patterns, reveal associations, and assess both the extent of existing inequalities, and their institutional origins. Here, Michal Grahn makes the case for deploying large-N methods to evaluate institutional rules, focusing on the impact of multiple candidate quotas from an intersectional perspective. Grahn's results provide clear evidence that the implementation of quotas has led to a gradual weakening and widening of the template of the "ideal" politician, with native women benefiting the most. Together, these chapters point to the continuing value and potential of both qualitative and quantitative methods in the FI methodological "toolkit."

Taking gender seriously fundamentally changes and enhances not only *how* we study party politics, but also *what* we study. The rapid expansion of specialist topics within the subfield of party politics has been matched by a proliferation of new parties, the gendered dimensions of which have often been overlooked. Green Parties, for example, are established features of many national party systems as well as a political group in the European parliament, yet their gender dynamics are largely unexplored. Here Petra Ahrens and Johanna Kantola contribute new research on the interplay between the national and the supranational, developing an FI intra-party and intra-political-group analysis of whether (and if so why) Green Parties are more gender equal than others. Kimberly Cowell-Meyers similarly provides new insights into a new party type that has received little systematic attention until recently—focusing on women's parties as "agents of contagion" seeking to promote women's representation. Drawing on examples from some of the largest and/or most successful women's political parties in Europe, Cowell-Meyers highlights the institutional conditions under which women's parties influence other political parties and affect women's representation, arguing that these parties operate in unique ways among niche parties.

7
Preventing and Handling Violence in Danish Political Parties

Karina Kosiara-Pedersen

The issue of harassment and violence toward (mostly) women candidates and elected representatives in established democracies has risen to prominence, largely due to the #MeToo campaigns that gained momentum in 2017, although scholarly research in this area predates these recent trends (Bjarnegård and Zetterberg 2023). One area within this field focuses on case studies of (top) women in politics, based either on single or small-n case studies, or on surveys (Krook and Sanín 2016, 2020; Krook 2020). Another area includes both men and women, revealing gender gaps such as a larger level of psychological and sexual harassment for women in politics, and a higher level of physical harassment for men (Herrick et al. 2019; Herrick and Franklin 2019; Bjarnegård et al. 2020; Collignon and Rüdig 2020, 2021; Håkansson 2021, 2023; Bjarnegård 2023). More recently, studies have emphasized the effects of harassment, some of which are gendered (Bardall et al. 2020). Harassment has negative effects on political ambitions (Bradley-Geist et al. 2015; Campbell and Lovenduski 2016; Dhrodia 2018; Haraldsson and Wängnerud 2018; Herrick et al. 2019; Castle et al. 2020; see also Davidson-Schmich, this volume) and on politicians' private lives—for instance, causing negative changes in personal relationships and raising concerns around going out in public or being home alone (Every-Palmer et al. 2015; Bjørgo and Silkoset 2018). Harassment also decreases politicians' mental well-being and increases psychological discomfort (Herrick and Franklin 2019), makes them feell less free to discuss all issues (Bjørgo and Silkoset 2018; Kosiara-Pedersen 2024), and reduces candidates' engagement in specific campaign activities with detrimental effects on election results, particularly for women (Collignon and Rüdig 2021). This chapter contributes to the subfield of harassment and violence in politics by turning

Karina Kosiara-Pedersen, *Preventing and Handling Violence in Danish Political Parties*. In: *Gendering Party Politics*. Edited by: Meryl Kenny and Elin Bjarnegård, Oxford University Press. © Oxford University Press (2025).
DOI: 10.1093/oso/9780197793985.003.0007

from individual experiences of violence to the institutional settings of its prevention and handling.

Democracy rests on a clear premise: elected representatives stand and act for the represented (Pitkin 1967). When (gendered) harassment and violence inhibit candidates and office-holders from campaigning and fulfilling their representative duties, then electoral integrity, democratic legitimacy, as well as descriptive and substantial representation are all harmed (Oskarsson and Wängnerud 1995; Phillips 1995; Young 2000; Mansbridge 2003; Mutz 2015; Krook 2017, 2020; Bjarnegård 2018b). A pertinent question to address, then, is whether—and how—parties (re-)organize to ensure that harassment, intimidation, and violence do not inhibit women's ability to participate and represent in democracies. In response to the #MeToo movement, many organizations and workplaces initiated discussions, implemented policies, and established mechanisms to prevent and address harassment, intimidation, and violence. The research questions this chapter explores are: (1) When and why do parties adopt regulations around harassment, intimidation, and violence? (2) What do these regulations look like in terms of their content, who they protect, and how they are implemented (through existing or new structures)?

Due to the gendered motivations, manifestations, and impacts of harassment and violence in politics (Bardall et al. 2020), studying parties' regulations on how to prevent and address this problem internally shows us whether and how political parties—as gendered organizations—can become more gender-sensitive. Gender-sensitive parties are understood here as ones that are re-gendered, meaning that they respond equally to the needs and interests of both men and women in their structures, operations, and work (see Childs, this volume). Few studies have explored gender-sensitizing efforts in party organizations beyond gender quotas (but see Verge, this volume, on action plans), and due to the relative newness of these efforts, even fewer have analyzed the institutional designs applied to prevent and address harassment, intimidation, and violence within parties. This chapter shows the fruitfulness of combining the studies of feminist institutionalism (FI) and traditional party theory—in particular, theories on party change.

The chapter proceeds as follows. First, in the section "Party Change, Party Organization, and Violence in Politics" I outline the analytical framework I use to study parties' adoption of regulations for preventing and addressing harassment, intimidation, and violence. Second, in the section "The Danish Parties, the #MeToo Campaigns, and Data Collection" I argue that the Danish case—with its relatively high level of women in politics and external pressure from #MeToo and public reports on harassment, intimidation, and violence in politics—is one where parties are most likely to adopt such regulations. In this section, I also describe the data collected in original interviews and party documents. Third, in the section "When and Why Do Parties Adopt New Regulations?" I show that some Danish parties have implemented regulations on sexual harassment specifically, and some also on other forms of harassment and intimidation. Finally, in the section "What Do These Regulations Look Like?" I discuss the implications of these findings. It seems that even in cases where parties have ample reasons to adopt regulations to prevent or minimize (the effects of) harassment, intimidation, and violence, parties are conservative—or "sticky" (Beckwith, this volume)—institutions only slowly accommodating the gendered need to reimagine how they organize. The results pave the way for future research to explore whether these findings apply more broadly, or whether other factors, such as intra-party entrepreneurs or innovative legislation, can overrule these conservative trends.

Party Change, Party Organization, and Violence in Politics

Drawing on FI's focus on the gendered foundation of political institutions (Krook and Mackay 2011; Chappell and Waylen 2013), the aim of this chapter is to study parties' adoption of regulations for preventing and addressing harassment, intimidation, and violence against elected representatives, candidates, and rank-and-file members. FI scholars are interested not only in studying institutions, but also in *transforming* them to be more inclusive, responsive, and egalitarian (cf. Celis and Childs 2020). An FI framework therefore calls for analyzing whether parties—in light of well-documented cases of harassment, intimidation, and violence—have set up new regulations to transform themselves as institutions that promote equal opportunities, in particular across gender, sexuality, ethnicity, and age. Through this lens, it is relevant to analyze whether regulations (that is, any rules, procedures, sanctions, or other mechanisms) aimed at preventing and addressing harassment, intimidation, and violence are institutionalized within existing organizations and power structures, or whether new institutions and/or external actors are brought in for this purpose. This chapter is an important first step toward these larger goals. It focuses on mapping formal regulations to show what institutional setups, if any, parties are formulating in this initial response phase (Bjarnegård 2013; Kenny 2013). This will allow future research to explore, for instance, whether such rules are being effectively implemented, to what extent they are being institutionalized, and the role of change agents.

The analytical framework combines both party and gender research, in particular theories on how parties organize and change, and theories on the types and targets of harassment, intimidation, and violence in politics. Party change is defined as changes in organization, policy, and/or strategy and tactics (Harmel and Janda 1994). A change in formal rules is a key aspect of how parties organize. Causes of party change may be both internal and external to the party. Harmel and Janda (1994) argue that external shocks to parties' primary goals (whether that be policy, votes, office-holding, or intra-party cohesion) are more likely than internal shocks to cause (dramatic) changes in parties' organization, policy, and/or strategy and tactics. On the one hand, due to the broadness of the #MeToo movement in general—and the campaign uncovering sexism in Danish politics, #enblandtos ("one among us," discussed in the following section), in particular—I expect all parties to have addressed the issue of sexual harassment and violence in some way. Even though the COVID-19 pandemic may have set these efforts back to some extent, parties have had almost three years (between September 2020, when the #enblandtos movement was ignited, and June 2023, when I collected the data) to act on the #metoo/#enblandtos campaigns. The theory would also predict that parties are more likely to change and adopt regulations if the #MeToo campaign hit closer to home—that is, when equality is part of their ideological commitment, and if they have themselves been struck by #MeToo cases. Furthermore, since this new institutionalism-based party change literature also contributes with the understanding that parties are generally conservative organizations not easily prone to change (Harmel and Janda 1994), I expect that new parties formed in 2020 or later are more likely to have adopted regulations than older parties. When new parties are formed, they have a window of opportunity to organize appropriately for the current context (see also Beckwith, this volume).

In this chapter, I focus on the adoption of formal regulations rather than changes in informal institutions. Formal regulations have, within party research, been seen as the structure within which de facto organization takes place (Katz and Mair 1992). This focus on formal regulations provides a hard test of whether parties adopt regulations in light of increased awareness of harassment, intimidation, and violence in politics. Such steps are often cumbersome to institutionalize and formalize in documents, so if parties have taken such actions, it is a good sign that they are taking the issue seriously. Furthermore, assuming all else equal, formal regulations may result in a faster cultural change than recommendations—as demonstrated by the example of quotas (see Meier, Lang, and Sauer, this volume). It should be noted, however, that some parties may adopt formal regulations mostly to signal action rather than ensure effective implementation, hence the need for future research to look at enforcement.

To assess who is protected by parties' regulations, I distinguish between the three faces of party: the party in public office, the party on the ground, and the party in central office (Katz and Mair 1992). While parties are in many ways regarded as unitary actors, they are made up of actors in these three separate arenas. The party in central office is the staff within the party headquarters. Their uniting characteristic is that they are employed by their party, and as such are protected by employment legislation. The party on the ground has traditionally been parties' membership organizations. With the blurring of the distinction between members and other party affiliates, parties' understanding of what is included in their party on the ground may be muddled. The third face of the party, the party in public office, are the groups of elected representatives in parliament, municipal councils, and so on. They are both party representatives as well as working within either a parliament or a specific municipal council—hence, their institutional context is not only the party but also the particular assembly where colleagues and staff may be perpetrators of harassment. Candidates for public elections are bridging the party on the ground and the party in public office. On the one hand, they are not elected (yet), meaning they are not part of parties' public office. However, they are much more out in public—that is, the electoral arena—than rank-and-file members in the party on the ground. Nevertheless, at election time, both party activists and candidates are campaigning in the public electoral arena, so both may potentially be exposed to harassment, intimidation, and violence from actors outside their party.

Finally, previous studies of harassment in politics provide the analytical categories to analyze which types of harassment, intimidation, and violence parties' regulations address. While Krook and Sanín (2020) distinguish between physical, psychological, sexual, financial, and semiotic violence, Bjarnegård and Zetterberg (2023) call for a continuum of physical, psychological, sexual, and online forms of violence. In this chapter,

I distinguish between sexual and non-sexual harassment, intimidation, and violence. Both categories may be psychological or physical in nature and may take place in a variety of arenas. The main reason for the rough distinction between sexual and non-sexual types of harassment is that it allows for an analysis of whether the external shock of the #MeToo movement led to regulations on sexual harassment and violence only, or whether it gave rise to protection against harassment more broadly.

To recap, the specific research questions addressed here are the following: (1) When and why do parties adopt regulations around harassment, intimidation, and violence; (2) What do these regulations look like in terms of their content, who they protect, and how they are implemented (through existing or new structures)?

The Danish Parties, the #MeToo Campaigns, and Data Collection

Denmark represents a most likely case for parties' adoption of regulations for preventing and addressing harassment and violence due to the relatively (compared to other countries) large presence of women among elected representatives, party staff, and party leadership, as well as the high level of media coverage of harassment, intimidation, and violence in general, and of sexism in the second #MeToo wave in 2020 in particular (Amnesty International 2017; Amnesty International & KVINFO 2018; Institut for Menneskerettigheder 2019; TV2 2020).

Denmark is widely considered to have achieved a decent level of egalitarianism compared to most other countries, in terms of the integration of women and other minorities in politics and in public life. Women have since 1990 made up 35–40 percent of Members of Parliament (MPs); in 2022, that share surpassed 40 percent for the first time. Women have held the keys to the prime minister's office in 2011–2015 and again since 2019, and around half the party leaders have been women for some time. Women are also more likely than men to vote (but not to enroll as members in political parties, most of which have long been and remain male-dominated). Hence, women are present in politics to a large extent.

The #MeToo movement began as a social media campaign to raise awareness about sexual harassment and assault in the workplace and gained momentum internationally following the sexual misconduct allegations against Hollywood producer Harvey Weinstein in October 2017. While the first #MeToo wave did not hit Danish institutions dramatically, the second one in 2020 did. It was ignited by television host Sofie Linde, who shared—during an awards show on August 26, 2020—her experience of harassment in the entertainment industry. Her revelation encouraged others in Denmark to come forward with their stories, using the #MeToo hashtag on social media platforms.

The #MeToo movement sparked widespread public debates, with social media playing a significant role in amplifying stories and experiences. It led to increased awareness of the issue of sexual harassment and prompted calls for change. It encouraged individuals to challenge and question existing power structures and norms, and it put pressure on institutions and organizations to prevent and address sexual harassment. Four young, politically active women even ignited a Danish politics branch of the #MeToo movement with its own hashtag, #enblandtos, which is translated as "one among us." On September 25, 2020, the broadsheet newspaper *Politiken* published an op-ed co-signed by more than 300 women across the political spectrum detailing 79 anonymous but specific cases of sexism in an appeal to the political leaders to end sexism in Danish politics (Friis et al. 2020). Since then, several cases of gendered harassment within politics have been uncovered, some of which have implicated prominent people, such as the party chair of the Social Liberals, two Conservative MPs, and the Social Democrat mayor of Copenhagen.

The parties represented in Danish parliament vary in size, age, and number of intra-party #MeToo cases, and they span the ideological spectrum from left to right: Red-Green Alliance (Enhedslisten), Green Left (Socialistisk Folkeparti [SF]), the Alternative (Alternativet), Social Democrats (Socialdemokratiet), Social Liberals (Radikale Venstre), Moderates (Moderaterne), Liberals (Venstre), Conservatives (Det Konservative Folkeparti), Danish People's Party (Dansk Folkeparti), Danish Democrats (Danmarksdemokraterne), New Right (Nye Borgerlige), and Liberal Alliance (Liberal Alliance).

The following analysis draws on two data sources: (1) eight original interviews with representatives from party headquarters; and (2) party documents collected both from party websites and directly from the interviewed representatives. The Social Liberals, Liberals, Danish Democrats, New Right, and Liberal Alliance have so far declined the invitation to be interviewed. Since neither of the latter three parties had any public documents at the time of data collection (June 2023), they are excluded from the analysis, while the Social Liberals and Liberals are included based solely on their publicly available documents. The interview and document sources used for the analyses can be found in the end of the chapter, whereas all other references can be found at the end of the book.

When and Why Do Parties Adopt New Regulations?

In this first part of the analysis of Danish parties' adoption of formal regulations on preventing and addressing harassment, intimidation, and violence, I focus on the interview data to understand when and why parties introduced such regulations.

The interviews revealed that Danish parties did not have rules and procedures for preventing and handling harassment, intimidation, and violence prior to the #MeToo and #enblandtos movements. However, in their wake, parties seem to have adopted regulations whether they have been hit with intra-party #MeToo cases or not. Action was firmly undertaken by the two left-wing parties, Red-Green Alliance and Green Left, who argued in the interviews that their actions were prompted by the public debate and awareness rather than specific incidents within the party. Both parties followed roughly the same procedure: first, an independent investigation into the extent of sexual harassment; second, a written report on the findings of the investigation (Red-Green Alliance 2022a; Green Left 2021a); and finally, the development of an action plan (Red-Green Alliance 2022b; Green Left 2021b). Both parties have established anonymous lawyer hotlines to ensure that the party headquarters is able to keep an arm's length from the party leadership, avoiding top-down interference. I did not identify any hesitation on the part of these party representatives; one of them was even appalled that their party had a declared feminist praxis but had not thought of institutionalizing regulations on preventing and addressing harassment, intimidation, and violence prior to #MeToo. In the case of these two established left-wing parties, it could be argued that #MeToo was an external shock due to their inclusive and feminist party ideologies; it touched upon their core goal and resulted in change.

The Moderates, a center party created by former Liberal Prime Minister and party chair Lars Løkke Rasmussen, first as a political network and formally as a party in 2022, gained representation at the general election on

November 1, 2022. This is therefore a new party formed *after* the heightened awareness of harassment, intimidation, and violence in politics. In the interview, the party representative argued that "in these times, it is unfortunately necessary to have a code of conduct to ensure that people know how to behave." This suggests that the theoretical expectation that new parties are likely to adopt regulations around harassment, intimidation, and violence is supported. Interestingly, the interviewee worried that the code of conduct does not address all aspects of harassment and violence, meaning members could theoretically argue that they were free to do whatever the code of conduct did not explicitly specify to be off-limits. Possibly due to the lack of a well-developed party culture in a new party, the Moderates appear to prefer formally institutionalizing rules rather than relying on a common understanding of general good behavior.

The interviews demonstrated that while the Red-Green Alliance, Green Left and Moderates were reacting to the #MeToo campaign in general, the Social Democrats were reacting to the multiple cases of sexual harassment brought forward in October 2020 against the then-mayor of Copenhagen and vice chair of the party, Frank Jensen, who ended up resigning. This shows that the Social Democrats adopted regulations against harassment, intimidation, and violence following a very specific and prominent #MeToo case, to mitigate damage to the party image.

Other parties are pursuing a more gradual and incrementalist approach to adopting such regulations. The center-right Danish People's Party is a good example of a party that has addressed the issue due to general awareness of the #MeToo and #enblandtos movements, but that is not pressured to a large extent by either their ideology or specific cases. As they argued, "We didn't need to signal that we are first movers ... there was some vote-maximizing on this agenda from some of the other parties." The interviewee stated that the party had a lawyer evaluate what was needed, and in this light formulated regulations against harassment, intimidation, and violence. At the time of interview, although they had informed the local party chairs about these new regulations, they were reluctant to announce them publicly. As the interview revealed, due to their lack of experience with #MeToo cases, they were unsure for instance about the division of responsibility between party and police for handling these cases, and were holding off to see what might happen, hoping that the opportunity might arise for a joint effort between the parties or that they might gain experience from other parties. Therefore, the Danish People's Party had neither the window of opportunity of a new party, nor intra-party cases of #MeToo, nor a party ideology driving the adoption of new rules and procedures. Rather, they followed suit slowly because "everybody else was doing it."

While most parties have adopted regulations, a quarter of the parties currently represented in parliament seem to have not (yet) adopted any specific regulations in regard to (sexual) harassment and violence within the party in light of the #MeToo and #enblandtos campaigns. Among these are new parties such as the New Right and Danish Democrats, who are forming and institutionalizing at a time with a high level of awareness about harassment, intimidation, and violence but who choose not to address this. This could very well be for ideological reasons. Both are right-wing parties, and when some #MeToo cases arose in other parties, New Right parliamentarians made an "anti-#MeToo" statement with a photo of the four MPs grabbing each other's thighs (Pedersen 2020). The party chair of Danish Democrats has explicitly argued that the #MeToo movement has gone too far (Gøttler and Vibjerg 2022).

Turning from the intra-party arena to harassment, intimidation, and violence experienced by elected representatives and candidates outside the party, parties have fewer formalized rules or procedures for prevention and handling of such cases. The interviews with party representatives show that parties are well aware that these kinds of incidents do take place, due to what they hear from their candidates and elected representatives, as well as (the media coverage of) reports from non-governmental organizations like Amnesty International & KVINFO (2017; 2018). However, most of the parties pursue an ad hoc strategy, deferring to their existing structures for handling these cases, which entails contacting the local party chair, or the party/general secretary. This demonstrates that parties rely on existing power structures to handle any issues that arise.

There is some help for elected representatives beyond the party apparatus, as both parliament and the association for municipalities (Kommunernes Landsforening 2023) work on awareness of the problems of harassment, intimidation, and violence, and on improving the support municipalities may provide for their elected representatives. However, due to being unelected, candidates are not included in this regulation meaning that absent any party action, they are left outside regulation.

Parties to varying extents emphasize that potential candidates may face harassment, intimidation, and violence. For some, it is tacit knowledge. For others, it is deliberately included in the recruitment process. As the interview revealed, since the newly created Moderates were recruiting candidates unfamiliar with politics, during their candidate training they made a special effort to emphasize the pressure and potential harassment and violence that potential candidates might face. This led to some potential candidates choosing to withdraw from the process, either because they found themselves unable to withstand the potential pressures of harassment and violence, or because they feared their personal circumstances, including their mental well-being, would leave them particularly vulnerable. Ironically, these potential candidates' experiences with the healthcare system may have drawn them into the Moderates in the first place, as the party put great emphasis on healthcare reform, but it also left them at larger risk. In sum, while most parties have adopted specific regulations in regard to (sexual) harassment and violence within the party in light of the #MeToo and #enblandtos movements, few have adopted anything in regard to harassment, intimidation, and violence in the electoral arena, instead relying largely on existing institutions and processes.

What Do These Regulations Look Like?

The second part of this analysis focuses on the substance of the adopted regulations, including what types of harassment and violence they address (sexual, other), who they protect (candidates in the electoral arena, rank-and-file members/the party on the ground, or staff and elected office-holders within the parliamentary arena), and which type of procedure is adopted (new or existing procedures). As expressed in their various wordings, the aim of these regulations is to ensure that members, elected representatives, and staff are safe and supported within the party. Most parties target their rules toward "offensive actions" more broadly, understood as behavior where one or more people rudely or repeatedly expose other people to behavior that is perceived by the targeted person or persons as degrading. Within that broad definition, they then specifically mention that this includes sexual harassment, intimidation, and violence. However, a few parties have singled out more specific procedures around sexual misconduct—e.g., when institutionalizing whistleblower arrangements (Red-Green Alliance 2022b, 2023; Conservatives 2023) or hotlines (Liberals 2023).

In terms of who is included, most parties include all members (party on the ground), elected representatives (party in public office), and staff (party in central office) in their codes of conduct, even though the latter is already protected through Danish employment law. Interestingly, the employment law serves as inspiration for the parties; given protecting staff is a legal requirement, this may have been their first step toward implementing further protections. However, not all parties include all members, elected/appointed representatives, and staff within these codes. The Liberals' arrangement includes staff both in parliament, Brussels and party headquarters, elected and appointed office-holders as well as all members of the youth organization (Liberals 2023)—but neither rank-and-file members nor candidates are mentioned. Similarly, the Social Democrat's legal arrangement includes office-holders and appointed people but does not state that it includes rank-and-file members nor candidates (Social Democrats 2022).

Turning to the types of regulations for preventing and addressing cases of harassment, intimidation, and violence within parties, various new regulations have been adopted. Many parties have adopted some kind of whistleblower arrangement; however, the level of institutionalization of these regulations varies. Some have hotlines with external firms, mainly legal firms. Others rely on existing structures—e.g., the party secretary (leader of party administration) or party leadership. However, when parties indicate collaboration with a legal firm, the degree of anonymity offered to the victims varies. For example, within the Danish People's Party, claims are to be made to the party secretariat, who will then contact lawyers to investigate (Danish People's Party 2020), whereas in the Red-Green Alliance, the legal firm organizes the party's anonymous sexism hotline, which all members can contact, independently of the party (Red-Green Alliance 2022b, 2023). Within the Liberals, if a conversation on the hotline indicates that legislation has been violated, a legal firm can be contacted for further actions (Liberals 2023). Hence, the role of lawyers and legal advice varies across parties; therefore, 'collaboration with a legal firm' is insufficient to assess the extent to which the procedures rely on and thus enforce existing power structures, or whether new formal institutions are created.

In addition to the party-assisted procedures, some parties also direct victims' attention to external actors. Victims are encouraged to contact the police in the case of severe incidents, but are also directed to other organizations, such as the Joan Sisters (Red-Green Alliance 2022b), who advise women victims of sexualized violence, and the Labor Supervision, the state institution that regulates working environments (*Arbejdstilsynet*)

(Moderates 2023). While some parties add an (external) whistleblower arrangement to their existing structures, others institutionalize new organs within the party. These institutional setups vary in the extent to which they affect existing power structures. Within the Social Liberals, the committee dealing with cases of misconduct consists of two members and two people who are not members but have expertise in, for example, counseling (Social Liberals 2020). They are there to help both witnesses to and those who have themselves experienced harassment within the party in complete confidence (Social Liberals 2023a, 2023b). The committee can recommend action but cannot themselves take action on cases of misconduct, since the Social Liberals rely on existing structures of decision-making power. Since the parliamentary group leadership is elected by MPs, the MPs are the ones deciding whether a member of the leadership is to be (temporarily) expelled from leadership due to misconduct, and misconduct by candidates is referred to the branch chair in the candidate's nomination district (Social Liberals 2020). Existing power structures are therefore strengthened with these new regulations intended to prevent and address harassment, intimidation, and violence.

This is also the case within the Social Democrats. This party has a disciplinary committee in which the party secretary (the highest-ranking person in the party office) and three members appointed by the national committee (*hovedbestyrelsen*) sit (Social Democrats 2022). When appointing members to the committee, emphasis is placed on competences within the fields of law and/or psychology, and that members must be widely respected within the party (Social Democrats 2022). Existing power structures may impact the composition of the Social Democrat's disciplining committee, since it is selected by the national committee, meaning its members are already well-integrated within the party. However, the advantage of specific committees is that members may become "experts" on cases of harassment, intimidation, and violence, and on how to prevent and address those within the party.

The institutional setup makes a particular difference if/when sanctions are to be implemented. While existing power structures may impact the composition of the Social Democrat's disciplining committee, the power invested in this new institution enables them to bypass existing power structures within the party. If the legal firm finds that there is a case of misconduct, the disciplinary committee can decide on sanctions, which include the following: criticism; a formal warning; quarantine from attending events/activities at the national, regional, and local levels; deprivation of intra-party office-holding; recommendation to parliamentary groups in the city council, regional council, parliament, or European Parliament to withdraw any committee memberships and spokesperson-roles; and ultimately withdrawal of the right to stand for election for the Social Democrats and exclusion from the party (Social Democrats 2022). The disciplinary committee acquires some power from its embeddedness in existing structures and may use this power to initiate change within the party.

Conclusion

In light of the well-documented cases of harassment and violence in politics in general, and the gendered dynamics of the #MeToo movement in particular, it is highly relevant to explore whether—and how—parties organize to ensure that (gendered) harassment and violence do not inhibit equal representation and participation among men and women in democracies. This chapter has taken a first step in analyzing this issue in the Danish context by posing the following research questions: (1) When and why do parties adopt regulations around harassment, intimidation, and violence? and (2) What do these regulations look like in terms of their content, who they protect, and how they are implemented (through existing or new structures)? Ultimately, I found that although many parties have adopted new regulations, there is great variation in how these regulations are applied and who they actually protect, leaving parties far away from fully re-gendering their party organizations.

Few parties have adopted regulations for physical and psychological harassment that candidates and elected representatives experience from political opponents and the public—i.e., the party in public office and from the public in the electoral arena—even though they are aware of its existence. The regulations adopted vary both in the type of harassment and violence covered, in who they protect, and in the institutional measures applied. Most parties with rules and regulations include a broader definition of harassment and intimidation; however, only a few address sexual harassment and intimidation. Some parties include members, office-holders, and staff, while others restrict their arrangements to office-holders and staff—that is, the party in central office. Candidates are largely excluded. As for the organizational changes, some have institutionalized new committees within the party with various measures of formal decision-making power, but most rely on existing structures. Organizational change is moderate.

Going forward, we need to turn to the core of FI and direct our attention to understanding which regulations are most valuable for the victims and bystanders of various kinds of harassment, intimidation, and violence—in particular, whether the formal regulations are actually implemented and how these regulations work in practice. Are these regulations enforcing the gendered nature of parties, or are they succeeding in re-gendering the parties? Setting out rules is not enough. If we are to ensure that harassment and violence are not inhibiting democracy, we need to analyze the interaction between formal and informal regulations and the experiences of members, candidates, and representatives. On the one hand, we may expect that experiences of violence are more common, and the negative effects of harassment are larger in parties without defined protocols, specified procedures, and cultures to prevent, limit, and handle violence. On the other hand, more common experiences of harassment may also prompt parties' adoption of protocols and procedures, as well as other efforts to change the party culture. In the Danish case studied here, a generally high level of harassment provides external pressure for all parties to adopt rules and procedures. However, marked variation among the parties could indicate that some of them may be more prone to adopt rules and procedures due to external shocks (e.g., media coverage of harassment of their members/candidates/representatives) or internal pressure due to ideological commitments and/or from those who have suffered from harassment, while others do not find it valuable or necessary. While potentially a driver for all parties to adjust their organization due to the general level of harassment and violence, several have not done so at the time of this research (2023); hence, party change of this sort is hard to achieve.

When structures for addressing harassment, intimidation, and violence are embedded into existing power structures, action may more easily be taken—for example, by hindering the renomination of perpetrators. The flexibility of existing structures aids the handling and possibly also the prevention of harassment and violence. However, if parties' formal and informal power holders do not recognize the need for preventing and addressing gendered harassment, existing power structures provide heavy barriers to change. Power structures are not challenged, and the organization remains intact. In such cases, more independent, external institutions may fare more efficiently.

Furthermore, a relevant question is whether "window-dressing" formal institutions are as effective as institutional change originating from intra-party demand. Are the Danish People's Party's rules more efficient in handling harassment, since nobody but party HQ has had a stake in their creation? Or are rules and regulations developed within the parties, respecting party tradition, such the Social Liberals' independent (expert) committee, more efficient? These are just some of the questions that future research can investigate, building on the findings presented in this chapter.

Democracy is inhibited at the individual, organizational, and societal levels if harassment and violence are left unprevented and unhandled and are seen simply as "the cost of doing politics." Efforts to enable full and equal political participation and representation free from gendered violence therefore need to focus squarely on political parties as pivotal actors in blocking or facilitating change efforts.

Party Documents

Alternative. 2023. *Alternativets samværspolitik med tilhørende handlingsplan. Vedtaget af Hovedbestyrelsen den 4. maj 2023 og revideres herefter efter hvert ordinære landsmøde.* Accessed June 9, 2023. https://alternativet.dk/application/files/6516/8389/6345/Alternativets_samvaerspolitik_godkendt_4_maj_2023.pdf

Conservatives. 2021. *Samværspolitik.* Accessed June 13, 2023. https://konservative.dk/organisationen/samvaerspolitik

Conservatives. 2023 *Retningslinjer til Medlemmer M.fl. om Whistleblowerordning hos Det Konservative Folkeparti.* Accessed June 13, 2023. https://konservative.dk/whistleblowerordning/retningslinjer

Danish People's Party. 2020. *Politik og retningslinjer om krænkende adfærd.* Accessed June 13, 2023. https://danskfolkeparti.dk/organisation/politik-og-retningslinjer-om-kraenkende-adfaerd

Green Left. 2021b. *Politik for imødegåelse af sexisme og forebyggelse og håndtering af seksuel chikane i SF's partiorganisation.* Accessed June 13, 2023. https://sf.dk/wp-content/uploads/2021/01/politik-for-forebyggelse-og-haandtering-af-seksuel-chikane-.pdf

Green Left. 2021a. *Undersøgelse af omfanget og karakteren af seksuel chikane og forskelsbehandling på baggrund af køn og seksualitet i SF. En undersøgelse blandt medlemmer.* Accessed June 13, 2023. https://sf.dk/wp-content/uploads/2021/04/endelig_rapport_sf_kvinfo_150421.pdf

Green Left. n.d. *Beretning for SF's Ligebehandlingsnævn.* Provided by the interviewed party representative.

Liberals. 2023 *Retningslinjer mod krænkende adfærd.* Accessed June 13, 2023. https://www.venstre.dk/partiet/retningslinjer-mod-kraenkende-adfaerd

Moderates (2023) *Adfærdskodeks.* Located 9 June 2023 at Code of conduct—MODERATERNE https://moderaterne.dk/code-of-conduct/.

Red-Green Alliance. 2018. *Feministisk praksis i Enhedslisten.* Provided by the interviewed party representative.

Red-Green Alliance. 2022a. *KVINFO rapport.* Provided by the interviewed party representative.

Red-Green Alliance. 2022b. *Handlingsplan*. Provided by the interviewed party representative.

Red-Green Alliance. 2023 *Uvildig advokatordning til henvendelser om krænkelser af seksuel karakter*. Accessed June 13, 2023. https://vores.enhedslisten.dk/om-enhedslisten/advokatordning

Social Democrats. 2022. *Retningslinjer mod krænkende adfærd, herunder chikane og seksuel chikane*. Accessed June 13, 2023. https://www.socialdemokratiet.dk/media/cxjbjwk3/retningslinjer-mod-kraenkende-adfaerd-002.pdf

Social Liberals. 2020. *Sanktionering af brud på samværspolitikken. Vedtaget af forretningsudvalget 20. oktober 2020*. Accessed June 13, 2023. https://www.radikale.dk/partiet/sanktionering-af-brud-pa-samvaerspolitikken

Social Liberals. 2023a. *Samværspolitik*. Accessed June 13, 2023. https://www.radikale.dk/partiet/samvaerspolitik

Social Liberals. 2023b. *Den uafhængige kontaktinstans*. Accessed June 13, 2023. https://www.radikale.dk/partiet/den-uafhaengige-kontaktinstans

Interviews

Alternative (Alternativet): Party founder. Interview conducted by the author, March 2023.

Alternative (Alternativet): Party secretary. Interview conducted by the author, June 2023.

Conservative People's Party (Det Konservative Folkeparti): General secretary. Interview conducted by the author, April 2023.

Danish People's Party (Dansk Folkeparti): Previous MP, current employee. Interview conducted by the author, April 2023.

Green Left (SF): Longtime employee. Interview conducted by the author, March 2023.

Moderates (Moderaterne): MP and active in party founding. Interview conducted by the author, March 2023.

Red-Green Alliance (Enhedslisten): Former MP and former political spokesperson (closest equivalent to party chair). Interview conducted by the author, April 2023.

Social Democrats (Socialdemokratiet): Party secretary. Interview conducted by the author, April 2023.

8

Young Women Aspirants and Gendered Ageism in Nigeria's Political Parties

Ọmọ́máyọ̀wá O. Àbàtì and Mayowa M. Adeniji

In most countries, women and young people are seldom nominated as party candidates and consequently are grossly underrepresented in political offices (Inter-Parliamentary Union 2023). This is despite several gender and age-related institutional reforms like gender and youth quotas, and reduction in candidacy and voting ages, among others. The gatekeeping role of political parties in this regard is particularly acute, especially in countries like Nigeria, where there is no legal provision for independent candidacy. As a result, despite nearly half of the country's population being women and more than 70 percent younger than 35 years, women and young people continue to be grossly underrepresented in Nigerian politics (Nkereuwem 2023; YIAGA Africa 2023), with young women appearing to be the most affected (Uzor 2019). Yet, it is still not clear how gender and age intersect in candidate selection practices, and what the consequences are for the political recruitment of different age categories of women (particularly young women).

This is because, for the most part, the fields of gender and youth politics have talked past rather than to each other, thus reflecting an underappreciation for the intersection of gender and ageism in the scholarship. Separately, obstacles to women's selection and election across the various stages of political recruitment are well documented (Norris and Lovenduski 1995; Madsen 2020; see also Davidson-Schmich, this volume). Youth scholars also highlight age-related discriminatory practices in the candidate selection process (Stockemer and Sundström 2022), ranging from high minimum candidacy age requirements that limit when they can legally

Ọmọ́máyọ̀wá O. Àbàtì and Mayowa M. Adeniji, *Young Women Aspirants and Gendered Ageism in Nigeria's Political Parties*. In: *Gendering Party Politics*. Edited by: Meryl Kenny and Elin Bjarnegård, Oxford University Press. © Oxford University Press (2025). DOI: 10.1093/oso/9780197793985.003.0008 contest for political offices even after they are granted voting rights (Krook and Nugent 2018), to the culture of ageism in politics that considers them as inexperienced and incapable of political leadership (Oyebode 2014). Yet, the pathway of young women, as a special category of marginalized groups facing both gendered and age-related discriminatory practices in parties, is scantily studied. Only a few studies have attempted to examine the gendered effect of being young candidates (Segaard and Saglie 2021; Belschner 2023); others have rather concentrated on young women's political interests (Briggs 2008; Grasso and Smith 2022), digital activism (Schuster 2013; Lixian 2020), or participation in party youth wings (Ammassari et al. 2023). In other instances where the political experience of young women has been examined, it has been in the context of the legislature (Erikson and Josefsson 2021).

This chapter, therefore, addresses this gap by focusing on the candidate selection experience of young women in parties, as it differs and/or resembles those faced by older women and young men. Specifically, we assess how informal norms and practices interact with formal rules and procedures at the party level to (re)produce generational and gendered recruitment challenges. This way, we further knowledge on whether and, if so, how women of younger age groups are subjected to greater levels of discrimination in parties.

The chapter continues in three main sections. The first section, "Political Recruitment of Women and Young People," highlights how feminist institutionalism (FI) may be expanded to theorize intersectional influences of gender and age in party politics. The second section, "Nigerian Party Context and Methods," contextualizes Nigeria as a good country case to examine such an intersection and outlines the methods used in the study. In the third section, "Young Women's Political Candidacies in Nigeria," we discuss the gendered and age-discriminatory character of the formal and informal rules as well as practices of political recruitment and their effects on young women within Nigeria's political parties, thus highlighting the implications of these dynamics for gender and party politics. Finally, we draw relevant conclusions.

Political Recruitment of Women and Young People

In theorizing the multiple structures of political inequalities that women and young people face, scholars of party politics have relied on the supply and demand framework (Norris and Lovenduski 1995), arguing that the outcome of a particular party's selection process is best understood in terms of the interaction between factors affecting the supply of aspirants for political office and the demands of selectors (see also Davidson-Schmich, this volume; Runderkamp and Kenny, this volume).

On the supply side, women and young people often have to strategically match their political drive, ambition, and interest with the constraints of resources such as time, money, and experience before they can decide to come forward (Norris and Lovenduski 1995). On one hand, women receive less encouragement to run for political offices due to cultural biases about gender roles (Fox and Lawless 2004) and to societal stereotypes that politics is not a woman's affair (Osori 2017). On the other hand, young people are often at a life stage where they are still building their professional careers, thus less likely to have acquired the financial resources or the political experience required to execute a political campaign (Ashe 2020), or even the time to dedicate to a campaign (Perron 2018). Young women, in addition to building their professional careers, are also likely to shoulder more of the labor involved in gendered roles like home management and childcare, which further limits their willingness and ability to come forward, in comparison to both young male and older women politicians (Joshi and Och 2021). Yet their inability to come forward is, in turn, interpreted by party leaders to justify their male-dominated recruitment outcomes, claiming that because too few women and young people come forward, they must therefore be less politically ambitious or politically inexperienced (Rehmert 2022; DeSmedt and Vandeleene 2024).

But even when women and young people do come forward, they may face direct and imputed discrimination from party selectors (Norris and Lovenduski 1995; see also Davidson-Schmich, this volume). Given that party selectors cannot know all aspirants on a personal level, they often have to consider "background characteristics as a proxy measure of abilities and character" (Norris and Lovenduski 1995, 14), with such shortcuts often leading to direct discrimination, where aspirants are judged based on the characteristics associated with their group, or indirect discrimination, where they are passed over by selectors based on unfounded fear that the party may lose votes if such aspirants are nominated. Some scholars have argued that these evaluations may also be connected to the scarcity of women in party high-status positions (Cheng and Tavits 2011). It is possible to make a similar argument for young people within Nigerian parties, as they rarely reach leadership party positions, despite constituting the largest member group (see Afrobarometer 2020). Aside from the positions of youth leader, which until recently were mostly occupied by older men (see Sahara Reporters 2012; Ibe 2014), Nigerian parties do not generally have young people holding high-status positions like party chairperson or secretary. This points to how gendered and age-biased demand and supply side factors can be, and to the need to examine them within their institutional contexts.

To achieve this, gender and party scholars rely increasingly on FI, a variant of new institutionalism that explores the interaction between gender and political institutions (Krook 2010; Bjarnegård and Kenny 2016). As Bjarnegård and Kenny (this volume) highlight, parties need to be examined beyond their formal rules, as informal norms and institutions both moderate their application or altogether sideline them to produce gendered outcomes (Bjarnegård and Zetterberg 2019). Women have been shown to lack access, support, and endorsements, as homosocial networks of men prefer to endorse only fellow men in their networks (Bjarnegård 2013; see also Josefsson, this volume). This is particularly acute in African party contexts where formal institutions are weak, giving room for such homosocial networks, in the form of 'godfathers' who anoint 'godsons' (Adeoye 2009, 269), and even go as far as substituting the names of female candidates who won party primaries (Omotola 2012). We contend that, if this argument is stretched further, a focus on informal party networks will also highlight a potential tendency for ageism, especially within the African party context, where old age is associated with sagacity and older people are thus accorded venerated places of authority as compensation for their wisdom (Oyebode, 2014).

By emphasizing the role of power in party institutional structures, party politics is rightly regarded as a site of unequal power relations. Yet these unequal power relations are not only manifested along gender lines. Given that some marginalized groups belong to more than one outgroup, from an intersectionality perspective, scholars highlight the need to account for more than one unequal power relation at a time—as age, race, and ethnic identities of women have been found to influence their institutional structures of opportunity (Celis et al. 2014; Stockemer and Sundström 2019; Belschner 2023). For instance, in the Netherlands and Belgium, some parties preferred minority women to minority men as part of what Celis et al. (2014, 47) call the "complementarity bonus"—being able to count them as both women and representatives of a minority ethnic group. A similar advantage is recorded by Stockemer and Sundström (2019), whose analysis of the persistent rise in women's representation in the European Parliament since 1979 showed that the youngest age group of women representatives accounted for most of the increases.

Yet, Grahn (this volume) cautions that the so-called complementarity advantage may be less of an advantage, as it is still part of the strategies of elite men to perpetuate their privileges. This explains, in part, why even when parties grant some form of gender or age-related concessions, they may not translate into improvements in the representation of women and young people. This may especially be the case in institutional contexts where the increased representation of a marginalized group implies a loss of political power for the dominant men, and where the desire to maintain the status quo may see these dominant men resorting to informal rules to circumvent formal reforms. In Nigeria, clientelist practices that pronounce the influence of godfathers, prebendal, party, and communal elites are often pointed as the main reason women and youths find it challenging to penetrate the party selection systems (Adeoye 2009; Uzor 2019).

This is further complicated by the fact that ageism is more context-dependent than gender, as it is both relative and temporal (Erikson and Josefsson 2021, 84). It is relative in that being 30 years old might have a different meaning in an urban setting of a high-income country where life expectancy might be over 70 years, compared to a rural setting in a low-income country where life expectancy would be far lower. And it is temporal in the sense that it changes with time, such that discrimination suffered at a youthful age may be reversed at older ages (Bidadanure 2015). As such, age discrimination may produce both positive and negative outcomes for a gendered category of people depending on the type of organization under examination and the age group being investigated. This is evidenced by mixed empirical results, even in contexts where gender and age are perceived as less politically salient than in Nigeria. For instance, contrary to Stockemer and Sundström (2019), Erikson and Josefsson (2021) found that younger ages reinforced negative gendered patterns for women in the Swedish parliament, and Belschner (2023) found that while being young provides a net electoral advantage for young men in Irish elections, young women, though advantaged by their age (compared to middle-aged women), were disadvantaged by their gender (compared to young men).

Nigerian Party Context and Methods

Given that Nigeria is a country where clientelist power relations are salient at the party level, our study focuses on the All Progressive Congress (APC) and People's Democratic Party (PDP) to tease out how ageism and gendered discrimination are manifested in candidate selection. These are the two major parties accounting for over half of the candidates in the candidacy pool and more than 90 percent of electoral victories, since the return to democratic practice in 1999. Both parties have alternated in government and opposition, with the PDP ruling the national government between 1999 and 2015, while the APC has kept dominance since then until now. This electoral dominance makes them the first point of call for all prospective aspirants in the country, whether for national or subnational elective offices (Osori 2017, 13). Furthermore, unlike other countries with two-party majorities, where either party has a divergent ideological orientation, the APC and PDP exhibit ideological convergence (Husaini 2019). Thus, though neither of them is ideologically opposed to nominating women or young candidates, still they do not need to nominate women and young candidates to differentiate themselves from other political parties, potentially making them less accessible to women and young people.

Importantly, both parties announced gender- and age-related concessions after the passage of the age-reduction bill in 2018 and in the build-up to the general elections of 2019 and 2023, suggesting their willingness to support women and young aspirants. Yet despite empirical evidence that reducing candidacy ages has a mobilizing effect on youth representation (Krook and Nugent 2018), many expressed doubts about it having any effect on youth and women inclusion in Nigeria, mainly because of the hurdle of candidate selection at the party levels (Ette and Akpan-Obong 2023). For example, the APC made the nomination form free for women, while youth were given a 50 percent discount (though for 2023 elections only) across elective positions (Akinwale 2022; Are 2022). Similarly, the PDP allowed female aspirants to pay for the expression of interest form only (Oyero 2022), while a 50 percent discount on nomination forms was given to young aspirants (Ndujihe 2022). While these concessions represented significant steps toward motivating women and young people to come forward, with young women expected to benefit significantly given that they fall under both age and gender categories targeted by the concessions, the proportion of young women candidates and elected representatives that emerged from both elections was disappointing, when compared to both young male and older women politicians (Àbàtì 2024). This called into question the extent to which formal concessions improved the chances of young women in both parties, and highlighted the need to examine the experiences of young women in the interplay of party formal rules and informal norms and practices.

Methodologically, we draw primarily on elite interviews and publicly available interviews (including newsletters) of young women and men aspirants of both parties for national and subnational legislative offices during the 2019 and 2023 general elections. We also interviewed party leaders across national and subnational levels, focusing on the Kwara and Oyo state chapters of APC and PDP. Kwara, an APC-led state at the executive and legislative subnational levels, and Oyo, a PDP-led state at the executive and legislative subnational level, make it possible to capture unique differences and similarities that may arise from an opposition party-led state at the subnational level and vice versa for the government party-led state. Interviews focused on individual experiences about the nature of party selection practices, the roles of gatekeepers, money, and godfathers, as well as what leverage aspirants used to navigate the selection process. Speaking with party leaders, we were interested in their statutory and non-statutory roles in selecting party candidates and how they decide which candidate selection method is to be used. While we triangulated the opinions gleaned from all interviews with relevant provisions of individual party constitutions, we also triangulated some of the opinions expressed by young aspirants about the influence of godfathers, delegates, and money in candidate selection processes with those of party leaders.

Young Women's Political Candidacies in Nigeria

To investigate the interplay of formal and informal rules, norms, and practices of parties, we focus on the gender–age biases in the candidacy requirements and selection practices of the two major parties—the APC and PDP. This way, we highlight the entry challenges that young female aspirants encounter both in their attempt to come forward and the effect of the various selection methods on their candidacy prospects.

Candidacy Requirements

The APC and PDP have a fairly similar set of formal rules on candidacy requirements, as contained in their party constitutions. Beyond the complementary provisions of citizenship, age, and educational qualification, aspirants in both parties must show financial good standing (All Progressive Congress 2014; People's Democratic Party 2014). While "financial good standing" literally means being up to date in payment of membership dues, it means far more than that in practice: it includes sponsoring party activities at the minimum. Simi, a young female aspirant at the 2023 Ekiti House of Assembly (HoA) election, recounts in her newsletter how, in addition to paying her dues, she "had to cover the costs for several [party] activities in my ward" (Olusola 2022a). All young aspirants interviewed for this research echoed this practice. Confirming the widespread nature of the practice, a party leader claimed that the financial donations count toward party recognition, especially for aspiring members: "Anytime the party has a programme, you attend, or you send a representative, and donate to the party because you must be a financial member of the party. This will make people recognise you and give you support."[1] Notice how recognition of financial membership is equated not just to the payment of party dues but more importantly to donating to party causes. It is on such a basis that party support and endorsement are given.

Elsewhere in her newsletter, Simi mentions where such recognitions come in handy:

> When declaring your intention to run for an elective position at the ward, you must be nominated by 20 persons from at least two-thirds of the Wards within the constituency; these persons must be registered party members and registered voters. Do you see why it is important for me to go on all those visits and donate towards party activities? Make dem no unlook my form wen time reach. [This can be loosely interpreted as, "So, they do not disappoint me when the time for nomination comes."]
>
> (Olusola 2022a)

The visits alluded to in this quote are another important informal ritual that aspirants are expected to perform even before buying nomination forms. Nothing in the constitutions of both parties mandates such visits. However, once aspirants decide to run for office, they must pay informal visits to key stakeholders within their party. The point of these visits is to get the endorsement of such stakeholders, at least in principle, such that when it comes up in their ward meeting that they are declaring their interest in contesting for an elective position, they can have some members who would back their aspirations. While these visits are not limited to young female aspirants, Simi's record of one such visit suggests how intimidating it can be for young female aspirants:

> I went with an "uncle" to meet this elderly party man. He asked me about my household, and I told him. He asked for my family name, etc., but he did not know my dad or grandparents. He then asked me where my husband is from, and when I said Òndó [another state in the Southwest], that even worsened matters. He straight up told me he could not introduce me to anyone or support me because how could I expect to come from Abuja, be married to an Ondo person, and not have my father resident here [Ekiti], yet wanting to hijack things? The person who took me to him kept trying to tell him about how I had been back in the town for a while; he did not even want to listen. However, he said he would make his findings and get back to me. When I left him, I heard he had asked my ward chairperson to meet with him on my matter ... This is Nigeria, where it is not your value that matters but who your father is, where the fact that my husband is from another state is a minus for me.
>
> (Olusola 2022b)

This anecdote presents multiple paradoxes. First, most of these party elites are men and difficult to reach/convince. Scheduling appointments to visit them requires having access to either their subordinates or knowing the right people to follow you, as did Simi, with the service of "an uncle." Yet many young female aspirants lack such access when compared to their young male counterparts, thereby missing out on the local politicking that goes into the candidate selection process. Several young women aspirants ended up consulting with the "wrong" people, resulting in them losing out before the candidacy race ever began, as the people they consulted with were not as influential as they had thought: "the real political stakeholders were not willing to meet with me, the ones who agreed to meet did not wield as much influence as they had pretended to have. So, I would say I consulted the wrong people and lost out of the nomination"[2] (cf. Bjarnegård and Kenny 2016, 384). Even when they agree to meet, due to the persuasive influence of an intermediary, they are also difficult to convince, as they are quick to dismiss young female aspirants as uncompetitive for unfounded reasons, as was the case with Simi.

Second, no consultation visit happens without aspirants giving away money and other material items—first to the subordinates, who introduce them to the party elites and schedule the appointment for the visit, and more importantly to the main party stakeholder during the visit. Given that such monies are unaccounted for, there is no threshold of how much money is appropriate. Political endorsement eventually becomes a matter of the highest bidder; with young women aspirants having limited access to informal networks that can provide them with such resources and political influence, they are often outwitted in the process. This is relatable to the instrumental resource component of homosocial capital where men are more likely to access the resources valuable to politics than women, simply because men are considered to be more preserving of the clientelist system (cf. Bjarnegård 2013, 171).

Aside from money, young female aspirants are also quizzed during these consultation visits on issues of ancestral roots and marital status—something their young male counterparts do not experience. While questions like "Who is your father?" could be directed at anyone without eliciting any undertone, being asked by a political stakeholder whom you visit to solicit political endorsement carries with it the sound of "Who do you think you are?" or "What is your claim to any authoritative privileges in our community?" For Simi, it did not matter that she was unequivocally a Yoruba lady seeking to represent a constituency in her father's state of origin; with such a question, her ancestral roots are doubted. This is because it is easy to doubt the ancestral lineage of female descendants especially because of marriage customs that require women to adopt their husband's family name, whereas a male descendant who continues in his father's family name makes it easy to trace the ancestral lineage of men in general.

Moreover, urbanization has created scenarios where most young millennials are born and raised in urban cities far away from their ancestral homes with little or no familiarization with the societal and political structures of their ancestral homes. Here lies the difference between young female and older female aspirants. Older female aspirants were not only born but to a large extent raised within their ancestral homes before the massive urbanization of the 1980s and 1990s, which saw families relocate to urban centers, like Lagos and Abuja. As such, older female aspirants can, for the most part, trace their familiar lineage and convincingly present their claims. While this is not a justifiable reason to exclude young female aspirants, it points to how gendered ageism can be manifested in informal practices of parties. Suppose Simi was to be unmarried or married to a non-Yoruba man, it might even have had other negative implications for her candidacy.

So, while neither party's constitutions outrightly outlaw young women from contesting on their platforms, the informal norms that guide the application of the formal candidate requirements make it doubly challenging for young female aspirants that come forward, when compared to the experience of their young male and older female counterparts. These findings mirror similar findings from Thai and Scottish parties, where Bjarnegård and Kenny (2016) found gendered local practices that distinguished outsiders from insiders, with women often viewed as unpredictable and as such not trusted to maintain patronage relations. Similarly, at the core of casting doubt on the ancestral route of young women is the fear and lack of trust in their ability to maintain patronage relations, resulting in an uneven playing field for young women.

Selection Practices

Both constitutions of the APC and PDP provide for three candidate selection methods—direct, indirect/delegate, and consensus primary—as specified in the country's electoral laws, and grant liberty to the party leadership to decide what methods to use at any level (All Progressive Congress 2014; People's Democratic Party 2014). The direct primary involves all card-carrying members of the party in voting decisions, the indirect/delegate primary requires only elected delegates to vote, and the consensus arrangement is such that only a few party elites decide who among the political aspirants would be the party candidate in the election. Placing the methods on a continuum of inclusiveness in participation, direct and consensus primaries would be considered the two extremes—as the most inclusive and most exclusive methods, respectively—while the indirect primary would be the middle of the spectrum.

Though indirect primary is the most preferred method among party leaders of both parties—out of 42 aspirants interviewed in this study, 13 emerged through a direct primary, 17 through an indirect primary, and 12 through consensus—it is doubtful that the relative inclusive nature of members' participation is the reason why party leaders prefer it. Instead, their preference for indirect stems mostly from its less expensive nature of organization for parties when compared to direct primary where all party members form the voting population. However, for young aspirants, direct primary is the most preferred for its perceived "cost-effectiveness" and propensity for a "reliable forecast" of primary voting outcome. Young female aspirants—who, on average, are not as financially buoyant nor as influential within the parties as their older counterparts—place more emphasis on the financial implications and the reliability of the selection method:

> Direct has advantages over indirect in that it could be cheaper as opposed to having to buy delegates because if you are running in an indirect primary, there is no amount of English you will speak. The Nigerian party system requires money. You must buy them, and there is still no guarantee that you give this money that you would get the [party] ticket. Though the direct would still cost you money to an extent, it would cost less than if you go to delegate one by one and do the job of convincing them. Another advantage of direct primaries is that it is easier to have a reliable forecast, you know, the wards where people will stand for you, as opposed to having delegates that could be compromised even one minute to cast their votes.[3]

Though with direct primaries, party aspirants engage in intensive campaigns (even before the main election) to convincingly get the support of ordinary members, young female aspirants consider it worthwhile for its predictability, knowing that such campaigns would serve them, eventually, should they emerge as party candidates. One of the young female aspirants, while narrating her campaign experience using direct primaries, said that "by the time I got to the main election, it was more like a walkover, I had already done the groundwork, I had covered areas that our opponents could not cover, during preparation for primaries."[4] This is not to say that direct primaries are devoid of political manipulations. For example, in both parties, opinion molders like the state governor, party leaders, and party financiers are believed to also shape the voting patterns of the party's ordinary members in direct primaries (Ifowodo 2021). Invariably, it also gives an advantage to the older money-bag aspirants, primary incumbents, or godfather-backed challengers, who are willing to give whatever is needed to buy the votes of the ordinary members. Nevertheless, as echoed by our interviewees, direct primaries still leave some room for young female aspirants to try their luck.

When indirect primary is the preferred method of candidate selection, the selection practice evolves like a multi-stage contest in both parties—starting with the election of party delegates at congresses, who then constitute the selectorate for later party primaries where party candidates are nominated. Husaini (2019) refers to such congresses as part of the "constituency building phase" due to how it offers opportunities for the party to reward its loyal party activists at various levels, as some of them get elected as party delegates. However, beyond getting rewarded with delegate positions, something else transpires during this phase. Prospective aspirants are informally expected to sponsor loyal party members into positions of party delegates, as a way to position themselves for the later party primary exercise: "Of course, you know how party delegates are selected in Nigeria; you have to sponsor your candidate [contestants for party delegate positions] to become a delegate."[5] Since party delegates constitute the selectorate for candidate selection in indirect primaries, aspirants who can influence the emergence of as many delegates are better positioned to get the support of enough delegates for their candidacy nominations.

While women and young people in general find it difficult to influence this process, young female aspirants particularly find it more challenging, given their limited access to the informal party networks. The only young aspirant who claimed to have been able to leverage such an informal arrangement was male: "In 2015, I was part of the party congress, i.e., how some executives and delegates emerged. I had some that I facilitated their emergence. So, in 2019, when the time came to lobby the party delegates since they were the ones to vote at the primary, it was effortless for me."[6] The inability of young female aspirants to influence the emergence of party delegates who are loyal to them, in turn, not only affects their ability to win the support of enough delegates but also their ability to get the endorsement of influential party stakeholders, with the cumulative negative effect on the outcome of the party primaries, not often in their favor. This way, indirect primaries, as the most preferred candidate selection method of both parties presents an unequal playing field for young female aspirants.

Last, when consensus is the preferred method of candidate selection, the decision of party candidacy is left to a few party elites, among whom the state governor is the most influential, as the unofficial leader of the party at that level. This implies that a young female aspirant will need to be a strong political ally of the governor or other political power brokers for such a person to be nominated, which is rarely the case:

> [W]here it is easy for a young female aspirant to scale through is when they are already in favour with the main power brokers. For instance, if the governor has a special interest in a particular community and says, I am giving you a female candidate, you know it is the governor, it is all the government that will secure and ensure that the candidate scales through. But for a female aspirant to scale through on her own, it is not that easy. I give it to them, and some of them made it through as a result of that I doff my cap to them, they really tried.[7]

In the build-up to the 2023 elections, to reduce this enormous power of the governor on the candidacy process at the subnational level, amendments were made to the electoral act requiring all other party aspirants who had indicated interest in the candidacy race to grant their consent by tendering their withdrawal and offering support for the adopted consensus candidate (Policy and Legal Advocacy Centre 2022; Electoral Act 2022, S.84[10]). Yet interviewees for this study opined that, in practice, this conditionality was either altogether ignored or other contenders had to grudgingly endorse the consensus candidates, as failure to endorse the consensus candidate would spell an act of indiscipline. But in instances where the consensus candidate is a woman, other contenders often explicitly declare their displeasure, forcing party leaders to resort to the adoption of an alternative method of candidate selection, as recommended by the Electoral Act (Policy and Legal Advocacy Centre 2022; Electoral Act 2022, S.84[9b]). This further evidences the arguments of Bjarnegård (2013) that homosocial networks are distrustful of women aspirants as highlighted by the varied reaction to the emergence of female consensus candidates compared to when it is a male consensus candidate.

Conclusion

In this chapter, we have shown how age- and gender-biased candidate selection practices of Nigeria's major political parties can be for young female candidates who seek party candidacy nominations. We did this by evaluating the interaction between informal norms and practices and formal rules of the country's two major parties. This way, this study has stretched further the application of FI in two main ways. Though previous research has always maintained that parties are gendered institutions (Bjarnegård and Zetterberg 2019), by introducing age to the evaluation of party selection mechanism, we have shown that parties can equally manifest gendered ageism. In line with this expectation, the two major political parties in Nigeria, despite regularly announcing gendered and age-related party concessions, are gendered and generationally biased toward their young female aspirants. This highlights the need to see young female aspirants as a distinct marginalized group that require extraordinary attention especially when institutional reforms are being designed to address age and gendered discriminatory practices of political parties.

By implication, scholars of gender and youth politics as well as party politics need to speak often with each other as against the hitherto speaking past another that has been the case in these scholarships. This will surely further our understanding of how women of different age categories are subjected to varying forms of discrimination (Erickson and Josefsson 2021). It is not enough to advocate for gender and youth quotas, or other forms of inclusive rules (Verge and Espírito-Santo 2016); it is also important to examine the dynamics of formal rules and informal norms, how gender may intersect with age in practical implementation, and whether such implementation privileges one category of actors over others.

Funding Statement

This research was supported by the South African National Research Foundation (NRF) Grantholder-linked bursary associated with Human and Social Dynamics in Development Grant (118,512). This chapter was supported by the University of Essex's open access fund.

News Sources and Empirical Material

Adeoye, O.A. (2009). Godfatherism and the future of Nigerian democracy. *African Journal of Political Science and International Relations*, 3(6), 268-272.

Afrobarometer. 2020. "Afrobarometer Round 8 Surveys: Summary of Results for Nigeria." Accessed January 28, 2023. https://www.afrobarometer.org/publication/summary-results-afrobarometer-round-8-survey-nigeria-2020-0/

Akinwale, A. 2022. "APC Declares Free Nomination Forms for Women Seeking Elective Office in 2023." Accessed May 15, 2025. https://www.arise.tv/apc-declares-free-nomination-forms-for-women-seeking-elective-office-in-2023/#google_vignette

All Progressive Congress. 2014. *The Constitution of the All Progressive Congress*. Abuja: APC Secretariat.

Are, J. 2022. "APC Slashes Costs of Nomination Forms by 50% for Persons Under 40 Years." Accessed May 15, 2025. https://www.thecable.ng/apc-slashes-cost-of-nomination-forms-by-50-for-persons-under-40-years

Ibeh, N. 2014. "Nigerians Condemn APC for Electing 52-Year-Old Youth Leader." *Premium Times*, June 17. Accessed April 10, 2023. https://www.premiumtimesng.com/news/163003-nigerians-condemn-apc-electing-52-year-old-youth-leader.html?tztc=1

Ifowodo, O. 2021. "Direct Party Primaries: Why President Buhari Is Right." *The Cable*. Accessed July 27, 2024. https://www.thecable.ng/direct-party-primaries-our-nervous-anxiety-and-why-buhari-is-right/

Ndujihe, C. 2023. "2023 Presidency: Where Are the Women?" Accessed May 15, 2025. https://www.vanguardngr.com/2022/04/2023-presidency-where-are-the-women

Olusola, S. 2022a. "Understanding the Naija Political System (2): Getting to the Primaries." Newsletter Email to O. Abati, August 21. Available email: *mrabatim@gmail.com*

Olusola, S. 2022b. "Campaign Trail Tales: Isinmi Ti De [Rest Has Come]." Newsletter Email to O. Abati, August 22. Available email: *mrabatim@gmail.com*

Oyero, K. (2023) "PDP Releases Timetable for By-Elections, Pegs Senate Form At N3.5m." Accessed May 15, 2025. https://www.channelstv.com/2023/12/26/pdp-releases-timetable-for-by-elections-pegs-senate-form-at-n3-5m

People's Democratic Party. 2014. *The Constitution of the PDP*. Abuja: PDP Secretariat.

Policy and Legal Advocacy Centre. 2022. *Electoral Act 2022: Including INEC Regulations and Guidelines for Conducting Elections*. Abuja: Policy and Legal Advocacy Centre.

Sahara Reporters. 2012. "Party of Gerontocrats: PDP's National Youth Leader Is 60 Years Old." *Sahara Reporters*, March 25. Accessed April 10, 2023. https://saharareporters.com/2012/03/25/party-gerontocrats-pdps-national-youth-leader-60-years-old

Uzor, D. 2019. "2019 Election: Why We should Support Youth Candidacy." Accessed July 26, 2022. http://yiaga.org/nottooyoungtorun/2019-election-why-we-should-support-youth-candidacy-darlingtonuzor

YIAGA Africa. 2023. *2023 Elections: Youth Representation in the Legislature*. Abuja: YIAGA Africa Publications.

Notes

1. Phone interview with an APC Party Leader in Kwara State, January 18, 2022.
2. In-person interview with a PDP young female candidate in Kwara state, January 15, 2022.
3. In-person interview with an APC young female candidate in Abuja, May 26, 2021.
4. In-person interview with a PDP young female candidate in Oyo State, December 8, 2021.
5. Phone interview with a PDP party leader in Oyo State, December 6, 2021.
6. In-person interview with a PDP young male candidate in Kwara State, January 20, 2022.
7. Phone interview with an APC young male candidate in Abuja, May 25, 2021.

9

Collective Candidate Strategies and Diverse Representation in Brazil

Malu A. C. Gatto and Kristin N. Wylie

As articulated in preceding chapters, party insiders—who tend to be, overwhelmingly, racial/ethnic majority men (Murray 2016)—often resist the gender equity project (Josefsson, this volume; Meier, Lang, and Sauer, this volume), employing informal institutions to undermine formal rules, to the detriment of women's political representation (Bjarnegård and Kenny 2017). In this chapter, we provide a feminist institutionalist (FI) account of how underrepresented groups can themselves make use of informal institutions as a means for circumventing insiders' resistance and promoting their own political representation. We posit that informal institutions can cultivate alternative incentives for more collectivist politics with positive implications for women's political representation. To this end, we chronicle the recent proliferation of the informal institution of *coletivos* (collective candidacies and collective mandates) in Brazilian legislative elections.

In Brazil, elections to federal, state, and municipal legislatures take place under open-list proportional representation (OLPR) rules. This system incentivizes candidate-centric campaigns and fuels personalist politics (Nicolau 2006). Under OLPR, candidates run against not only candidates from other parties but also their co-partisans. Due to a need to stand out from others in races with a high number of candidates, campaigns are expensive, and expenditure is a strong predictor of electoral success (Gatto et al. 2021, 83). Especially when candidates cannot rely on party funds—as tends to be the case with outsiders, whose share of party funds is much lower than for incumbents (Gatto et al. 2021, 88)—individual and self-contributions are key to campaign financing. The raced–gendered implications of that expense are clear amid stark wage and wealth gaps experienced by Afro-Brazilians and women across racial identities (Instituto de Pesquisa Econômica Aplicada [IPEA] 2015).

Malu A. C. Gatto and Kristin N. Wylie, *Collective Candidate Strategies and Diverse Representation in Brazil*. In: *Gendering Party Politics*. Edited by: Meryl Kenny and Elin Bjarnegård, Oxford University Press. © Oxford University Press (2025). DOI: 10.1093/oso/9780197793985.003.0009

Subverting the logic of candidate-centric elections, *coletivos* seek to overcome the high barriers to representation imposed by OLPR: by bringing together a group of people to campaign together in favor of a single (collective) candidacy, this informal institution aims to pool personal and social resources of individual members to strengthen the electoral chances of people who would, individually, likely be less electorally viable.

Their protagonists and goals make *coletivos* an innovative type of informal institution: instead of being enacted by political insiders (e.g., party leaders, incumbents) to protect the interests of those in power, *coletivos* are most commonly employed by individuals who have not previously held office, typically to increase the electoral visibility and viability of underrepresented groups, especially women. Studying *coletivos* can thus provide theoretical insights into how politically marginalized groups can themselves employ informal institutions to circumnavigate formal rules that hinder inclusion and/or supplement ineffective inclusionary formal rules.

Employing an FI approach to the literature on party politics, we theorize the gendered implications of personalist politics and how informal institutions can cultivate alternative incentives for more collectivist politics. We argue that contexts of weak formal rules provide opportunities for the emergence of informal institutions that are elite-driven as well as those that are bottom-up innovations. We then conceptualize *coletivos* and offer descriptive evidence on the raced–gendered patterns in their proliferation. The analysis demonstrates that *coletivos* constitute a mechanism for underrepresented groups to contest their exclusion—but that these groups' marginalization may itself hinder the capacity of the informal institution to achieve desired outcomes.

Overcoming Obstacles to Representation Through Informal Institutions

Among the gender and politics community, frustrations with the persistent obstacles confronted in efforts to advance equality by institutional design have fueled a return to the scene of party politics. After all, as the primary mediator of electoral rules and thus a key arbiter of political power, political parties are the central gatekeeper to women's electoral pursuits. Applying an FI lens, scholars have demonstrated how gender manifests in not only formal but also informal party rules, practices, and norms, and the implications for women's representation (Kenny et al. 2022; see Bjarnegård and Kenny, this volume). FI illuminates how seemingly gender-neutral formal rules like OLPR—which incentivizes personalist politics and thus expensive individualistic campaigns—deter newcomers who lack personal financial and political capital and/or prefer a more collectivist approach (Escobar-Lemmon and Taylor-Robinson 2008; Guadagnini 1993; Kittilson 2006; Wylie 2018). The FI approach has thus proven to be a compelling tool for awakening the party politics literature to the salience of gender (Kenny et al. 2022).

The literature on institutional change acknowledges its layered nature, discarding latent assumptions of the tabula rasa and pointing instead to the layers of generations of institutional design efforts (Krook and Mackay 2011; Mahoney and Thelen 2009), as well as of less legible yet "tenacious(ly)" persistent informal institutions (North 1990, 44–45). Informal institutions have often constituted mechanisms for shirking formal institutions—especially those promoting inclusion (Àbàtì and Adeniji, this volume; Bjarnegård and Kenny 2017; Kenny and Verge 2016; Verge and de la Fuente 2014; Waylen 2017). This is particularly the case "when formal rules are not actively maintained or enforced (which may leave) participants in selection processes ... with considerable leeway to circumvent and subvert regulations and reforms that clash with their interests—including gender quotas" (Bjarnegård and Kenny 2017, 215). Yet, informal institutions may also emerge as a supplement for weak formal institutions (Helmke and Levitsky 2004, 2006).

Helmke and Levitsky's (2004, 2006) account of interacting informal and formal institutions centers on the effectiveness of formal institutions and the extent to which the outcomes yielded by informal and formal institutions are convergent. Their resulting typology generates four ideal types: in the case of effective formal institutions, the interaction with informal institutions can be complementary (convergent) or accommodating (divergent); for ineffective formal institutions, the interaction with informal institutions can be substitutive (convergent) or competing (divergent). We apply that approach here, examining these interactions in two ways. In both cases, we focus on how marginalized groups can work through informal institutions to make the system more amenable and accessible.

First, we consider how informal institutions may interact with formal rules in an *accommodating* way. As articulated by Helmke and Levitsky (2004, 729), "Accommodating informal institutions are often created by actors who dislike outcomes generated by the formal rules but are unable to change or openly violate those rules. As such, they often help to reconcile these actors' interests with the existing formal institutional arrangements." Instead of highlighting how party elites and officeholders employ informal institutions to maintain their own power, however, we show that political outsiders can also make use of informal institutions to work around formal rules that undermine their political representation.

Second, we discuss how informal institutions may interact with ineffective formal rules in a *substitutive* manner. Per Helmke and Levitsky (2004, 729), "substitutive informal institutions achieve what formal institutions were designed, but failed, to achieve." We show that the failure of formal rules may actually open up opportunities for informal institutional innovation. In focusing on outsiders' employment of informal institutions to overcome their own marginalization, however, we caution that effective development and use of informal institutions will be challenged by disparities in access to privileged information and resources, and in knowledge about formal and informal rules of the game and how they function (Krook 2016)—which tends to be limited in weakly institutionalized party organizations that lack transparency and accountability. Especially in contexts of contested or weak formal institutions, the informal institutions that emerge to challenge or supplement them merit careful consideration. Next, we briefly discuss the Brazilian context, which is particularly well-suited for theorizing and analyzing these interactions.

The Brazilian Context

Brazil stands out as an exemplary case of the limitations of formal institutional fixes for women's underrepresentation. Despite employing proportional representation in lower-house legislative elections, a recently strengthened gender quota for candidacies initially implemented in 1996, and public financing and free air-time for parties during campaign season with judicially mandated reservations for women and Afrodescendant candidates proportionate to their candidacies, Brazil remains among the lowest in global standings of women's representation (Inter-Parliamentary Union 2024). With just 17.7 percent women elected to the Chamber of Deputies in 2022, Brazil ranks 131st, in stark contrast to the regional norm: when it comes to women's legislative representation, six of the top 15 countries in the world are in Latin America (Inter-Parliamentary Union 2024).

Accounts of the striking and persistent underrepresentation of women in Brazil point to the open-list character of its proportional elections, which incentivizes expensive individualistic campaigns, weakens parties, and undermines the gender quota, together fueling personalist politics, hyper party fragmentation, and an inchoate party system that perpetuates the status quo of white male dominance (Sacchet and Speck 2012; dos Santos and Wylie 2018; Wylie 2018). Campaigns are prohibitively expensive, with successful candidates in the 2010–2014 elections to the lower house (Chamber of Deputies) averaging over US$500,000 in campaign expenses, including a significant share from individual and self-contributions (Avelino and Fisch 2018; Sacchet and Speck 2012; Samuels 2001). Notably, even after a 2015 judicial decision ruling corporate contributions to campaign finance unconstitutional—which plummeted average campaign costs by around 50 percent—raced–gendered disparities in campaign finance have persisted, with white men on average reporting significantly and substantially more campaign funds than women and Afrodescendant candidates (Chaves and Mancuso 2020; Janusz et al. 2022; Wylie 2020).

Amid this rather unfavorable landscape, party elites keen to preserve their own power have deployed an inventive array of informal institutions to undermine the Brazilian gender quota and, more recently, the reservation of campaign funds. These efforts have included parties' nomination of phantom candidates to nominally comply with the gender quota without effectively increasing competition (Gatto and Wylie 2022; Wylie et al. 2019) and parties' delayed and disproportionate allocations of campaign finance to women (and Afrodescendant) candidates (Aflalo 2023; Sacchet and Wylie 2023). The capacity of targeted equity policies to level the playing field is thus hindered not only by their (often intentional) design flaws and compliance issues but also by competing informal institutions that emerge to thwart their impact.

While much of the literature on gender and institutional change emphasizes the debilitating effects of informal institutions on gender equity instruments (Àbàtì and Adeniji, this volume; Bjarnegård 2013; Bjarnegård and Kenny 2017; Gatto and Wylie 2022; Kenny 2013; Verge and de la Fuente 2014; Waylen 2017), informal institutions might also be wielded to advance women's representation in the face of formal institutions that perpetuate women's exclusion. Particularly in the context of formal institutions that are weak and/or hostile to women and people from historically excluded groups, informal institutions may offer an alternative route to promoting diversity in representation. The Brazilian case provides an opportunity to explore this possibility.

Conceptualizing Coletivos

First observed in the 1994 Brazilian elections, but increasing in number in the 2018 elections, and especially in the 2020 elections (Rede da Ação Política pela Sustentabilidade [RAPS] 2019; Instituto de Estudos Socioeconômicos [INESC] 2022; dos Santos 2023; Rezende de Almeida 2024), *coletivos* are an increasingly relevant type of informal institution operating in Brazilian legislative elections. Although the factors prompting their proliferation are not so well understood, existing studies point to generalized levels of public distrust in traditional elites (RAPS 2019, 16–22) and political parties' exclusion of outsiders—particularly those from marginalized groups (Bancada Ativista 2021, 8)—as motivations for the emergence of an alternative solution to promoting political renewal (Quintinho 2022). Bringing together these explanations, Rezende de Almeida (2024) contends that the growing presence of *coletivos* represent a new form of interaction between social movements and political parties, in which marginalized groups seek to overcome barriers imposed by political parties while acting strategically from within them, as dictated by electoral law. Regardless of what has prompted their proliferation, the fact is that this type of campaign (and office-holding) strategy has been in ascension, particularly since the 2020 elections (Russo 2020). And, importantly, contrary to many informal institutions associated with political elites, this growing type of informal institution is often employed by people from marginalized groups with the aim of improving diversity in political representation.

But what are *coletivos*, after all? To put it simply, collective *candidacies* consist of an electoral strategy whereby a group of individuals come together—pooling material and social resources—to campaign for the election of a single registered candidate. While this registered candidate has to abide by official eligibility criteria—such as be affiliated with a party and receive the candidacy nomination of the said party—other members of the *coletivo* are not required to comply with any official requirements. For example, they could be affiliated with a different party or no party at all (Rezende de Almeida 2024). If elected, *coletivos* typically promise to carry out collective *mandates*, with all group members exercising power over decision-making (cf. Bancada Ativista 2021).

On the one hand, by running as a group of candidates in an "elect-one-take-all" model, *coletivos* break with the individualist logic of candidate-centric campaigns. This is reflected in campaign materials, which instead of focusing on a single candidate, showcase all members of the *coletivo*, as well as on the collective commitment of members of *coletivos* to contribute to campaigns (RAPS 2019). In other words, unlike candidate-centric campaigns, where a single person's material resources and political and social networks shape their electoral viability, *coletivos* tap into the financial, political, and social capital of all of their members (RAPS 2019, 26). This strategy may disproportionately benefit people from marginalized groups, who often have lower levels of access to key campaign resources (Chaves and Mancuso 2020; Janusz et al. 2022; Wylie 2020). Bancada Ativista (2021)—the tenth most voted of 1,868 candidacies in the 2018 elections to São Paulo's state legislature—speaks to this benefit explicitly, presenting *coletivos* as an example of experimenting with new approaches that "strengthen and deepen democracy ... especially helping to confront inequalities by opening more space for those who have less financial resources" (Bancada Ativista 2021, 22).

On the other hand, by operating within the context of a candidate-centric system, *coletivos* function informally: the electoral law does not recognize the candidacy of groups, only of individuals (Rais and Alves Magarian 2021), so *coletivos* have to select one individual as the *porta-voz* (spokesperson), whose name is officially registered as a candidate; if elected, only that candidate (not their *coletivo* peers) is officially recognized as elected.

Collective candidacies therefore offer a workaround to formal institutions that pose a barrier to inclusion, but they do so through exploiting loopholes in formal rules. This, we argue, makes *coletivos* an informal institution with the aim of subverting the hostile and/or weak formal rules of the game to promote the political representation of marginalized groups. Reports authored by *coletivos* themselves reveal their recognition of informality and intent. For example, as the *Bancada Ativista* details about their experience carrying out a collective candidacy,

> Due to its potential to gather votes from several people who would not be elected alone, the collective candidacies have been gaining ground as a

> powerful formula for [the electoral participation of] new names, especially those who do not have a lot of financial resources to invest in the campaign. ... Collective candidacies are not yet foreseen by law, nor recognized by the TSE—that is, they are neither prohibited nor explicitly allowed. For these reasons, it is necessary to choose a person to legally assume the role of candidate, who will also officially be the parliamentarian if the candidacy is elected (Bancada Ativista 2021, 22, 29).[1]

If elected, the participation of all members of the *coletivo* in decision-making is also guided by informal arrangements. While these arrangements vary widely (RAPS 2019, 26), they often adapt to the formal institutions in place. For example, in their guidance for people seeking to run for office as part of *coletivos*, the *Bancada Ativista* recommends deciding the number of members of the collective candidacy based on the number of people that are allowed to compose the legislative office (*gabinete*) for the legislature to which they plan on running, as this would allow all members of the group, if elected, to be nominated for staff positions in the registered candidate's legislative office (Bancada Ativista 2021, 25).

Recognizing the opportunities, but also potential risks of engaging in this type of informal campaign and governing strategy—particularly for members of *coletivos* whose names are not the ones officially registered with the electoral authorities—many *coletivos* establish internal rules, and some go as far as to write up contracts to establish members' responsibilities and benefits (RAPS 2019; Rezende de Almeida 2024). Still, these measures can be insufficient. The recent experiences of some of the *coletivos* that broke down after taking office—with reports of the challenges in following horizontal decision-making when only one member of the group is officially recognized as an elected official (Agostine 2022)—raise concerns about the sustainability and functionality of informal arrangements that do not provide guarantees to individuals who actively contribute to the election of a candidacy, but who ultimately are not recognized by law as elected officials (INESC 2022, 4).

In spite of the risks imposed by informality, *coletivos* may provide an alternative avenue for the political representation of marginalized groups in a system where formal rules are largely exclusionary and those ostensibly aimed at inclusion have themselves been undermined by other informal institutions enacted by political elites. The next section examines whether this indeed seems to be the case.

Analyzing Coletivos

To explore the prevalence and employment of *coletivos* as a tool for the political representation of marginalized groups, we assemble a data set on collective mandates in the Brazilian 2020 municipal legislative elections and 2022 state and national legislative elections. These data allow us to offer descriptive analyses on demographic characteristics of *coletivos* and explore how they diverge from conventional candidacies.

Data

We build this data set with official data from the Tribunal Superior Eleitoral (Superior Electoral Tribunal, TSE) on valid candidacies (*candidaturas aptas*) for the 2020 races to municipal assemblies (N = 492,185) and for the 2022 races to state assemblies and the lower chamber of the National Congress (N = 25,353). These data include the names candidates choose to appear on the ballot in electronic voting machines.[2] Since *coletivos* are a new phenomenon, there is no standard practice to reliably identify these types of candidacies. To the best of our knowledge, however, candidates' chosen voting machine names serve as the point of departure for all existing analyses that have sought to identify *coletivos*.

To identify potential *coletivos* from these data, we employ a semi-supervised classification approach. We proceed in two steps. First, we created a dictionary of five key terms which explicitly signal the notion of a collective candidacy: (1) *coletivo (collective)*, (2) *coletiva (collective)*, (3) *mandato (mandate)*, (4) *mandata (mandate)*, and (5) *bancada (caucus)*.[3] Second, we use R function *str function* from the package *stringi* (Gagolewski 2022) to detect candidate voting machine names that employ at least one of these terms. With this procedure, we identify 229 *coletivos* running in the 2020 municipal legislative elections (representing 0.05 percent of all valid candidacies) and 173 candidacies running in the 2022 general elections (0.68 percent of all valid candidacies)—114 of which were for state-level races and 59 of which ran for the national-level Chamber of Deputies.

Relying on official electoral data to study an informal institution has a key limitation: since *coletivos* are not officially recognized by electoral authorities, the TSE's data do not officially label *coletivos* nor do they include information on all members of *coletivos*. In other words, these data only reflect information about the candidate registered to officially represent their group in elections (and take office, if elected). The challenge of capturing informal institutions is a recurring issue in this area of study (Bjarnegård and Kenny 2017)—and, in itself, a by-product of informality. To collect data on all members of *coletivos*, some analyses collected campaign materials and conducted extensive online searches (e.g., RAPS 2019; Rezende de Almeida 2024). Systematically collecting these materials outside of the electoral period (which is our case) is not possible, given that these are no longer available for many (if not most) candidacies. Our analyses are therefore restricted to analyzing the characteristics of the titular (i.e., officially named) candidate—or *porta-voz*—of *coletivos*.

Analyses

We begin our analyses by exploring whether *coletivos* are a type of informal institution largely employed by outsiders and, in particular, individuals from marginalized groups. Data demonstrate that *coletivos* are an emerging informal institution not (yet) employed by political elites: of the total 402 cases of *coletivos*, only two were headed by incumbent candidates. Prior studies found *coletivos* to be intentionally inclusive of voices historically excluded from formal politics, such as women and Afro-Brazilian, Indigenous, and LGBTQI+ people (Campos and dos Santos Almeida Costa 2022; da Silva et al. 2021; dos Santos 2023; RAPS 2019; Rezende de Almeida 2024). As shown in Figure 9.1, our data support that assertion.

Pooling together data from the 2020 and 2022 legislative races, we find that while women represent 34.6 percent of single candidacies, they are the officially registered candidate for 46.0 percent of *coletivos*. Although the political representation of other racial and ethnic groups is not higher in *coletivos* than in single candidacies, Black[4] candidates represent a much higher share of officially registered candidates for *coletivos*—28.4 percent—than for single candidates (11.1 percent). That pattern persists when looking exclusively at women candidates, with 11.3 percent of individual women candidacies and 32.4 percent of *coletivos* headed by women identifying as Black. For both single candidacies and *coletivos*, just under half of the candidates identified as white, which approximates population trends. The rate of white candidates (52.4 percent) was a bit higher among *coletivos* with women as their registered candidates.

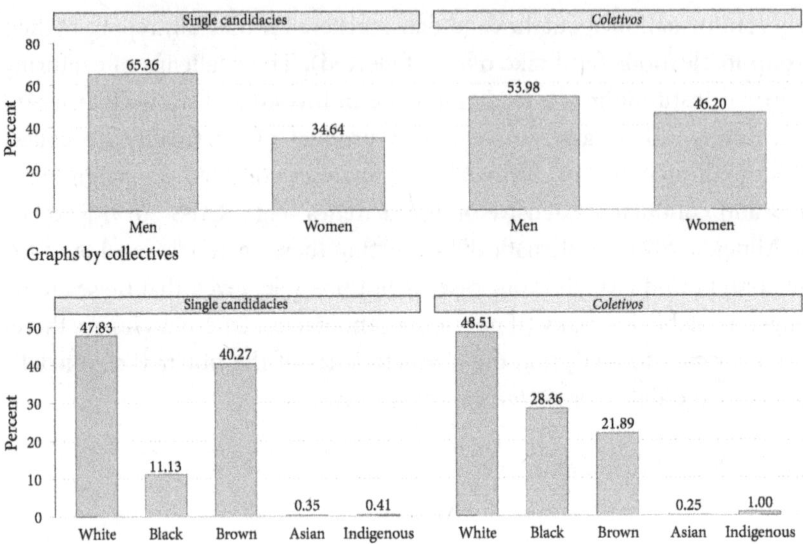

Figure 9.1 Gender and Racial Patterns in *Coletivos* (2020–2022 Legislative Elections)

Note: The unit of analysis is candidacy. Figure displays results from analyses with pooled data from the 2020 and 2022 legislative elections (N = 517,538).

Next, we look at the distribution of *coletivos* across parties, confirming prior studies that found the practice to be much more common among left-wing parties. INESC (2022) reports that 87.2 percent of *coletivos* in the 2020 elections were registered with left-wing parties, with just 5.2 and 7.6 percent registered with centrist and right-wing parties, respectively.[5] It is difficult to disentangle whether left-wing parties are more open to *coletivos* per se or to the types of candidates that tend to be part of *coletivos* (i.e., activists from social movements Rezende de Almeida [2024]).

One key factor in the concentration of *coletivos* among leftist parties is their prevalence among the Socialism and Liberty Party (Partido Socialismo e Liberdade, PSOL), a burgeoning socialist party that sits to the left of the governing Workers' Party (Partido de Trabalhadores, PT) and is known for launching the (single) candidacies of civil society activists. The PSOL elected the most prominent and exemplary *coletivo*, the Bancada Ativista (Quintinho 2022). Of the 402 *coletivos* analyzed here, a striking 135 (33.6 percent) were registered with the PSOL. The party with the second highest concentration of *coletivos* was the PT, with 76 *coletivos*, comprising 18.9 percent of *coletivos* but just 0.27 percent of their candidacies overall, significantly less pronounced than the PSOL, which had 3 percent of their candidacies in *coletivos*.

Coletivos hold promise for enhancing descriptive representation in part for their capacity for pooling resources and thus improving the electoral viability of candidates who typically confront resource disparities. The data offer strong evidence affirming that benefit—among women candidates, the average campaign expenditures was R$174,260 for single candidacies and R$1,085,502 for *coletivos*. For Black women candidates, the average campaign expenditure was R$260,301 for single candidacies and R$1,352,861 for *coletivos*. With some of those differences likely driven by state-level dynamics, especially given the concentration of *coletivos* in São Paulo's hypercompetitive elections, we also test for significant differences in resources among candidates in São Paulo (which had 32.1 percent of all *coletivos*), and find that the patterns hold.

Finally, we consider whether *coletivos* increase the electoral prospects of Black candidates and women across racial identities, relative to their chances when running as individual candidates. Of the 60 *coletivos* with Black women as the registered candidate, three were elected (5 percent). That success rate is almost double the rate among individual Black women candidates, with just 529/20,030 winning election (2.6 percent). With so few cases, however, the observed difference is not quite statistically significant ($p = 0.13$). Interestingly, the pattern is reversed for Black men candidates, who headed 54 *coletivos* but only elected one (1.9 percent), significantly lower than their success rate as individual candidates (8.5 percent). Among all registered women candidates, 6.5 percent of those running in *coletivos* won election, compared to 5.3 percent of those running individually, a statistically insignificant difference.

If we focus the analysis on just elected candidacies, however, we can see the representational benefits materialize. Of the 59,538 individual candidacies in our data set that won election, 16.1 percent were women. In stark contrast, the rate of women among elected *coletivos* candidacies was 4.4 times greater (70.6 percent). We also see a substantial difference when focusing on Black women, who comprised 0.9 percent of the elected individual candidates and 17.6 percent as elected *coletivos*.

Although our data preclude empirical consideration of the full slate of candidates presented informally by *coletivos*, instead limiting our analysis to the registered candidates, the findings presented here affirm what prior studies and *coletivos* themselves purport—*coletivos* provide resources (and visibility) to candidates from historically excluded groups, in particular, women and Afro-Brazilians. More intensive analyses on the full slate of members of elected *coletivos* reach similar conclusions; for example, Rezende de Almeida (2024, 19) finds that while women won election to only 16 percent of municipal assembly seats overall, women were the *porta-voz* in 22 of the 34 elected *coletivos* (64.7 percent) and were 87/120 co-councilors of those *coletivos* (72.5 percent). *Coletivos* are, then, a raced–gendered phenomenon, blazing a collectivist path for women and other outsiders to make their way into a system designed in their absence that has heretofore perpetuated their exclusion.

Conclusion

As cautioned by Mona Lena Krook (2016, 280), "The introduction of quotas thus represents only the beginning of (a) long, contested process to open up politics to women and guarantee their full and equal participation." Indeed, in Brazil, Uruguay (Josefsson, this volume), and elsewhere, quotas and other efforts to advance equality by institutional design have faced challenges and active resistance. Institutional interventions in lagging descriptive representation—such as the 1996 gender quota law and its subsequent reforms, as well as the judicially mandated reservation of public resources for the campaigns of women and Afrodescendant candidates—suffer from implementation issues and loopholes. Furthermore, elites seeking to preserve the (white, male) status quo have deployed informal institutions to undermine them, to the detriment of representative democracy.

Yet, in a system that incentivizes personalist, individualistic campaigns and perpetuates white male dominance, *coletivos* are emerging as a distinctly collectivist informal institution, with women and other outsiders tackling their underrepresentation from within by challenging the core logic of candidate-centric elections. *Coletivos* offer great promise but confront limitations, largely posed by their informality and formal rules around the official registration of candidacies. Calls for regulations could result in increased oversight of *coletivos* or even the formalization of collective candidacies, which might temper their power.

Studies of informal institutions confront methodological challenges, with their informality obscuring attempts to analyze them empirically. Research strategies include looking to proxies for or observable implications of informal institutions and conducting interviews with critical actors about their deployment. Such approaches would help to comprehend the conditions under which informal institutions could be effectively wielded in service of diversifying representation.

This analysis of the Brazilian case helps to advance the FI literature and mainstream party politics understanding of the interplay between formal and informal rules. We move beyond the recognition that resistant party elites can and will undermine gender quotas with more precision about *how* formal and informal institutions interact and to what effect. We underscore the importance of considering both the process and outcomes of institution creation, examining the common gap between their intended and actual effects, and identifying strategies for institutional innovation from below. Specifically, as we show, by launching collective candidacies, women work around the formal barriers to their representation and attempt to achieve what the gender quota has, for decades, attempted but failed to accomplish. In so doing, we show that *accommodating* and *substitutive* informal institutions (Helmke and Levitsky 2004, 2006) may not only be employed by party elites but can also be deployed by women and candidates from other marginalized groups keen to circumnavigate the formal institutions that perpetuate their exclusion.

News Sources and Empirical Material

Agostine, C. 2022. "Mandatos coletivos enfrentam desafios." *O Globo*, 28 January. Accessed July 13, 2023. https://valor.globo.com/politica/noticia/2022/01/28/mandatos-coletivos-enfrentam-desafios.ghtml

Bancada Ativista. 2021. "Guia Inspiracional: Como Estruturar uma Candidatura Coletiva." Accessed July 13, 2023. https://www.impulsa.voto/materials/como-estruturar-candidaturas-coletivas

Campos, B.L., and M dos Santos Almeida Costa. 2022. "Um Balanço de Quatro Eleições com Candidaturas Coletivas no Brasil." *Jota/Observatório das Eleições 2022*. Accessed July 13, 2023. https://www.jota.info/opiniao-e-analise/artigos/um-balanco-de-quatro-eleicoes-com-candidaturas-coletivas-no-brasil-24082022

Globo. 2023. "População que se declara preta sobe para 10,6% em 2022, diz IBGE," 16 June. Accessed July 13, 2023. https://g1.globo.com/economia/noticia/2023/06/16/populacao-que-se-declara-preta-sobe-para-106percent-em-2022-diz-ibge.ghtml

IBGE. 2018. "IBGE Mostra as Cores da Desigualdade." Accessed July 13, 2023. https://agenciadenoticias.ibge.gov.br/agencia-noticias/2012-agencia-de-noticias/noticias/21206-ibge-mostraas-cores-da-desigualdade

INESC. 2022. "#5: Candidaturas Coletivos." In *Perfil do Poder: Eleições 2022*. Brasília. Accessed July 13, 2023. https://www.inesc.org.br/candidaturas-coletivas-nas-eleicoes-2022

Instituto de Pesquisa Econômica Aplicada. 2015. *Retrato das Desigualdades de Gênero e Raça*. Brasília. www.ipea.gov.br/retrato/apresentacao.htm

Quintinho, R. 2022. "Propostas de mandatos coletivos são aposta para renovação na política." *Brasil de Fato*, 23 May. Accessed July 13, 2023. https://www.brasildefatodf.com.br/2022/05/23/propostas-de-mandatos-coletivos-sao-aposta-para-renovacao-na-politica

Rede da Ação Política pela Sustentabilidade. 2019. *Mandatos Coletivos e Compartilhados: Desafios e Possibilidades para a Representação Legislativa no Século XXI*. Accessed July 13, 2023. https://www.raps.org.br/2020/wp-content/uploads/2019/11/mandatos_v5.pdf

Notes

1. Translated by authors from Portuguese.
2. Official electoral data include information on candidates' full legal names, as well as their "voting machine names" (*nome de urna*), which are the names that candidates choose to use throughout their campaigns and display in electronic voting machines. Candidates are free to choose their "voting machine names," so many choose to include their professional titles, to signal their communities, or, in the case of *coletivos*, to showcase that the candidacy is not an individual one.
3. These keywords were also employed in the analysis conducted by Russo (2021). We favor this conservative approach over others that employ longer lists of terms for its lower likelihood of producing misclassifications (i.e., false positives). For example, our efforts to replicate INESC's (2022) methodology which employs 44 terms produced a high number of false positives. This, in large part, is due to their list including terms often used by single candidacies—such as, for example, the term "people" (used by many to signal they are "of the people").
4. Following Brazilian academics, government sources, and activists, we use the terms "Afrodescendant" and "Afro-Brazilian" as aggregated terms referring to people identifying as "preta/o" (black) or "parda/o" (brown or mixed race). We use "Black" to refer to people or organizations explicitly identifying as "preta/o" or "negra." The category "non-white" includes Afrodescendant people as well as Indigenous people and those of Asian descent. As of the 2022 census, 42.8 percent of the population identifies as "white," 45.3 percent as "parda," and 10.6 percent as "preta" (Globo 2023). The 2010 census found that 1.1 percent of the population identifies as "amarela" (of Asian descent) and 0.4 percent as Indigenous (Instituto Brasileiro de Geografia e Estatística [IBGE] 2018).
5. While the practice has been dominated by leftist parties and activists, a contagion effect of sorts has seen a spillover to right-wing candidates, such as those associated with the "*Bancada de Bala" (Bullet Caucus)*, which coalesces candidates affiliated with the military and police.

10

Women's Institutional Belonging and Self-Making in a Right-Wing Party in India

Proma Raychaudhury

As the chapters in this volume highlight, feminist institutionalism (FI) has proved to be a useful methodological tool to explore the formal rules as well as informal gendered norms and power relations that constitute the often-inaccessible "internal life" of formal political institutions such as political parties. This chapter illustrates how the concepts of "institutional belonging" and "self-making" can complement emerging FI research on gendered institutional cultures through an illustrative case study of women members of the Hindu right-wing Bharatiya Janata Party (BJP) in West Bengal, India. The experiential concepts of "institutional belonging" and "self-making" can assist in understanding how political party cultures condition women's integration ("fitting in") into such cultures by privileging models of political femininity that conform to gendered standards of appropriateness.

This chapter is divided into two main sections. The first section offers a brief review of FI interventions highlighting the importance of informal codes and contextual specificity in understanding the gendered institutional cultures of political institutions. It sets out the concepts of "institutional belonging" and "self-making" and highlights the ways through which the two concepts can aid FI research. After a brief discussion of methods, the second section illustrates these concepts with an in-depth focus on the BJP in West Bengal, drawing on semi-structured interviews with women party members and key party and political documents. It traces the requisites of institutional belonging in the BJP, assessing the influence of extra-institutional factors such as familial attachments, appeals to ideology, and social locations on women's experiences of belonging in the party. It further traces discursive practices of political self-making of women members of the BJP, focusing in particular on strategies of "defeminization." Recognizing the dynamic

Proma Raychaudhury, *Women's Institutional Belonging and Self-Making in a Right-Wing Party in India*.
In: *Gendering Party Politics*. Edited by: Meryl Kenny and Elin Bjarnegård, Oxford University Press.
 DOI: 10.1093/oso/9780197793985.003.0010

and co-constitutive relationship between institutions and actors, the chapter argues that such practices are key to the reproduction of institutional continuity in political party cultures, providing insights into the enduring attachment that marginalized actors can form with political institutions even in contexts of political exclusion.

Feminist Institutionalism, Women's Institutional Belonging, and Becoming

Institutions and their dominant gender regimes (Connell 1987) condition the behavior of individual actors. At the same time, the repeated performance (Butler 1997) and materialization of dominant gender norms by actors sustain institutional cultures. In recent decades, feminist research on political parties has particularly focused on how gendered "rules-in-form" (formal regulations) and informal conventions interact with and influence each other on an everyday level (Mackay et al. 2010; Verge 2015; Bjarnegård and Kenny, this volume). In investigating informal institutional norms and practices, FI research underlines the importance of context, and the "nestedness" of institutions within wider political and macro-social discursive formations (Mackay 2014; Beckwith, this volume). Such research can assist substantially in unpacking the subterranean gendered dynamics of power and hierarchy within formal institutional processes such as candidate selection. Moving away from both celebratory portrayals of agency and reductionist explanations of structural determinism, FI underlines the co-constitutiveness of institutions and the actors who inhabit them.

Similarly, the vast body of literature across disciplines on *belonging* explores it as a dynamic process—one that incorporates both individual and collective aspects and that shapes and is shaped by networks and relations of power in society (Ignatieff 1993; Castells 1996; Yuval-Davis 2006; Brubaker 2010; Yuval-Davis 2011). The experience of belonging connotes a sense of feeling "at home" and integration into a particular culture, institution, or a nation (Yuval-Davis 2006, 199). Distinguishing between three analytical aspects through which belonging is experienced and articulated, Nira Yuval-Davis draws attention to the importance of social locations, emotional attachments, and the ethico-political practice of marking boundaries to signify belonging and exclusion: "(P)eople can 'belong' in many different ways and to many different objects of attachments" (Yuval-Davis 2006, 199).

Studies of political institutions argue that women's belonging is shaped by their historical location in the peripheries of institutional culture. For example, in her sociological study of British racial and ethnic minority women parliamentarians, Nirmal Puwar highlighted the relationship between the conservative perception of women and ethnic minority legislators as "space invaders" and the historical exclusion of the bodies of women and racial/ethnic minorities from the higher echelons of power in particular, and from public spaces in general (Puwar 2004). Puwar identified the strategies through which women in political and institutional spaces are perceived as ill-fitting and unsuitable, while also demonstrating how these experiences of belonging are conditioned by the intersections of race, gender, class, and other social categories (McCall 2005; Yuval-Davis 2006; Yuval-Davis, Kannabiran, and Vieten 2006; Yuval-Davis 2007, 2011) that constitute their individual subjectivities.

Building on this work, this chapter traces the "requisites of belonging" (Yuval-Davis 2011, 20) in the Hindu right-wing BJP in West Bengal, India—that is, the formal and informal codes of gendered behavior and interpersonal interactions which serve to regulate access to power and facilitate belonging within party and institutional spaces. Drawing on interviews with women members of the BJP, the chapter explores their articulations of institutional belonging while being cognizant of the influence of their respective social positionings and ideological affiliations among other themes. As Rogers Brubaker points out, the question of "who belongs" to a nation, culture, association, club, or family can be a site of contestation (Brubaker 2010, 64). The politics of belonging in institutional cultures is similarly connected to practices of boundary-creation and contestation, and is often accompanied by the privileging of an idealized subjectivity over others. Actors who conform to such a practice are seen to experience a more wholesome integration into institutional cultures.

To explore the crafting of such an idealized subjectivity, this chapter also integrates the concept of "self-making" to enhance its analysis of the narratives of women members of the BJP. Expressed simply, *self-making* is an approach that helps to trace social change through a focus on the self. Michel Foucault, in his later works, explored the linkages between the modern "technologies of the self"—micro-social practices that equip individuals to cultivate themselves (Foucault 1980; Martin, Gutman, and Hutton 1988)—and larger historical developments in the state and society. Recent scholarship on self-making in South Asia adopts a more "processual" ethnographic understanding of the self that highlights the interconnectedness between the motivations and intentionalities of individuals and the external social, economic, cultural, political, and historical contexts they inhabit (Chandra and Majumder 2013). Rupturing the hegemonic model of the white, male, emancipated subject, contemporary conceptualizations of political self-making understand the self as embodied, gendered, and racialized (Rebughini 2014). This includes specific scholarship on the discursive strategies of self-representation deployed by party members, such as Tarini Bedi's study of Shiv Sena women cultivating "dashing" and locally influential political selves (Bedi 2016), or Srirupa Roy's study of Aam Aadmi Party workers developing themselves as active agents who "get things done" (Roy 2014, 49).

The related concepts of "institutional belonging" and "political self-making" can provide insights into the ways in which informal practices reproduce women's marginalization from positions of power within political parties—a core preoccupation of FI scholarship (see Bjarnegård and Kenny, this volume). Exploring the subjective experiences of belonging and discursive practices of self-making among women party members underlines not only the centrality of gender in the sedimentation of institutional "logics of appropriateness" (Chappell and Waylen 2013) but also the complex intersections between gender and other categories of social identity and oppression such as caste, class, and religious identity. Importantly, engaging with narratives of women's institutional belonging can offer possible answers as to why marginalized actors such as women and other oppressed social identities continue to participate in institutions instead of exiting them, illustrating the nature of agency exercised by the women. Following Naila Kabeer, the chapter understands agency as inclusive of not only autonomy but also a variety of deliberate practices such as bargaining, negotiation, deception, manipulation, subversion, or even reflection and analysis (Kabeer 1999, 4) that can both open up but also limit possibilities for change.

The twin concepts of institutional belonging and self-making therefore highlight the co-constitutiveness of agency and structure, demonstrating how expressions of agency by women party members are embedded in their historical location in the peripheries of institutional party cultures. Poststructuralist approaches can be particularly useful in understanding the emotional attachments that actors cultivate with the hegemonic institutional discourse while also highlighting the negotiations that women members undertake (or fail to undertake) with institutional (and social) standards of appropriateness. The study of women's experiences and articulation of institutional belonging within parties can also enhance FI scholarship by centering the perspectives on political party cultures offered by women members who are located at the lower echelons of such cultures. There are affinities here with sociological perspectives on "relations of ruling" in institutions from women and other actors in subordinate roles in such institutions (Smith 2005).

The adoption of poststructuralist and discursive approaches can thus deepen FI into the informal dynamics of political recruitment and candidate selection, and their interplay with formal rules. It also expands the feasibility of an FI research design, particularly in spatial contexts where data on institutional practices such as candidate selection in political parties are not accessible due to the lack of transparency in such institutions. An instance of such context is offered in this chapter with the research limitations that accompanied the case study of women members of the BJP in West Bengal, India. The limitations encountered during fieldwork included restricted access to the organizational processes that accompany political recruitment and candidate selection, reluctance among women interviewees to speak freely about their experiences of exclusion and marginalization, and an overarching lack of intra-party democracy in party cultures. Exploring the institutional belonging of actors and their discursive strategies of self-making can offer a window into how actors perceive the formal and informal institutional norms and practices that underpin and naturalize hierarchies and gendered ways of being and interacting. Together they offer a conceptual lens to further understand how institutions shape behavior, advancing FI understanding of how institutions (i) "regulate actors' behavior to produce gendered effects"; (ii) "obligate actors to behave in gendered ways"; and "narrate forms of gendered behavior and hence legitimize gendered political outcomes" (cf. Lowndes 2020, 11). Complementing FI research with studies of institutional belonging and self-making can augment our understandings of the durability and mutability of hegemonic institutional gender discourses and the emotive attachments with actors that sustain them.

Research Method and Data

This chapter draws on semi-structured interviews with women members of the BJP, as well as key party documents and other political texts. I conducted 14 semi-structured interviews in the state of West Bengal in three phases between 2018 and 2019, primarily in urban and peri-urban Kolkata. While insights offered by all the interviewees inform the analysis of the institutional belonging and self-making of women party workers, the chapter focuses on the narratives of primarily two interviewees due to the limited scope of the chapter. Covering women members across different layers of the party hierarchy, the interviews allowed for a sample of experiences of women at the grassroots as well as in the higher echelons of the party. Efforts were made to ensure a fair generational distribution among interviewees, although a focus on party functionaries and office-bearers at different levels have balanced the sample in favor of senior and middle-aged interviewees. Names of the interviewees have been changed to protect their anonymity. Of course, several of the interviewees may not agree with/recognize the concepts used to analyze their interpretations. Notwithstanding their limitations as a method of data collection—especially compared with an immersive method such as participant observation—the interviews highlight the informal processes that remain undocumented and yet are key to the reproduction of gendered institutions. The chapter adopts the method of poststructuralist discourse analysis, and the *logics* approach (Glynos and Howarth 2007) in particular, to identify and characterize the informal gendered codes that condition women's representation and participation within parties (*social logics*); to locate the gender binaries and antagonisms that undergird the institutional cultures of the parties (*political logics*); and to assess the appeal and the affective "grip" of hegemonic gender constructions in the self-makings of women party members (*fantasmatic logics*).

Social Locations, Ideology, and Loyalty to the Party: Women's Institutional Belonging and Self-makings in the BJP

Affiliated with a gamut of Hindu right-wing associations collectively designated as the Sangh Parivar ("Sangh Family"), the BJP represents the Sangh's political face. Within the institutional expanse of the Sangh, the BJP shares space with religious associations such as the Vishwa Hindu Parishad (VHP); cultural associations such as the Rashtriya Swayamsevak Sangh (RSS) and the Rashtrasevika Samiti (for women); trade unions such as the Bharatiya Mazdoor Sangh (BMS); and militant religious organizations such as the Bajrang Dal and the Durga Vahini (for women), among others. Founded on April 6, 1980, the BJP was a successor to the erstwhile Bharatiya Jana Sangh

(1951–1980)—a political organization established by the Hindu Nationalist political leader Shyama Prasad (S.P.) Mookerjee, who was closely connected to the RSS and the Hindu Mahasabha. The BJP describes itself as "The Party with a Difference" (Bharatiya Janata Party 2020b), underlining the party's commitment to its philosophical and ideological foundations in integral humanism[1] (Upadhyaya 2016; Bharatiya Janata Party 2020c) and Hindu nationalism/*Hindutva*[2] (Savarkar 2003; Sharma 2003; Bharatiya Janata Party 2019). Being the only non-communist political party in India with a strong and widespread network of cadres, the BJP's organization bears the influence of the structure of the RSS (Jha 2016; Andersen and Damle 2018; Bhattacharya 2020).

The BJP was one of the earliest among the political parties of India to pass a resolution in 1987 demanding 33 percent reservation of seats for women in the Parliament and state legislatures (Vajpayee 2000). The party constitution mandates 33 percent reservation of seats for women and up to 10 percent reservation for Scheduled Castes and Scheduled Tribes in every unit along the party hierarchy, including the state, district, and local units (Bharatiya Janata Party 2017). At the level of practice, however, the provision of constitutional regulations affirming the party's formal commitment to gender quotas have not always translated into adequate descriptive representation for women. In the current National Executive, only six out of 82 members are women—constituting a measly 7.31 percent. Out of a total of 72 National office-bearers, 14 are women (19.44 percent) (Bharatiya Janata Party 2020a). The only post in the party which approximates gender parity is that of the National Vice President, where five out of 12 vice presidents are women (41.66 percent).

In West Bengal, the BJP has emerged as the primary opposition to the ruling All India Trinamool Congress (AITC) government in the state after the 2021 state Assembly election. In recent years, newcomers and turncoat leaders have been elevated to prominent positions in the party's mainstream organization and its women's wing. This organizational practice of allocating elevated party positions to newcomers and rival party turncoats, coupled with an increasing personalized concentration of authority in the central leadership of the party, constitute a crucial electoral strategy devised by the party elite to expand the BJP's organizational network in states such as West Bengal. This practice, however, has generated open disaffections among the old-timer members and leaders in the West Bengal unit of the BJP (Bhattacharya 2020; Daniyal 2020; Kundu 2020; Ramaseshan 2020;

Sarkar 2020; Singh 2020) and has been blamed for the party's electoral defeat in the 2021 West Bengal Assembly elections (Datta 2021). Such discontent among party old-timers at the rapid elevation of newcomers was expressed by some women members of the BJP during their interviews with me. Perceiving a dilution of the party's ideological core, the interviewees also expressed concern with what they perceived was a policy that denied old-timers their due dignity.

Illustrating the operation of the "social logics"—disciplinary gendered codes of being and behavior that constitute the institutional culture of the party—several interviewees from the BJP underlined the determinative and abiding influence of their respective families in the inception and development of their political careers. Whether their close relatives were active political workers, or their families were politicized along ideological lines, many interviewees identified their families as the primary spaces of their political socialization. Demonstrating inter-institutional linkages and transfer of social values, the interviewees also often characterized their party as an extended family—the party culture being imbued with the values associated with the dominant patriarchal and heteronormative construction of South Asian familial culture.

Family ties with politics often extended beyond the arena of electoral party politics and involved deeper connections with particular social and cultural associations affiliated with the political parties. While such cultural networks often serve as springboards for the recruitment of women and men into electoral politics, they also comprise affective investments that in turn contribute toward developing a strong sense of institutional belonging among the members of the BJP vis-à-vis their party culture. Emotional identifications with the cultural associations such as the RSS—and driven by family ties—therefore often strengthen belonging with the affiliated political party. Such attachments are also conditioned by the particular social and cultural positionalities and ethical values of members (Yuval-Davis, Kannabiran, and Vieten 2006; Yuval-Davis 2007, 2011). Several women members of the BJP highlighted their long-term familial connections with the RSS to explain the depth of their involvement and integration in the party as well as the larger Sangh Parivar universe, illustrating the prestige that associations with the RSS have historically been accorded in the BJP's institutional culture.

An instance of such affective investments can be located in the narrative of Debasmita Banerjee[3], a BJP Member of Parliament (MP), who identified her family connections with the RSS as being formative to her political socialization. Banerjee highlighted her Brahmin (upper-caste) Hindu social location while speaking of her relationship with the party's ideology. Distinguishing the BJP's ideological grounding in Hindutva from the ideologies of the communist parties in India and that of the Indian National Congress, Banerjee subscribed to the official self-description of her party as "a party with a difference." In this view, her religiosity and caste identity were not seen as obstacles to her political participation but were central to the construction of her institutional belonging and conformity to the ideological framework of the BJP:

> Ignoring my *Puja* [Hindu ritual worship], assaulting my religious sentiments, this I couldn't take. I am a daughter of a typical Hindu family, a Hindu Brahmin family. *Hindutva* is in my flesh, blood, and genes! Most importantly, my uncle and father had to come here as refugees from East Bengal [now Bangladesh] only because they were Hindus. This suffering, this overnight transformation into a homeless refugee from being landlords, all of this has happened under Congress and communists. Congress and communists together broke apart this country, which is why their hateful politics has never attracted me.

In the process of articulating her Brahmin Hindu social location, Banerjee attempts to establish it as the archetypal, "typical" Hindu identity, thus contributing to an invisibilization of lower-caste social locations. Banerjee's invocation of her upper-caste identity illustrates her privileged subjectivity as well as the hegemonic "social logic" that frames the conditions behind such privileging of upper-caste identity in the party organization. At the same time, by referring to her organic ties with Hindutva, she equates the political doctrine of Hindutva with the practice of Hinduism. While her familial legacy of the historical trauma of mass displacement stemming from the Partition was by no means unique, Banerjee's experiential narrative can be distinguished by its peculiar interpretation of the history of Partition and the resultant refugee crisis. Taking care to highlight her feudal upper-caste, upper-class inheritance, Banerjee lays the onus of Partition squarely on the Communist Party of (then-undivided) India and the Indian National Congress, erasing the influential roles of the Hindu right-wing association Hindu Mahasabha (the ideological predecessor of the BJP) and upper-caste Bengali Hindus in the historical circumstances that led to the Partition

(Sarkar 1989; Chatterji 1994; Datta 1999; Bose and Jalal 2004; Chandra, Heierstad, and Bo Nielsen 2015; Sen 2018; Mukherjee 2019). Banerjee's positive evaluation of and emotional attachment to her upper-caste Hindu identity situates her belonging within the institutional culture of the BJP in relation to her privileged positioning along the extra-institutional hierarchy of social locations (Yuval-Davis, Kannabiran, and Vieten 2006; Yuval-Davis 2011).

The social locations of individual actors thus condition their institutional belonging and contribute to the naturalization of the gendered institutional party culture. At the core of such processes of naturalization is the construction of certain discursive binaries which constitute the "boundaries of belonging" (Yuval-Davis, Kannabiran, and Vieten 2006; Yuval-Davis 2011). Involving the privileging of an idealized gendered subjectivity against others, this creation of boundaries privileges an idealized gendered subjectivity against others through elements of repetitive performance (Butler 1993, 1997; Yuval-Davis 2011). Within the context of the BJP's party culture in West Bengal, women's articulation of their experiences of belonging and their self-makings demonstrates this politics of boundary-creation—with women creating and expanding spaces for themselves in male-dominated party cultures, while also distinguishing themselves from other women who did not meet the institutional and social standards of "appropriateness."

For example, Debasmita Banerjee's interview illustrated the significance of these discursive strategies of "defeminization" in the articulation of her institutional belonging and her self-making. Stating that during her long association with the BJP, she had never faced isolation or exclusion from the party on the basis of her gender, Banerjee attempted to distinguish her personal experience as a possible exception stemming from her growing up in a joint family with several brothers and cousins. Her positive perception of the party's institutional culture can be understood in the context of her swift ascension along the party and ministerial ranks. She credited the elevation of her career entirely to the benevolence of her "respected mentors" ("*gurujon*") in the party. During the interview, while describing a particular incident involving the state president and other office-bearers of the BJP, Banerjee sought to highlight her close, exclusive association with the predominantly male party leadership:

> Our state president was making fun of me about something, and I was saying, "How can you say this to your sister?" He said, "Huh, since when

> are you our sister?" I was flustered and started thinking—"What just happened? Why is he saying this?" Everyone was looking. He said, "You are our brother!"

On the one hand, this incident—chosen by her to portray her place of privilege in the party—also served to center her defeminized integration within the homosocial and male-dominated party environment. On the other hand, it also served to reinforce her distance from her more "feminine" women colleagues, a sentiment also echoed in her opening statement in the interview: "Since childhood, I was a little desperate,[4] not like other girls."

A similar perspective was offered by Manisha Ghosh[5]—a state-level leader of the BJP. Ghosh's narrative further illustrates the operation of the conforming and disciplinary "social logics" in the party culture. Ghosh additionally expressed open dismay at the present state of affairs within the party, where newcomers and defectors from the AITC and other parties were being given prestigious party offices at the expense of "committed old-timers" such as herself.

Having expressed her disaffection with her party's recent situation, however, Ghosh took care to underline her persistent loyalty to the party ("Over the years, I have proved my loyalty to the party, and they have realized that whatever you do to her, she will not leave"), as well as her special privileged access to the top leadership. Despite her recent exclusion from rewarding party positions and the allocation of responsibilities such as fund-collection to her ("It is a bad work I have to do, fund-collection is horrible"), Ghosh chose to focus on her continued close association and "personal rapport" with the party elite. Ghosh's institutional belonging was, therefore, tied to her personal equations with the party leadership which, in her opinion, aided her in tiding over the experience of institutional marginalization.

Emphasizing her close personal access to the top layer of the party leadership, Ghosh—in a similar vein as her party colleague Debasmita Banerjee—demarcated her distinction from her fellow women colleagues, and in doing so, indicated her subscription to a model of political subjectivity that is privileged in the institutional culture of her party. While expressing dissatisfaction with the present state of the BJP, Ghosh consistently invoked her self-effacing display of loyalty to the ideological core of the party and asserted that she was not someone who would take her discontent outside the party.

Underlining her distance from her fellow party members who choose to negotiate differently with their experiences of exclusion and discrimination from the party, Ghosh also casts aspersions on the characters of some of her women colleagues who have been promoted to higher party positions while distinguishing herself from the "compromising type":

> I want to make it very clear that there are some women who have utilized their charms, so to say, to get wherever they are, I'm not going to take names there, but in my case, it has never happened, mainly because I'm not the compromising type and I have always been treated with a lot of love and respect in the party.

Ghosh and Banerjee's sense of belonging and the connected practice of self-making are predicated upon the repetitive performance of distinguishing themselves from an identified Other, a gendered subjectivity that is not privileged under the institutional "requisites of belonging" (Yuval-Davis 2011, 20) in their party and the wider social context. Their responses to discrimination under the male-dominated homosocial institutional cultures of the party involve developing defeminized and desexualized subjectivities marked by their self-effacing loyalty to the party leadership. Viewed under the analytical lens of political logics (Glynos and Howarth 2007)—which, in this case, constitutes mutually opposed models of gendered subjectivity—the sense of belonging that the aforementioned interviewees articulated illustrates their conformity to the institutional construction of discursive antagonisms and binary models of gendered subjectivity that undergird the dominant institutional cultures of the BJP.

Despite their relatively privileged institutional belonging, Banerjee and Ghosh also have to contend with navigating their experiences of institutional marginalization—a practice wherein their emotional attachments to the dominant institutional culture of their party are tested. Under the lens of the logics approach, the emotional appeal of dominant gender constructions to actors in institutional spaces is illustrated through fantasmatic logics (Glynos and Howarth 2007). The political self-makings that Banerjee and Ghosh perform also subscribe to the fantasmatic logic that it was possible for women party members to overcome gender-based discrimination and have successful political careers if they affirmed their distinction from other women, while at the same time defeminizing themselves. By shielding the party leadership and the dominant institutional cultures of the party from the pull of institutional change, the logic of defeminization places the obligation of addressing women's underrepresentation in the party on the women party members themselves. The prevalence of such a logic contributes to the stability and institutional continuity of the party by absorbing and concealing the disaffections arising from the structural gender discrimination and lack of intra-party democracy in the BJP in West Bengal. At the same time, practices of defeminization in the self-makings of women party members accord a degree of agency to their practitioners.

While defeminization assists Banerjee and Ghosh to create and expand spaces for themselves in their respective male-dominated party cultures, it also allows them to negatively distinguish and isolate themselves from other women colleagues in the party—as well as from women more broadly who are perceived as lacking in political capital, moral scruples, and loyalty, thus failing to meet the institutional and social standards of appropriateness. Practices such as defeminization can also underline the resilience of dominant gender constructions as well as indicate how women actors can continue to persist in institutional spaces despite their experiences of institutional marginalization.

Conclusion

This chapter presented an FI interpretive study of the institutional belonging and political self-makings of women interviewees from the BJP. The analysis traced the play of discursive institutional logics and processes of gendered exclusion that go on to constitute systemic coherence and continuity in the "secret garden" (Gallagher and Marsh 1988; Bjarnegård and Kenny 2015) of the BJP in West Bengal. Employing the concept of institutional belonging, the chapter elaborated on the ways through which the respective social locations, ideological affiliations, and personal loyalties to the party leadership shaped women's articulations of their belonging in or exclusion from the institutional spaces of the party. In doing so, women party members engaged with practices of political self-making to frame their political subjectivities. Such practices included constructing their political selves by othering women who were imagined as representing dissident subjectivities.

The chapter argues that institutional continuity—marked by women's underrepresentation and marginalization in political party cultures such as the BJP—is sustained through the reproduction of antagonistic models of political femininity. An ideal model of a self-effacing, deferential, and often defeminized woman party worker undergirds the gendered institutional culture of the BJP. The concepts of institutional belonging and self-making therefore can assist FI and party scholars in understanding the enduring emotional attachments that marginalized actors can forge with hegemonic institutional cultures, illustrating why women political party members continue to persist in their vocation in the face of institutional exclusion.

News Sources and Empirical Material

Bharatiya Janata Party. 2017. "Party Constitution, Bharatiya Janata Party." Accessed December 11, 2020. https://www.bjp.org/en/constitution

Bharatiya Janata Party. 2019. "About the Party, Bharatiya Janata Party West Bengal." Accessed December 8, 2020. https://bjpbengal.org/about

Bharatiya Janata Party. 2020a. "Bharatiya Janata Party Homepage." Accessed December 17, 2020. https://www.bjp.org

Bharatiya Janata Party. 2020b. "BJP Bengal, Bharatiya Janata Party." Accessed December 8, 2020. https://bjpbengal.org

Bharatiya Janata Party. 2020c. "Integral Humanism, Bharatiya Janata Party." Accessed November 27, 2020. https://www.bjp.org/en/integralhumanism

https://www.bjp.org/en/ourphilosophy

Daniyal, S. 2020. "The BJP Is Making Sure Its West Bengal 2021 Campaign Is Controlled from Delhi." *Scroll*. Accessed October 15, 2020. https://scroll.in/article/975669/the-bjp-is-making-sure-its-west-bengal-2021-campaign-is-controlled-from-delhi

Datta, R. 2021. "Witch-Hunt Within the BJP." *India Today*. Accessed June 26, 2021. https://www.indiatoday.in/india-today-insight/story/witch-hunt-within-the-bjp-1817963-2021-06-22

Jha, D.K. 2016. "BJP Takes the First Step to Adopt the Organisational Structure of the RSS." *Scroll*. Accessed December 11, 2020. https://scroll.in/article/815309/bjp-takes-the-first-step-to-adopt-the-organisational-structure-of-the-rss

Kundu, I. 2020. "Mukul Roy's Elevation Irks BJP's West Bengal Unit, Party Leader Rahul Sinha Revolts." *India Today*. Accessed December 16, 2020. https://www.indiatoday.in/india/story/mukul-roy-s-elevation-irks-bjp-s-west-bengal-unit-rahul-sinha-says-nothing-more-painful-than-this-1725775-2020

Mukherjee, I. 2019. "Battle for the Bhadralok: The Historical Roots of Hindu Majoritarianism in West Bengal." *The Caravan*. Accessed December 15, 2019. https://caravanmagazine.in/politics/historical-roots-of-hindu-majoritarianism-in-west-bengal

Ramaseshan, R. 2020. "BJP's Bengal Game Plan." *The Tribune*. Accessed December 8, 2020. https://www.tribuneindia.com/news/comment/bjps-bengal-game-plan-175364

Sarkar, S. 2020. "Dropped in Reshuffle, Bengal BJP Leader Rahul Sinha Says Defectors from TMC Favoured." *Hindustan Times*. Accessed October 15, 2020. https://www.hindustantimes.com/india-news/dropped-from-top-party-post-in-favour-of-tmc-defectors-bjp-bengal-leader-rahul-sinha-on-rejig/story-mHFyt0AAdDVcQhBHOGHZPN.html

Sen, D. 2017. "How the Dalits of Bengal Became the 'Worst Victims' of Partition." *The Wire*. Accessed September 30, 2020. https://thewire.in/165508/partition-dalits-bengal

Singh, S.S. 2020. "Former TMC Leaders Get Top Slots in Bengal BJP." *The Hindu*. Accessed December 8, 2020. https://www.thehindu.com/news/national/other-states/former-tmc-leaders-get-top-slots-in-bengal-bjp/article31750083.ece

Notes

1. Propagated by the RSS leader and ideologue Deen Dayal Upadhyay, Integral Humanism endorses an organic conception of society, state, and the individual while privileging the society over and above the state (Bharatiya Janata Party 2020a, 2020b; Jaffrelot 1993, 2007; Upadhyaya 2016). Contrasting an essentialized conception of "Bharatiya (Indian) culture" with Western philosophical concepts such as "dialectical materialism," integral humanism posits the theory that non-dualism and cooperation with nature and each other are the foundations of human existence. Under such a worldview, conflict and contestations of any kind, including anti-caste movements, are viewed as a "sign of cultural regression" (Upadhyaya 2016, 14).
2. Advocated by the Hindu Mahasabha ideologue Vinayak Damodar Savarkar, Hindutva promotes the vision of India as an essentially Hindu Nation (a "Hindu Rashtra") and maintaines that the Hindus are to be identified not only by their common religious practice but also by their territorial and racial origins (Bhatt 2001; Savarkar 2003).
3. Interviewed on November 10, 2018.
4. The English term "desperate" in the Bengali common parlance carries the distinctive connotation of being untamed and adventurous. It is often used as a pejorative adjective for women who lead socially and culturally transgressive lives.
5. Interviewed on November 24, 2018.

11

Quantifying Gender and Immigrant Bias in Swedish Candidate Selection

Michal Grahn

Supplying candidates for elected office is one of the core functions of political parties (Gallagher and Marsh 1988; Katz and Mair 1995; Norris and Lovenduski 1995; Rahat 2007). The way political parties exercise this function has consequences for important political outcomes, including descriptive representation (Norris and Lovenduski 1995; Rahat 2007; Bjarnegård and Kenny 2016; Sundström and Stockemer 2021a). (Feminist) institutionalist research has proved to be crucial in shedding light on institutional barriers that perpetuate enduring inequalities between women and men in accessing elected office (Zetterberg 2008; Murray 2010; Bjarnegård 2013; Kenny 2013; Smrek 2020). Due to the elusive and partly context-specific nature of these barriers, the bulk of this research has taken the form of in-depth, mostly qualitative cases studies (Zetterberg 2008; Murray 2010; Kenny 2013; van Dijk 2023). In the past decade, large-N approaches to studying gendered outcomes of candidate selection have gained momentum (Folke, Freidenvall, and Rickne 2015; Folke and Rickne 2016; Smrek 2020; Stauffer and O'Brien 2018; Bjarnegård and Zetterberg 2019). By analyzing a broad spectrum of data, these methods can be especially adept at uncovering the extent of persistent inequalities in accessing elected office (Folke, Freidenvall, and Rickne 2015; Folke and Rickne 2016; Smrek 2020). Importantly, large-N approaches have also proven adept at identifying the institutional origins of these inequalities. For instance, there are studies that examine how politically valuable resources are allocated within the political arena (Folke and Rickne 2016; Verge and Claveria 2018; Smrek 2022; Grahn 2023), or those that zoom in on the formal rules that are particularly detrimental to women's political inclusion (Bjarnegård and Zetterberg 2019). Recently, experimental research has shed light on the prevailing archetypes

Michal Grahn, *Quantifying Gender and Immigrant Bias in Swedish Candidate Selection*. In: *Gendering Party Politics*. Edited by: Meryl Kenny and Elin Bjarnegård, Oxford University Press. © Oxford University Press (2025). DOI: 10.1093/oso/9780197793985.003.0011 of an ideal politician, which influence the preferences of those involved in candidate selection (Bauer 2018; Devroe and Wauters 2018; Doherty, Dowling, and Miller 2019; Rehmert 2022; Schwarz and Coppock 2022; Grahn and Håkansson 2025).

This chapter highlights the usefulness of large-N methods in evaluating the impact of rules aimed at mitigating enduring disparities in access to elected positions (Bhavnani 2009; De Paola, Scoppa, and Lombardo 2010). Political parties globally strive to rectify inequalities in elected office access for both normative and strategic reasons (Hughes 2011; Krook and Zetterberg 2017; Hughes et al. 2019). Typically manifested as candidate quotas, these rules compel individuals involved in candidate selection to recruit a specified number of candidates from targeted groups. In some cases, political parties put in place multiple candidate quotas, each targeting a different politically underrepresented group (Celis et al. 2014; Bird 2016; Freidenvall 2016; Hughes et al. 2019; Joshi and Och 2021). It is unclear which groups benefit and which groups lose out when political parties attempt to tackle several dimensions of political inequality simultaneously. There is a possibility that the politically privileged class may subvert the intended purpose of the new quotas to preserve their own political advantages (Celis et al. 2014; Janssen, Erzeel, and Celis 2020). Alternatively, the quotas may be genuinely implemented in ways that benefit multiple groups traditionally excluded from political office.

This chapter demonstrates the suitability of large-N approaches for examining the impact of multiple candidate quotas from an intersectional perspective (Joshi and Och 2021; Belschner 2023). It focuses on Sweden, where relatively strict quotas for women coexist with more flexible quotas for candidates with an immigrant background (Folke, Freidenvall, and Rickne 2015; Freidenvall 2016). By identifying the beneficiaries of these two quotas *and* those disadvantaged by them, the chapter also aids in understanding how different forms of discrimination, such as sexism and immigrant biases, intersect in the Swedish candidate selection process.

Candidate Recruitment Through an Intersectional Lens

Past research has examined the impediments to accessing elected office faced by women and other social groups, shedding light on both the supply-

and demand-related explanations (Norris and Lovenduski 1995; Norris 1997; Bjarnegård and Kenny 2016). Political parties typically seek candidates they believe will garner voter support and effectively advocate the party's agenda in the parliamentary sphere (Carey 2007; Rahat 2007; Siavelis and Morgenstern 2008). The perceptions of political party recruiters about who is best suited for these tasks shape who is recruited as candidates (Gallagher and Marsh 1988; Norris and Lovenduski 1995; Norris 1997). On the supply side, varying degrees of political ambition and the resources needed for a successful political career affect who is inclined to pursue candidacy (Davidson-Schmich, this volume; see also Fox and Lawless 2010; Anzia and Berry 2011; Pruysers and Blais 2017; Josefsson 2020; Piscopo and Kenny 2020). Feminist institutionalist scholars argue that the underrepresentation of women in politics is due to both the demand for and the supply of women candidates being shaped by gendered institutions (Krook 2010; Bjarnegård 2013; Kenny 2013; Kenny and Verge 2016). On the demand side, the widely shared template of an ideal candidate tends to highlight qualifications and character traits more commonly associated with men (Murray 2010; Bjarnegård 2013, 2018a; Kenny 2013; Bauer 2018; Grahn and Thisell 2024). On the supply side, there are empirically substantiated reasons to believe that women aspirants are conscious of the discrimination they might face in the political arena, which serves as a significant deterrent to their political involvement (Fox and Lawless 2004, 2010; Anzia and Berry 2011; Fulton 2012).

Institutionalist explanations for the political underrepresentation of women focus on institutions: prescribed roles and behaviors, which, though often formally codified or socially enforced, present challenges for study (Chappell 2006; Mackay, Kenny, and Chappell 2010; Kenny 2014). Consequently, a typical institutionalist inquiry frequently merges the analysis of human accounts of rules and norms with the analysis of human practices (Bjarnegård 2013; Kenny 2013; Gains and Lowndes 2014; Grahn 2023). A growing body of literature suggests that large-N methods are well-suited for both objectives: identifying gendered practices and tracing their institutional origins (Stauffer and O'Brien 2018; Smrek 2020). Experimental studies, for example, have proven effective in defining the nature of gender bias that women political aspirants encounter in party-led candidate recruitment (Bauer 2018; Rehmert 2022; Schwarz and Coppock 2022; Grahn and Thisell 2024; Håkansson and Grahn 2025). Additionally, large-N studies have been instrumental in highlighting gender bias within parliamentary settings by demonstrating that positions and tasks of political merit are disproportionately assigned to men Members of Parliament (MPs) (O'Brien 2015; Verge and Claveria 2018; Smrek 2022; Grahn 2023). In a different approach, cross-national studies of codified rule prescriptions have been utilized to identify specific formal rules that are especially harmful to women's political inclusion (Bjarnegård and Zetterberg 2019). In most cases, it remains necessary to consult local discursive material for a complete institutionalist analysis (Grahn 2024), but advances in large-N techniques hold the promise of making the process of studying institutions more efficient.

One avenue where the merits of large-N approaches to studying institutions comes to the fore most strikingly is the study of candidate quota implementation (Beaman et al. 2009; Bhavnani 2009; De Paola, Scoppa, and Lombardo 2010; Krook 2010; Hughes 2011; Folke, Freidenvall, and Rickne 2015; Belschner and Garcia de Paredes 2021; Grahn and Håkansson 2025). Candidate quotas are often put in place in recognition of structural inequalities at the heart of the candidate recruitment process. By mandating the selection of candidates with a targeted trait or characteristic, candidate quotas have a potential to transform the template of an ideal politician within the political realm (Beaman et al. 2009). Large-N approaches are helpful in verifying whether the quotas function as intended and thus evaluating whether the introduction of a new rule has a tangible effect on the institutions that govern candidate selection processes. De Paola et al. (2010), for instance, examine whether party selectors keep recruiting women candidates after a gender quota has been withdrawn and find this to be the case. This finding provides a relatively straightforward indication that the quota has succeeded in transforming and widening the template of an ideal politician. This chapter focuses on political parties that, in their effort to make their candidate body more representative, choose to address more than one source of inequality by implementing multiple candidate quotas (Celis et al. 2014; Folke, Freidenvall, and Rickne 2015; Bird 2016; Joshi and Och 2021).

Insights from an intersectional perspective enhance the theorizing process regarding the potential effects of enacting multiple candidate quotas. This perspective, originating from the pioneering work of Black feminist scholars (Crenshaw 1989, 1991), encourages scholars to examine the interplay of overlapping, structurally marginalized identities when analyzing group-based inequalities (Weldon 2006; Freidenvall 2016; Reingold, Haynie, and Widner 2021). For instance, Black women confront both gender- and race-based discrimination, leading to additional structural barriers compared to their white counterparts. Additionally, young Black women face youth bias on top of sexism and racism. Utilizing these insights in the context of multiple quotas, two plausible effects of such policies emerge.

First, there is a possibility that the politically privileged class of native-born men will resist the prescriptions introduced by new quotas, as these prescriptions challenge them to relinquish seats traditionally held by individuals who, in their eyes, epitomize the dominant ideal of a politician (Celis et al. 2014; see also Josefsson, this volume). To preserve as many of these "ideal politicians" as possible, party selectors might prefer candidates who embody both quota-targeted characteristics (e.g., immigrant women) over those with just one (e.g., immigrant men or native women). This approach enables party selectors to meet quota requirements without significantly reducing their preferred candidate pool (Celis and Erzeel 2017; Janssen 2021). This strategy, often described in literature as the "complementarity advantage," suggests that by recruiting immigrant women, party selectors can adhere to quota mandates while minimizing the impact on their favored candidate demographics (Celis and Erzeel 2017; Janssen, Erzeel, and Celis 2020). Despite its name, this is not an actual advantage that propels individuals facing gender and immigrant biases into power positions. Instead, it is a tactic enabling native-born men to maintain their numerical dominance in politics, thereby preserving the institutional structures that perpetuate their privileges (O'Brien 2015; Verge and Claveria 2018; Verge and Astudillo 2019; Smrek 2022; Grahn 2023).

The alternative scenario suggests that political actors genuinely commit to the principles underpinning quota policies. In this case, party selectors actively recruit a diverse range of candidates with different combinations of quota-targeted attributes, without attempting to minimize their numbers. Here, all groups targeted by quotas would see improved access to political candidacy and elected office, while native-born men might experience more limited opportunities compared to the pre-quota status quo. This scenario is based on the belief that candidate recruiters acknowledge the purpose behind the quotas: to correct past practices that have led to structural imbalances in political representation. Such acknowledgment would initiate a shift toward expanding the definition of an ideal politician.

Three groups of candidates stand as potential beneficiaries of quota targeting candidates' gender and immigrant status: native-born women, immigrant men, and immigrant women. By comparing the electoral fortunes of candidates belonging to these groups to those of native men candidates over time, this chapter illustrates the capacity of large-N methods to adjudicate between two competing institutional explanations of the outcome of multiple quota enactment. By demonstrating whether and how gender and immigrant biases converge and interact, the chapter also demonstrates the effectiveness of large-N approaches for uncovering heterogeneities in privilege and discrimination that hide within large social groups, like women or immigrants.

Sweden: Multiple Candidate Quotas in a Proportional Representation Setting

Sweden serves as an excellent case study to illustrate the potential of large-N methodologies for examining whether candidate quotas for women and people with an immigrant background have a potential to change the "face" of candidate selection.

Swedish Electoral System

Sweden employs a proportional representation (PR) system across its three administrative tiers. Voters cast their ballots for political parties and seats are allocated to parties in proportion to their vote share. To ensure proportional seat allocation, all electoral districts in Sweden are multimember districts. Consequently, political parties present voters with candidate ballots consisting of multiple candidates. The multicandidate nature of the ballots grants political parties the flexibility to select a diverse pool of candidates, each with the potential to appeal to different segments of the electorate (Folke, Persson, and Rickne 2016; Widenstjerna 2020). Moreover, a relatively high rate of voluntary retirements creates openings for new candidates. However, with eight relevant political parties competing for the seats, most parties can only expect to secure one or two seats in most districts. Thus, if the first seat is occupied by an entrenched incumbent with no intention of leaving office, competition for the remaining safe ballot spots can become fierce (Freidenvall 2016). Under conditions like these, the mechanism of complementarity advantage can be triggered, especially within political parties that prioritize diversity not only among their candidates but also among their elected officials.

The responsibility for candidate selection is delegated to local and regional selection committees, consisting of party veterans and representatives from various internal interest organizations (Widenstjerna 2020). The committees are tasked with selecting candidates and preparing draft ballots. In certain districts, quasi-primaries are conducted, enabling party members to indicate their preferences for the candidates proposed by the selection committee (Folke, Persson, and Rickne 2016). However, it is important to note that the results of these primaries—if they are held at all—do not carry any binding authority over the committee. As a matter of consequence, considerable power resides in the hands of committee members, whose views on an ideal candidate and their understanding of the requirements imposed by different candidate quotas can profoundly influence candidate selection and placement on electable ballot positions.

Candidate Quotas in Sweden

Starting in the 1980s, Swedish political parties experienced mounting internal pressure from various factions to take seriously the lack of diversity within their candidate pools (Freidenvall 2021). Following a drop in women's descriptive representation in the early 1990s, the women's wings of the two major political parties—Social Democrats and Moderates—threatened to create separate women's parties if their demands for greater representation on party ballots was not met (Burness 2000). This campaign represented the dawn of the zipper quota—a placement mandate quota that reserves every other spot on the ballots for women. The first major party to enact the zipper quota was the Social Democrats in 1993, and the quota was embraced by the rest of the party spectrum by the end of the decade (Freidenvall 2021; Freidenvall and Krook 2011). Following the successful enactment of gender quotas, other interest organizations also campaigned for greater inclusion, leading to a gradual proliferation of recommendations to include youths and immigrants on the ballots, among other groups. These quotas vary in specificity as well as the degree of codification. This chapter focuses on immigrant quotas which, contrary to gender quotas, take the form of more vague recommendations for the inclusion of candidates with an immigrant background (Folke, Freidenvall, and Rickne 2015).[1]

Using Register Data to Study Inequalities in Access to Elected Office

Swedish administrative data are a collection of population-wide registries that is administered by Statistics Sweden (SCB). Pertaining to the study at hand, the data contain a registry of all the candidates for elected office starting in 1982 and onward. The registries also contain detailed information about each person's immigrant background and gender, among other crucial characteristics. These data are available for research, pending a lengthy ethical review process and payment of a substantial fee.

Measuring Gender and Immigrant Background

To measure gender identity, I rely on the records from the Swedish Tax Authority, which is responsible for maintaining an updated record of individuals' gender. Sweden officially recognizes two gender identities. In 1972, Sweden became the first country in the world to permit transgender individuals to change their assigned sex at birth in the national registry (Regeringskansliet 2018). As a result, the data used here accurately represent the gender identity of those who identify with their assigned sex at birth, as well as those who have changed their gender identity in the registry. However, it is important to note that this inquiry misgenders transgender persons who have not yet updated their public records or those who do not identify with the binary gender identities. While this limitation exists, its impact on this inquiry should not be overstated due to this group's relatively small size.

Measuring individuals' immigrant status is less straightforward, primarily due to the vagueness of the Swedish quotas for the inclusion of individuals with an immigrant background. These recommendations do not explicitly differentiate between those who were born abroad and those whose parents have an immigrant background. Swedish administrative data can help to accurately ascertain whether a person was born abroad or whether she has one or two foreign-born parents. This is a wealth of information that can be used to study disparities in access to elected office based on immigrant status. Given the ambiguity concerning the quota's scope of applicability, deciding who should be counted as part of the quota's target group is not self-evident. Different rules of exclusion (e.g., people with a non-European background, people with an accent, people with a foreign-sounding surname, etc.) return different potential beneficiary populations. However, this does not necessarily pose a limitation, as large-N methodologies offer the benefit of rapidly employing multiple operationalizations of the concepts under study. These alternative operationalizations can be presented in an online appendix. This chapter treats those who were either born abroad or have two parents who were born abroad as individuals with an immigrant background.

Measuring Group-Based Access to Elected Office

The quality of the Swedish administrative data makes it possible to analyze how likely it is for an average woman/individual with an immigrant background to get elected compared to an average man/individual with a native background. The chapter defines the 1998 election as a turning point: by 1998, most political parties enacted quotas for women and immigrants (Freidenvall 2021; Folke, Freidenvall, and Rickne 2015). Harnessing the power of a full panel of candidates running for municipal office between 1982 and 2022 (12 elections in total), I estimate election- and group-specific likelihoods of getting elected for candidates belonging to three groups that stand to be affected by the two quotas of interest: (1) native-born women; (2) immigrant men; and (3) immigrant women. Each of these three groups is compared to the reference category of native-born men.

In the main analysis, I rely on linear regression. The primary dependent variable is a binary indicator of whether a candidate is elected (1) or not (0). I interact three dummy variables—identifying native-born women, immigrant men, and immigrant women candidates—with election-specific dummies, using the 1998 election as the reference category. This approach yields a descriptive analysis of group-specific probabilities (in percentage points) of being elected, relative to native-born men, for each election in the study. All models include fixed effects for municipality, party, and election (as an interaction) to ensure comparisons are made among candidates assessed by the same selection committee at the same time. Robust standard errors are clustered at the candidate group level.

The analyses focus on the municipal level because it is considered to be a stepping stone into a political career (Folke, Persson, and Rickne 2016). Being a municipal legislator is not a full-time employment, which means that the level of turnover between elections is relatively high at this level. This means that party recruiters often need to find new candidates to replace retiring incumbents, giving party selectors a better opportunity to comply with quota demands. Municipal councilors also tend to receive less media attention, which allows political parties to try out new practices without risking their overall competitiveness. If candidate quotas are to make an early breakthrough, it will be at the municipal level.

The Winners and Losers of Gender and Immigrant Quotas

Before assessing who benefits or is disadvantaged by the introduction of gender and immigrant quotas, I begin by illustrating over-time changes in the demographic makeup of the Swedish population, municipal candidates, and local elected councilors. Figure 11.1 presents data on the population at large, Figure 11.2 on candidates for municipal office, and Figure 11.3 on elected councilors.

Figure 11.2 shows a consistent decrease in the proportion of native men among municipal candidates, dropping from over 60 percent in 1982 to approximately 50 percent in 2022. This declining trend is also observed among elected municipal councilors (see Figure 11.3). Nonetheless, when comparing the representation of native-born men within the candidate pool and among incumbents to their proportion in the general population (Figure 11.1), it is evident that native men have remained numerically overrepresented throughout the study period. The representation of native women in both candidate and incumbent roles saw a marked increase in the 1990s, likely influenced by the implementation of gender quotas, and has stabilized at around 40 percent. This boost has aligned native women's political representation with their overall demographic share. Concurrently, both immigrant men and women have experienced a modest rise in their representation among candidates and incumbents, with immigrant men having a slight advantage. Despite these improvements, both groups have been consistently underrepresented during the study period. The reduction in the numerical representation of native men and the improvement seen by the other groups lend support to the notion that quotas have initiated a gradual broadening of the template of an ideal politician. There is no evidence of a complementarity advantage, as the substantial part of the improvement observed among the three quota-targeted groups primarily benefits native women, rather than women with an immigrant background.

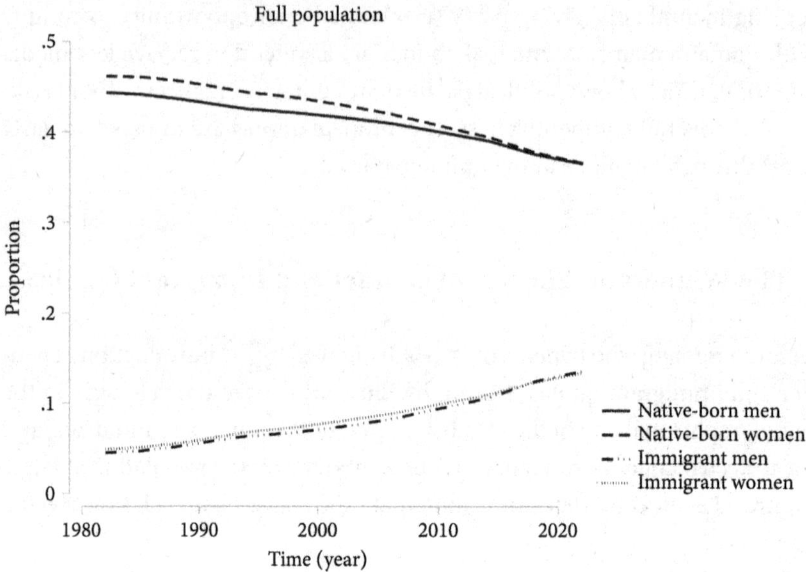

Figure 11.1 Composition of the Population of Sweden over Time

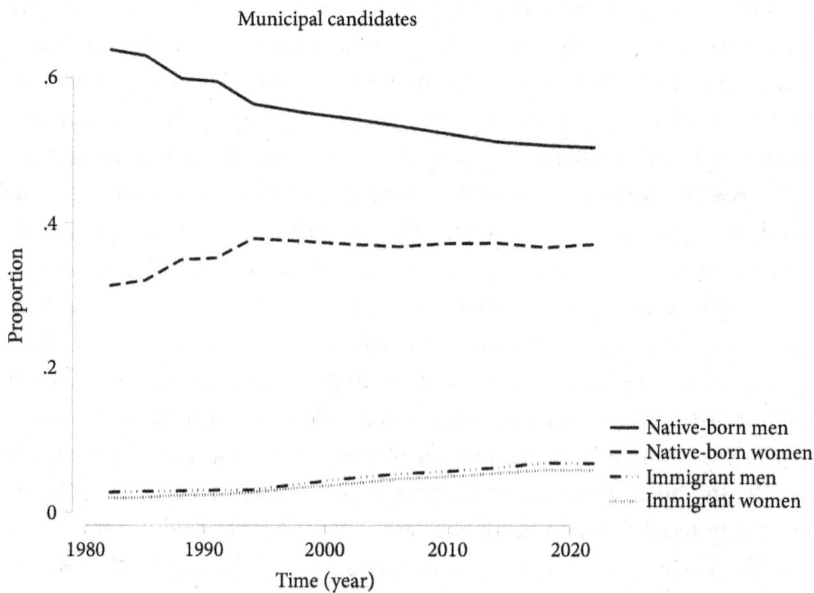

Figure 11.2 Composition of the Population of Swedish Municipal Candidates over Time

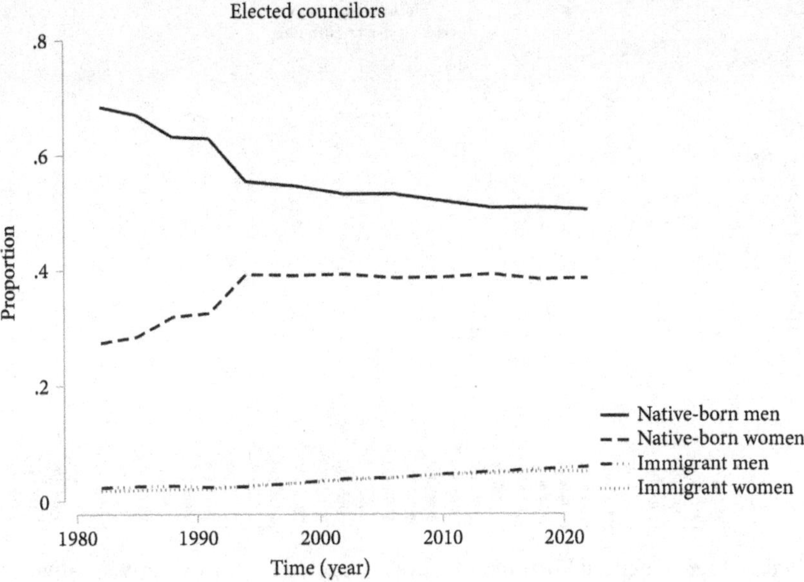

Figure 11.3 Composition of the Population of Swedish Municipal Councilors over Time

The main analysis involves estimating group-specific chances of being elected over time using the regression model, described above. Figure 11.4 captures the results. This model includes the entire body of municipal candidates running for office between 1982 and 2022, amounting to approximately 600,000 individual-election observations. For each group of candidates, I estimate election- and candidate group-specific chances of getting elected compared to the reference group of native men candidates. I leave out the 1998 election as a reference category. I expect that by 1998, both the quota for women candidates and the less stringent recommendations for the inclusion of candidates with immigrant backgrounds are in place in all major Swedish political parties. While my chosen method cannot isolate the precise effect of candidate quotas on the electoral prospects of different groups, it does allow for a robust analysis of how their electoral fortunes evolve over time.

The results suggest that some candidate groups benefit in a quota-rich environment, while others are disadvantaged. First, native women saw substantial improvements in their access to elected office in a quota-rich environment. Throughout the 1980s and in the 1991 election, the average native

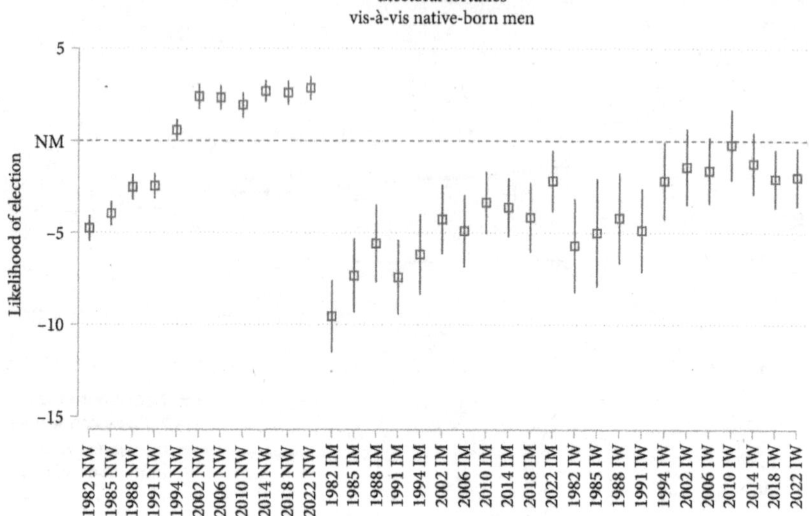

Figure 11.4 Electoral Fortunes of Quota-Targeted Groups Vis-à-vis Native Men over Time

Note: The figure captures group- and election-specific likelihoods of getting elected compared to native men, represented by the dashed line. The results are reported in percentage points. Ninety-five percent confidence intervals are reported around the point estimates. N = 594,241 observations. NW = native women. IM = immigrant men. IW = immigrant women. NM = native men.

woman candidate was less likely to get elected than her men counterparts. However, the fortunes of native women candidates began to shift following the enactment of the zipper quota by the Social Democrats in 1993, and again in the late 1990s as other major parties followed suit. Immigrant men and women candidates also see a modest improvement in the likelihood of getting elected in a quota-rich environment, but they remain less likely than native men candidates to be elected.

On the whole, the results do not lend support to the complementarity advantage thesis. Native men candidates have seen their electoral chances diminish compared to native women candidates, indicating a weakening demand for this group of candidates in a quota-rich environment. Immigrant men and women candidates have also seen their electoral fortunes improve following quota enactment, but their modest boost does not match that encountered by native women candidates. The results provide strong evidence that the implementation of quotas has contributed to a gradual expansion of the dominant template of the ideal politician—rather than merely reflecting a strategic use of the 'complementarity advantage' to preserve the dominant status of native men.

Conclusion

One of the most significant advantages of large-N approaches is their ability to uncover patterns of behavior that are conditioned by institutions (Stauffer and O'Brien 2018; Verge and Claveria 2018). With a substantial volume of empirical evidence at their disposal, large-N methods are adept at showing how deep-rooted various practices are and how susceptible they are to change. What is more, large-N approaches can be used to unpack hidden heterogeneities in privilege that hide within large social groups or examine intersectional effects of institutional interventions (Weldon 2006; Folke, Freidenvall, and Rickne 2015; Reingold, Haynie, and Widner 2021). Increasingly, large-N methods are being used to organize and analyze large amounts of textual data that include descriptions of institutions, and experimental studies are conducted to understand the norms guiding processes such as candidate recruitment. This chapter highlights the efficacy of large-N approaches in assessing the impact of rules designed to address persistent inequalities in access to elected positions. In most electoral systems, political parties play a critical role in guarding access to elected office by managing the candidate selection process. The chapter focuses on political parties that voluntarily adopt new rules for their candidate selection process. It asks whether such quotas have a potential to reduce gender and immigrant biases inherent in the recruitment process or whether they are met with resistance from those whose privileges are most threatened by these new rules.

The chapter hypothesized that if quotas are resisted by the politically privileged group of native men, then immigrant women would be the primary beneficiaries. By selecting candidates who meet both quota criteria, native men could maximize the remaining candidacies available to them. Conversely, if quotas are genuinely enforced, they are expected to benefit all quota-targeted groups at the expense of native men. The findings strongly support the latter scenario. All quota-targeted groups have seen an improvement in access to elected office, with native women benefiting the most. There is therefore clear empirical evidence that the ideal politician's template is amenable to change in contexts where key political actors appear to be committed to quota implementation. While the quotas did not break native men's political dominance, they help to tangibly weaken the demand for this group of candidates.

This chapter shows that large-N approaches can, when conditions are favorable, allow researchers to rapidly adjudicate between competing—yet equally plausible—institutional accounts of a particular phenomenon. In our case, our analyses helped to shed light on the consequences of multiple quota enactment. This analysis is merely an introduction to what quantitative methods can reveal about the impact of candidate quotas. A logical next step would be to apply a more direct causal design—such as a difference-in-differences approach or one of its dynamic extensions. Further analysis could also test whether the differences in electoral success between native and immigrant women candidates are due to income or education disparities (they are not). It could also investigate whether some aggregate findings shown in Figure 11.4 vary according to party ideology or municipality size (they do not significantly). The essence is that higher-quality data allow for a more detailed examination of the structural explanations behind observed practices.

This chapter highlights the potential of large-N methods for exploring both gendered practices and their institutional origins. Large-N approaches can be employed to assess whether some known political inequalities originate from structural resource disparities (Lindgren, Oskarsson, and Persson 2019), thereby offering a swift means to refute or corroborate plausible explanations for observed gendered practices. These approaches can also help to identify the intricacies of the shared templates of an ideal politician (Berz and Jankowski 2022; Everitt and Horvath 2021; Rehmert 2022), and to determine how resistant to change these templates are. The rapid development of artificial intelligence tools might soon allow for more automated sweeping of large volumes of text with the purpose of identifying accounts of rules and norms within this text. A growing body of literature shows that quantitative analysis is a vital part of feminist scholars' methodological toolkit, helping us to build ever more complete models of institutions that perpetuate inequalities within the political realm.

Note

1. Foreign-born immigrants constituted approximately 20 percent of Sweden's population in 2023. This chapter centers on individuals who are either immigrants themselves or have two foreign-born parents, making up about 30 percent of the population.

12
Green Parties and Gender Equality in the European Parliament

Petra Ahrens and Johanna Kantola

The European Parliament (EP) with its multi-national political groups, the EP version of a "parliamentary party," provides a unique setting for studying the relationship between gender, institutions, and political parties. EP political groups are conglomerates of national party delegations, each of them arriving with nationally imprinted gendered structures, practices, and rules. Political groups thus constantly (re)negotiate gendered supranational party politics and democratic practices, and their attention and positions on gender equality differ considerably (Kantola and Rolandsen Agustín 2016, 2019; Ahrens and Kantola 2022; Kantola 2022).

In this chapter, we engage with the political group most systematically committed to gender equality, the Greens/European Free Alliance (Greens/EFA) (Ahrens and Kantola 2022; Ahrens, Gaweda, and Kantola 2022; Elomäki and Ahrens 2022; Elomäki and Kantola 2022; Kantola 2022; Kantola, Elomäki, and Ahrens 2022). Extant research demonstrated that Green Parties in general have often been pioneers in promoting gender balance (Keith and Verge 2018; Bick 2019) and that woman-led parties (such as many Green Parties) are more apt in promoting progressive political agendas (Kröber 2021). Whether such strong parity commitments translate into similar well-developed gender equality practices in internal party organization has been less often researched (but see Jackson 2017).

Applying Gains and Lowndes's (2014) four-part framework of analyzing (1) rules about gender, (2) rules with gendered effects, (3) gendered actors working with rules, and (4) gendered outcomes, we discuss how gender shapes the structures, practices, and rules of Greens/EFA. Our chapter provides an intra-party and intra-political-group analysis through a feminist institutionalist (FI) lens to scrutinize if (and if so why) Green Parties are

Petra Ahrens and Johanna Kantola, *Green Parties and Gender Equality in the European Parliament*. In: *Gendering Party Politics*. Edited by: Meryl Kenny and Elin Bjarnegård, Oxford University Press. © Oxford University Press (2025). DOI: 10.1093/oso/9780197793985.003.0012 more gender-equal than others—in other words, whether their structures, practices, and rules can be characterized as feminist politics. We explore potential tensions originating from adopting rules about gender equality at the level of political group versus individual party. Engaging with party organization, intra-party democracy, as well as candidate and leader selection, we ask if Green Parties are indeed gender-equal, and what challenges and opportunities the interplay between the national and the supranational adds to these dynamics.

Analyzing electoral data, party statutes, and 18 semi-structured interviews with Greens/EFA Members of the European Parliament (MEPs) and political-group staff originating from the 8th (2014–2019) and 9th (2019–2024) EP legislatures, the chapter engages with the European Green Party (EGP) and its EP Greens/EFA.[1] Greens/EFA are home to 17 Green Party national delegations and thus allow tracing how different national regulations play out, how gender parity is discussed and regulated, and whether the usual gendered segregation of policy fields is tackled.

We first sketch the broader context of the EP as a space where the supranational and national needs to be renegotiated before explaining our FI theoretical approach, data, and methods. In our empirical analysis of Greens/EFA, we apply the four-fold framework by Gains and Lowndes (2014) to quota rules and the role of national party delegations, and then to intra-party gender equality provisions and the influence of national party delegations. We conclude by discussing effects for gender equality through supranational party politics.

Parties and Gender Equality in the Supranational EP

Supranational European party politics comprise two overlapping party organizations: Europarties and EP political groups. While the former are transnational European party organizations which often include non-European Union members, the latter are formed after each EP election in line with the EP Rules of Procedure stipulating a minimum of 23 MEPs, originating from at least seven member states and demonstrating political affinity (Ahrens and Rolandsen Agustín 2021). Gender plays out differently for political groups when formed after elections, when distributing leadership positions and in their policy-making (Ahrens and Kantola 2022; Kantola and Miller 2022; Elomäki et al. 2022; Elomäki et al. 2023).

In the 2019–2024 legislature, the political groups are, in order of size, the center-right conservative European People's Party (EPP), the center-left Progressive Alliance of Socialists and Democrats (S&D), the liberal Renew Europe (previously ALDE), the radical-right-populist Identity and Democracy (ID, previously ENF), the Greens/EFA, the radical-right European Conservatives and Reformists (ECR), and the Left of the EP (GUE/NGL). Extant research covers well gendered descriptive representation in the EP (Fortin-Rittberger and Rittberger 2014, 2015; Lühiste and Kenny 2016; Aldrich and Daniel 2020; Dingler and Fortin-Rittberger 2022; Sundström and Stockemer 2021b). Regarding gender equality policies and practices, political groups are often compared (Kantola and Rolandsen Agustín 2016, 2019; Kantola and Lombardo 2021b; Ahrens and Kantola 2022), yet we know little about how political groups attend to gender issues in their internal rules and practices (but see Kantola 2022).

Unquestionably, Greens/EFA were since their first formation in 1989 (the EGP was founded in 1983[2]) the leading political group regarding parity in representation, with women's and men's respective shares fluctuating around 45–55 percent (see Figure 12.1 for results starting with the first direct

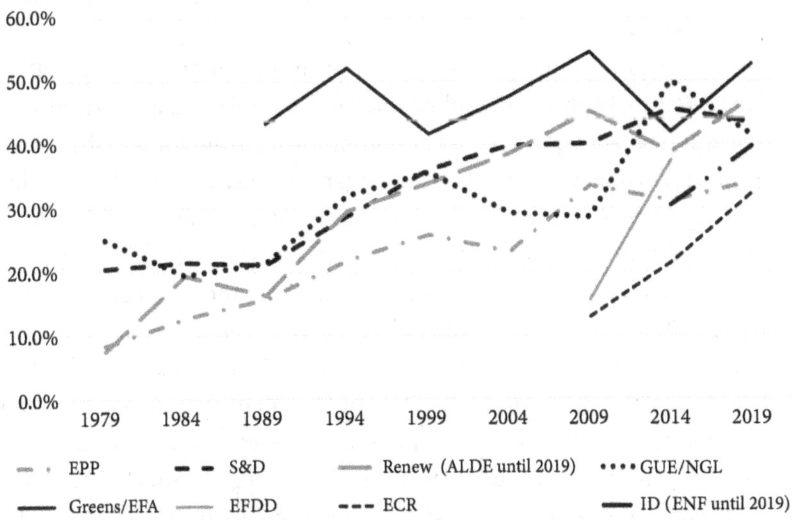

Figure 12.1 EP Gender Composition by Political Group (1979–2019)

Source: The authors' own calculation based on EP data (European Parliament n.d.).

EP elections), percentages considered as constituting gender equality or parity in political representation (Abels 2020). Other left-leaning and liberal political groups (S&D, The Left, ALDE/Renew) only selectively managed to cross the 45 percent parity zone, while all conservative and radical-right populist parties (EPP, ECR, ID) remain below 40 percent. Thus, in the EP, Greens/EFA are indeed the leading political group regarding gender parity.

Despite their uncontested lead in women's political representation (Keith and Verge 2018; Bick 2019), Green Parties are surprisingly among the least explored regarding gender quotas (but see Bick 2019) or are studied without a specific emphasis on women's representation (Richardson and Rootes 1995; Bomberg 1998; van Haute 2016). Coverage also differs across countries, with those Green Parties represented in parliament or even in government receiving more attention, although mostly compared to other national parties (Verge 2012, 2020; Abels 2020; Ahrens et al. 2020). Jackson (2017) provides one of the few historical accounts of Green Parties from a gendered perspective, highlighting strong parity compliance and successful promotion of women into leadership, but also arguing that internal party practices were often less feminist. Hierarchical campaign structures persisted with dominant men leaders and women in subordinated roles and with cooperative and consensual decision-making replaced by non-consensual decision-making (Jackson 2017, 307, 312).

In a comparative study covering 20 European countries, Bick (2019) demonstrated that throughout all countries, Green Parties are indeed gender equality leaders with higher commitments regarding leadership, quotas, powerful women's party member organizations, and gender equality policy than the average party in their national parliaments. This holds true even if only compared to radical left parties, with ideology as a "greater determinant of representation than geographical region" (Keith and Verge 2018, 397, 407). In the EP, though, political-group numbers are aggregated and may hide crucial differences in national party delegations and their actual commitments to gender equality, an issue addressed in this chapter. While previous studies focused on either national contexts or the whole Greens/EFA group, we compare Green Parties in the EP with each other—a setting where they need to develop a supranational political group (Kantola and Rolandsen Agustín 2016, 2019; Warasin et al. 2019).

Theoretical Framework: Gendering the Rules of Political Parties and Political Groups

We use the four-fold framework suggested by Gains and Lowndes (2014; see also Lowndes 2020) on how political institutions, such as political parties, may be gendered in relation to the rules that shape their workings. FI studies into the gendered dynamics of political parties mainly focus on single parties at national levels. The unique contribution of this chapter is to take this theoretical framework to a more complex supranational level, where the EP's Green Party group, the Greens, brings together 17 national-level Green Parties. As a result, the political group's politics and practices are shaped by interacting national and supranational rules. We ask: What are the effects of the diversity and the links between national and transnational? Are the rules at national and transnational levels competing or complementary?

First, political institutions can be shaped by *rules about gender*. These evidently include gender quotas but also a range of other norms and practices surrounding, for example, maternity and parental leaves or regulating hateful speech in parliamentary settings. Second, political institutions can operate on the basis of *rules with gendered effects*. Seemingly "neutral" rules in political institutions can have differentiated effects on women and men politicians and staff within the institutions. For example, the rules surrounding seniority or merit when allocating leadership positions within parliaments may appear neutral yet be based on masculine norms and favor men politicians (Kantola and Miller 2021).

The third dimension of gendered political institutions focuses on *gendered actors working with rules* (Gains and Lowndes 2014; Lowndes 2020, 54). The rules come into effect and shape the actions of the people within the institutions. The concept "rules in use" puts the analytical focus on the "interactions between specific institutional rules and the actors who interpret and enact them" (Gains and Lowndes 2022, 397). The positionalities, positions, and agency of these actors to represent their constituents, undertake parliamentary work, or work as political staff within institutions is shaped by the rules. In a constitutive process, the actors can also shape, change, or ensure the continuity of these rules. Finally, the fourth dimension aims at capturing the *gendered outcomes of action shaped by rules*. Some rules—such as gender quotas—help to take actions which foster gender equality successfully. Others—such as traditional gender norms—can compromise positive change implied by the rules (Lowndes 2020, 547).

Both rules about gender and rules with gendered effects involve not just formal codified practices that can be read from laws, rules of procedure, or statutes but also informal practices such as customs, habits, and norms that can be less easily identifiable and accessible for both practitioners and researchers (Chappell and Waylen 2013; Chappell and Mackay 2017; Waylen 2017). At the level of political parties, practices for advancing gender equality may include aspects such as gender action plans based on identifying gendered inequalities; institutionalizing the position of gender mainstreaming in all policy-making; gender training for policy-making and countering sexual harassment and obtrusive behavior; equal allocation of speaking time and other political resources (offices, staff); commitments to gender equality in all decision- and policy-making; and measures against sexual harassment (Kantola 2022; see also Verge, this volume). FI provides the tools to ask whether these institutions are formal or informal and examine their interplay, and current empirical studies show that while formality adds to the visibility, transparency, effectiveness, and accountability of the measures, informal practices for gender equality can be effective too in some cases (Kantola 2022; Ahrens and Kantola 2022; see also Gatto and Wylie, this volume).

Data and Methods

For analyzing parity issues in Greens/EFA along national lines—or in other words, their feminized politics—we rely on electoral data from the EP, websites by the EGP and national parties, as well as party statutes and secondary literature. We compiled data on electoral and voluntary party quota regulations via the International Institute for Democracy and Electoral Assistance (IDEA) website and used it to compare formal provisions on parity and the result for the EP elections. Importantly, several national Green Party delegations could only send one MEP to the EP, which makes it harder (or must at least be viewed with some reservations) to comprehensively judge the implementation of formal parity provisions.

To cover the complex ways in which political groups construct their views on gender equality and practices, the chapter draws on 18 semi-structured interviews with Greens/EFA MEPs and staff[3] conducted over the course of the 8th and 9th EP legislature. The interviews are part of a larger set of 140 interviews with MEPs and staff from all political groups about their gendered practices and policies. The team of the ERC-funded EUGenDem project conducted them; all the interviews were recorded, transcribed, anonymized, and coded using AtlasTi (see Berthet et al. 2023). For this chapter we extracted the Greens/EFA interviews and examined the code material for "gendered practices" and "gender equality practices" with subcodes on discrimination, division of labor, hierarchies, inappropriate behavior, gendered interaction, sexist language, gendered expertise, and sexual harassment. Additionally, we analyzed the most recent political-group statutes.

Green Parties and Descriptive Representation in the EP

The national members of the EP's Green Party group are often characterized as particularly committed to securing parity (Bick 2019; Keith and Verge 2018). We compare the national party *rules about gender*, and the EP intraparty practices. These vary considerably and result in *gendered outcomes*, not least mediated through *rules with gendered effects* such as EP election laws. Finally, we discuss how Greens/EFA as *gendered actors working with rules* actively seek to implement their parity commitment in EP electoral laws.

Rules About Gender

The EGP statutes stipulate as aim and objective in Article 3.8 that the EGP "applies the principle of gender-balance in all its elected and appointed bodies and external representation" (European Green Party 2023, 5). The EGP also requires in Article 4.2 that all full and associate members are "applying a gender balance principle" (European Green Party 2023, 5). Yet, there are no formal rules as to how national parties should implement this requirement, and our analysis demonstrates that there is a large variation of formal and informal rules.

We compiled different quota regulations—electoral gender quotas, voluntary party quotas—that apply to Green Parties in EU member states and to EP elections. Electoral rules for EP elections were successively harmonized and follow different forms of proportional representation (closed lists, preferential voting, single transferable vote), independent from the national electoral system. Table 12.1 provides an overview of applicable electoral and voluntary party quotas (or lack of both); there are no full members in Lithuania, Malta, and Slovakia. Likewise, some parties are subject to both electoral and voluntary party quotas.

Eleven[4] national delegations must comply with electoral gender quotas ranging from 33 percent to 50 percent, although implementation and sanctions for quota violation vary (European Parliamentary Research Service [EPRS] 2021)—with Romania, for instance, only requiring that each list is composed of both men and women. Six national parties operate with voluntary party quotas for electoral lists aiming at parity in outcome—yet, at different effectiveness levels. For instance, the Polish and German Greens adopted very strict quotas with a zipper system and securing a minimum of 50 percent women: in Poland, men's share is limited to 50 percent maximum, including for first-list places; in Germany, every electoral list shall

Table 12.1 Quota Regulations for Green Parties in EP Elections (Quota Threshold in %)

	Electoral gender quota	**Voluntary party quota**	**No formal quota regulation**
Countries	Belgium (50%); Croatia (40%); France (50%); Greece (40%); Italy (50%); Luxemburg (50%); Poland (35%); Portugal (33%); Romania (no all-men or all-women lists); Slovenia (40%); Spain (40%)	Austria (50%, zipper); Belgium (50%, zipper); Germany (50%, all uneven places for women, even places open for everyone); Hungary (maximum two repeated candidates of the same sex); Netherlands (50%); Poland (zipper, 50% limit for men; plus max 50% of first places for men); Spain* (50%, vertical and horizontal zipper) Sweden (40% minimum, each sex aiming at gender balance)	Bulgaria; Cyprus; Czech Republic; Denmark; Estonia; Finland; Ireland; Latvia; Romania

*Spain: Iniciativa per Catalunya Verds/Initiative for Catalonia Greens

Sources: EPRS 2021; International Institute for Democracy and Electoral Assistance (IDEA) n.d.; Lang et al. 2023; own data.

be led by a woman, uneven places are reserved for women, even places are open for everyone. Austria and Belgium also adopted a 50 percent quota and a zipper system, but without rules for who heads the list. Interestingly, the Belgian Greens kept their voluntary party quota despite legislated quotas. Sweden and the Netherlands stipulate 50 percent without any specific further rules. Hungary also adopted a kind of zipper quota with a maximum of two repeated candidates of the same sex, but in effect this may also result in only a 33 percent share for men/women if, for instance, two men (or women) alternate with one woman (or man). The remaining nine EU EGP members with a wide geographic spread operate without formal quota rules. Thus, despite the gender balance requirements in the statutes, not all EGP members opted for formal rules for their national party, which might be acceptable if informal rules ensure gender balance.

Gendered Outcomes

Looking at election results for the 8th and 9th EP, we can see that the Greens as a political group are located in the "parity zone," yet outcomes vary for national delegations (see Table 12.2).

Overall, there is no clear pattern for countries that would suggest that either men or women are advantaged. The (non)existence of quotas also appears insignificant. For instance, for Austria and Belgium, men dominated in the 8th EP, women in the 9th EP; one-MEP countries can go either direction. As the other delegations often arrive with only one to three MEPs, the two biggest national party delegations, Germany and France, are better suited to judge parity performance, and their delegations were gender-balanced. Nevertheless, maintaining parity is thus somehow also a bit by chance: if instead of the current balancing out between countries it had happened that in each legislature all small party delegations were composed predominantly of women (or men), Greens would have missed parity at large.

Rules with Gendered Effects and Gendered Actors Working with Rules

Our Greens/EFA interviewees were aware of different quota regulations and considered differences in national party delegations as a consequence of different national rules rather than resistance (see Josefsson, this

Table 12.2 Overview of Women MEPs in EP National Party Delegations

Party	EP 8th (2014–2019)			EP 9th (2019–2024)		
	MEPsM	MEPsW	W%	MEPsM	MEPsW	W%
EGP Greens	17	16	48.5%	26	32	55.2%
Austria Grüne	2	1	33.3%	1	2	66.6%
Belgium Écologie	1	–	0%	1	1	50%
Belgium Groen	1	–	0%	–	1	100%
Czech Republic Zelení	–	–	–	2	1	33.3%
Denmark SF—Green Left	–	1	100%	–	2	100%
Germany Bündnis '90/Die Grünen	5	6	54.5%	10	11	55%
Germany ÖPD	–	–	–	–	1	100%
Ireland Green Party	–	–	–	1	1	50%
France Europe Ècologie	3	3	50%	6	5	45.5%
Italy Europa Verde	–	–	–	–	1	100%
Lithuania Peasants and Greens Union*	(1)	–	0%	(1)	–	0%
Luxemburg Les Verts	1**	–	0%	–	1	100%
Hungary LMP—Magyarország Zöld Pártja	1	–	0%	–	–	–
Netherlands GroenLinks	1	1	50%	1	2	66.6%
Finland Vihreä Liitto	–	1	100%	1	2	66.6%
Sweden Miljöpartiet de Gröna	2	2	50%	2	1	33.3%

*The Lithuanian Peasants and Greens Union is currently not a member of the EGP. We included them because of their official label as Green Party and their membership in the political group.
**Replaced by a woman in 2018.

Source: The author's own calculation based on EP data (European Parliament n.d.).

volume). Or, as one Greens/EFA interviewee explained, "It is not the case that the European Green Party would have the tools to enforce something on national parties. The power to do so is simply totally somewhere else" (Greens/EFA Staff F 010419). As this quotation illustrates, ensuring parity is considered national and not EGP business, and, as they further explained, certainly not that of any national delegation: "So, we Germans encourage everyone to switch to our system—and no one really wants to hear this" (Greens/EFA Staff F 010419). Next to quota rules and despite all national electoral laws following proportional representation for EP elections, the general rules may impair parity ambitions. For instance, preferential voting or single transferable vote systems offer voters the chance to change party preferences, often to the disadvantage of women (Millard et al. 2011).

On the other hand, Greens/EFA have tried to change electoral rules with potential gendered effects by changing supranational regulations. In 2022, Greens/EFA were successful in mobilizing other political groups to support gender equality amendments when revising the EP electoral law (personal communication with an EGP representative). If successful, Europarties would be required to adopt a gender equality plan and a (sexual) harassment protocol, provide data about the gender balance of their member parties (including candidates and MEPs), and publish an annual report. This would extend the Greens/EFA rules and practices to all other groups.

Greens/EFA and Gender Equality Within the Political Group

In this section, we focus on the intra-group practices for gender equality of the Greens/EFA group in the EP. The political group cannot determine national-level candidate selection processes. Nevertheless, this section illustrates the rules and practices it can use to advance gender equality. We thereby identify political-group-specific *rules about gender* and show that these are usually formal codified rules. This is striking in relation to other political groups of the Parliament, which do not have as extensive formal rules about gender equality (Kantola 2022). We discern a multitude of important *rules with gendered effects*, which both undermine gender equality in the group but also support it. Finally, we pinpoint some of the *gendered outcomes of action shaped by rules* as well as illustrations of *gendered actors working with rules.*

Rules About Gender Within Political Groups

First, the strong norm of upholding gender equality in relation to both intra-group practices and the political group's policies is the overarching *rule about gender* we identify. Gender equality as a fundamental principle and a key facet of the political group's identity was discussed in the interviews by all genders and by both MEPs and staff (Kantola 2022). The Greens/EFA statutes institutionalize the principle into an array of formal gender equality practices. In the bureau, half of the chair posts were to be held by women (article 3.9). The statutes stated that the group shall have an ombudsperson as a mechanism for reporting and solving complaints/conflicts (article 4.–4.3). The ombudsperson writes a report every two years and is an MEP elected by group staff (Greens/EFA Staff F 210319). The group also commits "to full gender equality" in staff practices (article 5.3) (see Kantola 2022).

Informally too and beyond the statutes, gender balance was a strong norm for the way in which the group operated when nominating and selecting MEPs for different positions. This was described as follows: "We have a lot of internal rules which are not in the statutes and are implementing rules which are not in the statutes, where practically the question of the gender balance is completely, completely covered" (Greens/EFA Staff F 200319) (Kantola 2022).

The Greens/EFA were—next to the Left group—the only political group that formally committed to implement gender mainstreaming internally (Elomäki and Ahrens 2022; Kantola 2022). Gender mainstreaming is the responsibility of everyone rather than of few gender experts. The group implemented a practice whereby all the policy briefings produced by staff were to include a section on gender impacts. This was accompanied by trainings on gender equality issues for all staff members (Greens/EFA Staff F 100320; Greens/EFA Staff F 210319). Additionally, as an informal practice, Committee on Women's Rights and Gender Equality group members can amend group positions if gender perspectives are insufficiently integrated (Greens/EFA 130320). There was also mention of the need to develop a monitoring process at the next stage to assess whether this was implemented, thereby making the practices more effective (Greens/EFA Staff F 100320).

In addition, the group held mandatory training for MEPs and staff on sexual harassment (Greens/EFA Staff F 210319), an approach considered highly controversial in many other groups who did not consider sexual harassment an serious enough issue to merit mandatory measures for all MEPs (see Berthet and Kantola 2020). The group had also created a "network of confidential counselors" consisting of two women and two men as "first entry points" in harassment cases (Greens/EFA Staff F 210319).

The Greens/EFA approach can thus be characterized as proactive and not just reactive in relation to gender equality practices and policy, and consisting of a wide range of progressive rules about gender put in place to ensure gender equality (Kantola 2022). Other groups oppose such gender mainstreaming and also gender budgeting efforts, as illustrated by a Greens/EFA MEP quote on committee work: "The rest of the people just sort of sat there looking at me, 'oh God, the Green, the gender budgeting,' you know ... 'There comes the crazy one'" (Greens/EFA F 300919).

Rules with Gendered Effects

Remaining gendered inequalities within the group can be discerned by analyzing the *rules with gendered effects*. For example, one Greens/EFA MEP suggested that agriculture is "quite a men's issue" in EU politics in general as well as in the political group, as were the environment, finance, industry, and research; however, "human rights and FEMM, gender aspects, social things, then you will have much more women" (Greens/EFA MEP F 100320) (see also Ahrens et al. 2022; Kantola 2022).

One of the central problems emerging from many of the interviews with the Greens/EFA MEPs was that speaking time was unequally divided in group meetings, with men dominating (Kantola 2022). This was systematically mentioned in a number of interviews variously describing how and why men felt entitled to "talk, talk, talk" and do it in a "competitive way" (Greens/EFA MEP F 130320; Greens/EFA MEP F 190319; Greens/EFA MEP F 210120; Greens/EFA MEP F 300919).

> I think the only issue ... is speaking time. Because as everybody knows men tend to speak more, feel more important and the way the list is, the speaker's list is done ... And if you don't have a limitation of speaking time, time might be up [laughs]. So I've requested speaking time limitations several times and ... I brought it up with the bureau member that I wasn't quite happy with the way speaking time was distributed.
>
> (Greens/EFA MEP F 300919)

> I realized when I really want to speak, actually speaking time's up usually. So, you have to say you want to speak even before knowing what exactly you're going to say, where this debate is going ... [T]hen I realize that three

> or four men are speaking in a row and each taking a lot of time. And then there's the speaking list of 25 speakers and I don't feel like speaking anymore because like two hours and I'm like, well let me go home, I have some work to do ...
>
> (Greens/EFA MEP F 300919)

> [S]ometimes I wish that ... some people were cut short, and it was limited to two minutes for everybody. There are a few French colleagues who particularly rabbit on ... So actually, in a way, for me, that's an equality issue.
>
> (Greens/EFA MEP F 210120 Brexit)

The interview material contained different explanations, with some being related to beliefs about "how women and men are," while others explained that it was a consequence of speaking time being distributed by national delegations chaired mainly by men (Greens/EFA MEP F 300919). The position of the heads of national delegations (HoDs) exemplifies an *informal rule*—heads of national delegation speaking first—undermining a general commitment to gender equality (Kantola and Miller 2022). For the Greens/EFA, the biggest delegation (German) is headed by a man, and the second biggest (French) has two HoDs, one woman and one man (Elomäki et al. 2023).

Interestingly, the Greens/EFA is the only group in the EP which plays down the role of national delegations and instead emphasizes the supranational and European level Green identity and cooperation. For instance, unlike all other groups (except for S&D) the Greens/EFA does not have national delegation-based representation in its top decision-making body, the Bureau. Playing down the importance of national delegations potentially creates space for upholding other aspects than nationality in selection processes, also for employees, including competence and gender equality norms (Elomäki et al. 2023) as shown in the previous section in relation to the rules that the political group has on gender balance. In strong contrast to the conservative EPP group, which also has a large German national delegation, the Greens/EFA has in place measures and practices that mitigate against German dominance in the way that positions, particularly leadership and committee membership, are handed out in the political group (Elomäki et al. 2023).

Gendered Outcomes and Gendered Actors Working with Rules

As evidence of achieving gender equality for the group, the interviewees typically mentioned the gender balance in terms of the MEPs numbers they had reached; the fact that the group was co-chaired by a woman and a man; the secretary general being a woman and gender balance being sought when filling key positions, including the bureau, coordinators, committee chairs, and different working groups (Kantola 2022). The norms and rules about gender equality were most upheld in everyday interactions of the group, even without a formal gender equality plan (see Verge, this volume). One interviewee pointed to two male French MEPs as not being very good on gender equality, but that overall, men would not dominate Greens/EFA. Instead, the working environment was described as "throughout supportive" and not requiring specific "sisterhood" (Greens/EFA MEP F 250220).

Despite their overall strong commitment to gender equality, Greens/EFA, like other political groups, struggle with adhering to it given their national party delegations. Interviewees explained that gender parity is the main factor in composing speaker lists. Yet, when it comes to high-level events, such as the inaugural speech of Ursula von der Leyen as Commission president, the picture changed. Then, like in other political groups, the HoDs—all men for the biggest Green NPDs—get the first speaking slots.

> And then we had the key debate when Ursula von der Leyen was presenting her speech. And what happened [was] that we had a really serious imbalance within the group of speakers, we had ten speaking slots and seven of them were given to men ... I mean for German Greens this is not possible, it doesn't happen ... You know then the Green group having all these men speaking ... so we protested against that, against the bureau and against the person who had decided on speaking time ... And then, the problem is that the distribution is according to national delegations as well.
>
> (Greens/EFA MEP F 300919)

Important to note though, the interviewee stated that for the Germans, the high number of men was "not possible" but—given they are the biggest delegation—it was their male HoD who spoke first. One might say that if gender parity was their priority, they could have changed the picture themselves instead of (only criticizing) their political group.

Showing *gendered actors working with rules*, one of the interviewees complained about the violation of gender equality rules to the Secretary General, who saw their hands bound with view to formal criteria, and the issue was then scheduled for debate at the next political-group retreat.

> Speaking time in the key debates must be distributed equally. Because I thought that was obvious and then I went to the Secretary. And she said well, it's not a criteria, it's not among my criteria. I have to take into account, thematic, the topic, the issue and ... nationality ... But that shows how difficult it is, even if you have the rules in place.
>
> (Greens/EFA MEP F 300919)

The citation illustrates how, even within the Greens/EFA, other rules with gendered effects, such as issue salience or the importance of nationality representation, can at times trump the rule about gender equality.

Finally, studying the EP's political groups in relation to gendering the EU economic governance and policy shows that there are policy fields—such as the strongly masculine field of economic policy—where the Greens/EFA also fail to implement gender mainstreaming in their committee and policy work in the EP (Elomäki 2023). Another field where the political group does not live up to its high norms in relation to equality is political-group-specific antiracism work. The internal practices for antiracism within the group remain weak or non-existent in a parliamentary context, which is characterized by normative whiteness and racism (Kantola et al. 2022).

Conclusion

Using Gains and Lowndes (2014) four-part framework, we found that the EP's Green intra-party and intra-political-group commitment to gender equality is indeed quite comprehensive, characterizing their structures, practices, and rules as feminist politics (Childs and Webb 2011; Childs 2013a). This holds true for formal and informal parity rules as well as the internal intra-group practices for gender equality.

For instance, the EGP requires a parity commitment from its members and Greens/EFA aim to establish parity as a formal rule for European elections. Likewise, some national delegations actively try to diffuse their strict parity rules to all EGP members, though this has been so far unsuccessful. Yet, despite this formal commitment, parity seems to happen by chance given the many national delegations with only one or three MEPs, who could in any election arrive all with only women (or men). So far, and despite being the most supranational political group, the EGP does not coordinate between national party members to secure parity for, for example, the first-list position, which is often the only successful one. In other words, the parity rules by national delegations so far have resulted in gender equality outcomes at the supranational level, but the outcomes are not necessarily set in stone.

The intra-group political-group practices of the Greens/EFA demonstrate a strong normative commitment to gender equality, which is translated into formalized intra-group practices that hold up the norm in everyday political work of the group (as rules about gender). Our analysis of the intra-group rules with gendered effects shows that some gendered inequalities still persist and that these relate to masculine norms of expertise or behavior. The analysis of the gendered outcomes of the rules and actors working with the rules showed how the formal rules about gender equality result mostly in gender-equal outcomes. Yet, the Greens/EFA fail to hold up equality in all policy fields and in relation to all equalities, pointing to the intra-group work for equality which remains to be done.

Overall, our chapter points to considerable consistency between the national and the supranational party politics of the Greens in relation to gender equality. Parties and the political groups all work toward the same direction, with some gaps and discrepancies but within an overall positive picture for gender equality. This analysis was done using the four-fold FI framework: formal and informal (i) rules about gender and (ii) rules with gendered effects, the actual (iii) outcomes of these rules, and how the (iv) actors use them (Gains and Lowndes 2014; 2022). It is a complex and comprehensive analytical framework, which, we conclude, could usefully be applied and extended to intersectional inequalities too.

Funding Statement

This research has received funding from the European Research Council (ERC) under the EU's Horizon 2020 research and innovation program (Grant agreement 771676). Petra Ahrens' work was supported by the Academy of Finland, grant number 338556.

Notes

1. In this chapter, we reflect on the EFA where appropriate regarding internal political-group organization but disregard EFA parties when analyzing descriptive representation, because their parties are not members of the EFA.
2. See Acabo (2024) for a historical review of the Greens' political-group formation and relevant gender issues.
3. Eight women MEPs, two men MEPs; six women staff, two men staff.
4. Ireland's electoral gender quota does not apply to EP elections.

13
Women's Political Parties as Agents of Contagion

Kimberly Cowell-Meyers

The decisions of parties to recruit, train, and promote female candidates are critical to how many women run for office and how many are elected (Lovenduski and Norris 1993; Caul 1999; Kittilson 2006; Bjarnegård 2013; Kenny 2013). As Lovenduski notes, the power of political parties "means that activity to increase women's representation and the effects of its increase are first and foremost felt within parties" (Lovenduski 2005, 245). But parties do not make these decisions in a vacuum. Instead, they form their policies and practices in response to other parties in the system, following successful parties, reacting to new dynamics and competing with each other for issue space and voters (see inter alia Meguid 2005, 2008; Green-Pedersen 2007; see also Beckwith, this volume). This chapter examines the role of women's political parties as agents of contagion that can promote women's representation in politics by altering the behavior of other political parties.

This chapter will first give a brief overview of the history and key features of women's political parties, which scholars have referred to as a "new party family" akin to liberal, conservative, workers', ecological, or Christian-Democratic parties (Cowell-Meyers, Evans, and Shin 2020). Then, the chapter will use four case studies of the largest and/or most electorally successful women's political parties in Europe (the Icelandic Women's List, Swiss Frauen Macht Politics, Northern Ireland's Women's Coalition, and Sweden's Feminist Initiative) to consider how and under what institutional conditions women's parties can influence other political parties and affect the representation of women.

The case studies indicate that the gendered dynamics of party competition give women's parties disproportionate influence over other political parties in ways unique among niche parties. They also demonstrate that

Kimberly Cowell-Meyers, *Women's Political Parties as Agents of Contagion*. In: *Gendering Party Politics*. Edited by: Meryl Kenny and Elin Bjarnegård, Oxford University Press.
DOI: 10.1093/oso/9780197793985.003.0013

these niche parties can produce institutional change in ways that are underappreciated in the literature on parties. And, finally, the examples of these four women's parties indicate that these movement–party hybrids can alter the pattern of women's representation and the types and scope of issues addressed by parties—thus helping to shape distributions of power in the systems in which they emerge.

Overview of the History and Key Features of Women's Political Parties

Women's parties, as I have defined elsewhere, are "autonomous organizations of or for women that run candidates for elected office" to "advance the volume and range of women's voices in politics" (Cowell-Meyers 2016, 4). They differ from other political parties in that their principal goal may not be to recruit or run candidates but to increase women's representation in politics through a variety of mechanisms. They differ from women's wings or branches of established political parties because gender is their principal organizing strategy and focus, and their independence means they do not have to fit into the issues or structures of broader organizations. They are also distinct from social movements, though most arise from established movements and represent efforts to increase the reach and resources of the movement by giving it formal tools—or, in the words of Elisabeth Joris, member of Frauen Macht Politik! in Switzerland, "double feet" (interview with author, 2015). Most are, in fact, movement–party hybrids. Although they advocate for a diversity of substantive issues and not all are explicitly feminist, all use a gendered analysis, focusing on women's marginalization, embrace female leadership in their organizations even when the leadership structures are horizontal, and demand greater access to power for women through their inclusion in the political sphere. Like other party families, they are joined by their shared orientation and sociological origins, their emergence in dialectical opposition to mainstream dynamics and parties, and often their party name, which usually includes some form of "women" or "feminist" (Cowell-Meyers, Evans, and Shin 2020).

More than 100 parties with "women" or "feminist" (or their non-English equivalents) in their names have stood for election for national legislatures in all regions of the world, according to online electoral records. At least 50 of these have appeared in Europe, and at least 35 emerged in the 1990s, during the institutional reconfiguration precipitated by the collapse of the Soviet Union. Most have not crossed the commonly used 4 percent threshold to be considered competitive or a potential coalition partner (Sartori 1976; Kitschelt 1988), but some have had remarkable success (the Shamiram Women's Party in Armenia won 17 percent of the vote in a single election, and Iceland's Kwennalisten earned 10 percent). Most are short-lived (Shamiran disappeared in the next election), although there are notable exceptions such as Gabriela Women's Party in the Philippines, which won seats in five congresses, and the German Feminist Party, which campaigned in national and European Union (EU) elections for more than 20 years.

There is little scholarship on these parties, but those that emerged in Europe since the end of the Cold War tended to arise, as would be expected, where structural conditions (e.g., multiple parties, proportional representation, large district magnitudes, and low elective thresholds) favored the rise of small parties (see Cowell-Meyers 2016). However, there are also unique gendered dynamics that appear to contribute to their emergence; they are more likely where women's labor force participation is high and either their descriptive representation low or no major party in the system employs a gender quota. This suggests that these parties, in the European context at least, are expressions of frustration at the failure of mainstream parties to empower women politically relative to their economic empowerment.

Though women's parties run election campaigns, their central goal may be less to win seats than to draw attention to their cause. In other words, the purpose may not be to act as established parties do but to embarrass the other parties for their lack of attention to the issues of women's representation (Levin 1999; MacKenzie 2005; Tavits 2008). Given that they are only niche parties (Meyer and Miller 2015), their opportunity to affect policy may be limited but they may still be able to present a choice for mainstream parties, which have to respond strategically to issues the party raises by either "accommodating"/adopting them or diverging from them (Meguid 2005, 2008; van der Wardt 2015). The ability of niche parties such as left (mostly Green) or radical right parties to shift the agenda and behavior of established parties is well-documented (see the reviews in Green-Pedersen and Mortensen 2010; Vliegenthart, Walgrave, and Meppelink 2011; Lefevre, Tresch, and Walgrave 2015). Taking advantage of these processes, women's parties can increase women's representation overall by improving women's status in the other parties, even without winning many votes/seats. And women's parties may have a unique ability to trigger a process of contagion relative to other niche parties, as inclusiveness and equity are difficult for mainstream parties to oppose or avoid when their salience is raised and public opinion is supportive (Matland and Studlar 1996; Davis 1997; Caul 2001). As Freidenvall has noted, small parties that introduce new measures on gender representation can "trigger approximately all parties in the political spectrum to comply with the new norms" (Freidenvall 2003, 6). This means the women's parties do not need to be durable or large to improve women's representation.

Examining the experiences of the largest and/or most successful of these parties in Europe can illustrate this process and the conditions under which this kind of accommodation or contagion is most likely. In all four cases the parties won seats in legislatures above the local level, two at the national level, one at the European level, and one in peace talks and the subsequent devolved assembly. The case studies rely upon close scrutiny of election records, archived party and campaign materials, local; national; and international news coverage, and, where possible, interviews with participants and observers, including other parties' politicians. What follows is a brief discussion of their history and some of the common themes in their experiences.[1]

The Cases

The first of these parties to emerge was the Icelandic Women's List (Kvennalisten), which grew from an energized women's movement that had successfully run candidates for local office in Iceland's larger cities. In 1983, KL won three seats in the Althingi (national parliament). In 1987, it would go on to win more than 10 percent of the vote at the national level and almost 20 percent in Akureyri, one of Iceland's largest cities. The party lasted until 1999, when it allied itself with a couple of other small parties and dissolved its separate apparatus.

In Switzerland, Frauen Macht Politik! (or FraP!) arose in 1986, contesting elections for the cantonal parliament (Kantonsrat) and the Council of States (Ständerat) in Zürich for the first time in 1987. The party was a "loose, heterogeneous coalition of women's groups, autonomous feminists and members of political parties" (quoted in Neue Zürcher Zeitung 1990, 94, translated by Google), which grew out of the activist and anti-establishment culture of civil society in Zürich. The party never topped 5 percent in any election but won seats in the cantonal legislature beginning in 1987 and seats at the municipal level beginning in 1990, and held one seat in the national parliament in 1991–1999 until its National Councilor quit the party and took her mandate to the Social Democratic Party (SPS). The party held on to its local representation until 2002.

Northern Ireland developed a women's party in 1996, in the weeks immediately preceding the elections to the Forum for Political Understanding and Dialogue, from which participants in the peace talks were drawn. Frustrated that the existing political parties did not respond to requests for women's representation from the Northern Ireland Women's European Platform (Holland 1996), women active in grassroots organizations in both communities formed the Northern Ireland Women's Coalition (NIWC). The NIWC earned two seats in the Forum, and thus two seats at the talks. They went on to campaign for local councils and also for the new Assembly created out of the peace agreement in 1998. The NIWC won two seats in the Assembly in 1998, although it lost them when the center more generally collapsed in Northern Ireland politics in 2003 and the party folded in 2006.

The Swedish Feminist Initiative (F!) emerged considerably later than the other three parties and had a slower start. F! was created in 2005 and began contesting elections in 2006. Though they never crossed the 4 percent threshold for representation in the national parliament, they won 5.5 percent support in the EU elections in May 2014 and seats on 13 local councils the same year, securing 9 percent support in one Swedish city (Simrishamn). The party did not retain its Member of the European Parliament (MEP) in 2019, and its municipal support collapsed at approximately the same time, although it founded sister parties in Norway and Finland before that.

Mechanisms: Worrying the Other Parties

As agents of contagion, women's parties tend to influence the representation of women primarily by triggering a process of transformation in the mainstream parties. All of the four parties in this study were small but each pressured the other parties in the system, starting with those on the left, to respond to their issues and accommodate the demand to increase women's representation. There is abundant evidence of this in media coverage of these parties. The NIWC, for example, was seen to have "forced the male-dominated main parties to take the size of their female contingent seriously" (Sharrock 1996, 6) and pushed the mainstream parties "to wake up and realize that they needed women on the ticket" (Purdy, interview with author, 2009). In the Swedish case, national and international press asserted that F!'s "poll success must put pressure on mainstream parties" (Lundin 2014, 13), noting that as F! "has grown, the parties' interest in gender has done the same" (Svenska Dagbladet 2014, para 36).

And figures from some of the mainstream parties themselves acknowledged the effects of the women's parties on their parties, although this was usually an opinion voiced primarily by female politicians. In Iceland, for example, Salome Thorkelsdottir, Conservative Party MP and former president of the Parliament stated that KL "worried all the other parties" (see Einarsdottir 2015); while interviews conducted by Edward Schneier in Iceland indicated that "more than one PA [People's Alliance] leader agreed that Kvennalisten was 'helping to move the political dialogue to the left'" (Schneier 1992, 430–431). In Northern Ireland, figures in the Progressive Unionist Party and Social Democratic and Labour Party (SDLP) repeatedly talked about the NIWC as "highlighting" the underrepresentation of women in interviews with the author. Even Arlene Foster, former head of the Democratic Unionist Party, commented in an opinion piece in the *Irish News* in 1997 that, as an election agent for the Ulster Unionist Party in 1996 just after the NIWC was formed, "above all other questions the one which kept popping up again and again was why there were not more women in politics" (Foster 1997).

FraP!'s influence on the other parties was manifest in part when its work promoting women's representation was co-opted by women in the SPS, the main center-left party in Switzerland (Isele 1996; Stump, interview with author, 2015). And the women in SPS leaned on FraP! to pressure the male leadership of their party. Multiple times women in the SPS threatened to break off and set up their own party, mimicking FraP! (Stump, interview with author, 2015) as did women in Sweden's SPS (see the "Support Stockings" as described by Jansson 2021). These points drive home the sense of the women's parties as useful means to advance women's inclusion by goading the mainstream parties into changing their behavior.

Descriptive Representation: Who Is Included/Excluded

In Iceland, Switzerland, and Northern Ireland, the effect on the emergence of the women's party on women's descriptive representation was profound.[2]

In Iceland, women made up 5 percent of the Althingi through the 1970s. That number jumped to 15 percent in 1983, when Kvennalisten first ran for national office, to 21 percent in 1987, and to 24 percent in 1991. It hovered between 24 and 30 percent until the party folded in 1999, remaining at approximately that level until 2009, when the first female Prime Minister was elected. This dramatic change was made possible, as explained above, by the women's party "worrying" the mainstream parties into making marked alterations to their selection patterns. In 1987, the first election after KL won seats, the four parties ran 15 percent more candidates on average than they did in 1979, immediately before KL appeared. The two parties that already had the highest proportion of female candidates (the PA and the Social Democrats) only added 8 percent more, but the two more right-leaning parties (the Progressives and the Independence Party), both of which started with less than 20 percent female candidates, added 13 and 17 percent respectively between 1983 and 1987. The Alliance, which already had an internal party quota but, according to Schneier (1992), "found it difficult either to persuade women to run, or to convince its constituent organizations to cast aside prominent males with long records of party service in favor of untested women" (424), suddenly found it easier to overcome these barriers, running 47 percent female candidates in 1987.

The situation in Northern Ireland and Switzerland is more complicated because both have multiple, nested institutions of either federalism or devolution; however, both cases saw a sizable jump in female candidates and/or female representation. Though there were no women elected to Westminster from Northern Ireland until 2001, the proportion of female candidates in Northern Ireland Westminster elections from left and center parties jumped in the first election after NIWC emerged. From 1992 to 1997, the number of female candidates from the two left-of-center parties Sinn Féin and the SDLP surged (Sinn Féin from 7 to 18 percent, and the SDLP from 0 to 17 percent). And, while the proportion of women elected at the local level ticked up only slightly over the 1990s, the percentage of female SDLP candidates for local election in 1997 nearly doubled from 1993 and also doubled between 1993 and 2001 in the Democratic Unionist Party and Sinn Féin. There was also a dramatic change in the ability of female candidates at the local level in many of the parties to win seats, meaning that parties took their candidacies more seriously and listed them in winnable seats, beginning in 1997. Though these gains could have been due to changes occurring throughout the British

Isles at the time, these changes only occurred in Northern Ireland and not in Westminster more generally or in the Irish Oireachtas.[3] In addition, Sinn Féin, the only party that campaigned in all three jurisdictions—Northern Ireland, the Westminster Parliament in London, and the Irish Oireachtas in Dublin—only altered its percentage of female candidates in Northern Ireland and not in the other jurisdictions in this window of time, suggesting it was responding to pressures that were unique and specific to Northern Ireland.

Women's descriptive representation in Zürich was also dramatically transformed after the women's party emerged. In Zürich, from the time immediately before FraP! formed in the mid-1980s until it declined in the late 1990s, women's representation increased by 17 percent at the municipal level (from 20 to 37 percent), by 14 percent at the cantonal level (from 15 to 29 percent), and by 24 percent at the national level (from 17 to 41 percent). Though this was a moment of tremendous transition for women in Swiss politics generally, the change was much more intense where FraP! existed than in other cantons. Zürich began the period with approximately 7 percent greater female representation at the local and national levels than the rest of Switzerland but finished it 15 percent higher than other cantons on average at the local level and 20 percent higher at the national level. Furthermore, the behavior of the parties shifted specifically around the emergence of FraP!. Swiss electoral law, for example, permits parties to run specialized lists of candidates; however, the Social Democrats (SPS), the main left-of-center party, ran a separate women's list only once in Zürich, in 1991, which was the first election after FraP! campaigned at the national level. The SPS was already using internal quotas for women by 1983 but raised them from 33 to 50 percent in 1995. And, though women were 33 percent of SPS candidates at all levels by 1986, they were more than 60 percent of all SPS representatives at the municipal, cantonal, and national levels in Zürich by 1998. The Green Party in Zürich also adopted their own quotas in 1991, just as FraP! gained seats at all three levels. And, neither party used gender-balanced zippered lists of alternating male and female candidates until after FraP! emerged. As a leading female figure from the SPS explained, women from the other parties leveraged the pressure coming from FraP! on these parties to achieve gains for women from their parties' leadership (Stump interview with author, 2015).

Substantive Representation

These parties were all tiny, meaning that they typically lacked opportunity to initiate or pass policy. However, each was able to prompt improvements in women's substantive representation. As part of the peace negotiations, the NIWC is widely credited for getting certain passages included in the Good Friday/Belfast Agreement such as those on gender equality, victims, integrated education, integrated living, community development, and the Civic Forum—but this was a highly unusual institutional opportunity. The Icelandic party was involved in negotiations to take part in a coalition government on two occasions in the 1980s but did not participate, thus none of these parties ever exercised executive authority at the national level beyond ceremonial posts. Lacking the power to create policy, what the parties did succeed in doing was adjusting the political stances of the other parties—and thus shaping the norms of the political system. This process is evident in the adjustments the mainstream parties made to their election manifestos in response to the women's party emergence or their competitive pressure.

This is where the Swedish party, which campaigned in a context of already elevated women's descriptive representation, especially shone. F! campaigned on addressing economic inequality and structural inequities related to gender, mainstreaming a gendered perspective, combating violence against women, and using a feminist foreign policy, alongside some traditional left ideas such as shortening the workday, investing in public transport, and limiting use of fossil fuels. Of the 17 issues listed in the election manifesto of F!, the other seven parties averaged only six mentions in the three elections that preceded F!'s breakout success in the May 2014 European Parliament elections. In the run up to the 2014 parliamentary elections that fall, when polls showed F! closing in on the four percent national support they needed for a seat in the Riksdag, mentions of F! priority issues by the other parties jumped to 10 on average. That election cycle, the Moderates produced a five-point economic program for greater gender equality, the Liberals crafted a banner of "Feminism without Socialism," the Greens campaigned on free contraceptives for women under 26, and SAP advocated for a ban on sexualized advertising (Wikstrom 2014). The parties on the right also gave greater attention to these issues in recent elections though not as much as those on the left.

In Northern Ireland, a sharp uptick in attention to the women's party's issues is also clear after their emergence. In fact, none of the mainstream parties made any mention of the issues identified as key concerns of the NIWC until after the party campaigned on them in 1996—with the exception of Sinn Féin, the SDLP, and Alliance—referring to the need for human rights protections. There was a surge in interest in the other issues of the NIWC manifesto, starting with the general election in 1997; four of the five main parties (plus the Progressive Unionists) referred to women's equality, the gender (im)balance in public appointments, and the necessity of gender-mainstreaming. Four of these also called for greater support for childcare for working parents. Three of the five main parties even produced separate documents on women in politics shortly after the NIWC emerged but not before.

In Switzerland, the outcomes were more mixed although the research is more difficult to conduct because the parties do not issue the same kind of direct communications with voters such as manifestos used elsewhere and there is no repository of cantonal election materials. Of the 17 issues FraP! discussed in their election and media materials, 14 pertained specifically to women's status or condition, and the remainder were related to the environment and immigrants. Many were already on the SPS agenda by 1983, so the party did not so much introduce them as increase the pressure on SPS to follow through on them. In a kind of backlash, the bourgeois parties appeared to cede this space to the left parties in the 1990s. Though the bourgeois parties professed the need for gender equality, environmental protection, and the integration of immigrants from 1987 to 1999, and picked up 40–50 percent of FraP!'s issues in the 1980s, they fell silent on them by 1995. The Greens, however, transformed themselves entirely from silence on the issues in 1983 to mentioning 59 percent of them and calling for the restructuring of traditional gender roles and endorsing quotas for their internal bodies and all public bodies by 1991.

Conditions for Success

The four parties analyzed in this chapter were chosen as the largest or most successful parties in Europe electorally. They were included because they did not just run candidates but also succeeded in stealing votes from other parties and gained seats.

As the case studies reveal, the women's parties influenced the representation of women by getting other parties to take up their issues and/or include more or different types of women in prominent positions within their organizations. This is a process centered on competition and the opportunities and risks present in conditions of uncertainty where multiple parties vie for seats in small contexts. In each of these cases, party shifts, new institutions, and/or electoral uncertainty drove parties to adapt and accommodate the women's parties (see also Beckwith on "newness," this volume).

Intense party competition is a key part of the equation. For example, in Sweden, eight major and many minor parties compete for 20 seats in the European Parliament. In Northern Ireland, five parties and multiple other more minor ones competed for seats in the Assembly, although 10 were permitted seats in the Forum where the NIWC first landed. Frap! competed against the five prominent national parties and multiple smaller ones, some with sizable local support. Iceland had only four main parties but gained four new ones in 1987, including one that earned 10 percent of the vote, alongside KL's 10 percent. As many as 11 ran candidates in one election when KL was in office. The point is that the parties in these contexts were especially desperate to gain votes and/or were wary of losing them.

The parties also competed in very small contexts where district magnitudes tended to be high and thresholds to affect electoral outcomes were very small. The importance of these factors is underscored by the fact that even though women's parties emerged in seven of Switzerland's German-speaking cantons in the 1980s and 1990s, Zürich's large district magnitude (34 in the Nationalrat where the average was seven members per canton) meant FraP! alone gained a national seat and the changes in women's representation in Zürich subsequently far outpaced other cantons, even those where women's parties were elected at the cantonal level.

Uncertainty and the need to accommodate the women's parties were also fueled by other factors, including new institutions in two of the cases. In Northern Ireland, a more proportional electoral system (single transferable vote in 18 six-seat districts) and the uncertainty that accompanied the establishment of a new institution clearly made parties wary about the appeal of their own campaigns. The Icelandic system underwent dramatic restructuring as its two legislative chambers were combined into one in 1995. And, at the time F! earned an MEP, all the parties worried about the rise of the Sweden Democrats and strove to distinguish themselves from them.

The pressure to accommodate these parties was typically felt most intensely among proximate parties, meaning parties on the left and center. In Iceland, Dominelli and Jonsdottir (1988, 47) note that "left politicians were worried enough about the threat posed by KF to make overtures to KF women," asking them to join their coalition. In Switzerland, whereas FraP! had been a coalition partner of the Socialists at the cantonal level, they became a direct competitor in the national elections in 1991 elections, costing both the Socialists and the Greens one seat (Strech 1995). At the municipal level, it even appeared that FraP! might by 1994 supplant the Greens, whose delegation declined by half between 1990 and 1994. In Northern Ireland, the system of transfers makes it easy to see this pressure on proximate parties; the women's party was elected through transfers from every party except the far-right DUP.

And features of the other parties played a role in their adaptation. In at least three cases (Northern Ireland, Switzerland, and Sweden), there were women's wings in many of the other mainstream parties, particularly those on the left, that could reinforce the claims of the women's parties within their own, though women in the mainstream parties often faulted the other women for organizing outside of the established party structures and siphoning off support. These women were commonly the first people that the male leadership of the parties elevated in response to the pressure from the women's parties. When, for example, the SDLP in Northern Ireland were "scrambling" to "push women in front of tv cameras" (Haughey 1997, 13), the party turned to its women's wing, elevating its profile and increasing its budget for programming. This pre-existing institutional resource made it easier for those parties to adapt.

All four parties also drew from supportive exoteric environments. In 1991, the women's movement in Switzerland organized a national Frauenstreik to protest women's pay, which became the largest strike in Switzerland since 1918 (Kaiser 2011). FraP! became almost the political expression of this informal social movement, deploying the slogan of the Frauenstreik at the center of their subsequent election manifestos. Iceland too had a women's strike to protest gender discrimination in 1975, in which approximately 90 percent of women participated (Schneier 1992, 419). These events—combined with the election of the first female president, Vigdís Finnbogadóttir (see Eimieho 2022) in 1980—created momentum for the movement. F! undoubtedly benefited from several prominent court decisions pertaining to sexual offenses and also from mass anti-racist demonstrations that occurred all across Sweden in 2013 and 2014. These environments of mass mobilization outside of formal politics and protest against established practices increased the ability of these parties to embarrass the mainstream parties for having failed to address these issues.

Finally, all four parties styled themselves as outsider, novel, and connected to informal grassroots mobilizations. At least two of the parties, KL and FraP!, were true movement–party hybrids, drawing on deep and extensive women's movements and networks outside of formal politics (Lundin 2014). The Icelandic party evolved from an entity organized in multiple cities at the local level to rethink the boundaries of the political and engage women in the formal political process through nontraditional pathways such as theater, visual arts, and economic exchange. The party also used its public services around rape and domestic violence to draw women into formal politics. They even described themselves as "in but not of politics" (Einarsdottir 2015). This bridging of social movement and political party was key to KL's fresh and outsider character. In Zürich, the party also originated in informal groupings, and its membership crisscrossed many other civic organizations. Its repertoire was very social movement–like even inside the legislatures, which gave their small party a novel set of tools compared to other parties. The party gave the movement new resources, and the movement proved useful for garnering public attention and support/votes for the party. Together, they brought new actors into politics and introduced new approaches to the formal conduct of politics. The unwillingness or inability to take on formal party structures, however, turned into a liability at times for these parties. Both were internally divided over how to govern themselves and make decisions. Both struggled to produce policy statements and do the daily work of legislating. The other two parties lacked the grassroots depth, informal character, and street-level presence of the Swiss and Icelandic parties but had more professional leadership. At least for F!, the lack of community partners seems to have meant that the impact of the party receded with its electoral fortunes more than it did in the other cases.

Conclusion

These case studies clearly indicate that women's parties can trigger a process of competition and reform that increases women's inclusion, draws attention to new sets of issues, and shapes expectations of what politics is about and who participates. In short, these parties, even when short-lived and marginal, can contribute to a process that can be described as re-gendering parties in more equal directions (Beckwith 2005; Childs and Webb 2012; Celis, Childs, and Kantola 2016).

The experiences of these parties highlight the dynamic interplay between parties, legislative institutions, and gender. This process not only expands our understanding of the history of parties' treatment of gender in European democracies but also underscores the fact that, sometimes, institutional change is possible when formal politics mixes with the informal, or new institutional opportunities are manipulated by women's movements (see also Beckwith, this volume).

As Laurel Weldon notes, social movements can alter the inclusiveness of a political system by producing a collective consciousness, expressing and spreading the views of the marginalized, and enhancing the effectiveness of other institutions (Weldon 2011). Because every other party also includes women and campaigns to win the votes of women, the issues of women's parties are especially contagious and difficult to ignore. Thus, women's parties have a unique opportunity relative to other niche parties to shape the behavior of other parties and enhance the effectiveness of their representation of women.

These experiences, however, with the exception of the Swedish case, date to times when women's descriptive representation was especially low (less than 15 percent). The presence of gender quotas in many political systems in Europe may mean women's parties are less likely to emerge or be successful there in the future. Evans and Kenny (2019), in their study of the Women's Equality Party in the United Kingdom, note the difficulties of women's parties making an impact in contexts where parties are already at least partially feminized, have party quotas in place, and/or are already competing over women's representation.

As scholars and activists around gender equality know, however, the campaign for gender equality is ongoing and mainstream attention to it often only episodic. Given the power of these examples, even the threat to mobilize separately can be a useful tool in the repertoire of women's movements everywhere.

Notes

1. More extensive development of these cases can be found in Cowell-Meyers 2011, 2014, 2017, 2020.
2. This is less true of the Swedish party, where descriptive representation was already some of the highest in the world.
3. There was a significant jump in the number of women in the Westminster Parliament when the Labour Party introduced all-women short lists in 1997, but the increase was not repeated in subsequent elections or in other parties.

Notes

PART III
TRANSFORMING POLITICAL PARTIES

Debates around the relevance and real-world impact of political science as a discipline have increasingly entered the field of party politics, presenting challenges and opportunities for engagement. Here, mainstream party scholarship has much to learn from gender party researchers, many of whom were never in the academic "ivory tower" to begin with. Here the "feminist" moniker of feminist institutionalist (FI) studies reflects an imperative to both investigate but also redress gender and other inequalities in political parties and institutions (cf. Campbell and Childs 2013). In this part, we shift the focus to the gender politics academic as change actor—evaluating both the opportunities for and constraints to "re-gendering" political parties and drawing on research and reflections from FI scholars involved in change efforts.

First, Tània Verge—a gender politics academic and the former (and first) Minister of Equality and Feminisms in the Catalan Government—looks beyond gender quotas to explore the adoption and implementation of party gender action plans in Spain, focusing not only on the feminization of party organizations in terms of women's numerical representation, but also the femin*ist*ization of parties in terms of transformative gender-equitable change. In the context of broader feminist networks between activists, party members, politicians, and academics (including her own movement back-and-forth between these different categories), Verge highlights how FI concepts and insights have made their way into these kinds of strategies, shaping wider understandings of the interplay between the formal and the informal, and of gendered and intersectional party power dynamics.

Building on this contribution, Sarah Childs makes the case for a Gender-Sensitive Political Parties (GSPP) approach as a new way of approaching the re-gendering of political parties, drawing on the growing body of practitioner and academic work on gender-sensitive parliaments (GSP). Drawing on her experiences over the last decade as a *feminist academic critical actor* engaging in GSP work in the UK Parliament, she draws out the wider lessons learned from this work for gender-sensitive reform of political parties, and outlines the potential dilemmas that gender politics academics seeking to undertake this kind of work may face in their endeavors.

Finally, Carmen Geha sounds a cautionary note, drawing on her experiences and research as a Lebanese scholar, activist, and practitioner to outline the limits of change in ethno-nationalist power-sharing systems amid multiple ongoing "man-made" crises. Her contribution vividly highlights the tensions between international agendas around "women's empowerment" and the realities of male-dominated political parties, which are often the preferred partners of international development organizations. Arguing that international narratives of "empowerment" ultimately marginalize women—placing the onus for change on women themselves, rather than on discriminatory and un-democratic formal and informal institutions—she ends with a call for a feminist "re-imagining" of empowerment, centered around feminist principles of co-creation and collective mobilizing.

14

From Feminization to Femin*ist*ization Through Party Gender Action Plans

Tània Verge

Most research on gender and political parties has addressed the question of how parties are gendered organizations that (re)produce multiple inequalities and power dynamics with effects on candidate selection processes (see, among others, Norris and Lovenduski 1995; Kittilson 2006; Kenny 2013; Bjarnegård 2013), intra-party democracy (Childs 2013a), and, more broadly, their day-to-day functioning (Verge and de la Fuente 2014; Verge 2015). As discussed earlier in this volume (see Meier, Lang, and Sauer), this has relevant normative implications for assessing how and to what extent parties do act in practice as a vehicle for democratic equality and inclusion. Scholars have also examined the process of (and resistance to) feminizing party decision-making bodies and electoral candidacies through the adoption of quotas (Kenny and Verge 2016; Lang et al. 2023; see also Josefsson, this volume). Yet, studies on more comprehensive reforms aimed at re-gendering the party organization are still few and far between (Dean and Maiguashca 2018; Verge 2020).

Furthering our knowledge on these specific types of change trajectories and their encompassing processes is crucial, since political parties are the "major distributors" of traditional masculinity in politics and, therefore, "the work of equalizing men's and women's representation must begin in the political parties" (Lovenduski 2005, 56–57). Indeed, gender-sensitizing efforts in parliaments are limited if political parties do not undergo their own gender-sensitizing process (see Childs, this volume). Building on feminist institutionalism (FI), this chapter fills such a gap by focusing on how the gendered nature of political parties can be recast by adopting new rules that seek to displace their "institutional sexism"—i.e., the naturalization of male biases underpinning personnel, policy, and organizational arrangements

Tània Verge, *From Feminization to Feministization Through Party Gender Action Plans*. In: *Gendering Party Politics*. Edited by: Meryl Kenny and Elin Bjarnegård, Oxford University Press.
DOI: 10.1093/oso/9780197793985.003.0014

(Lovenduski 2005, 52). More specifically, given the scarcity of statutory measures in national constitutions or party laws to further gender equality in politics beyond electoral gender quotas (Childs 2013b), this chapter delves into how party organizations can be femin*ist*izized or depatriarchalized from within in order to redistribute power.

International organizations recommend gender action plans in political parties as a "roadmap" not only to increase women's political participation but also as a broader gender sensitization process of internal policies and procedures (Organization for Security and Co-operation in Europe 2016, 50; see also Organization for Security and Co-operation in Europe 2014; United Nations Development Programme & National Democratic Institute for International Affairs 2012). Whereas this strategic reform is still rare across the world, it has flourished in Spain among political parties ranging in the ideological spectrum from social democracy to the radical left.

The first section of the chapter, "From the Feminization to the Feministization of Party Politics," conceptualizes feministization processes in mainstream parties and the power-distributional implications of the gendered rules configuring the various dimensions of the party regime that such processes must target. The second section, "Feministization in Practice Through Gender Action Plans," identifies the feminist innovations in this direction devised by several parties in Spain, mainly through the adoption of gender action plans and other reforms introduced in party bylaws. The documentary analysis also surveys electoral manifestos and resolutions from party congresses. While assessing the extent to which the various measures are effectively implemented and the resistance they may meet would merit an analysis in its own right (see Verge 2020; Josefsson, this volume; Childs, this volume) and cannot thus be covered in this chapter, the facilitating factors leading to the adoption of gender action plans are nonetheless discussed.

From the Feminization to the Feministization of Party Politics

Feministizizing, rather than merely feminizing, politics is gaining momentum in the Left (Dean and Maiguashca 2018; Roth, Zugasti, and de Diego Baciero 2020). Indeed, the political integration of women and its impact on the introduction of women's policy concerns in political party or parliamentary decision-making processes—that is, feminization—cannot be equated to feministization. For one thing, women's interests are diverse, including both feminist and non-feminist (or even anti-feminist) policy platforms. Furthermore, FI scholars have also cautioned against deterministic accounts of the relationship between descriptive and substantive representation (Celis et al. 2014; Campbell and Childs 2015).

While quotas have the capacity to modify the gendered distribution of positions in electoral tickets or party decision-making bodies, expectations about a direct relationship between women's presence and policy outputs or organizational changes are both unrealistic and unjust. On the one hand, meriting inclusion should not carry the burden of having to make a difference (Lovenduski 2005, 177). On the other hand, women may be included but not integrated in terms of substantive power (Childs 2013a, 93; see also Meier, Lang, and Sauer, this volume). Several forms of inequality, exclusion, and even harassment are still found in gender-balanced institutional or organizational settings, where women elected representatives and party officers often remain outsiders on the inside (Verge and de la Fuente 2014; Martínez-Cantó and Verge, 2023; see also Kosiara-Pedersen, this volume). In addition, gender-equitable change efforts are usually met with resistance in political parties and parliaments (Franceschet 2010; Kenny and Verge 2016; see also Josefsson, this volume).

Subverting parties' gender regimes, including women's unequal access to resources, organizational gender blindness, and the multiple gender biases entrenched in the informal norms and practices that underpin their daily functioning (Verge 2015) requires an explicitly feminist redesign. Feministization is thus a conscious re-gendering process of party politics aimed at displacing the deeply entrenched "institutional sexism" that produces ingroup and outgroup logics, and at locking in new rules that promote gender justice. In a nutshell, feminist reengineering in political parties requires setting in motion an institutional transformation to depatriarchalize the organization and to institute feminist political practices, building on an inherently feminist vision of political change. Given the diversity of feminist currents, the ways in which feminist-inspired change may unfold in political parties will differ. However, liberal feminism's ethos falls short in the analysis of power dynamics, particularly from an intersectional perspective, and is thus a limited approach to develop strategies to subvert them (Roth, Zugasti, and de Diego Baciero 2020, 13; see also Arruzza, Bhattacharya, and Fraser 2019).

Feministization processes will not happen in a vacuum but are likely to be shaped by party cultures and the broader context. Despite the historical tension between the Left and feminism, left-wing political parties can be expected to be more permeable to feminist innovations (Dean and Maiguashca 2018). They are more likely to adopt gender quotas that are effectively implemented, carry out feminist policy analyses, and have party women's organizations with an explicitly feminist vision. On their part, feminist social activists and scholars are more likely to advise left-wing parties on how to "instigate" and "institute" feminist-inspired reforms (see Childs, this volume). Also, while the strength of the feminist movement in a given polity might be a source of external pressure and inspiration for the incorporation of feminist practices into parties' inner lives, feministization processes require a thorough understanding by party actors of how patriarchy is embedded in their organization and the ways in which gender—and its intersections with class, race, age, sexuality, or ableness—is productive of power inequalities.

Accordingly, the leading change agents can only be feminist actors who seek to transform gradually *but* also radically the rules of the game working in partnership with others. The latter include male allies from within the party, particularly in times of party renewal, and feminist academic critical actors who help change agents read the situation and accompany their reform efforts (see Childs, this volume). To have better chances of success, actors promoting change need a formal organizational structure from which to launch and sustain over time their strategic reforms. They also need to obtain the support of the party leadership, to resource the process, involve the whole organization in the implementation of the new rules, and deter open resistance that could harm change promoters' political trajectories within the party or in the institutional arena. In this regard, participatory self-assessments or gender audits of party procedures and practices can raise institutional awareness on extant biases and outgroup dynamics, building new alliances and legitimizing the call for action (Verge 2020).

Due to the significant transformation of party politics it pursues, feministization will be a "fluid, contested and complex" process in which "feminism is simultaneously endorsed and contained" (Dean and Maiguashca 2018, 384, 387). Feminist party actors do not have enough power to produce an outright displacement of the formal and informal rules sustaining institutional sexism. Thus, feministization is inevitably a "nested" process through which "the new is embedded in time, sequence, and its institutional environment" (Mackay 2014, 552). The implementation of the newly designed feminist institutional blueprints may face instability and uncertainty, with past legacies and inertias leading actors to "remembering the old" and "forgetting the new" (Mackay 2014, 550; see also Beckwith, this volume), even in new parties (Evans and Kenny 2020), or to deploying different forms of resistance (Kenny and Verge 2016). This is very likely to occur when feminist reforms target core elements of parties' gender regime (Verge 2020, 240). After all, political parties may be keener on incorporating new ideas than on reorganizing the distribution of power (cf. Kittilson 2006, 41).

Signing up to a feminist redesign entails at least three main transformations that confront the main dimensions of parties' gender/inequality regimes: personnel, organizational arrangements, and policy (Lovenduski 2005, 52–55):

(i) *Radical parity (or parity everywhere).* Feministization will not just happen in political parties simply because their executive bodies are gender-balanced, but the latter is a necessary condition (Roth, Zugasti, and de Diego Baciero 2020, 18). Parity in the distribution of all positions is fundamental to challenge and eventually displace male-centered institutional practices that yield segregation and hierarchies patterned through gender. A substantive participation of women across the various party's structures and activities can be regarded as an indicator of the "institutionalization of women's power" (Childs 2013a, 95). The latter can also be measured through the existence of formal feminist organizational sites with sufficient political weight and material support (funding, personnel, etc.) to influence decision-making processes. From an intersectional perspective, parity also means reflecting societal diversity, particularly of those groups whose lack of representation overlaps with historical patterns of socioeconomic marginalization (Phillips 1995, 175).

(ii) *Feminist intra-party democracy (or developing feminist ways of doing things).* For women (as the outgroup) to gain power relative to men and relative to where power lies (cf. Childs 2013a, 98), a feminist notion of gender balance must be coupled with a comprehensive understanding of presence and inclusion that seeks to subvert male dominance in organizational arrangements. This includes the informal rules that sustain pervasive biases toward certain kinds of masculinity in recruitment practices, the gendered division of labor, super-surveillance of women politicians, and ideas of gender-appropriate behavior in leadership styles and participation modes (Lovenduski 2005; Raychaudhury, this volume). A substantive change in this domain requires a feminist approach to more sustainable participation norms and practices and a more hospitable organizational culture so that women do not have to face double binds,[1] disregard for their interventions in party meetings, or exclusion from informal networks, leading them to retreat from politics or forgo career opportunities (Verge and de la Fuente 2014; Davidson-Schmich, this volume). It also entails addressing sexual harassment and other forms of violence against women in politics, which constitute a severe infringement of women's right to participate in political life (Krook and Restrepo Sanín 2020, 13; Kosiara-Pedersen, this volume). Feministizizing intra-party democracy should also entail identifying the outgroup logics grounded on race, class, ableness, age, sexual orientation, or gender identity, thereby addressing the "inequality regimes" (Acker 2006) and the corresponding intersectional inequalities that configure the organization (e.g., gendered–raced and gendered–class processes). Likewise, it should take into account the different participatory styles of individuals with subordinate identities, such as racial minorities (Brown 2014; Hawkesworth 2003) and disadvantaged social classes (Alcaraz Coca 2022).

(iii) *Acting for feminist interests.* Putting party policy at the service of societal transformation necessarily requires intersectional feminist analytical frameworks rather than non-gendered or neutral approaches in party manifestos, parliamentary and governmental activity, in order to address the needs of all women and avoid marginalizing some groups of women (Sanders et al. 2021). For this to occur, mechanisms guaranteeing that a feminist intersectional perspective is mainstreamed in party policy and communication strategies must be developed, such as coordination mechanisms between the women's sections and the various party committees or secretariats, external gender consultancy, or the provision of training for party members, party officers, and elected representatives on gender equality, feminism(s), and intersectionality.

Feministization in Practice Through Gender Action Plans

As Table 14.1 shows, starting in 2001, several left-wing parties in Spain have adopted gender action plans.[2] Prior to their adoption, these organizations had long-standing gender quotas for both electoral candidacies and party bodies that predated and surpassed the statutory electoral quotas in force in Spain—a minimum of 40 percent and a maximum of 60 percent of positions for either gender in candidate tickets—alongside strong women's sections and other types of specific organizational structures for women's participation. In the case of new parties, parity quotas were adopted upon their foundation (Verge 2023). Over time, the women's sections managed to gender the debates on equal political participation, establishing a tension between formal quota rules and male-biased organizational practices. This included shifting the focus from "why women participate less than men" to "why women are disincentivized to participate" in the party organization. In doing so, they strategically framed the needed transformation as a means to improve intra-party democracy, and, on some occasions, party leadership change presented a window of opportunity to align the reform with new leaders' vision of a renewed organization (Verge 2020, 241–242).

Participatory gender audits, led by the women's sections—often accompanied by feminist scholars and supported by the party leadership—preceded

Table 14.1 Political Parties' Gender Action Plans

Name of party (acronym in the original language)	Party type	Date of approval
Party of the Socialists of Catalonia (PSC)	Social Democrat, Catalonia[a]	2001
Spanish Socialist Workers' Party (PSOE)	Social Democrat, Spanish-wide	2002
Republican Left of Catalonia (ERC)	Social Democrat, Catalonia	2017
Podemos (Ps)	Populist Left, Spanish-wide	2020
Coalition Euskal Herria Bildu (EH Bildu)	Radical Left, Basque Country	2021
United Left (IU)	Radical Left, Spanish-wide	2022

[a] PSC is PSOE's sister-party in Catalonia.
Note: Only a few of these gender action plans are available online: ERC (2017), Podemos (2020a) and IU (2022).

the drafting of the plans. Such auditing process was instrumental in raising awareness and building feminist alliances among women party members and with some men local party officers, who volunteered to implement the gender reforms right away with a view to setting an example for the whole organization. The plans were approved by central party bodies (the executive committee or the party congress), thus becoming a formal rule that granted statutory legitimacy to the feminist-inspired redesign. While women's sections coordinate the implementation of the plans, the political responsibility for their effective enactment is assigned to central party bodies, in accordance with the collective dimension of the commitment emphasized in the very same plans.

Next, I move to outlining the actions seeking to instill the three main transformations discussed in the section "From the Feminization to the Feministization of Party Politics."

Parity Everywhere

With regards to electoral tickets, all parties under examination alternate women and men throughout party lists (vertical zipping) and select an equal share of both genders in position number one (horizontal zipping). This double zipping, which is the most effective quota under proportional electoral systems (Verge 2023), has been introduced in the respective party constitutions or the formal rules for drafting electoral tickets, and central party bodies supervise its implementation. Indeed, parity has become a taken-for-granted norm. Parity is also established for all types of institutional representation (i.e., gender-balanced cabinets and municipal councils) and party executive bodies. Some parties have even introduced a correction mechanism in their party constitution for the composition of party bodies when using open lists (Podemos) or when the presence of ex officio members in a party body may distort parity—e.g., extra seats for women are added until they reach at least 50 percent (IU). Exceptions on term limits are allowed for women to consolidate female leaderships in some parties (Podemos).

Emphasis is put as well on gender balance in those party offices with higher status and public visibility, such as spokespersons, secretariats for organization, or regional and local party chairs, which have traditionally been more masculinized (Martínez-Cantó and Verge 2023), thereby addressing both vertical and horizontal segregation. Reports on performance in this domain must be presented periodically before the parties' highest executive bodies. Parity representation is sought too among political advisors as well as in political events (ERC, IU, Podemos). Some parties plainly forbid their representatives to participate in all-male panels (IU), and others (PSC and ERC) have created an internal database of women experts on different domains to preclude excuses when party branches organize events. To attract more women members, some of the plans contain actions to feminize the party on the ground (IU, ERC), such as introducing a reduced membership fee for women (for instance, in ERC, the reduction is equivalent to the extant gender pay gap in Catalonia) and for single-parent families.

Although only one organization has formalized in its party constitution the principle of social diversity (IU), the latter is increasingly gaining traction as an informal norm. All parties admit that their representatives should reflect much more diversity, and they have elected or appointed "political firsts" from various political minorities in all institutions, which is a symbolic act that broadens the social imaginary of which bodies belong to institutional politics. PSC-PSOE's parliamentary group included the first LGBTIQ+ persons of the Spanish lower house (a gay Member of Parliament [MP] in 1999 and a lesbian MP in 2011), the PSOE elected in 2019 the first transgender woman MP in a regional assembly, and Podemos' parliamentary group included in 2016 the first Black women MP of the Spanish lower house. In Catalonia, ERC appointed in 2018 the first minister (Labor and Social Affairs portfolio) with migrant origin, and in 2021 it appointed the first Roma person in a senior position (director of the Office for Equal Treatment and Non-Discrimination) as well as the first director general of migration policies who was herself a migrant.

Concerning organizational structures, women's sections are included in the highest party bodies as a secretariat in its own right—Secretariat for Feminist Policies (PSC), Secretariat for Equality (PSOE), Secretariat for Intersectional Feminisms and LGBTIQ+ (Podemos), Secretariat for Feminism (IU), Secretariat for Feminisms and LGBTIQ+ (ERC), or Feminist Secretariat (EH Bildu).[3] In some organizations, the party constitution sets out that this secretariat must be present in all decision-making bodies at all party levels (Podemos and ERC). In half the parties, LGBTIQ+ policies also fall under the purview of these secretariats (Podemos, ERC, and EH Bildu).

In all parties, women's sections actively seek to engage with feminist social organizations and feminist scholars.

Furthermore, half the organizations have a coordinating structure that integrates the federal, regional, and local women's sections of the party (EH Bildu, ERC, and Podemos). Formal sites for women members' networking and for the adoption of feminist political proposals also exist across the board—namely, the Women's Assembly (ERC), the Women's Space (EH Bildu), the Network of Feminism (IU), the Feminist Working Group (Podemos), and the Socialist Feminist Council (PSC).[4] Migrants' participation or antiracism is channeled through a long-standing party sectoral branch or area, most commonly named Citizenship (PSC) or Citizenship and Migrations (ERC), but also Migration Policies (PSOE) and Cultural Diversity (EH Bildu). Yet, as will be discussed in the subsection "Acting for Feminist Interests" most women's sections have assumed intersectional feminism in their analytical frameworks and policy proposals (Podemos, IU, ERC, and EH Bildu).

Feminist Intra-Party Democracy

The feminist analysis underpinning party gender action plans has also helped put the focus on recasting organizational arrangements, so that parties' inner life is more hospitable to women and participation is more sustainable for everyone. The plans thus include actions aimed at debunking expectations of time-intensive activism (EH Bildu), including problematizing hyper-activism in social networks (Podemos); facilitating online connections (ERC and PSC); establishing more horizontal and less hierarchical debates; counting who participates in meetings and establishing mechanisms for equilibrated interventions by gender or an equitable distribution of speaking time; paying attention to the implicit gender biases that may occur during meetings (IU, EH Bildu, and Podemos); and monitoring that an equal share of human and material resources are allocated to men and women party officers to perform their responsibilities (PSC). Some party constitutions explicitly mandate the removal of obstacles that may hinder women's active participation (Podemos and IU).

Moreover, care values are defined in the action plans as a key organizational feature and as integral to feminist participation modes. To start with, party congresses and conferences must provide childcare and playrooms in all left-wing parties under examination. Furthermore, time uses are identified as crucial to guaranteeing the right to political participation, recognizing that time availability varies across members and that the pace of participation must be inclusive, in order to make it compatible with everyone's life, regardless of age, type of job, and family responsibilities. For this reason, all plans establish that starting and ending times must be set up for the meetings of all party bodies at all levels (local, regional, and national) taking into consideration work–life balance concerns. Likewise, agile intervention methods are to be used in order to guarantee both that women participate in the discussion and that time schedules are respected. Whereas all plans include as an action the collection of sex-disaggregated data in all areas of party work, no specifications are made on which body is tasked with this function except in the case of the IU, where an annual report on the participation climate is to be drafted by the Commission for Care.

To tackle the higher turnover rates of new women members and women elected officers, mentoring and training programs are devised. For instance, in IU, new women members are to be welcomed by a senior women member, with a view to identifying and channeling her interests into participation within the party as well as to help her navigate organizational processes; in EH Bildu, peer groups of new members are to be created. The setting up of informal networks among women is also defined as a goal. In this light, ERC launched in 2021 a feminist leadership training program aimed at building intra-party sorority networks and at providing feminist knowledge (on intersectional feminism and on the mainstreaming of gender in public policy), leadership, and communication skills to women party officers and elected officials. Spanning over six months, the number of applications has substantially overcome the 20 positions offered each year by the program, according to party sources. Specific training programs and sessions are also run in some parties for the women occupying the secretariats of equality/feminism at the local and regional levels (PSOE and ERC).

Regarding anti-harassment policies, the PSOE was the first party to impose a membership suspension for those party representatives facing gender-based violence complaints, including sexual harassment. Nowadays, all left-wing parties under examination have adopted internal anti-harassment protocols,[5] including a specific reporting, investigation, and sanctioning procedure, which is managed or supervised by the women's section. IU's plan also includes as an action setting up "purple points" in its recreational activities (public events, concerts, or fairs) to inform about the zero-tolerance policy of the party and assist potential victims, and ERC has established a counseling service for party women members who have suffered political violence or discrimination inside or outside the party—e.g., attacks on social networks. EH Bildu's plan is the only one that foresees specific training to party members aimed at reinforcing prevention against gender-based violence.

Analyses of raced (or raced–gendered) party rules are virtually missing in the self-assessments preceding the action plans, which yields no specific action to subvert them, with the exception of Podemos, which calls for the adoption of an antiracist perspective in the functioning and organization of the party in terms of visibility, representation, recognition, and reparation. Yet, there is no concretization of this goal, and the only actions that make an explicit reference to antiracism are the creation of spaces for cultural exchange and the provision of training on diversity, which are, at best, soft antiracist measures.

Acting for Feminist Interests

Feminism appears in the party constitution of all six organizations as a core principle, as a feature of their self-identity. An analysis of party manifestos, party positionings for International Women's Day (March 8th), or resolutions from party congresses indicates that these left-wing parties align with different feminist currents. PSOE and PSC subscribe to radical feminism, with very few references made in their documents and policy proposals to the heterogeneity of the subject "women" or their diverse needs. Moreover, various women party officers and elected or appointed representatives have publicly expressed their discomfort with the expectation that feminism has to "bear the burden" of LGBTIQ+ or antiracist vindications, and they have increasingly adopted a trans-exclusionary position.[6] In sharp contrast, the remaining political parties embrace intersectional feminism and an understanding of feminism as a political project for global justice, with references to "feminism for the 99%" (Arruzza, Bhattacharya, and Fraser 2019) along with explicit antiracist and transinclusive standpoints being repeatedly found in their party documents and public discourses.[7]

The women's sections of these six parties are integrated in the committees tasked with drafting electoral manifestos, thereby guaranteeing that feminist policies are included. Typically, these policies tend to be grouped into a specific section, rather than being mainstreamed throughout the manifesto. This strategy has pros and cons. On the one hand, it helps voters identify the party's feminist pledges. On the other hand, it may fail to mainstream a feminist perspective into "core" policy fields, such as the economy or security—which tends to be the case. Intersectionality is still poorly developed in party manifestos, although it is increasingly present and has been gradually introduced in institutional action.

Feminist policies have been prominent in governing plans, and specific portfolios that stand on equal footing with the rest of cabinet portfolios were created. The so-called progressive coalition pact for the Spanish Government (2019–2023), signed by PSOE, Podemos, and IU, included a section on feminist policies (PSOE-Unidas Podemos 2019), and the Catalan government led by ERC defined the "feminist transformation" (Generalitat de Catalunya 2021) as one of the four axes that structured the legislature's policy roadmap (2021–2024). These feminist platforms were coupled with the creation of a Ministry of Equality in the Spanish Government (led by Podemos) and a Ministry of Equality and Feminisms in the Government of Catalonia (led by ERC). Both designed antiracist policies and other non-discrimination measures beyond gender equality and LGBTIQ+ policies, and also counted with specific directorates-general for LGBTIQ+ rights and antiracism. Furthermore, the exchange of feminist blueprints or best practices implemented by local governments has been set up by some parties to promote their emulation by other city councils they led (ERC and EH Bildu).

Last, the plans mandate that external communications should emphasize the ways in which parties work for gender equality in various policy domains (PSC, ERC, and EH Bildu), and specific campaigns are to be regularly run on feminist policies to raise social awareness and increase the party's appeal to women voters and potential new members. For example, in 2022, ERC ran the campaign "Stop the Gender Pay Gap" through social networks as well as on-site in over 20 municipalities throughout Catalonia. Likewise, with a view to making members cognizant of women's contributions to the party's political project and to broadening the collective imaginary, some plans establish communication actions to make visible historical women figures of the party (PSC and ERC).

Conclusion

This chapter has shown that feminist-inspired reforms can be undertaken by mainstream political parties through gender action plans that aim at displacing the institutional sexism underpinning their organizational culture. Given the broader feminist networks shared by social activists, party members, politicians, and scholars, and the back-and-forth movement of the latter—including the author[8]—between these categories (cf. Childs and Dahlerup 2018, 187), it is hardly a coincidence that both gender audits and action plans draw on feminist institutionalist contributions. For instance, explicit references to gender-biased informal norms and practices feature quite prominently in these documents.

The feminist transformation processes outlined here provide several insights for various strands of scholarship, including FI, gender and parties, and mainstream party politics, on how party change can occur, even in the absence of major constitutional, electoral, or party system changes. Likewise, insights on how equality and inclusion can be furthered in political parties have practical implications for candidate selection, intra-party democracy, parties' day-to-day functioning, and institutional politics and policy. In essence, the feministization of political parties warrants feminist agency, but setting in motion an institutional change aimed at displacing institutional sexism needs a sufficiently strong intra-party feminist organizational structure to launch such a reform. Equally crucial, change agents need key alliances with the party leadership to preclude open resistance. Whereas some feminist innovations can take root in the short-term, involving the whole organization in this reengineering process and having reforms effectively implemented requires both time and resources along with a sustained commitment to feminist change.

While the magnitude of the goal and the "nested newness" (Mackay 2014) character of feministization processes unavoidably entail incremental rather than overnight changes, substantial feminist outputs have been achieved, particularly with regards to radical parity and acting for feminist interests. The organizational arrangements dimension, which is the core of parties' gender regime, is transforming at a slower pace. Yet, we must not lose sight of the fact that it *is* changing, and that women party members have learned to identify and denounce instances of exclusion and marginalization as eminently political, which is in itself disruptive and collectively empowering. Political intersectionality is also making significant inroads in most parties, although it still requires further development, particularly with respect to the analysis of how party regimes are shaped by multiple axes of inequality and their interlocking dynamics.

To conclude, when initiated, the feministization of mainstream political parties may be a work in progress for a while, but it is not utopian, and its impact is significant in both party and institutional politics and policy.

Notes

1. These include the tension between time-intensive participation norms and social gender norms regarding care responsibilities, or between intra-party activism on feminist substantive representation and chances for successful political careers (see Verge and de la Fuente 2014).
2. While gender action plans are mandatory in Spain since 2007 for all public administrations and for companies with over 250 workers, and since 2019 for companies over 50 workers, this measure was only recently extended to political parties. The first legal obligation of this sort was introduced by the Parliament of Catalonia in 2020, when the region's gender-based violence law was updated(Verge 2021). The Constitutional Court, though, annulled this measure on the grounds that only an organic statewide law can impose obligations on political parties, but by then the Government of Catalonia had already managed to introduce political party gender action plans in the Spanish-wide bill on gender-balanced representation, which was passed in August 2024 (Act 2/2024).
3. The use of the word "feminism(s)" rather than "equality" or "women" in these sections' name is relatively recent.
4. The Socialist Feminist Council is the only body of this sort opened to men's participation—since 2011. The PSC is also the only party with organized men for equality, the so-called Egalitarian Socialist Men group. Originally it was a sectoral party branch sponsored and mentored by the women's section that later on became a collateral organization.
5. While anti-harassment protocols are statutory since 2007 in all workplaces in Spain, only the Catalan law against gender-based violence established this obligation for political parties in 2020. As in the case of gender-action plans, the Constitutional Court suspended such measure. This notwithstanding, since 2022, the Spanish-wide Act 10/2022 mandates parties to adopt anti harassment protocols, thanks to an amendment to the bill submitted by the Government of Catalonia. Furthermore, The Catalan law is the first law in the European context to recognize violence against women in politics (Verge 2021), which has led the Parliament of Catalonia to adopt as well an anti-harassment protocol that includes the staff, MPs, political advisors, interns, external contractors, journalists, and visitors.
6. This opinion was expressed on the eve of 2023 International Women's Day by Carmen Calvo (eldiario.es 2023), former vice president of the Spanish Government (2018–2021), chair of the parliamentary committee on equality, and Secretary for Equality of the PSOE (2017–2021).
7. See, for example, Podemos's 2020 party congress resolution "A Feminist Transition" (Podemos 2020b) or ERC's 2023 party congress resolution, with a specific section titled "Feminist Sovereignty" (ERC 2023).
8. In the last decade, the author of this chapter has accompanied two of the political parties examined here in their internal gender auditing processes and coordinated the elaboration of the Equality Plan of the Parliament of Catalonia. Between May 2021 and August 2024, she was the Minister of Equality and Feminisms in the Government of Catalonia, a cabinet portfolio created for the first time in that term.

15

Gender-Sensitizing Political Parties and the Feminist Academic Critical Actor

Sarah Childs

I am sitting next to Prof. Meryl Kenny in a Committee Room of the Scottish Parliament. We are academic Members of Holyrood's Gender-Sensitive Parliament (GSP) Advisory Board, job-sharing the role with our colleague Fiona Mackay. We have just discussed the Audit's four-part foci with the Presiding Officer and a number of elected representatives (MSPs), parliamentary officials, and Scottish women's civil society group actors.[1] The Audit, and the final Report *A Parliament For All*, are to be structured around the following themes: (i) women's representation and participation in parliament; (ii) institutional infrastructure; (iii) parliamentary culture; and (iv) women's substantive representation/policy outcomes. Specifically, Meryl and I underline that *as an audit of the Parliament*, the research and most importantly its attendant recommendations will target *what Parliament can do* to embed the principle and practices of gender sensitivity at Holyrood.

The discussion immediately turns to political parties and their recruitment processes that gatekeep candidate selection. To keep the GSP Advisory Board MSPs' attention on the actions that Parliament can undertake, Meryl and I *have* to respond. I have been here before: when I was seconded at Westminster in 2015–2016. Neither of us disagree with the MSPs about the many ways in which political parties—and the dynamics of party politics—determine women's participation and representation. Rather, it is appreciation that parliaments frequently have limited capacity to instruct political parties to behave in certain ways that is foremost in our minds. Parties operate to lesser or greater degrees independently, and in some places largely as private organizations, reflecting country-specific legislative and regulatory frameworks. In contexts of light regulation, as in the United Kingdom, GSP

Sarah Childs, *Gender-Sensitizing Political Parties and the Feminist Academic Critical Actor*. In: *Gendering Party Politics*. Edited by: Meryl Kenny and Elin Bjarnegård, Oxford University Press.
DOI: 10.1093/oso/9780197793985.003.0015

actors are constrained in what they can require of political parties. Unless political will is mobilized for new gender-sensitive laws and regulations, GSP recommendations directed at parties will almost certainly end up relying on exhortation and any associated incentives, and in so doing, lack prescriptive and/or strong accountability and enforcement measures. This was very much the case with regards to the UK House of Commons. *The Good Parliament* Report's numbered recommendations aimed at parties can only be adjudged slight—overwhelmingly indirect and vague (Childs forthcoming, Chapter 4; Childs 2016; see also Lovenduski 2017).

If the potential of GSP audits is frequently limited vis-à-vis political parties, a complementary approach is to advocate for parties themselves to undergo gender-sensitizing processes. Parliaments lacking sufficient authority and/or political will might, as before, not be able to mandate this, but gender-sensitive audits of parties should be in any GSP "shopping basket" of recommendations, nonetheless. In line with this rationale, a recent Inter-Parliamentary Union (IPU) GSP assessment included the following among its many recommendations: Undertake 'gender sensitive' political party audits, and develop 3–5 year action plans, including reviews of party constitutions to include substantive commitment to gender equality.

In making recommendations for gender sensitive political party audits there is a notable, and explicit, extension from a GSP to a Gender-Sensitive Political Parties (GSPP) approach. That this recommendation was made by the international organization most responsible for the promotion of GSP work over the last decade or so, may prove particularly significant, if others also active on GSP, such as the Commonwealth Parliamentary Association (CPA), the European Institute for Gender Equality (EIGE), Organization for Security and Cooperation in Europe (OSCE), and UN Women, follow suit.

Against this contemporary backdrop, I make the case for considering GSPP a new way of conceiving of and approaching the feminization or re-gendering of political parties—the classic Politics and Gender (P&G) terms for the reform of traditional, male-dominated, and masculinized political parties.[2] A working definition of GSPP is provided below (see also Verge, this volume), following a brief introduction to the concept and practices of GSP. That said, my contribution here is less about detailing the specifics or the operationalization of a GSPP approach.

Instead, and having spent a considerable amount of time since 2005 and especially since 2015 undertaking impactful research (i.e., advising party women's activists, Members of Parliaments [MPs], and parliamentary officials), my central goal is to show how lessons learned as a *feminist academic critical actor* engaged in GSP work in the UK Parliament have wider application to gender-sensitive reform of political parties. My new category of "critical actor" (Childs and Krook 2006, 2008), is at times quite different from the "gender expert/advocate" form of *feminist critical friend* who has worked with political actors in the past (Chappell and Mackay 2021; Childs and Dahlerup 2018). There are practical, tactical, and strategic, as well as potentially risky or harmful dilemmas that almost certainly need to be considered and worked through before deciding whether to adopt such a role, but the putative feminist academic critical actor is helpfully guided and bolstered in their efforts by the insights of feminist institutionalism (FI). Accordingly, I contend that undertaking GSPP work constitutes the kind of impactful work that some P&G scholars might—and in my opinion should—turn their attention to as a worthwhile undertaking that augments existing feminist work on political parties (see also Verge, this volume)—and one that, in bringing about party and party-system change, should have positive knock-on effects for parliaments too.

To Gender-Sensitive Political Parties, via Gender-Sensitive Parliaments

The concept of a GSP dates back to 2001 and the CPA's "Gender-Sensitizing Commonwealth Parliaments" Report, although it took the IPU twin publications, authored by Sonia Palmieri (Inter-Parliamentary Union 2011, 2012), to popularize it. Distilling its core elements, and appreciating the necessity of an intersectional approach, we define GSP as a parliament that

> Values and prioritizes gender equality as a social, economic and political objective and reorients and transforms a parliament's institutional culture, processes and practices and outputs towards these objectives.
>
> (Childs and Palmieri 2023, 177)

A GSP four-dimensional framework is detailed in Table 15.1.[3]

Table 15.1 Four Dimensions of Gender-Sensitive Parliaments

Dimension	Definition
Dimension 1: Equality of participation in parliament	Ensuring a diverse composition and achieving equality of participation.
Dimension 2: Parliamentary infrastructure	How parliament organizes itself and supports the work of Members.
Dimension 3: Parliamentary culture	Making the culture of the parliament more inclusive.
Dimension 4: Gender-equality policy/women's substantive representation	Subjecting the political work of parliament—its outputs—to gendered analysis.

Source: Amended from Childs and Palmieri 2020, 475.

To make the case for extending GSP concept and practices to political parties depends, in the first instance, upon its reframing and reorientation. One might, for example, make the following IPU GSP questions applicable by removing the old object—parliament—and inserting a new object—political parties:

- Are *party* facilities suited to men and women?
- Is the culture of a *party* non-sexist, or does it privilege traditional masculinized ways of operating?
- Are men—*party leaders, members, and activists*—shouldering their responsibilities in respect of gender equality?
- Is there a *party* plan of action for gender equality?

Alluding variously to mothering, the domestic division of labor, unequal socioeconomic resources, and the gendered use of public spaces, the following, illustrative sub-questions are suggestive of the form and substance of an ideal, gender-sensitive political party across the four dimensions of gender sensitivity. Inter alia:

Are *party* recruitment processes delivering gender-equal opportunities and outputs, in respect of elected, appointed, and/or official party positions? Is there attention to women and men's retention and promotion across these positions? (Dimension 1).

Are local party offices and meeting places, or conference locations and buildings, accessible to all? Is there affordable, safe, and reliable public transport? Are *party* activities (what is undertaken, where activities take place, how they are undertaken) suited to both men and women? What childcare and breast/infant feeding provisions are available, and to whom? Are policy workshops three hours long with toilet breaks scheduled for only five minutes? (Dimension 2)

Are the "normal ways of doing things" *within the party* assuming or privileging a masculinized ideal of a party member, activist, elected or appointed, and/or official? (Dimension 3).

Do *parties* elide the "good constituency member" with availability to "door-knock" on weekends, precisely when parents are shuttling children between various social and sporting activities? What "outreach activities" are rolled out, and do these reproduce traditional assumptions about gender and politics? "Politics and a pint" may on first blush seem inclusive of previously excluded groups but will disproportionately reach (certain kinds of) mostly men. Does the *party* code of conduct name sexual harassment, and is it accompanied by an effective and independent complaints procedure, with which party members and workers have confidence? And, to what extent are *party policies* responsive to the perspectives, needs, and interests of women, and champion gender equality? (Dimension 4)

Does the *party* place gender equality as a priority on its policy platform or manifesto? How much of this re-gendering work is left to "willing women," rather than a formalized, institutional priority of *party* leaders and officers, irrespective of gender?

At this point, the reader may be asking what the advocacy of a GSPP approach would bring to existing P&G scholarship on political parties and party change (cf. Young 2000; Childs 2008). Very much in sympathy with Verge (this volume), who details party gender action plans as an important, albeit to-date under-utilized mechanism of political party re-gendering, or in her words, "feministization" (Verge 2024; OSCE 2014; 2016), my answer is three-fold. The first part lies in the systematic and holistic assessment of the gender *in*sensitivity of political parties, which underpins the production of a comprehensive reform agenda and attendant, and resourced, change strategy. This is not just a tinkering around the edges of parties' organization and structures, practices and cultures, and ideas and practices, but ultimately provides for their radical re-gendering.

The second part lies in the potential for the concept of gender sensitivity—as an increasingly high-profile international democratic norm—to confer status (and thus, in turn, political will) on the re-gendering of political parties in respect of what they are and the work that they do, which to-date is relatively limited and with a much lower profile and focus. There is an important debate to be had about what is "gained and lost"—in theory and on the ground, and especially beyond left parties—when one appeals to ideas of gender and/or diversity sensitivity, feminization and feministization, gender equality and de-patriarchialization (Verge, this volume; Ahmed 2012; Childs forthcoming). The third part of my answer lies in what GSP work can tell us—again both theoretically and empirically—about the critical actors, processes, and effects of GSPP, the central focus of this chapter.

The full translation work needed for the development of a comprehensive and intersectional GSPP framework, including the development of party-oriented standards, toolkits, guidelines, and field guides akin to that which exists for GSP, is a key task for future research. This work can only benefit from collaborations between academics, international organizations, and political party actors. These collaborations would not only cement, and importantly expand, current connections but also learn from the real world lessons of GSP interventions to-date (Palmieri 2019; Verge 2020; Childs and Palmieri 2023). Such collaborations will also better showcase GSPP work internationally and thereby lift the concept and practices of party feministization—audits/assessments, recommendations and reforms, and action plans and accountability measures—up the global political agenda, making this the twin and not the Cinderella of gender-sensitizing work.

Lessons from a GSP Feminist Academic Critical Actor

In the remainder of this chapter, I focus on the final part of my answer for bringing GSP to political parties in terms of what the former can tell us—theoretically and empirically—about the actors and drivers of feminist change. This is not to say that actors are absent from feminist institutionalist or indeed new institutionalist theory; they are not, but they have gone by many different names which at times renders them less well-defined (Childs forthcoming). As a direct consequence of reflecting on my own GSP work in the UK House of Commons between 2015 and 2018, I explicitly insert the P&G concept of critical actor within FI theory and broaden its meaning.

It is in the blurring of (i) the academic who studies and (ii) the practitioner who acts on and in parliaments that the new type of critical actor—the feminist academic one—emerged. Distinct, accordingly, from the MP depicted in the original conceptualization (Childs and Krook 2006, 2008), she is also distinct from Chappell and Mackay's (2021) feminist critical friend (FCF), as gender expert/advocate. If the FCF is characterized by her criticism of the institution she is *studying* and through her supportive actions regarding internal actors, the feminist academic critical actor is critical in the sense of being *essential* to instigating and instituting institutional change. Having accepted the feminist impact imperative to act on the political world (Campbell and Childs 2013), the status of the feminist academic critical actor is dependent upon documenting how—*as a consequence of their direct acts*—they worked within and on an institution to realize change. In addition, then, to applying a classic formulation of an FI inquiry to political parties (following Chappell 2006; Kenny 2013)—when and under what conditions, and in respect of which reforms, institutional change happens—I also want to know when and under what conditions the putative feminist academic critical actor is allowed "into a party" to undertake GSPP work—what agency she has, with whom she allies within and outside the institution, and in the face of what response (cf. Waylen 2014, 219; Franceschet 2017, 141; see also Puwar 2004, 80–81, 94; Miller 2021).

It was only while embedded in the House of Commons that I realized that FI was my *methodological toolkit.* It told me that the "feminist art of the possible" is (more than) okay; that the feminist academic critical actor's responsibility is to identify and exploit institutional "soft spots" and "internal contradictions" (Chappell and Mackay 2021, 2); and that dead-ends and blocked paths are to be expected (Mackay 2021; Ahmed 2012). To achieve critical but nevertheless institutionally grounded knowledge, the feminist academic critical actor combines her academic expertise with new observations in situ. She may look at first to the existing comparative parties literature. These analyses will, however, require a feminist re-reading before they can be of much use. Party scholars rarely analyze the presence or absence of women in parties—as members, activists, and leaders—or how gender structures and mediates (understandings of) the forms of and relationships between voters, members, and leaders (and civil society); intra-party organizations; intra-party democracy; party policy making processes and outcomes; and party formation (Kenny et al. 2022; see also Bjarnegård and Kenny, this volume). Pre-sensitized to gendered institutional rules/norms and interactions between actors from her

FI schooling, the feminist academic critical actor, reconsiders through her academic feminist lenses all that she is observing and feeling in the institution or organization that she is seeking to act upon. But first she must, of course, get access.

Access

The feminist academic critical actor knows that women in general, and feminists in particular, are less likely to be "invited in" (following Geddes 2018). Unlike some parliaments, party approval is more likely to be on the basis of an informal arrangement, even if it still requires a formal "signing off."[4] Established, esteemed, and more mainstream scholars might be considered advantaged over the neophyte and/or (perceived) critic, although the young academic may at the same time be regarded as less threatening and therefore more welcome. Some political parties will simply be more amenable than others on ideological grounds whereas others may stoutly refuse to engage.[5] Where the feminist academic critical actor is (perceived to be) associated with one party, access to others might be thwarted, although inter-party competition might yet come into play.[6] Making overt reassurances regarding fairness and reasonableness—drawing attention to esteemed research records, cross-party relationships, and/or to previous consultancies or (in)formal advisory roles—are excellent access strategies, but they may not persuade the skeptical party actor. We may need to agree to delay publications or even to not publish—a price some putative feminist academic critical actors may not be willing or able to pay. At the same time, such strategies, nay "deals," risk complicity in constructing colleagues as the feminist "other"—that is, the excludable critical actor. Initial access is in any case only the first step. Achieving impactful change is unlikely to be the result of a one-off interaction and so sustained relationships are premised upon the ongoing performance of acceptability. All of the above is, then, a repeated performance.

Authority, Legitimacy, and Knowledge

Daily traversing the outsider/insider border, the feminist academic critical actor's two prefixes compound: her authority to be present *and* speak is very much open to question on both grounds, separately and combined.

The academic title might be only begrudgingly given respect; "knowing" in an academic fashion is all too often considered abstract and theoretical. Any assumption that the Professor "ranks" higher than the Dr. and PhD candidate should not be accepted uncritically; as previously stated, authority may be inversely related to tenure and rank. When depicted as elite, the academic is placed both out of step with the people as well as the political class. "Classic" fieldwork practices of professionalism, objectivity, and groundedness may only temper party actors' tendencies to perceive partisanship, intellectualism, and critique (i.e., leftist ivory tower-ness or even a simple "them vs. us").

The feminist prefix is likely regarded as more disturbing still: biased in a "shiny, metropolitan café, feminist way."[7] The feminist academic critical actor might try to hide or dilute her feminist politics, although university ethics procedures, departmental websites, and/or social media will usually publicize our politics. Working with feminist party insiders, the feminist academic critical actor is also likely to find herself accused of attracting and associating with the wrong kind of informants and making inappropriate friendships with institutional "sisters," who are themselves mistaken in what they think about the institution or organization (Childs forthcoming). In such instances and/or where we are otherwise regarded as the puppets of others, the feminist academic critical actor becomes someone who might be heard (if only for the optics and to show she was not excluded), but who, nevertheless, the institution need not listen to.

Agency and Persuasion Work

The putative feminist academic critical actor is engaged in a *double performance*—research *and* persuasion work. In respect of the latter, she must convince critics and supporters alike that hers are the right and not just technically appropriate solutions. In this, more is asked of her than the usual day job. Rarely, if ever, are academics formally taught how to be changemakers. At the same time, what differentiates the feminist academic critical actors' GSPP work from the work of feminist party insiders and from outsider activists engaged in institutional transformation, is precisely our *dual location* in the academy and, albeit temporarily and precariously, "in" an institution or an organization. In undertaking GSPP work we are working with academic feminist knowledge about parties as well as "live," situated knowledge of the party—observing opportunities and obstacles that internal party actors may be blind to or unable to address. It is in precisely the intertwining of the feminist understanding and imagining of what parties can—and should—deliver for diverse women, cut with lived experience of the party—observations of its structure and practices, as she interacts with multiple party actors—that makes the feminist academic critical actor well placed to act. In this, and in other words, her job is to mediate between the ideal, preferable, and feasible, mindful of what is gained and lost by asking for something and not another thing, at this particular or later moment in time, and working with these allies within and beyond the institution or organization.

Accountability

The feminist academic critical actor must judge what gender insensitivities she can address given her context, and the extent to which she can exploit any conduciveness, and bypass or overcome critics' counteractions or wider constraints. Recognizing the identity and positionality of those who occupy particular party posts and roles, and how they act within these places—which (in)formal rules they enact "day in and day out"—will guide the feminist critical actors' strategic and tactical acts. Once again FI is instructive, guiding her to work with institutional norms and align with institutional practices, and when to act otherwise. For example, when encountering resistance that frames the obstacles faced by women as the same as those faced by men, or when told that gender is but one of many issues to be considered, the feminist academic critical actor might accept that the arguments are made in good faith by the genderblind or she might regard them as disingenuous attempts at dismissal and/or silencing (Childs and Palmieri 2023).

Ultimately, the feminist academic critical actor will have to "live with" her GSPP recommendations and strategy. (Extra)institutional actors of various kinds—including feminist ones in the academy and in civil society—will no doubt hold her to account for what gender insensitivities are included and excluded, how, and within what time frame. At Westminster I leaned heavily on my Advisory Board and MPs' Panel, and "feminist in residence" and "secret clerk," and I would advise the putative feminist academic critical actor to properly build a feminist design coalition, with other academic, political party, and civil society feminists to act as a collaborative sounding board at the very least (Lowndes and Roberts 2013). For, when one's approach, analysis, and recommendations are questioned, and especially when criticism comes from those whose feminist stance you share, whether within the academy or from the political world, it is reassuring to know one's decisions of GSPP "red lines" have already been tested.

Personal and Professional Risks

The feminist academic critical actor seeking gender-sensitive ends will almost certainly "invite" resistance if not backlash (see also Josefsson, this volume). This is because she does what the institution or organization has been unwilling or unable to do (Ahmed 2012, 25). Parties, like parliaments, are empirically the places of elite men, with proven records of exclusion, marginalization, and harassment. In parliaments, elected representatives might be formally "above the law," protected by privilege or bolstered by claims to their electoral mandate. Absent workplace or organizational protections, the feminist academic critical actor engaged in GSPP acts is also at risk and perhaps even in danger. We know, for example, that gendered political violence is experienced at higher rates by women of color, and we can unfortunately expect the same for impactful researchers from these and other minoritized communities (see also Kosiara-Pedersen, this volume). In a hotel bar meeting with a party election campaign manager, the need to maintain access to information about his party "outweighs" the harm of the thigh rubbing, and/or the harm that comes with calling it out. And didn't he just know this when he decided to sexually harass? If such abuse is toward one end of the spectrum, the feminist academic critical actor also risks reputational damage from actors—political, media, academic—who question her political/ideological impartiality and/or her professionalism (Stoker 2013). The precariousness of the contemporary academic post, increasingly an issue for the Early Career Academic, will further influence one's "freedom" to undertake this work. Such are the realities of becoming a feminist academic critical actor—costs that bear not just on the individual but also on the very gender-sensitizing actions she is able to undertake.

Conclusion

The subfield of comparative party politics has recently been accused of having lost its focus on the "bigger" picture (Gauja and Kosiara-Pedersen 2021). The same, as Kenny et al. (2022) make clear, is simply not true for P&G scholars (see also Dahlerup 2017; Lovenduski 2019; Celis and Childs 2020). We are acutely sensitive to the harm that anti-democratic, populist and authoritarian politics causes women and other marginalized and minoritized groups (Verloo 2018; Kantola and Lombardo 2021b; Lombardo, Kantola, and Rubio-Marin 2021). Because our parliaments, and the political parties and politicians that comprise them, can take away rights and further inequalities, many P&G party and parliamentary scholars hold that electoral politics must remain an important site of feminist resistance. Contending, too, that as parties and parliaments become more gender-sensitive, representative democracy will become more responsive to the good representation of women and regain stronger health. These claims are additional drivers for the feminist imperative to change the political worlds that we study. The central claim in this chapter is a simple one: that gender-sensitizing interventions undertaken by feminist academic critical actors have the potential to substantially re-gender political parties, akin to GSP work on parliaments. Reflections on questions of agency and institutional change based on my experiences undertaking GSP work are, in my opinion, translatable to GSPP acts. Admittedly, becoming a feminist academic critical actor may not be possible or desirable for all or even most P&G scholars. Our identities and positions—academic and other—mediate access to and the success of the embedded, gender-sensitizing work we engage in. That said, by offering up observations *as* a feminist academic critical actor, and in presenting the case for other P&G scholars to take up the mantle in respect of political parties, the intention is to start a new conversation about how we as academics might make political parties feminist.

Notes

1. I use the terms "audits" and "assessments" interchangeably, in part because on the ground the terms are used interchangeably—but also because I do not regard the former as inherently or necessarily more quantitative, objective, or "tickbox" nor the latter as more qualitative, subjective, or "deeper."
2. Regrettably, feminization/re-gendering has rarely been addressed by the comparative parties subfield. Kenny et al. (2022) offer a critique and a large bibliography of P&G research.
3. NB, in *The Good Parliament* I chose to analyze only the first three dimensions, due to Dimension 4 falling mostly under the purview of the government, and also because of a lack of resources. I also worked with the concept of "diversity"-sensitive parliaments in response both to the challenge of intersectionality and to the questioning of "gender" as exclusive of men and ignoring men's "family" commitments, as well as in recognition of other groups who are also underrepresented in the UK parliament. A qualified defense of this shift is made in Childs forthcoming.
4. Access to a parliament is more likely to be by a formal scheme. (https://www.parliament.uk/get-involved/research-impact-at-the-uk-parliament/academic-fellowships/.) There is a significant advantage when gatekeepers require only minimal knowledge rather than a full breakdown of a project.

5. For example, when they agreed to participate in interviews, the EUGenDem team (https://projects.tuni.fi/eugendem/) were stymied by Popular Radical Right parties' stonewalling.
6. This might seem a substantive difference to gaining entry to a Parliament—multi-party arenas—but one should not assume that access determined by an independent Speaker or Presiding Officer automatically negates such partisan criticism (Childs forthcoming). I would like to thank Tània Verge for emphasizing the point about parties linking the feminist critical actor with their opponents.
7. As one woman MP once said to me (Childs forthcoming).

16

Exploiting Empowerment in Lebanon's Sectarian Political Parties

Carmen Geha

Political parties are major organizational vehicles for the promotion of gender equality as a set of policies as well as the representation of women in politics. In contexts where women's representation continues to be dismal, local and international organizations and donors have placed resources and expertise in attempts to empower women to enter politics. This chapter argues that women's political empowerment is untenable within the context of sectarian political parties and corrupt electoral practices. Pursuing political empowerment and representation when women are not offered protection and equal rights can be a cumbersome task falling on the shoulders of the oppressed while inadvertently "empowering" those who oppress them. A political empowerment agenda that places the onus on women themselves also personifies the struggle for representation and moves it from the realm of collective struggle to the realm of the individual's capacity. When reduced to a set of skills and individual capabilities, political empowerment becomes illusive and largely removed from a broader institutional context that places formal and informal constraints on women's access to political rights.

This chapter is empirically set in Lebanon and specifically in the period from 2019 to 2023, offering insights from activists, electoral candidates, and gender experts. It is based on research that explores how foreign-funded women's political empowerment programs influence, or are influenced by, the nature of Lebanon's sectarian political parties. The chapter advances a feminist institutionalist (FI) critique of Lebanese political parties as instrumentalizing women's political empowerment while blocking key reforms for women's rights. A century-old sectarian power-sharing agreement among male leaders has prevailed despite civil war, occupations, and the most

Carmen Geha, *Exploiting Empowerment in Lebanon's Sectarian Political Parties*. In: *Gendering Party Politics*. Edited by: Meryl Kenny and Elin Bjarnegård, Oxford University Press. © Oxford University Press (2025). DOI: 10.1093/oso/9780197793985.003.0016 recent economic and public sector. This power-sharing agreement even survived the October 17 Revolution in 2019, allowing sectarian warlords to co-opt, oppress, and discredit hundreds of thousands of people that called for reform and accountability. Political parties and party leadership in Lebanon draws support and legitimacy from religious authorities, foreign allies, and networks of clientelism (Cammett and Issar 2010). The path-dependency of power-sharing has shaped the development of sectarian political parties for over a century. The chapter concludes by calling for a re-imagining of political empowerment through feminist principles of co-creation and collective mobilizing.

I am writing this as a Lebanese scholar, activist, and practitioner who worked on women's political participation in various capacities. As an academic, I researched and wrote about this using tools of co-creation and participatory action research. I was also extremely active in Lebanon's 2019 revolution, often blurring the lines between scholarship and street activism and advocacy. I also experienced first-hand and organized collective feminist action following the explosion in the Beirut port on August 4, 2020. I have deep friendships, ties, and histories with many of the participants and audiences affected by this study and with whom we co-created the questions and reflections that went into this analysis. I write this chapter two years after my migration from Lebanon following the multiple crises and continued state of impunity across the nation. This chapter is based on findings and reflections from 15 interviews, conducted in 2023 and 2024, with Lebanese feminist political activists and participants in political empowerment programs. To protect the anonymity of participants, all quotes are presented without identifying names. Each participant is coded numerically (e.g., P1, P2, P3), with the code indicated after each quotation. When quotes were originally in Arabic, I translated them into English.

Impunity as an Antidote to Empowerment

The empowerment of women as a group, historically marginalized from politics, is usually geared toward the involvement of a larger number of women in decision-making (Moghadam 2010). But the process of empowerment should not be removed from the wider institutional and political context that causes disempowerment and marginalization. Lebanon's sectarian political parties have blocked potential reforms for women's rights for over a century and sustained a grip over government, including through critical junctures that could have shaken their power base.

Lebanon is governed through a sectarian power-sharing system that bolsters the role of sectarian leaders as guarantors of peace and survives through resources from outside the state itself. Formally, sectarian power-sharing requires that top positions of president, prime minister, and speaker of parliament can only be held by a Maronite, a Sunni, and a Shia respectively (Krayem 1997). Seats in the military, public administration, and justice system are likewise appointed through a system of patronage and consensus among ruling parties. Essentially, parties are run by a male leader and his close aides, often his family and business partners. Political parties are not institutional spaces of deliberation and contestation, and candidate selection for elections is done in closed secretive circles and heavily negotiated through foreign intervention. Gatekeepers for electoral candidates, basic services, and foreign relations are male-dominated and passed on to close family members or business associates (Cammett 2011).

Sectarian political leaders maintain a grip over public offices and dominate informal channels that mediate access to public benefits, rendering citizens as subjects who need to express loyalty to receive benefits (Cammett 2015). Women's formal political participation and representation is contingent—like men's—on their belonging to a sect. Sectarian affiliation bolsters the role of male guardians; when it comes to politics, these guardians are gatekeepers for elections, "The focus on individual choice is my problem, it is not my choice whether or not I have the backing of my family and the leader of my party. I barely even know him, I shake hands with him on occasion, that's it, he does not consult me on candidates and ministry nominations" (P15). A few men decide on voting patterns in their district as one participant explained, "I am very proud of the (few) women who made it to parliament last time. But so many of us who did things right did not stand a chance at winning because those districts had been swayed by the sectarian leader who tells them who to vote for, when to attack, and when to boycott" (P11).

The postwar Ta'if agreement in 1990 cemented sectarianism and did not include women at the negotiations table. Like in other consociational ethnonationalist contexts, gendered cleavages and women's issues were ignored (Kennedy et al. 2016). Completely genderblind, the amnesty law offered a clean slate to the warring factions and, through religious and geo-political backing, sidelined women from subsequent political dialogue. With nobody held accountable in the public realm, gender-based violence relegated to the private realm is also sustained through impunity.

The mainstream political parties in control of the country today and that were in power during the last five years of multilayered collapse are the product of this century-old sectarian power-sharing system. Participation and representation in this political system is predicated upon belonging and being loyal to one's sect, with sects represented by political parties that have a homogenous sectarian base. These political parties are formally registered at the state but do not abide by internal democratic bylaws. There is no way for people to hold political parties accountable because these party leaders operate outside state structures through informal negotiations and bargaining, often paralyzing state institutions for months and years to achieve partisan gains. For example, at time of writing, Lebanon's political parties have still not agreed on naming a president for over 18 months and have sabotaged parliamentary deliberations leaving the country without a head of state for more than a year and a half. Political parties also leverage foreign relations to maintain their local political status—including their relationships with international organizations, donors, and United Nations (UN) agencies—and draw legitimacy from these foreign alliances, religious leaders, and corruption.

Sectarian political parties therefore mediate the relationship of women with state and political institutions. Lebanon has held parliamentary and municipal elections since 1947, which have effectively excluded all "outsiders" to the power-sharing system, including women. Corruption privileges closely-knit circles of men who are seen as the norm in politics (Bjarnegård 2018c) through several institutionalized mechanisms that exhibit elements of continuity in each election. These include widespread and well-documented bribery and coercion, as well as gerrymandering districts into sectarian homogenous groups (Corstange 2012). The uncompetitive nature of the electoral system in Lebanon gives the upper hand for men to appoint other men on lists in return for funding and favors. The 2009 parliamentary election had one of the highest recorded bribes per vote, and only four women, out of 128 total seats, were elected to parliament. Under a new proportional law, sectarian political parties added more women into their lists in 2018, with the exception of the Iran-backed Hezbollah party, which publicly announced that parliamentary activities were not considered an appropriate place for women. But even though more women were nominated, the share of women elected only rose from 3 to 5 percent.

In 2022, inspired by the revolution and subsequent new political parties that emerged after 2019, there were many lists and candidates opposing the mainstream sectarian parties. However, the number of women elected only rose to eight out of 128, a mere 10 percent. During the election campaigns, women's participation and representation in the media as candidates comprised only 12 percent of the coverage (Women in News 2022), while online digital violence and hate campaigns were almost entirely directed toward women (Maharat Foundation 2023). Lebanon still maintains one of the lowest rates of women's economic and political participation worldwide (Inter-Parliamentary Union 2024).

Creeping "Man-Made" Crises

I deliberately use the term "creeping man-made crises" to refer to the context of Lebanon as an "extreme context" characterized by uncertainty and a proneness to eruption. An extreme context is one where crisis begins to denote the new normal and render it almost impossible for people and organizations to plan and anticipate challenges (Wilson et al. 2010). This context requires coordination and responses that are of large magnitude, and a strong level of monitoring and adaptation. At the same time, such overlapping unresolved crises are not synonymous with an emergency context; Lebanon exhibits a form of "slow-burning" or "creeping crisis" (cf. Boin et al. 2020, 121) as a result of multiple unresolved challenges that remainunaddressed by political parties in control of state institutions.

Lebanon's current crises are rooted in institutional policies and practices that sustain sectarian power-sharing. Despite failing public institutions, economic collapse, the devastating port explosion, and a majority of the population reeling under poverty, decisions still require a consensus among ruling parties. Political parties acquiesce on the form of governing through sectarianism and electoral gerrymandering but lack consensus over reforms. In the absence of consensus, as for instance the election of a president, vacuum and paralysis prevail. A "no" decision by political parties halts the functioning of state institutions, but is no obstacle to political parties themselves, which continue to deliver services through clientelist networks.

In October 2019, an unprecedented wave of protests led to a revolution that lasted several months, marked by a systematic role for women and feminist collectives which took the lead to demand an end to the sectarian regime. The revolution was met by oppression and violence that culminated with the advent of the pandemic in March 2020 and the utter collapse of Lebanon's public institutions and banking system. The aftermath was not the political empowerment of women but a sense of defeat, described by one participant, "When we were all out on the streets, the issue of women's representation was a collective demand, we shouted together and tried to make it to politics altogether. Right now it is an individual thing, great for those who can make it as a candidate but most of us cannot" (P4). The port explosion on August 4, 2020, killed over 200 people, destroyed 300,000 buildings, and devastated any remaining infrastructure including schools and hospitals. But political parties succeeded in blocking a national investigation, and at the time of writing not a single official has been held accountable. As one participant explains, "We have lost the public spaces we once occupied, the streets where we marched, the media attention we once commanded. Now it is all these men, those murderers back on screen and still in power" (P2).

The aftermaths of the explosion were politically similar to the aftermaths and regional context that coincided with the end of the civil war in 1989. The port explosion did not break the pattern from past "business as usual" but instead cemented a historical pattern of oppression, exclusion, and corruption that we can trace back to over a century of man-made deals by sectarian leaders. In many ways, the postwar impunity granted to warlords has been granted to the explosion culprits. This dissuaded many feminist activists from politics broadly and elections more specifically: "I do not want to even be near those men" (P13).

Widely recognized as "man-made," these crises are leading to rapidly deteriorating mental health conditions, particularly among the most vulnerable and isolated groups in Lebanon (Farran 2021). For experts and activists, like me, there appears to be no vision for the end of any of the multiple crises. Participants describe an increased sense of insecurity, leading many (including myself) to retreat from confrontation of those in control. As one participant explained, "You can be the most empowered and capable woman in Lebanon, look at me, who is stronger than me? But empowerment does not protect me from warlords and their followers who raid our streets at night" (P12). In fact, at the time of writing, an impending war between Israel and Hezbollah has led to an estimated 100,000 displaced. Unprecedented and mounting backlash on women's rights and gender equality is also taking place (Mendelek 2022). This has set back the work of feminist organizations: "The war in the South of Lebanon puts us again in emergency mode, daily news of attacks, sounds of Israeli drones above our heads, we are back into victim mode" (P4).

Universities teaching gender studies are accused of promoting delinquency in society. Long-standing organizations working to stop gender-based violence have come under attack by religious authorities. One expert explains, "We had worked collectively so hard for many years to make the state assume responsibility for women's rights and protection, this was our aim before the collapse, and now this feels like it has gone down the drain. We are back to being isolated in our homes" (P8). Queer-friendly spaces and bars have been physically attacked by self-organized local religious mobs. In addition to blocking reforms, Lebanon's political parties continue to instrumentalize these crises to sustain their power base and extend their time in power. According to one participant, "We are facing daily micro and macro-aggressions making it impossible to imagine being in politics right now. We went from wanting to be represented in politics to just keeping our heads down and wishing for good health" (P6).

Exploiting Empowerment, Evading Reform

Against this backdrop, Lebanon is also home to a long-standing feminist and gender-equality history of resistance and mobilization. The feminist movement in Lebanon—centuries-old and rooted in decades of war and conflict—has mobilized against sectarian politics and for equality during all critical junctures of modern history, including in the wake of the Beirut port explosion. From university campuses, hospitals, schools, businesses, theater, and arts, and across conflict zones, feminist activists have built networks of solidarity and advocacy seeking to transform Lebanon's deeply rooted obstacles to gender equality. Since the 1920s, this movement has accompanied nation-building and grown to a more inclusive form of organizing with greater assertion around equality and inclusion for LGBTQ+ community, and not only for women's rights (Stephan 2014). In the absence of a functioning state and in the shadow of sectarian political parties, feminist collectives have worked on sexual and reproductive health, established new public health services, offered free litigation, protested and slept on the streets, and established social businesses to help impoverished communities. I have been one of the actors in this context and initiated several campaigns on anti-corruption, gender equality, and freedom of assembly.

While this chapter is not focused on taking stock of all of the spaces and forms of activism, it is important to foreground women's political empowerment within an indigenous movement that has long demanded equality in politics and sought political representation, although its efforts have largely remained confined to informal grassroots politics. Although we managed to construct safe spaces of mobilization and solidarity, reforms for women's rights have remained blocked. Lebanon's electoral system continues to favor sectarian political parties and clientelism at the expense of women, and other independent candidates from outside the ruling parties. What appeared possible, in terms of activism and participation, before these crises is now farfetched, according to one participant: "The economic crises take up all our energy, every month I battle with rent, and my female friends accept jobs in bad conditions just to put food on the table. The idea that we can run for elections and miraculously fix things does not work here" (P4).

While sectarian parties are responsible for the marginalization of women and entrenched corruption in elections and governmental appointments, they also accept women's political empowerment workshops and participate in them, especially around election time. These workshops remain politically neutral when it comes to state responsibility and the role of sectarian political parties in perpetuating the status quo. Indeed, in the lead up to the parliamentary elections of May 2022, as political parties were burying evidence of the port explosion, and in the wake of a new wave of assassinations, sectarian political parties still nominated women to attend political empowerment programs. In fact, political parties were the main target groups for women's political empowerment programs and campaigns funded by international donors and UN agencies. This empowerment took two forms mainly: candidate-training and awareness-raising for a women's quota. But candidate-training can be a burden on the women themselves, especially those women from outside the sectarian parties, as one participant explained: "It's like they are telling us we need to do more, be better, be stronger. It is not enough that we battle our own survival every day, now we need to run for elections and fix the system that is run by the same criminals who cause our suffering" (P8).

Experts and activists also criticize the ways in which political parties instrumentalize programs, for example, "We attend these workshops knowing very well that the women attending represent parties that are oppressing us, that sent armed groups to shoot at us, and that have no interest in our freedom. At the end, they go back to their parties, and we go back to being alone and utterly controlled by their leaders" (P5).

To understand why true political empowerment cannot be promoted by sectarian parties, three institutions that work together to maintain women's *dis*empowerment should be highlighted. First, each Lebanon ruling party is led by a male political leader known as the *za'im* (pl. *zu'ama*), who represents a sectarian community and is legitimized by the religious leader of that sect. Male zu'ama prefer male candidates and party loyalists; according to one expert, "The parliamentary agenda is pre-set, that is if parliament even meets, and so even if you have the most ambitious agenda for change, it is near impossible to put our own issues on the table. Decisions to convene or boycott the Parliament are made by a handful of men, most of whom are not even parliamentarians" (P9). The za'im is the spokesperson, deal-broker, and decision-maker on behalf of his community and is responsible for nominating candidates for elections and government. Parliamentary politics in Lebanon are pre-set by male zu'ama through deals often secured outside of parliament. In fact, some of the most powerful political leaders are not Members of Parliament: "When women do win, they are really left on their own. Parliament is dysfunctional and the men there are ... settling scores and stamping all over our Constitution. Empowerment without help in moments of threat is useless, we need a women's movement not a training workshop" (P14)

Second, as already highlighted, sectarian political parties have sustained clientelistic electoral processes for decades and gerrymandered districts to obtain a majority vote from specific sectarian communities. According to one participant, running for elections is not appealing, "Preparing a campaign agenda is very important and having expertise on certain issues is essential. But elections here are not about knowledge and fairness, they're about blood and settling scores, it is no place for women like me to be in" (P13). Political parties secure votes way before any election through a web of services and benefits that extend to municipalities at the local level. In reference to trainings on political participation, one participant explains, "These kinds of campaign processes work in a democracy, and Lebanon is not a democracy. It is not true that if we work hard, we will make a difference, and we keep creating hope and then proven wrong, over and over again" (P11).

Third, parties use religious courts to maintain women's legal subjugation. Despite decades of campaigning for a unified civil status law, Lebanon's parliament continues to block such a proposal, leaving women at the mercy of the religious court assigned to them upon birth into a sect, not a nation. This legal framework favors men in all aspects including custody and inheritance. Child marriage laws differ on the basis of each religious court, with some courts allowing marriage as early as nine years old. Sectarian courts promote male dominance of women since they are born. The legal system has worsened amid recent crises, leaving women without protection from violence and harassment. Even women who win parliamentary seats are not immune to violence: "We see the women Members of Parliament every day under attack, such violence, such vile male behavior, and such dirty politics. I do not want to ever run for politics in this context and risk being harassed every day and disappointing my voters" (P2).

These institutions are sustained by all political parties equally. While their foreign allies might differ, their stances on local women's rights are the same. Sectarian parties extend their governance through male patronage over state resources. Lebanon's collapse economy has made it easier for (some) men, who are allies to sectarian leaders, to win, because for the rich and powerful the depreciation of local currency presents an opportunity to sustain bribes and services, whereas for the marginalized local depreciation has taken food off the table. Women—historically underpaid compared to men, legally disadvantaged, and politically marginalized—are expected nevertheless to be "empowered" to carry these burdens and enter a system that was designed to keep them at bay.

Amid the current crises, whatever state capacities were left have been depleted, leaving women at greater risk of gender-based violence that manifests in discrimination in the political and public spheres. Participants describe elections as risky: "Running and winning could be dangerous, who will hire me after this and especially if I go against the men in my party? I would consider it if we were a large and coordinated movement, but alone I am not going to stand against the men in my party. I prefer to sit aside in this period and hopefully this dark cloud will pass" (P6). Even for those women who were active in feminist organizations, the current context is impossible to navigate: "The police stations and court system are not working, with no fuel or electricity and constant strikes, it is not realistic to expect women to stand up to the daily violence and harassment we face in politics" (P5).

Despite local and international pressure for reform following the port explosion, political party leaders and zu'ama did not undertake a single reform to combat corruption. Without such reforms, the International Monetary Fund and World Bank will not extend any loans to Lebanon. The gendered effect of this non-reform is that political parties continue to govern through rules and practices that are essentially anti-women's rights.

To provide women equal and fair rights would require a strengthening of the judiciary, a democratization of elections, and a capacity-building for public institutions to protect women. Instead, political parties simply agree to training programs aimed at empowering women to run as electoral candidates. This, in fact, is dissuading many from taking on such a role: "What happens after women win? We are thrown into a lion's den of shouting men, murderers, and warlords that are too invested in obstructing justice to let anyone do their work. Running and winning depletes our energy while they [the men] continue growing stronger" (P14). For some women, these trainings' focus on women's roles in mitigating peace were divorced from the reality of a system based on consensus among a handful of men: "I am not convinced that simply more women in power will make Lebanon better, we are being trained to be pigeons of peace in the face of warring factions. I am not sure this is the right messaging, and I am not convinced that more women would make Lebanon safer" (P12).

Finally, the narratives in this study show how political parties have misused empowerment to empower themselves while leaving women isolated. Despite a negative transformation in the political and security context, candidate-training for elections remained largely similar in both content and format. Political parties were asked to nominate women who attended a series of seminars and skill-building workshops in the lead up to the 2022 parliamentary elections. Most of the content of training workshops and seminars are focused on the formal electoral aspects of competition and good governance. Participants are trained on key political and public administration issues in Lebanon including for example fiscal policies, decentralization, and public debt. The general assumption here is that if women do well, they stand the same chance at winning as men, and that state institutions actually work to serve women. As I have written elsewhere,

> The logic of fair competition, in addition to being utterly normative, places the blame entirely on women and does not consider the noncompetitive institutional characteristics that keep the same men in power.
>
> (Geha 2019, 17)

This idea that women who work hard will have a chance at winning is largely misguided in a context where self-confident women can be attacked with no way of seeking justice: "I threw myself into running in the last election because of my deep convictions that this country deserves better. But I was not prepared for the wave of online and offline attacks against me, my family, my private history, and the worst part is that it worked, voters were swayed, and my personal credibility was tarnished" (P9). At the time of writing, the municipal elections continue to be at risk of being canceled by Lebanon's caretaker government, while ongoing trainings for women to run for municipalities are still taking place. None of the participants in this study negated the importance of bringing women together for support, but they all pointed out to the disengaged nature of these activities: "The trainer stressed the importance of women running and women's vital role in governance. We know this, but it is not up to us to run. If it were, trust me, we would be taking over" (P3).

Conclusion

This chapter has questioned the feasibility of women's political empowerment within a sectarian power-sharing system, plagued by multiple ongoing man-made crises. While much FI research focuses on when and why change happens, I explore when and why it does not happen, delineating the gendered (formal and informal) institutions that sustain the status quo in Lebanon and expanding the reach of feminist institutionalism to consider the limits of change in ethno-nationalist power-sharing systems. Focusing on women's political empowerment programs and women's experiences as the units of analysis is very consequential to our ability to theorize political parties from a gender lens. The gendered character and gendering effects of Lebanon's anti-women parties and political system have been highlighted through the narratives of the women interviews. In turn, their experiences add evidence to the argument that it is not women's ambition that keeps them away from politics but rather the gendered dynamics of politics and candidate selection (Piscopo and Kenny 2020). All of the participants in this study were politically engaged and aspired for a role in politics (me included) but argued that such a role would be impossible for most and dangerous too.

The findings here align with research in other parts of the world showing that political institutions and parties are gendered in terms of the distribution of political power and resources. Women can have ambition, but the plausibility of their choice to run remains guided by "relationally embedded" risk assessment, constrained by the masculinized ethos of political parties (Wylie 2020), which in the Lebanon case are male sectarian leaders relegating women to second- and third-class citizens. The chapter also expands a gendered understanding of clientelism within an ethnonationalist, sectarian political system and expands existing research on men's political dominance and male-dominated networks of corruption (Bjarnegård 2013, 2018c).

Where do we go from here? The chapter's guiding question on whether women can be truly empowered leads us to undertake a new project inspired by feminist institutionalism. For political empowerment to achieve its stated goals, we need to listen to women, including those who tried to enter politics and those who refuse to try. To that end, I have sought to co-create the questions and ideas together with participants in this research, recognizing also my own positionality as a longtime scholar-activist who recently joined scores of people who migrated from Lebanon due to the multiplicity of challenges outlined in this chapter. The women's narratives in this study, and my experience, provide a roadmap for re-imagining political empowerment along three lines.

First, the empowerment project should focus on easing the burden from the shoulders of women. Empowerment without access to justice and equal rights is not possible. We cannot expect women to continue to exhibit defiance in the face of extreme injustice. To accelerate empowerment, this project should be directed toward accountability of the men in charge—in Lebanon, this includes accountability across the continuum of violence, from civil war crimes, to the port explosion, to the daily aggressions that women face.

We need to reimagine empowerment as firmly rooted in feminist praxis and ethics of care amid multiple ongoing purposefully unresolved crises. Empowerment programs and efforts can build on existing networks of solidarity across the country and the world—networks that were so visible in the wake of the port explosion. The local and global mobilization against corrupt men in charge helped businesses reopen, staffed hospitals, removed bodies from under the rubble, and cleaned the streets from glass after the explosion. That mobilization is the continuation of a history of inclusive organizing that women have modeled throughout Lebanon's violent history.

Finally, women's political empowerment ought to be re-politicized and linked to Lebanon's prospects, or not, for democratic reforms. Nondemocratic sectarian political parties have not been the champions of women's rights (although some may continue to wish that they will have a change of heart). Politicizing political participation starts with the very structures of political parties, including their formal and informal decision-making processes. Empowerment can begin to take place when parties have democratic and functional internal bylaws that are not only written down but actually followed, protection mechanisms against harassment and other aggressions, and inclusive and transparent processes of decision-making around candidate selection and campaign finance. To even begin to conceive of such emancipatory possibilities for women's political empowerment, we need to advocate for an ethic of co-creation of what empowerment means; recognize the intersection of the formal and the informal; and focus on political and institutional reform, rather than reforming women. Without these commitments, political empowerment programs will continue to impede rather than facilitate women's participation and leave them to their individual fates.

CONCLUSION

17

Looking Back, Moving Forward

Editors' Conversation with Joni Lovenduski and Pippa Norris

Joni Lovenduski, Pippa Norris, Elin Bjarnegård, and Meryl Kenny

We end this volume not with a conventional conclusion but with a conversation with leading political scientists Joni Lovenduski and Pippa Norris, authors of foundational books that have profoundly impacted the gender and party politics subfield. Their contributions range from the first systematic contemporary edited volume on women and political parties, *Gender and Party Politics* (Lovenduski and Norris 1993), to the definitive work on candidate selection, *Political Recruitment: Gender, Race and Class in the British Parliament* (Norris and Lovenduski 1995, named by *The Guardian* in 2017 as one of the best books ever published on British politics), to later work on gender, political institutions, and representation like *Feminizing Politics* (Lovenduski 2005).

Together, and crossing different generations of scholars, we look backward as well as forward, reflecting on the field's development over time and the opportunities and challenges that lie ahead for researchers.

Building Foundations

MERYL KENNY: One of our touchstones for doing this project [the book *Gendering Party Politics*] was your work—*Gender and Party Politics* and *Political Recruitment* are foundational texts for most of us. What brought you individually as scholars, but also together collectively, to the study of gender and party politics?

JONI LOVENDUSKI: Well, I think we were on a train. We were going from somewhere to somewhere. We just decided that we wanted to get

Joni Lovenduski, Pippa Norris, Elin Bjarnegård, and Meryl Kenny *Looking Back, Moving Forward*. In: *Gendering Party Politics*. Edited by: Meryl Kenny and Elin Bjarnegård, Oxford University Press. © Oxford University Press (2025). DOI: 10.1093/oso/9780197793985.003.0017 involved in a large empirical project. From my point of view, I had published five books and various articles, essays and reports based on document analysis, textual exegesis, and interviews with local government and government agencies. I had a lot of field work experience but very little history of survey research and data analysis. So I was interested in doing that kind of work, which was also a good fit with Pippa's skills. And we both wanted to do some research on candidates for elected office, which we thought was the key to many of the questions feminists were asking about political representation. We thought it had legs, if we designed the right sort of application. And it took off from there.

PIPPA NORRIS: The Women and Politics Group in the UK Political Studies Association [PSA] was the network, I think, which brought us together.

JONI: The group, when first founded, had few members, and half were sociologists who popped into our meetings to offer moral support from time to time ... but it was about both empowering women and trying to get the subject on the agenda, so it had two manifestations. It took a long time before it started to have a critical mass of people working on women and politics.

In the PSA we were organizing, networking, figuring out how the institutions we were in worked, trying to get our people elected to leading positions, trying to get panels at conferences, etc. I took what I learned there to the ECPR [European Consortium of Political Research], and it was a very similar history and trajectory of trying to get people together. As in the UK, women doing PhDs on women and politics were being told by their supervisors that they should stop, otherwise they'd never get a job. That's what it was like.

PIPPA: And there were no women mentors anyway. So that didn't help.

I got involved in by-elections and then served as Principal Investigator for the 1992 British Election Study (BES), with John Curtice, Antony Heath, and Geoff Evans. I was interested in developing survey-based research on the relationship between mass public opinion in the British electorate and the attitudes of political elites, including grassroots party members and activists, parliamentary candidates, and elected Members of Parliament [MPs]. So that was part of the reason why we started work on candidates, to bring the two studies together. The BES focused on social class, at the time, with very little interest in many other forms of diversity. And we wanted to talk about how candidates were selected.

ELIN BJARNEGÅRD: Did you see yourself as women and politics scholars? Or was it rather that there was so much on parties and elections that just looked at class, and didn't have the gender aspect in there? Or was it really bringing both fields together?

JONI: I think it's fair to say that at the time, you would have had to have a colossal imagination and optimism to think that there was a big future in studying women and politics. So you had to hedge your bets. We were trying to convince other political scientists. I was also very interested in how to make things better for women, which I thought would be helped by increased political representation. But in those days if you framed a question about women from the outset you were accused of being biased, so you had to learn how to reframe. Looking back on it, I am amazed that we were being asked to buy an argument about value-free social science that no one had believed for decades.

PIPPA: There was always the long tradition of research on occupational class in British politics and sociology, starting with Butler and Stokes (1974). And the "secret garden" of candidate selection had been studied by others, including Gallagher and Marsh (1988). And so we could build on and expand on this foundation.

JONI: We had to secure party cooperation to get access to and conduct fieldwork on processes of political recruitment, including observing and conducting surveys of participants attending selection meetings. It's very different from the kind of studies you now get, which are general population studies with subsets on party politics. And I think that's an important shift and one of the reasons why the gender work and the so-called mainstream work hasn't come together.

We did *consider* studying sexuality and we decided that we wouldn't be allowed to. But we did pop in some sexuality questions in the survey so at least we got a little idea about attitudes.

MERYL: And how were you perceived as actors by the parties?

PIPPA: So here we have to bring in the anecdote of Joni's conservative shoes, which I vividly remember. We went to one of the selection meetings and we were meant to be the neutral observers sitting back ... using the qualitative work to inform our quantitative surveys. And before we went in, Joni changed into her Tory shoes, which were somewhat more conservative.

JONI: They were blue pumps, navy blue pumps.

PIPPA: And then we went in.

JONI: I used to keep them in the back of my car [for each political party]—red boots and blue pumps.

PIPPA: I think they thought we were [party members].

JONI: They asked us routinely if we wanted to be candidates. But I know from people who've gone and done candidate selection studies since that that always happens.

PIPPA: This was also the time when scholars in other countries were also interested in candidate selection processes and the barriers facing women in winning elected office. The network included, for example, Marian Simms in Australia and Linda Erickson in Canada, as well as colleagues in Europe.

And there was *also* interest amongst those who were just starting to study party members because, again, our project was designed as a multi-level survey. In our work, the "ladder of recruitment" included the incumbent MPs at the top, the nominated parliamentary candidates, and the activists who didn't get selected—often an excluded group in empirical studies of the political pipeline. And then, of course, the subset of selectors nominating candidates, the ordinary party membership, and voters in the electorate, at the bottom of the party organization. We always wanted to compare different levels in the ladder of recruitment. This also helped to build bridges from our work to related studies which didn't really focus on gender per se.

JONI: One of my favorite moments was at one of the first meetings of the PSA's Elections, Public Opinion and Parties Specialist Group, where two women and 100 men met at Worcester College in Oxford. And, at our invitation, following our meetings with him about the project, Tom Arnold came to speak. He was the Conservative Vice Chair for Candidates who had reformed their selection process at Margaret Thatcher's behest. It was a very supportive thing from him to do and it was a big coup. And when he got up, he made this speech, which he started off with saying that you should all be doing the kind of work that Joni Lovenduski and Pippa Norris are doing. And, you know, all these faces around the room just collapsed.

Gendering Parties and Political Recruitment

JONI: I recently re-read *Gender and Party Politics*, which I haven't done for a long time. And when you read the first and the last chapters, it's textbook institutionalism. It just pages through organization, structures, processes, cultures, formal and informal rules, patterns of logics of appropriateness, although we didn't call it that.

And as editors we gave all the contributors a detailed template and we made them stick to it for each country ... and that meant that the way the book came out, it was possible to make a systematic comparison.

PIPPA: I think the strengths of the books, and our collaboration, has always been that we come from different methodological angles. We gathered a lot of details from the candidate surveys about X, Y, and Z, but understanding what was going on behind these responses was difficult. And I think that's true also cross-nationally, for example when you talk to somebody in Japan or in Canada, they make certain assumptions about how the candidate selection process works in their cases. But then to supplement the surveys, we could also incorporate insights from the personal interviews that we recorded. And those proved very powerful because they told us a lot more about what was going on behind the scenes ... So, as I remember, we battled a little bit about the strengths of both approaches, the quantitative and the qualitative. But between us, we brought the two things somewhat together.

MERYL: Even though it's come under some critique, the "supply and demand" model outlined in *Political Recruitment* is still the dominant framework for talking about political recruitment, and especially gender and political recruitment. Why do you think it's still so useful?

JONI: I think it's because it's systematic. I think you can build out from it in various ways.

PIPPA: Yes, the model is a set of heuristic ideas. Basically, all my research follows a similar approach. I usually focus on a topic which is [i] theoretically interesting, where there remain unresolved scholarly debates; [ii] where further empirical evidence can be gathered; and [iii] where scholarly insights are policy relevant for tackling social problems in the real world.

Political recruitment met all three criteria. So, in the early-to-mid-1990s, the party selection process in the pathway for elected office remained the classic "secret garden" which was poorly understood. The research was "do-able" because we got UK Economic and Social Research Council (ESRC) funding and we used alternative approaches and a combination of skills and empirical backgrounds to conduct the study, which I think brought this area together. And key officials in British political parties opened the doors to us, because party leaders wanted to reform the selection process to include more women and ethnic minority parliamentary candidates to expand their party's electoral appeals.

The supply and demand model also struck a chord, particularly in Europe. In America, party control of the nomination processes was greatly weakened in the 1970s by the expansion of direct primary elections, weakening control by party activists. Other potential gatekeepers are often a hidden world difficult to identify and study systematically, like the role of campaign consultants, financial donors, volunteer networks, and newspaper editorial endorsements. As a result, American scholars of state and congressional recruitment have largely focused on studying the "supply-side" factors associated with candidate "ambition," including the social psychological attitudes and resource constraints, like time and money, helping to explain why women fail to gain office in state and federal primary and general elections.

But the more comprehensive "market" model we advanced proved more useful in the cross-national contexts where political party officials, party selectorates, and ordinary party members continue to be the main gatekeepers for gaining nomination to local and parliamentary office. Our heuristic model suggested that there is both the supply of the candidates willing to come forward, and the demand from gatekeepers, as well as the context of formal institutional rules that constrains both of those actors. This was the fundamental heart of the approach which others have adapted to each local and national context.

MERYL: It's interesting how that frame of ambition has also been imported (uncritically sometimes) to other contexts where parties have much stronger gatekeeping powers. This notion has shaped strategies to get women into politics and training women to become better candidates, but, ultimately, in most contexts, if you're not selected by a party, you're not going anywhere.

JONI: There's also the underlying assumption that women candidates have to be trained because there's something wrong with them, there's nothing wrong with the party.

ELIN: And that's still everywhere, I think.

PIPPA: And of course, this influences so much of the developmental work that's been done. Training projects hire international consultants to swoop in (it's basically a parachute model) two or three weeks before an election and teach women how to become better candidates. And of course, all we're doing is training women to fail half the time, because we don't understand the local structural constraints. Or the role of gatekeepers.

JONI: In Britain, a lot of the people who were against proposals for quotas, which they saw as power grabs by second wave feminists, changed their mind as less powerful initiatives repeatedly failed to deliver more women candidates.

PIPPA: The democratization process was also expanding, of course, in the late '80s–early '90s. So, it was a time of progressive hope that newly competitive multiparty elections would provide an opening for women and for other groups who were previously underrepresented. One of the things to emphasize today, decades later, is that processes of democratization and women's rights are heading rapidly in the reverse direction.

MERYL: So, what would you think now about the potential of parties as a vehicle for inclusion and women's representation?

PIPPA: One of the big things about institutional change is that it's sticky. We've seen the third wave era of progressive advance in democratization and women's rights from the mid-1970s through to about 2005. The subsequent process of democratic backsliding, and challenges to a whole range of rights for women and girls, can be observed since then in many, although not all, countries. But formal institutions are a partial brake on those reversals. Once you introduce a constitutional, legal, or party candidate gender quota, for example, it becomes more difficult to get rid of it, but not impossible by any means.

But then how the formal institutions work, and how the rules are implemented in practice, are closely associated with the cultural attitudes, values, and norms within any political party or society. Institutions like constitutional conventions, laws, party rules, and administrative agencies can function as a buttress against multiple types of gender backsliding, from issues of women in elected office to gender-related violence and reproductive rights, sexuality, and gender education. But when formal provisions for gender equality are rolled back, exemplified by the US Supreme Court's June 2022 decision to topple the constitutional right to abortion, abandoning *Roe v. Wade*, then a lot of other dominoes can fall quite fast as well.

Opportunities, Challenges, and Future Directions

ELIN: Are we still asking the right questions and are those that were the pertinent questions 10 or 15 years ago still the ones we need to ask? Are there new challenges we need to tackle?

JONI: What we're ultimately talking about is exchanges of power. What you're trying to do is change power relationships of a particular kind within an institution. And what seems to happen is that institutional actors learn how to reinstate those power relationships very quickly. So, it becomes difficult to predict trajectories of long-term change even in Western democracies. In less stable situations, obviously, the changes can be even more dramatic. What's embedded in this institutional-process approach are ideas about power that need to be drawn out more than they have been in the past. In the end, a focus on power is what we've got as political scientists. It's the thing we're supposed to understand.

PIPPA: I think that is a weakness of our intellectual work as well. We're still stuck in a lot of current research in the progressive era of advances in democratization and women's rights. The implicit question is, therefore, how to nudge this trajectory further and faster. Whereas in fact, any further progress may not be the case. If we look at more systematic trends, a plateau can be observed in terms of the proportion of women in parliament and broader dimensions of women's political empowerment, which suggest that dark times may well be ahead.

MERYL: The *Political Recruitment* text is also path-breaking in that it looks at gender, race, and class. As the intersectional imperative has become more important in gender and politics over time, what do you see as the opportunities and challenges for intersectional work on gender and parties specifically, or parties more broadly?

JONI: Well, at base level, you can actually ask questions about it now ... it's become much more researchable. So that is an opportunity.

PIPPA: And, while there is a tremendous research literature on the role of ethnicity and race in political representation in the US, there remain many questions where we lack systematic knowledge about these issues around the globe. Years and years ago, I tried to get the Inter-Parliamentary Union (IPU) to establish a new database to examine this topic. The IPU monitors how many women are elected to national parliaments worldwide every year, providing an invaluable resource. I urged them to produce an equivalent annual monitoring database in terms of ethnic minority and indigenous representation. The assumption is that diversity in parliament should reflect the social diversity of the population in terms of gender, language, religion, ethnicity, or other politically significant characteristics. Although an initial survey was undertaken in selected cases, and the IPU recognizes the important value of diversity and inclusion in parliament, the organization had technical and political difficulties in following up on the pilot study. These issues arose partly because of the complex way that the multidimensional concepts of "ethnicity" and "race" are defined and measured in different countries and global regions, without any standard harmonized international classificatory codes. There are also legal constraints, where in some cases surveys cannot ask about these identities. It remains a field which still needs further systematic work.

ELIN: What do you think is the future of merging what we see now as feminist institutionalism and gender and politics with political party research? We have a very strong gender and politics community, we can now go to the wonderful ECPG [European Conference on Politics and Gender] conferences, there's a vibrant and dynamic discussion going on, lots of good research coming out... But there's still, to some extent, silos—which is in many ways the way that research works these days, with increasing incentives to specialize. What would you say is the way forward? Is there a way in which we can bring feminist institutionalist research into "mainstream" party politics research?

JONI: I think that there is now a wide ranging and relevant feminist agenda that has institutionalist dimensions at its core. We can now interrogate things that were once beneath the radar or off the agenda, such as violence against women in politics, heteronormativity across and within parties and systems, intersectionality in women's and men's political representation. I am very curious about how masculinity varies, which kinds are powerful, how diversity plays out in different groups, and in different ideological settings. I would really like to know why incoming diverse groups seeking representation tend to compete with other incoming or recently arrived diverse groups rather than the dominant group, which is, and always has been, itself a minority. It is a logical development of our research questions. But these are gaps that are even now being filled. More fundamentally, I think feminist scholars of political representation have to deal with a considerable tension between, on the one hand, wanting to understand the barriers to representation in contemporary democratic institutions and, on the other, needing to confront and understand the hollowing out of organizations that we once thought contributed to democracy, including political parties. This is an area of interest on which feminist and other party politics scholars should insist on meeting, as they have considerable common ground. There are some major research questions here about political power and processes that are saturated with aspects of gender, race, class, and sexuality, and with ideas about equality, entitlement, representation, and accountability.

PIPPA: I hate, hate, hate silos, and I refuse to be in any because I move from one field to another. But the trouble is, few in the younger generation attempt to cover multiple disciplinary subfields now, in part because of processes of professional training and employment incentives. When early-career scholars first come into a graduate PhD program, they often have broader interests. And then the training process narrows the subfield down, of course, to get a PhD and [get] published. Within each of the disciplinary subfields, there are clear boundaries, so scholars tend to only read and cite others within a particular area. But it's the overlaps among subfields which are often the most interesting.

MERYL: Joni and Elin and I and others wrote a piece a couple of years ago [Kenny et al. 2022] where there had been a review of the state of the field of party politics research in Western Europe, and it didn't cite any gender research, including your books. So, how do you work at the intersections of subfields if people aren't listening? What happens when the dialogue isn't two-way?

PIPPA: I think it's naive to assume that there's a flat playing field. There isn't. The center is the place where the "mainstream" goes, and the periphery is where everybody else has their subfield. And you can either say, "Well, I'm happy in the periphery, because I've got my colleagues in my networks, and I know the field well," or you can try and dissolve boundaries. And I don't think political science can break down silos by itself. When politics changes in the world, then the intellectual divisions often change as well—for example, Americanists are currently interested in learning more about topics like proportional electoral systems, far-right parties, and authoritarian leaders, which were once the province of comparativists.

JONI: I think the "nobody's listening" problem is very, very serious. I don't think that it's something that you can hit young scholars with and say, "OK, you guys, we've left you this mess. Go along and fix it. You know, you be all-embracing. You wait 10 years to get a tenured position, if that. And then one day your reward will be that somebody might listen to you." It is not just about silos, it's also about careers, about how universities work, how journals work, and how people access resources.

Of course, the worst thing that can happen mostly used to be that nobody listened. I think now it's a little riskier than that. I don't know really how it is at home with you, Pippa, but there is a real closing down in the UK of the basis of intellectual inquiry. Not only does nobody listen, many are afraid to speak at all.

PIPPA: The way I frame this issue is to distinguish between orthodox and heterodox. So, the "heterodox" (outside the mainstream views in any social group) don't feel comfortable speaking up in departmental meetings or in academic classrooms, or in a variety of other academic contexts, as well as on social media, so they self-censor. As a result, we're getting a very skewed vision of academic life. And I think, for example, when we think about feminism and the 1970s, when you started this work, when I first started entering academic life, feminists were very much the heterodox group. Nowadays they're not. I think they've become the orthodoxy.

JONI: Believe me, they're not yet anything other than the heterodox group.

PIPPA: In political science, Joni? You don't think that in our lifetime it's changed in terms of what's the norm, attitudes, and values predominant in the culture of political science?

JONI: I think that it's possible to get a job, a good job, and have a good career studying gender and politics now. And there is some support for that within the profession. But it doesn't mean that women are treated equally around the systems and structures. They're not.

PIPPA: That's different, though. I'm talking about the intellectual ideas, feminist assumptions, and values of gender equality. You don't think that's become mainstream in political science?

JONI: I think it might be there, but I don't think anybody who isn't doing gender and politics is reading it.

PIPPA: The citations are another matter, absolutely. But the fact that gendered norms appear to have shifted in a more progressive direction during our lifetimes means that there's more visibility for the study of gender, and women and politics, in the discipline, and in the ability for scholars to publish in these fields, which is important.

JONI: I think that we're kind of at cross-purposes here because you're talking about the difference between whether things have got better and whether things have got equal.

Our discipline, however defined, has been accommodating in the sense of, after a considerable struggle, allowing us space. But I do not see the continuing intellectual engagement that would be truly transformative. More generally I think there is growing resistance to feminist success, and this will creep into the academy. In some ways it already has.

In terms of candidate selection, for example, I was recently told by an influential woman how sad it was that a man who had cultivated a Labour safe seat all his political life had been "tragically" ruled out, thus ruining his career, when it became an all-woman shortlist. This is nonsense. Yes, it was disappointing, but he was never entitled to that seat. Such stories about how improvements for women have "gone too far" are resistances, and we hear more and more of them.

ELIN: So, given the progress you've outlined, but also ongoing and new challenges, do you have any advice for early-career scholars who are interested in the intersection of party politics and gender in current times?

JONI: We are either confident about the foundations we've laid for how to go about it and how to develop it or we're not. I don't think there's any other way. The methods of observation and substantiation and comparison are as they ever were. And the other thing, which has certainly been the case with my students, is that you just have to do something you're passionate about, otherwise you're not going to be successful.

PIPPA: Yes, you have to have passion. You have to have a genuine interest and follow your heart as well as your head in pursuing your academic dreams. Maybe it will work out in your scholarly career. Maybe it won't. *Fortuna* plays a role—alongside *necessitas* and *virtù*. You have to take risks, in political science as well as in life.

References

Àbàtì, O.O. 2024. "Beyond #NotTooYoungToRun: Party Candidacy, Political Representation, and Legislative Effectiveness of Young Politicians in Nigeria's Fourth Republic." PhD dissertation. Stellenbosch: Stellenbosch University.

Abels, G. 2020. "Gender and Descriptive Representation in the 2019–2024 European Parliament." In *Die Europawahl 2019*, edited by M. Kaeding, M. Müller, and J. Schmälter, pp. 407–421. Wiesbaden: Springer VS.

Acabo, M. 2024. "Beyond Ballots: Paths to an Analysis of the Political Uses of Parliamentary Groups Beyond Their Legislative Activity." Paper presented at the European Consortium for Political Research (ECPR) Standing Group on the European Union, Universidade NOVA, Lisbon, Portugal, June 19–21.

Acker, J. 2006. "Inequality Regimes: Gender, Class, and Race in Organizations." *Gender and Society* 20(4): 441–464.

Adeoye, O.A. 2009. "Godfatherism and the Future of Nigerian Democracy." *African Journal of Political Science and International Relations* 3(6): 268–272.

Aflalo, H.M. 2023. "The When and What of Electoral Funds and Why They Matter for Gender and Racial Political Equality." Paper presented at the annual conference of the International Political Science Association, Buenos Aires, Argentina, July 15–19.

Ahmed, S. 2012. *On Being Included: Racism and Diversity in Institutional Life*. Durham: Duke University Press.

Ahmed, S. 2017. *Living a Feminist Life*. Durham: Duke University Press.

Ahrens, P., K. Chmilewski, S. Lang, and B. Sauer. 2020. *Gender Equality in Politics: Implementing Party Quotas in Germany and Austria*. Cham: Springer.

Ahrens, P., B. Gaweda, and J. Kantola. 2022. "Reframing the Language of Human Rights? Political Group Contestations on Women's and LGBTQI Rights in European Parliament Debates." *Journal of European Integration* 44(6): 803–819.

Ahrens, P., and J. Kantola. 2022. "Political Group Formation in the European Parliament: Negotiating Democracy and Gender." *Party Politics* 29(5): 817–828.

Ahrens, P., and L. Rolandsen Agustín. 2021. "Party Politics." In *Routledge Handbook on Gender and EU Politics*, edited by G. Abels, A. Krizsan, H. MacRae, and A. van der Vleuten, pp. 235–249. London: Routledge.

Alcaraz, C.N. 2022. "Les Relacions de Gènere a les Organitzacions Polítiques Temps, Treballs i Transformacions." PhD dissertation. Barcelona: Universitat Autònoma de Barcelona.

Aldrich, A.S., and W.T. Daniel. 2020. "The Consequences of Quotas: Assessing the Effect of Varied Gender Quotas on Legislator Experience in the European Parliament." *Politics & Gender* 16(3): 738–767.

Allen, P. 2013. "Last in, First out: Gendered Patterns of Local Councillor Dropout." *British Politics* 8(2): 207–224.

Ambrosio, T. 2016. *Authoritarian Backlash: Russian Resistance to Democratization in the Former Soviet Union*. London: Routledge.

Ammassari, S., D. McDonnell, and M. Valbruzzi. 2023. "It's About the Type of Career: The Political Ambition Gender Gap Among Youth Wing Members." *European Journal of Political Research* 32(3): 675–1004.

Amnesty International. 2017. "Kvindelige politikere: Had og trusler er hverdag." Accessed April 8, 2020. https://amnesty.dk/nyhedsliste/2017/kvindelige-politikere-had-og-trusler-er-hverdag

Amnesty International & KVINFO. 2018. "DIGITAL VOLD: Kvindelige folketingspolitikere mødertrusler og chikane online." Accessed May 23, 2020. https://amnesty.dk/en-ud-af-fem-danske-kvinder-oplever-chikane-paa-nettet/

Andersen, W.K., and S.D. Damle. 2018. *The RSS: A View to the Inside*. Gurgaon: Penguin Random House India.

Annesley, C., I. Engeli, and F. Gains. 2015. "The Profile of Gender Equality Issue Attention in Western Europe." *European Journal of Political Research* 54(3): 525–542.

Antić Gaber, M., and I. Selišnik. 2022. "Legislative Gender Quotas in Slovenia: Implemented but Not Internalized." In *Party Politics and the Implementation of Gender Quotas*, edited by S. Lang, P. Meier, and B. Sauer, pp. 321–340. Basingstoke: Palgrave Macmillan.

Anzia, S.F., and C.R. Berry. 2011. "The Jackie (and Jill) Robinson Effect: Why Do Congresswomen Outperform Congressmen?" *American Journal of Political Science* 55(3): 478–493.

Are, J. (2022). APC slashes costs of nomination forms by 50% for persons under 40 years, https://www.thecable.ng/apc-slashes-cost-of-nomination-forms-by-50-for-persons-under-40-years/

Arendt, C.M. 2018. "From Critical Mass to Critical Leaders: Unpacking the Political Conditions Behind Gender Quotas in Africa." *Politics & Gender* 14(3): 295–322.

Arnold, R.D. 1990. *The Logic of Congressional Action*. New Haven: Yale University Press.

Arruzza, C., T. Bhattacharya, and N. Fraser. 2019. *Feminism for the 99%: A Manifesto*. New York: Verso.

Ashe, J. 2020. *Political Candidate Selection: Who Wins, Who Loses, and Under-Representation in the UK*. London: Routledge.

Avelino, G., and A. Fisch. 2018. "Money, Elections, and Candidates." In *Routledge Handbook of Brazilian Politics*, edited by B. Ames, pp. 161–174. London: Routledge.

Baer, D.L. 1993. "Political Parties: The Missing Variable in Women and Politics Research." *Political Research Quarterly* 46(3): 547–576.

Baldez, L. 2007. "Primaries v. Quotas: Gender and Candidate Nominations in Mexico, 2003." *Latin American Politics and Society* 49(3): 69–96.

Bale, T., P. Webb, and M. Poletti. 2020. *Footsoldiers: Political Party Membership in the 21st Century*. London: Routledge.

Bardall, G., E. Bjarnegård, and J.M. Piscopo. 2020. "How Is Political Violence Gendered? Disentangling Motives, Forms, and Impacts." *Political Studies* 68(4): 916–935.

Barnes, T.D. 2016. *Gendering Legislative Behavior: Institutional Constraints and Collaboration*. New York: Cambridge University Press.

Barnes, T.D., and M.R. Holman. 2020. "Gender Quotas, Women's Representation, and Legislative Diversity." *The Journal of Politics* 82(4): 1271–1286.

Bauer, G., and A.K. Darkwah. 2020. "We Would Rather Be Leaders than Parliamentarians: Women and Political Office in Ghana." *European Journal of Politics & Gender* 3(1): 101–119.

Bauer, N.M. 2018. "Untangling the Relationship Between Partisanship, Gender Stereotypes, and Support for Female Candidates." *Journal of Women, Politics & Policy* 39(1): 1–25.

Beaman, L., R. Chattopadhyay, E. Duflo, R. Pande, and P. Topalova. 2009. "Powerful Women: Does Exposure Reduce Bias?" *The Quarterly Journal of Economics* 124(4): 1497–1540.

Beauregard, K., and J. Sheppard. 2021. "Antiwomen but Proquota: Disaggregating Sexism and Support for Gender Quota Policies." *Political Psychology* 42(2): 219–237.

Beckwith, K. 1981. "Women and Parliamentary Politics in Italy, 1946–1979." In *Italy at the Polls*, edited by H.R. Penniman, pp. 230–253. Washington: American Enterprise Institute.

Beckwith, K. 2005. "A Common Language of Gender?" *Politics & Gender* 1(1): 128–137.

Beckwith, K. 2007. "Numbers and Newness: The Descriptive and Substantive Representation of Women." *Canadian Journal of Political Science* 40(1): 27–49.

Beckwith, K. 2015. "Before Prime Minister: Margaret Thatcher, Angela Merkel, and Gendered Leadership Contests." *Politics & Gender* 11(4): 718–745.

Bedi, T. 2016. *The Dashing Ladies of the Shiv Sena: Political Matronage in Urbanizing India*. New York: SUNY Press.

Belschner, J. 2023. "Youth Advantage Versus Gender Penalty: Selecting and Electing Young Candidates." *Political Research Quarterly* 76(1): 90–106.

Belschner, J., and M. Garcia de Paredes. 2021. "Hierarchies of Representation: The Re-Distributive Effects of Gender and Youth Quotas." *Representation* 57(1): 1–20.

Bergqvist, C., E. Bjarnegård, and P. Zetterberg. 2013. "Analysing Failure, Understanding Success: A Research Strategy for Explaining Gender Equality Policy Adoption." *NORA—Nordic Journal of Feminist and Gender Research* 21(4): 280–295.

Bernhard, R., S. Shames, and D.L. Teele. 2021. "To Emerge? Breadwinning, Motherhood, and Women's Decisions to Run for Office." *American Political Science Review* 115(2): 379–394.

Bernstein, J.L., and J. Wolak. 2002. "A Bicameral Perspective on Legislative Retirement: The Case of the Senate." *Political Research Quarterly* 55(2): 375–390.

Berthet, V., B. Gaweda, J. Kantola, C. Miller, P. Ahrens, and A. Elomäki. 2023. *Guide to Qualitative Research in Parliaments: Experiences and Practices*. Basingstoke: Palgrave.

Berthet, V., and J. Kantola. 2020. "Gender, Violence and Political Institutions: Struggles over Sexual Harassment in the European Parliament." *Social Politics* 28(1): 143–167.

Berz, J., and M. Jankowski. 2022. "Local Preferences in Candidate Selection: Evidence from a Conjoint Experiment Among Party Leaders in Germany." *Party Politics* 28(6): 1136–1149.

Besley, T., O. Folke, T. Persson, and J. Rickne. 2017. "Gender Quotas and the Crisis of the Mediocre Man: Theory and Evidence from Sweden." *American Economic Review* 107(8): 2204–2242.

Bhatt, C. 2001. *Hindu Nationalism: Origins, Ideologies, and Modern Myths.* Oxford: Berg.

Bhattacharya, S. 2020. *Mission Bengal: A Saffron Experiment.* Noida: Harper Collins India.

Bhavnani, R.R. 2009. "Do Electoral Quotas Work After They Are Withdrawn? Evidence from a Natural Experiment in India." *American Political Science Review* 103(01): 23–35.

Bick, N. 2019. "Women's Representation and European Green Parties: Unlocking the Connection." *International Journal of Feminist Politics* 21(5): 789–813.

Bidadanure, J. 2015. "Better Procedures for Fairer Outcomes: Youth Quotas in Parliaments." *Intergenerational Justice Review* 1(1): 1–7.

van Biezen, I., and D.R. Piccio. 2013. "Shaping Intra-Party-Democracy: On the Legal Regulations of Internal Party Organizations." In *The Challenges of Intra-Party Democracy*, edited by W.P. Cross and R.S. Katz, pp. 27–48. Oxford: Oxford University Press.

van Biezen, I., and E.R. Rashkova. 2013. "Introduction: Gender Politics and Party Regulation. Quotas and Beyond." *Representation* 49(4): 393–400.

Bird, K. 2016. "Intersections of Exclusion: The Institutional Dynamics of Combined Gender and Ethnic Quota Systems." *Politics, Groups, and Identities* 4(2): 284–306.

Bjarnegård, E. 2013. *Gender, Informal Institutions and Political Recruitment.* Basingstoke: Palgrave Macmillan.

Bjarnegård, E. 2018a. "Men's Political Representation." In *Oxford Research Encyclopaedia of Politics.* https://doi.org/10.1093/acrefore/9780190228637.013.214.

Bjarnegård, E. 2018b. "Making Gender Visible in Election Violence: Strategies for Data Collection." *Politics & Gender* 14(4): 690–695.

Bjarnegård, E. 2018c. "Focusing on Masculinity and Male-Dominated Networks in Corruption." In *Gender and Corruption: Historical Roots and New Avenues for Research,* edited by H. Stensöta and L. Wängnerud, pp 257–273. Basingstoke: Palgrave.

Bjarnegård, E. 2023. "The Continuum of Election Violence: Gendered Candidate Experiences in the Maldives." *International Political Science Review* 44(1): 107–121.

Bjarnegård, E., and M. Kenny. 2015. "Revealing the Secret Garden: The Informal Dimensions of Political Recruitment." *Politics & Gender* 11(4): 748–753.

Bjarnegård, E., and M. Kenny. 2016. "Comparing Candidate Selection: A Feminist Institutionalist Approach." *Government & Opposition* 51(3): 370–392.

Bjarnegård, E., and M. Kenny. 2017. "Who, Where and How? Informal Institutions and the Third Generation of Research on Gendered Dynamics in Political Recruitment." In *Gender and Informal Institutions,* edited by G. Waylen, pp. 203–221. London: Rowman & Littlefield.

Bjarnegård, E., and P. Zetterberg. 2016a. "Political Parties and Gender Quota Implementation: The Role of Bureaucratized Candidate Selection Procedures." *Comparative Politics* 48(3): 393–417.

Bjarnegård, E., and P. Zetterberg. 2016b. "Gender Equality Reforms on an Uneven Playing Field: Candidate Selection and Quota Implementation in Electoral Authoritarian Tanzania." *Government & Opposition* 51(3): 464–486.

Bjarnegård, E., and P. Zetterberg. 2019. "Political Parties, Formal Selection Criteria, and Gendered Parliamentary Representation." *Party Politics* 25(3): 325–335.

Bjarnegård, E., and P. Zetterberg. 2022. "How Autocrats Weaponize Women's Rights." *Journal of Democracy* 33(2): 60–75.

Bjarnegård, E., and P. Zetterberg. 2023. *Gender and Violence Against Political Actors.* Philadelphia: Temple University Press.

Bjarnegård, E., S. Håkansson, and P. Zetterberg. 2022. "Gender and Violence Against Political Candidates: Lessons from Sri Lanka." *Politics & Gender* 18(1): 33–61.

Bjørgo, T., and E. Silkoset. 2018. *Threats and Threatening Approaches to Politicians: A Survey of Norwegian Parliamentarians and Cabinet Ministers.* Politihøgskolen: PHS Forskning.

Blofield, M., C. Ewing, and J.M. Piscopo. 2017. "The Reactive Left: Gender Equality and the Latin American Pink Tide." *Social Politics* 24(4): 345–369.

Bogaards, M. 2022. "Feminist Institutionalism(s)." *Italian Political Science Review* 52(3): 418-427.

Boin, A., M. Ekengren, and M. Rhinard. 2020. "Hiding in Plain Sight: Conceptualizing the Creeping Crisis." *Risk, Hazards & Crisis in Public Policy* 11(2): 116–138.

Bolin, N., A. Backlund, and A.C. Jungar. 2023. "Attracting Tomorrow's Leaders: Who Joins Political Youth Organisations for Material Reasons?" *Party Politics* 29(3): 527–539.

Bomberg, E.E. 1998. *Green Parties and Politics in the European Union.* New York: Routledge.

Borders, R., and C. Dockery. 1995. *Beyond the Hill: A Directory of Congress from 1984–1993.* Lanham, MD: University Press of America.

Bos, A.L., J.S. Greenlee, M.R. Holman, Z.M. Oxley, and J.C. Lay. 2022. "This One's for the Boys: How Gendered Political Socialization Limits Girls' Political Ambition and Interest." *American Political Science Review* 116(2): 484–501.

Bose, S., and A. Jalal. 2004. *Modern South Asia: History, Culture, Political Economy.* London: Routledge.

Bourdieu, P. 1984. *Distinction: A Social Critique of the Judgement of Taste.* Cambridge: Harvard University Press.

Bradley-Geist, J., I. Rivera, and S.D. Geringer. 2015. "The Collateral Damage of Ambient Sexism: Observing Sexism Impacts Bystander Self-Esteem and Career Aspirations." *Sex Roles* 74(1–2): 29–42.

Brennan, M., F. Buckley, and Y. Galligan. 2022. "Ireland: Understanding Gender Quotas as a Stepping-Stone to Gender Transformation and Empowerment." In *Party Politics and the Implementation of Gender Quotas*, edited by S. Lang, P. Meier, and B. Sauer, pp. 231–248. Basingstoke: Palgrave Macmillan.

Briggs, J.E. 2008. "Young Women and Politics: An Oxymoron?" *Journal of Youth Studies* 11(6): 579–592.

Broockman, D.E. 2014. "Do Female Politicians Empower Women to Vote or Run for Office? A Regression Discontinuity Approach." *Electoral Studies* 34: 190–204.

Brown, N.E. 2014. "Political Participation of Women of Color: An Intersectional Analysis." *Journal of Women, Politics & Policy* 35(4): 315–348.

Brown, N.E., and P.K. Dowe. 2020. "Late to the Party: Black Women's Inconsistent Support from Political Parties." In *Good Reasons to Run*, edited by S.L Shames, R.I. Bernhard, M.R. Holman, and D.L. Teele, pp. 153–166. Philadelphia: Temple University Press.

Brubaker, R. 2010. "Migration, Membership, and the Nation-State." *Journal of Interdisciplinary History* XLI(I): 61–78.

Buchanan, I. 2025. *Women in Politics and Public Life*. London: House of Commons Library.

Burness, C. 2000. "Young Swedish Members of Parliament: Changing the World?" *NORA—Nordic Journal of Feminist and Gender Research* 8(2): 93–106.

Bush, S.S. 2011. "International Politics and the Spread of Quotas for Women in Legislatures." *International Organization* 65(1): 103–137.

Butler, D.M., and J.R. Preece. 2016. "Recruitment and Perceptions of Gender Bias in Party Leader Support." *Political Research Quarterly* 69(4): 842–851.

Butler, D. and D. Stokes. 1974. *Political Change in Britain: Basis of Electoral Choice*. 2nd ed. Basingstoke: Palgrave Macmillan.

Butler, J. 1993. *Bodies That Matter: On the Discursive Limits of "Sex."* New York: Routledge.

Butler, J. 1997. *Excitable Speech: A Politics of the Performative*. New York: Routledge.

Byrne, C., and K. Theakston. 2016. "Leaving the House: The Experience of Former Members of Parliament Who Left the House of Commons in 2010." *Parliamentary Affairs* 69(3): 686–707.

Cammett, M.C. 2011. "Partisan Activism and Access to Welfare in Lebanon." *Studies in Comparative International Development* 46: 70–97.

Cammett, M.C. 2015. "Sectarianism and the Ambiguities of Welfare in Lebanon." *Current Anthropology* 56(S11): S76–S87.

Cammett, M.C., and S. Issar. 2010 "Bricks and Mortar Clientelism: Sectarianism and the Logics of Welfare Allocation in Lebanon." *World Politics* 62(3): 381–421.

Campbell, R., and J. Lovenduski. 2016. *Footprints in the Sand: FIVE Years of the Fabian Women's Network Mentoring and Political Education Programme*. London: The Fabian Society.

Campbell, R., and S. Childs. 2013. "The Impact Imperative: Here Come the Women :-)" *Political Studies Review* 1(2): 182–189.

Campbell, R., and S. Childs. 2014. "Parents in Parliament: 'Where's Mum?'" *The Political Quarterly* 85(4): 487–492.

Campbell, R., and S. Childs. 2015. "Conservatism, Feminisation and the Representation of Women in British Politics." *British Politics* 10(2): 148–168.

Carey, J.M. 2007. "Competing Principals, Political Institutions, and Party Unity in Legislative Voting." *American Journal of Political Science* 51(1): 92–107.

Carroll, S.J., and K. Sanbonmatsu. 2013. *More Women Can Run: Gender and Pathways to State Legislatures.* Cambridge: Cambridge University Press.

Carty, R.K. 2013. "Are Political Parties Meant to Be Internally Democratic?" In *The Challenges of Intra-Party Democracy*, edited by W.P. Cross and R.S. Katz, pp. 11–26. Oxford: Oxford University Press.

Cassese, E.C., and M.R. Holman. 2018. "Party and Gender Stereotypes in Campaign Attacks." *Political Behavior* 40(3): 785–807.

Castells, M. 1996. The Information Age*: Economy, Society and Culture,* vol. 1. Oxford: Blackwell Publishing.

Castenmiller, P. 2015. *Rust en onrust: Beperkte vernieuwing van het Provinciaal bestuur in 2015.* The Hague: Stichting Decentraal Bestuur.

Castenmiller, P., M. Leijenaar, K. Niemöller, and H. Tjalma-den Oudsten. 2002. *Afscheid van de Raad: Een terugblik op het raadslidmaatschap.* Den Haag: SGBO.

Castle, J.J., S. Jenkins, C.D. Ortbals, J. Poloni-Staudinger, and J.C. Strachan. 2020. "The Effect of the #Metoo Movement on Political Engagement and Ambition in 2018." *Political Research Quarterly* 73(4): 926–941.

Catalano Weeks, A. 2022. *Making Gender Salient: From Gender Quota Laws to Policy.* Cambridge: Cambridge University Press.

Caul, M. 1999. "Women's Representation in Parliament: The Role of Political Parties." *Party Politics* 5(1): 79–98.

Caul, M. 2001. "Political Parties and the Adoption of Candidate Gender Quotas: A Cross-National Analysis." *Journal of Politics* 63(4): 1214–1229.

Celis, K., and J. Lovenduski. 2018. "Power Struggles: Gender Equality in Political Representation." *European Journal of Politics and Gender* 1(1–2): 149–166.

Celis, K., and S. Childs. 2018. "Conservatism and Women's Political Representation." *Politics & Gender* 14(1): 5–26.

Celis, K., and S. Childs. 2020. *Feminist Democratic Representation.* Oxford: Oxford University Press.

Celis, K., and S. Childs. 2024. "Feminist Democratic Design & The Redress of Intersectional Representational Problematics." *Politics & Gender* 20(3): 734–739.

Celis, K., S. Childs, and J. Kantola. 2016. "Regendering Party Politics: An Introduction." *Party Politics* 22(5): 571–575.

Celis, K., S. Childs, J. Kantola, and M.L. Krook. 2014. "Constituting Women's Interests Through Representative Claims." *Politics & Gender* 10(2): 149–174.

Celis, K., and S. Erzeel. 2017. "The Complementarity Advantage: Parties, Representativeness and Newcomers' Access to Power." *Parliamentary Affairs* 70(1): 43–61.

Celis, K., S. Erzeel, L. Mügge, and A. Damstra. 2014. "Quotas and Intersectionality: Ethnicity and Gender in Candidate Selection." *International Political Science Review* 35(1): 41–54.

Chandra, U., and A. Majumder. 2013. "Introduction: Selves and Society in Postcolonial India." *South Asia Multidisciplinary Academic Journal* 7: 1–16.

Chandra, U., G. Heierstad, and K. B. Nielsen, eds. 2015. *The Politics of Caste in West Bengal.* London: Routledge.

Chappell, L. 2006. "Comparing Political Institutions: Revealing the Gendered 'Logic of Appropriateness.'" *Politics & Gender* 2(2): 223–235.

Chappell, L. 2014. "'New,' 'Old,' and 'Nested' Institutions and Gender Justice Outcomes: A View from the International Criminal Court." *Politics & Gender* 10(4): 572–594.

Chappell, L., and F. Mackay. 2017. "What's in a Name? Mapping the Terrain of Informal Institutions and Gender Politics." In *Gender and Informal Institutions*, edited by G. Waylen, pp. 23–44. London: Rowman and Littlefield.

Chappell, L., and G. Waylen. 2013. "Gender and the Hidden Life of Institutions." *Public Administration* 91(3): 599–615.

Chatterji, J. 1994. *Bengal Divided: Hindu Communalism and Partition, 1932–1947.* Cambridge: Cambridge University Press.

Chaves, B.M., and W. Pralon Mancuso. 2020. "Raça e Gênero nas Eleições Brasileiras: Uma Análise sobre a Corrida Eleitoral de 2018." Boletim de Políticas Públicas 6. Observatório Interdisciplinar de Políticas Públicas EACH-USP, São Paulo. Accessed July 23, 2023. https://sites.usp.br/boletimoipp/wp-content/uploads/sites/823/2020/10/Chaves_Mancuso.pdf

Cheng, C., and M. Tavits. 2011. "Informal Influences in Selecting Female Political Candidates." *Political Research Quarterly* 64(2): 460–471.

Childs, S. 2000. "The New Labour Women MPs in the 1997 British Parliament: Issues of Recruitment and Representation." *Women's History Review* 9(1): 55–73.

Childs, S. 2008. *Women and British Party Politics.* London: Routledge.

Childs, S. and P. Webb. 2012. *Sex, Gender and the Conservative Party: From Iron Lady to Kitten Heels.* London: Palgrave Macmillan.

Childs, S. 2013a. "Intraparty Democracy: A Gendered Critique and a Feminist Agenda." In *The Challenges of Intra-Party Democracy*, edited by W.P. Cross and R.S. Katz, pp. 81–99. Oxford: Oxford University Press.

Childs, S. 2013b. "In the Absence of Electoral Sex Quotas: Regulating Political Parties for Women's Representation." *Representation* 49(4): 401–423.

Childs, S. 2016. *The Good Parliament Report.* Bristol: University of Bristol.

Childs, S. Forthcoming *Designing Feminist Institutions: The Making of the Good Parliament.* Oxford University of Press.

Childs, S., and D. Dahlerup. 2018. "Increasing Women's Descriptive Representation in National Parliaments: The Involvement and Impact of Gender and Politics Scholars." *European Journal of Politics & Gender* 1(2): 185–204.

Childs, S., and M. Hughes. 2018. "'Which Men?' How an Intersectional Perspective on Men and Masculinities Helps Explain Women's Political Underrepresentation." *Politics & Gender* 14(2): 282–287.

Childs, S., and M.L. Krook. 2006. "Gender and Politics: The State of the Art." *Politics* 26(1): 18–28.

Childs, S., and M.L. Krook. 2008. "Critical Mass Theory and Women's Political Representation." *Political Studies* 56(3): 725–736.

Childs, S., and P. Webb. 2011. *Sex, Gender and the Conservative Party: From Iron Lady to Kitten Heels.* Basingstoke: Palgrave Macmillan.

Childs, S., and S. Palmieri. 2020. "Patience Ladies: Gender Sensitive Parliamentary Responses in a Time of Crisis." *European Journal of Law Reform* 22(4): 468–483.

Childs, S., and S. Palmieri. 2023. "Gender Sensitive Parliaments: Feminizing Formal Political Institutions." In *Handbook of Feminist Governance*, edited by M. Sawer, L.A. Banaszak, J. True, and J. Kantola, pp. 174–188. Cheltenham: Edward Elgar.

Čičkarić, L. 2022. "Legislative Quotas and Political Representation in Serbia." In *Party Politics and the Implementation of Gender Quotas*, edited by S. Lang, P. Meier, and B. Sauer, pp. 303–320. Basingstoke: Palgrave Macmillan.

Claessen, C., S. Bailer, and T. Turner-Zwinkels. 2021. "The Winners of Legislative Mandate: An Analysis of Post-Parliamentary Career Positions in Germany and the Netherlands." *European Journal of Political Research* 60(1): 25–45.

Claveria, S. 2014. "Still a 'Male Business'? Explaining Women's Presence in Executive Office." *West European Politics* 37(5): 1156–1176.

Claveria, S., and T. Verge. 2015. "Post-Ministerial Occupation in Advanced Industrial Democracies: Ambition, Individual Resources and Institutional Opportunity Structures." *European Journal of Political Research* 54(4): 819–835.

Clayton, A. 2021. "How Do Electoral Gender Quotas Affect Policy?" *Annual Review of Political Science* 24: 235–252.

Cockburn, C. 1991. *In the Way of Women: Men's Resistance to Sex Equality in Organizations.* Ithaca: Cornell University Press.

Coffé, H., and C. Bolzendahl. 2010. "Same Game, Different Rules? Gender Differences in Political Participation." *Sex Roles* 62(5–6): 318–333.

Coffé, H., and L.K. Davidson-Schmich. 2020. "The Gendered Political Ambition Cycle in Mixed-Member Electoral Systems." *European Journal of Politics and Gender* 3(1): 79–99.

Collier, C.N., and T. Raney. 2018. "Canada's Member-to-Member Code of Conduct on Sexual Harassment in the House of Commons: Progress or Regress?" *Canadian Journal of Political Science/Revue Canadienne de Science Politique* 51(4): 795–815.

Collignon, S., and W. Rüdig. 2020. "Harassment and Intimidation of Parliamentary Candidates in the United Kingdom." *The Political Quarterly* 91(2): 422–429.

Collignon, S., and W. Rüdig. 2021. "Increasing the Cost of Female Representation? The Gendered Effect of Harassment, Abuse and Intimidation Towards Parliamentary Candidates in the UK." *Journal of Elections, Public Opinion and Parties* 31(4): 429–449.

Collin, F. 1999. *Le différend des sexes: De Platon à la parité.* Nantes: Editions Plein Feux.

Connell, R.W. 1990. "The State, Gender, and Sexual Politics." *Theory and Society* 19(5): 507–544.

Connell, R.W. 1987. *Gender and Power: Society, the Person and Sexual Politics.* Cambridge: Polity Press.

Conroy, M., and J. Green. 2020. "It Takes a Motive: Communal and Agentic Articulated Interest and Candidate Emergence." *Political Research Quarterly* 73(4): 942–956.

Corstange, D. 2012. "Vote Trafficking in Lebanon." *International Journal of Middle East Studies* 44(3): 483–505.

Cowell-Meyers, K. 2011. "A Collarette on a Donkey: The Northern Ireland Women's Coalition and the Limitations of Contagion Theory." *Political Studies* 59: 411–431.

Cowell-Meyers, K. 2014. "The Social Movement as Political Party: The Northern Ireland Women's Coalition and the Campaign for Inclusion." *Perspectives on Politics* 12(1): 61–80.

Cowell-Meyers, K. 2016. "Women's Political Parties in Europe." *Politics & Gender* 12(1): 1–27.

Cowell-Meyers, K. 2017. "The Contagion Effects of the Feminist Initiative in Sweden: Agenda-Setting, Niche Parties and Mainstream Parties." *Scandinavian Political Studies* 40(4): 481–493.

Cowell-Meyers, K. 2020. "The Women's Movement Knocks on the Door: Theorizing the Strategy, Context and Impact of Frauen Macht Politik (FraP!) on Women's Representation in Swiss Politics." *Politics & Gender* 16(1): 48–77.

Cowell-Meyers, K., E. Evans, and K. Shin. 2020. "Women's Parties: A New Party Family." *Politics & Gender* 16(1): 4–25.

Crenshaw, K. 1989. "Demarginalizing the Intersection of Race and Sex: A Black Feminist Critique of Antidiscrimination Doctrine, Feminist Theory and Antiracist Policies." *University of Chicago Legal Forum* 1: 139–167.

Crenshaw, K. 1991. "Mapping the Margins: Intersectionality, Identity Politics, and Violence Against Women of Color." *Stanford Law Review* 43(6): 1241–1299.

Cross, W.P., and R.S. Katz, eds. 2013. *The Challenges of Intra-Party Democracy*. Oxford: Oxford University Press.

Crowder-Meyer, M. 2013. "Gendered Recruitment Without Trying: How Local Party Recruiters Affect Women's Representation." *Politics & Gender* 9(4): 390–413.

Crowder-Meyer, M. 2020. "Baker, Bus Driver, Babysitter, Candidate? Revealing the Gendered Development of Political Ambition Among Ordinary Americans." *Political Behavior* 42: 359–384.

Dahlerup, D. 2017. *Has Democracy Failed Women?* Cambridge: Polity Press.

Dahlerup, D., and L. Freidenvall. 2005. "Quotas as a 'Fast Track' to Equal Representation for Women: Why Scandinavia Is No Longer the Model." *International Feminist Journal of Politics* 7(1): 26–48.

Dahlerup, D., and M. Leyenaar. 2013. *Breaking Male Dominance in Old Democracies*. Oxford: Oxford University Press.

Datta, P.K. 1999. *Carving Blocs: Communal Ideology in Early Twentieth-Century Bengal*. New York: Oxford University Press.

Davidson-Schmich, L.K. 2006. "Implementation of Political Party Gender Quotas: Evidence from the German Länder 1990–2000." *Party Politics* 12(2): 211–232.

Davidson-Schmich, L.K. 2016. *Gender Quotas and Democratic Participation: Recruiting Candidates for Elective Offices in Germany*. Ann Arbor: University of Michigan Press.

Davidson-Schmich, L.K. 2018. "Addressing Supply Side Hurdles to Gender Equal Representation in Germany." *Femina Politica* 2: 53–69.

Davis, R.H. 1997. *Women and Power in Parliamentary Democracies: Cabinet Appointments in Western Europe 1968–1992*. Lincoln: University of Nebraska Press.

Dean, J., and B. Maiguashca. 2018. "Gender, Power, and Left Politics: From Feminization to 'Feministization.'" *Politics & Gender* 14(3): 376–406.

Devroe, R., and B. Wauters. 2018. "Political Gender Stereotypes in a List-PR System with a High Share of Women MPs: Competent Men Versus Leftist Women?" *Political Research Quarterly* 71(4): 788–800.

Devroe, R., and S. Van Trappen. 2022. "Keeping Women in Their Place? The Prevalence of Gender Role Attitudes Among Local Party Chairs in Flanders." *Acta Politica* 57(3): 472–488.

Dhrodia, A. 2018. "Unsocial Media: A Toxic Place for Women." *IPPR Progressive Review* 24(4): 380–387.

van Dijk, R.E. 2023. "Playing by the Rules? The Formal and Informal Rules of Candidate Selection." *Women's Studies International Forum* 96: 1–8.

Dingler, S.C., and J. Fortin-Rittberger. 2022. "Women's Leadership in the European Parliament: A Long-Term Perspective." In *Women and Leadership in the European Union*, edited by H. Mueller and I. Toemmel, pp. 74–91. Oxford: Oxford University Press.

Dittmar, K. 2015. "Encouragement is Not Enough: Addressing Social and Structural Barriers to Female Recruitment." *Politics & Gender* 11(4): 759–765.

Doherty, D., C.M. Dowling, and M.G. Miller. 2019. "Do Local Party Chairs Think Women and Minority Candidates Can Win? Evidence from a Conjoint Experiment." *The Journal of Politics* 81(4): 1282–1297.

Dominelli, L., and G.J. Jonsdottir. 1988. "Feminist Political Organization in Iceland: Some Reflections on the Experience of Kwenna Frambothid." *Feminist Review* 30(1): 36–60.

dos Santos, P.A.G., and K.N. Wylie. 2018. "The Representation of Women." In *Routledge Handbook of Brazilian Politics*, edited by B. Ames, pp. 57–71. London: Routledge.

Durovic, A. 2023. "Rising Electoral Fragmentation and Abstention: The French Elections of 2022." *West European Politics* 46(3): 614–629.

Duverger, M. 1954. *Political Parties*. London: Methuen.

Eimieho, S. 2022. "Facts About Women's Rights in Iceland." Borgen Project, 4 April. Accessed January 15, 2024. https://borgenproject.org/womens-rights-in-iceland

Einarsdottir, H.K. 2015. *The Kitchen Sink Revolution*. Reykjavik: Krumma Films.

eldiario.es. 2023. "Carmen Calvo critica que el feminismo tenga que 'cargar' con las reivindicaciones LGTBI: 'También podríamos unirnos a los que diseñan tractores.'" Accessed April 23, 2025: https://www.eldiario.es/politica/ultima-hora-actualidad-politica-directo_6_10010205_1097941.html

Elomäki, A. 2023. "'It's a Total No-No': The Strategic Silence About Gender in the European Parliament's Economic Governance Policies." *International Political Science Review* 44(3): 403–417.

Erikson, J. 2017. *Criminalising the Client. Institutional Change, Gendered Ideas and Feminist Strategies*. London: Rowman & Littlefield.

Elomäki, A., B. Gaweda, and V. Berthet. 2022. "Political Dynamics, Power Struggles and Intraparty Policy-Formation in the European Parliament." In *European Parliament's Political Groups in Turbulent Times*, edited by P. Ahrens, A. Elomäki, and J. Kantola, pp. 73–96. Basingstoke: Palgrave.

Elomäki, A., and J. Kantola. 2022. "Feminist Governance in the European Parliament: The Political Struggle over the Inclusion of Gender in the EU's Covid-19 Response." *Politics & Gender* 19(2): 327–348.

Elomäki, A., J. Kantola, P. Ahrens, V. Berthet, B. Gaweda, and C. Miller. 2023. "The Role of National Delegations in the Politics of the European Parliament." *West European Politics* 47(6): 1251–1275.

Elomäki, A., and P. Ahrens. 2022. "Contested Gender Mainstreaming in the European Parliament: Political Groups and Committees as Gatekeepers." *European Journal of Politics & Gender* 5(3): 322–340.

Erikson, J., and C. Josefsson. 2021. "Equal Playing Field? On the Intersection Between Gender and Being Young in the Swedish Parliament." *Politics, Groups, and Identities* 9(1): 81–100.

Erikson, J., and C. Josefsson. 2022. "The Parliament as a Gendered Workplace: How to Research Legislators' (UN)Equal Opportunities to Represent." *Parliamentary Affairs* 75(1): 20–38.

Erikson, J., and C. Josefsson. 2025. "Leaders' Desires to Lead: Progressive Ambition and Norms Around Gender Balance in the Swedish Parliament." *Politics, Groups, and Identities* 13 (2): 325-345.

Erikson, J., and T. Verge. 2022. "Gender, Power and Privilege in the Parliamentary Workplace." *Parliamentary Affairs* 75(1): 1–19.

Erzeel, S., and K. Celis. 2016. "Political Parties, Ideology and the Substantive Representation of Women." *Party Politics* 22(5): 576–586.

Escobar-Lemmon, M., and M. Taylor-Robinson. 2008. "How Do Candidate Recruitment and Selection Processes Affect Representation of Women?" In *Pathways to Power*, edited by S. Morgenstern and P. Siavelis, pp. 345–370. University Park: Penn State University Press.

ERC. 2017. "Pla per la Igualtat." Accessed May 20, 2025. https://static.esquerra.cat/arxius/textosbasics/pla-igualtat.pdf

ERC. 2023. "Ponència Política. 29è Congrés Nacional." Accessed May 20, 2025. https://esquerrarepublicana.cat/documents/29cgn-ponencia-politica.pdf

Ette, M., and P. Akpan-Obong. 2023. "Negotiating Access and Privilege: Politics of Female Participation and Representation in Nigeria." *Journal of Asian and African Studies* 58(7): 1291–1306.

European Green Party. 2023. "Statutes of the European Green Party." Accessed June 26, 2023. https://www.datocms-assets.com/87481/1734351623-adopted-revised-egp-statutes-copenhagen-4-dec-2022-with-annexes.pdf

European Parliament. No date. Advanced Search. Accessed May 16, 2025. https://www.europarl.europa.eu/meps/en/search/advanced?name=

European Parliamentary Research Service. 2021. "Women in Politics in the EU: State of Play." Accessed June 26, 2023. https://www.europarl.europa.eu/RegData/etudes/BRIE/2021/689345/EPRS_BRI(2021)689345_EN.pdf

Evans, E., and M. Kenny. 2019. "The Women's Equality Party: Emergence, Organisation and Challenges." *Political Studies* 67(4): 855–871.

Evans, E., and M. Kenny. 2020. "Doing Politics Differently? Applying a Feminist Institutionalist Lens to the U.K. Women's Equality Party." *Politics & Gender* 16(1): 26–47.

Evans, E., and S. Reher. 2024. "Disability and Representation in British Politics." *Political Insight* 15(3): 45–47.

Everitt, J., and L. Horvath. 2021. "Public Attitudes and Private Prejudices: Assessing Voters' Willingness to Vote for Out Lesbian and Gay Candidates." *Frontiers in Political Science* 3. https://doi.org/10.3389/fpos.2021.662095

Every-Palmer, S., J. Barry-Walsh, and M. Pathé. 2015. "Harassment, Stalking, Threats and Attacks Targeting New Zealand Politicians: A Mental Health Issue." *Australian & New Zealand Journal of Psychiatry* 49(7): 634–641.

Faludi, S. 1991. *Backlash: The Undeclared War Against American Women*. New York: Crown.

Farran, N. 2021. "Mental Health in Lebanon: Tomorrow's Silent Epidemic." *Mental Health & Prevention* 24: 200–218.

Flood, M., M. Dragiewicz, and B. Pease. 2018. *Resistance and Backlash to Gender Equality: An Evidence Review*. Brisbane: Crime and Justice Research Centre.

Folke, O., and J. Rickne. 2016. "The Glass Ceiling in Politics: Formalization and Empirical Tests." *Comparative Political Studies* 49(5): 567–599.

Folke, O., L. Freidenvall, and J. Rickne. 2015. "Gender Quotas and Ethnic Minority Representation: Swedish Evidence from a Longitudinal Mixed Methods Study." *Politics & Gender* 11(2): 345–381.

Folke, O., T. Persson, and J. Rickne. 2016. "The Primary Effect: Preference Votes and Political Promotions." *American Political Science Review* 110(3): 559–578.

Fortin-Rittberger, J., and B. Rittberger. 2014. "Do Electoral Rules Matter? Explaining National Differences in Women's Representation in the European Parliament." *European Union Politics* 15(4): 496–520.

Fortin-Rittberger, J., and B. Rittberger. 2015. "Nominating Women for Europe: Exploring the Role of Political Parties' Recruitment Procedures for European Parliament Elections." *European Journal of Political Research* 54(4): 767–783.

Foster, A. 1997. "Ulster Unionist." *Irish News*, 14 April.

Foucault, M. 1980. *Power/Knowledge: Selected Interviews and Other Writings 1972–1977, New York*, edited by C. Gordon. New York: Pantheon Books.

Fox, R.L., and J.L. Lawless. 2004. "Entering the Arena? Gender and the Decision to Run for Office." *American Journal of Political Science* 48(2): 264–280.

Fox, R.L., and J.L. Lawless. 2010. "If Only They'd Ask: Gender, Recruitment, and Political Ambition." *Journal of Politics* 72(2): 310–326.

Franceschet, S. 2005. *Women and Politics in Chile*. Boulder, CO: Lynne Rienner Publishers.

Franceschet, S. 2010. "The Gendered Dimension of Rituals, Rules, and Norms in the Chilean Congress." *Journal of Legislative Studies* 16 (3): 396–406.

Franceschet, S. 2017. "Disentangling Informality and Informal Rules." In *Gender and Informal Institutions*, edited by G. Waylen, pp. 115–135. London: Rowman and Littlefield International.

Francis, W.L., and J.R. Baker. 1986. "Why Do U.S. State Legislators Vacate Their Seats?" *Legislative Studies Quarterly* 11(1): 119–126.

François, A., and E. Grossman. 2015. "How to Define Legislative Turnover? The Incidence of Measures of Renewal and Levels of Analysis." *The Journal of Legislative Studies* 21(4): 457–475.

Freidenvall, L. 2003. "*Women's Political Representation and Gender Quotas: The Swedish Case." The Research Program: Gender Quotas—a Key to Equality.* Stockholm: Department of Political Science, Stockholm University. Working Paper Series 2003:2". The link is here: https://www.niyf.org/wp-content/uploads/2016/05/zipping.pdf.

Freidenvall, L. 2016. "Intersectionality and Candidate Selection in Sweden." *Politics* 36(4): 355–363.

Freidenvall, L. 2021. *Equal Representation Without Legislation.* London: Rowman & Littlefield International.

Freidenvall, L. 2022. "Implementing Special Measures for Political Representation and Gender in Sweden." In *Party Politics and the Implementation of Gender Quotas*, edited by S. Lang, P. Meier, and B. Sauer, pp. 113–130. Basingstoke: Palgrave Macmillan.

Freidenvall, L., and M.L. Krook. 2011. "Discursive Strategies for Institutional Reform: Gender Quotas in Sweden and France." In *Gender, Politics and Institutions*, edited by M.L. Krook and F. Mackay, pp. 42–57. Basingstoke: Palgrave Macmillan.

Friis, S., F. Fokdal, C. Søe, M. Gudme, et al. 2020. "322 kvinder står frem i opråb: 'Sexisme, seksuel chikane og magtmisbrug er overalt i vores samfund, også i de politiske partier.'" Politiken. Accessed February 28, 2024. https://politiken.dk/debat/debatindlaeg/art7938422/»Sexisme-seksuel-chikane-og-magtmisbrug-er-overalt-i-vores-samfund-også-i-de-politiske-partier«

Fulton, S.A. 2012. "Running Backwards and in High Heels: The Gendered Quality Gap and Incumbent Electoral Success." *Political Research Quarterly* 65(2): 303–314.

Fulton, S.A., C.D. Maestas, L.S. Maisel, and W.J. Stone. 2006. "The Sense of a Woman: Gender, Ambition, and the Decision to Run for Congress." *Political Research Quarterly* 59(2): 235–248.

Gagolewski, M. 2022. "A Framework for Benchmarking Clustering Algorithms." *SoftwareX* 20: 101270.

Gains, F., and V. Lowndes. 2014. "How Is Institutional Formation Gendered, and Does It Make a Difference? A New Conceptual Framework and a Case Study of Police and Crime Commissioners in England and Wales." *Politics & Gender* 10(4): 524–548.

Gains, F., and V. Lowndes. 2022. "Identifying the Institutional Micro-Foundations of Gender Policy Change: A Case Study of Police Governance and Violence Against Women and Girls." *Politics & Gender* 18(2): 394–421.

Galais, C., P. Öhberg, and X. Coller. 2016. "Endurance at the Top: Gender and Political Ambition of Spanish and Swedish MPs." *Politics and Gender* 12(3): 596–621.

Gallagher, M., and M. Marsh, eds. 1988. *Candidate Selection in Comparative Perspective.* London: Sage.

Gaspard, F. 1994. "De la parité: Génèse d'un concept, naissance d'un movement." *Nouvelles Questions Féministes* 15(4): 29–44.

Gatto, M.A.C. 2016. "Endogenous Institutionalism and the Puzzle of Gender Quotas: Insights from Latin America." PhD dissertation. Oxford: University of Oxford.

Gatto, M.A.C., G.A. Russo, and D. Thomé. 2021. "+Representatividade." São Paulo. Accessed July 13, 2023. https://discovery.ucl.ac.uk/id/eprint/10139751/1/UpdateRepresentatividade_Relatorio-1.pdf

Gatto, M.A.C., and K.N. Wylie. 2022. "Informal Institutions and Gendered Candidate Selection in Brazilian Parties." *Party Politics* 28(4): 727–738.

Gauja, A. 2017. *Party Reform: The Causes, Challenges, and Consequences of Organizational Change.* Oxford: OUP.

Gauja, A., and K. Kosiara-Pedersen. 2021. "Decline, Adaptation and Relevance: Political Parties and Their Researchers in the Twentieth Century." *European Political Science* 20(1): 123–138.

Gaweda, B. 2022. "The Least That Could Have Been Done? The Ambiguous Effects of Gender Quotas in Polish Parliamentary Elections." In *Party Politics and the Implementation of Gender Quotas*, edited by S. Lang, P. Meier, and B. Sauer, pp. 267–284. Basingstoke: Palgrave Macmillan.

Geddes, B. 1995. "A Comparative Perspective on the Leninist Legacy in Eastern Europe." *Comparative Political Studies* 28(2): 239–274.

Geddes, M. 2018. "Committee Hearings of the UK Parliament: Who Gives Evidence and Does This Matter?" *Parliamentary Affairs* 71(2): 283–304.

Geha, C. 2019. "The Myth of Women's Political Empowerment Within Lebanon's Sectarian Power-Sharing System." *Journal of Women, Politics & Policy* 40(4): 498–521.

Generalitat de Catalunya. 2021. "Pla de Govern de la XIV Legislatura." Accessed May 20, 2025. https://govern.cat/govern/docs/PdG.pdf

Geissel, B., and E. Hust. 2005. "Democratic Mobilisation Through Quotas: Experiences in India and Germany." *Commonwealth & Comparative Politics* 43(2): 222–244.

Giger, N. 2009. "Towards a Modern Gender Gap in Europe? A Comparative Analysis of Voting Behavior in 12 Countries." *The Social Science Journal* 46(3): 474–492.

Gilardi, F. 2015. "The Temporary Importance of Role Models for Women's Political Representation." *American Journal of Political Science* 59: 957–970.

Glick, P., and S.T. Fiske. 1996. "The Ambivalent Sexism Inventory: Differentiating Hostile and Benevolent Sexism." *Journal of Personality and Social Psychology* 70(3): 491–512.

Glick, P., and S.T. Fiske. 2001. "An Ambivalent Alliance: Hostile and Benevolent Sexism as Complementary Justifications for Gender Inequality." *American Psychologist* 56(2): 109–118.

Glynos, J., and D. Howarth. 2007. *Logics of Critical Explanation in Social and Political Theory.* London: Routledge.

Gøttler, S.Ø., and T. Vibjerg. 2022. "Inger Støjberg kalder til kamp mod MeToo-bølgen: 'Ingen skal udsættes for overgreb, det er vi da alle enige om, men lad os nu komme videre.'" Jyllandsposten. Accessed February 29, 2024. https://jyllands-posten.dk/politik/ECE14182362/inger-stoejberg-kalder-til-kamp-mod-metooboelgen-ingen-skal-udsaettes-for-overgreb-det-er-vi-da-alle-enige-om-men-lad-os-nu-komme-videre

Goertz, G. and A. Mazur. 2008. "Mapping Gender and Politics Concepts: Ten Guidelines." In *Politics, Gender and Concepts. Theory and Methodology*, edited by G. Goertz and A.G. Mazur, pp. 14-43. Cambridge: Cambridge University Press.

Gouglas, A., B. Maddens, and M. Brans. 2018. "Determinants of Legislative Turnover in Western Europe, 1945–2015." *European Journal of Political Research* 57(3): 637–661.

Gougou, F., and S. Persico. 2017. "A New Party System in the Making? The 2017 French Presidential Election." *French Politics* 15: 303–321.

Government Offices of Sweden. 2018. "Chronological Overview of LGBT Persons Rights in Sweden." Ministry of Employment. Accessed April 18, 2023. https://www.government.se/articles/2018/07/chronological-overview-of-lgbt-persons-rights-in-sweden

Grahn, M. 2023. "Apprentices or Outsiders? Age-Driven Heterogeneities in Access to Political Capital and Reelection." *Research & Politics* 10(2). https://journals.sagepub.com/doi/10.1177/20531680231186840

Grahn, M. 2024. "Gendered Institutions and Where to Find Them: A Critical Realist Approach." *Politics & Gender* 20(2): 449–473.

Grahn, M. and S. Håkansson (2025). "Inclusive or exclusive? Candidate selection methods do not affect descriptive representation." *West European Politics*, https://doi.org/10.1080/01402382.2025.2504296

Grahn, M., and T. Thisell. 2024. "Are Minorities in Politics Held to a Higher Standard? Experimental & Observational Evidence from Candidate Selection." *Journal of European Public Policy*: 1–25. https://www.tandfonline.com/doi/full/10.1080/13501763.2024.2398770

Grasso, M., and K. Smith. 2022. "Gender Inequalities in Political Participation and Political Engagement Among Young People in Europe: Are Young Women Less Politically Engaged than Young Men?" *Politics* 42(1): 39–57.

Green-Pedersen, C. 2007. "The Growing Importance of Issue Competition: The Changing Nature of Party Competition in Western Europe." *Political Studies* 55(3): 607–628.

Green-Pedersen, C., and P.B. Mortensen. 2010. "Who Sets the Agenda and Who Responds to It in the Danish Parliament? A New Model of Issue Competition and Agenda-Setting." *European Journal of Political Research* 49(2): 257–281.

Guadagnini, M. 1993. "A 'Partitocrazia' Without Women: The Case of the Italian Party System." In *Gender and Party Politics*, edited by J. Lovenduski and P. Norris, pp. 168–204. London: Sage.

Gunther, R., and L. Diamond. 2003. "Species of Political Parties: A New Typology." *Party Politics* 9(2): 167–199.

Håkansson, S. 2021. "Do Women Pay a Higher Price for Power? Gender Bias in Political Violence in Sweden." *Journal of Politics* 83(2): 515–531.

Håkansson, S. 2023. "The Gendered Representational Costs of Violence Against Politicians." *Perspectives on Politics* 22(1): 1–16.

Håkansson, S. & M. Grahn (2025). The Cost of Debating Harassment Against Politicians: Are Women and Men Affected Equally? *Political Behavior*. https://doi.org/10.1007/s11109-025-10039-1

Haraldsson, A., and L. Wängnerud. 2018. "The Effects of Media Sexism on Women's Political Ambition: Evidence from a Worldwide Study." *Feminist Media Studies* 19(4): 525–541.

Harmel, R., and K. Janda. 1994. "An Integrated Theory of Party Goals and Party Change." *Journal of Theoretical Politics* 6(3): 259–287.

Haughey, N. 1997. "Northern Machismo: Women Are Notable Only by Their Absence in Northern Ireland's Political Front Line." *The Irish Times*, 9 October, p. 13.

van Haute, E., ed. 2016. *Green Parties in Europe*. London: Routledge.

van Haute, E., and A. Gauja, eds. 2015. *Party Members and Activists*. London: Routledge.

Hawkesworth. M. 2003. "Congressional Enactments of Race-Gender: Toward a Theory of Raced-Gendered Institutions." *The American Political Science Review* 97(4): 529–550.

Hay, C., and D. Wincott. 1998. "Structure, Agency and Historical Institutionalism." *Political Studies* 46(5): 951–957.

Hazan, R.Y., and G. Rahat. 2010. *Democracy Within Parties*. Oxford: Oxford University Press.

Heidar, K., and K. Kosiara-Pedersen. 2019. "Why Do Members Join Parties?" In *Nordic Party Members*, edited by M. Demker, K. Haidar, and K. Kosiara-Pedersen, pp. 51–72. Colchester: ECPR Press.

Heinsohn, T., and M. Freitag. 2012. "Institutional Foundations of Legislative Turnover: A Comparative Analysis of the Swiss Cantons." *Swiss Political Science Review* 18(3): 352–370.

Helmke, G., and S. Levitsky. 2004. "Informal Institutions and Comparative Politics: A Research Agenda." *Perspectives on Politics* 2(4): 725–740.

Helmke, G., and S. Levitsky, eds. 2006. *Informal institutions and democracy: Lessons from Latin America*. Baltimore: The Johns Hopkins University Press.

Herrick, R., and L. Franklin. 2019. "Is It Safe to Keep This Job? The Costs of Violence on the Psychological Health and Careers of US Mayors." *Social Science Quarterly* 100(6): 2047–2058.

Herrick, R., S. Thomas, L. Franklin, M.L. Godwin, E. Gnabasik, and J.R. Schroedel. 2019. "Physical Violence and Psychological Abuse Against Female and Male Mayors in the United States." *Politics, Groups, and Identities* 9(4): 681–698.

Hinojosa, M. 2012. *Selecting Women, Electing Women*. Philadelphia: Temple University Press.

Högström, J. 2016. "The Effect of Gender Quotas in the First Decade of the Twenty-First Century: A Global Comparison." *Comparative Sociology* 15(2): 179–205.

Holland, M. 1996. "Women Emerge as New Ulster Force." *The Observer*, 5 May, p. 7.

Hollander, J.A., and R.L. Einwohner. 2004. "Conceptualizing Resistance." *Sociological Forum* 19(4): 533–554.

Holman, M.R., and M.C. Schneider. 2018. "Gender, Race, and Political Ambition: How Intersectionality and Frames Influence Interest in Political Office." *Politics, Groups, and Identities* 6(2): 264–280.

Htun, M., and S.L. Weldon. 2010. "When Do Governments Promote Women's Rights? A Framework for the Comparative Analysis of Sex Equality Policy." *Perspectives on Politics* 8(1): 207–216.

Hughes, M.M. 2011. "Intersectionality, Quotas, and Minority Women's Political Representation Worldwide." *American Political Science Review* 105(3): 604–620.

Hughes, M.M., P. Paxton, A.B. Clayton, and P. Zetterberg. 2019. "Global Gender Quota Adoption, Implementation, and Reform." *Comparative Politics* 51(2): 219–238.

Husaini, S. 2019. "Beyond Stomach Infrastructure: Party Membership and Political Ideology in Nigeria's Fourth Republic." PhD dissertation. Oxford: University of Oxford.

Ignatieff, M. 1993. *Blood and Belonging: Journeys into the New Nationalism.* Ontario: Penguin Canada.

Institut for Menneskerettigheder. 2019. "Undersøgelse af chikane og trusler mod folketingskandidater 2019." Accessed September 11, 2020. https://menneskeret.dk/nyheder/folketingskandidater-oplever-chikane-trusler

International Institute for Democracy and Electoral Assistance (IDEA). No date. Gender Quotas Database. Accessed May 5, 2025. https://www.idea.int/data-tools/data/gender-quotas-database

Inter-Parliamentary Union. 2011. "Gender Sensitive Parliaments: A Global Review of Good Practice." Accessed September 2024. https://www.ipu.org/resources/publications/reports/2016-07/gender-sensitive-parliaments

Inter-Parliamentary Union. 2012. "Plan of Action for Gender-Sensitive Parliaments." Accessed September 2024. http://archive.ipu.org/pdf/publications/action-gender-e.pdf

Inter-Parliamentary Union. 2023. *Youth Participation in National Parliaments.* Geneva: International Parliamentary Union.

Inter-Parliamentary Union. 2024. "Monthly Ranking of Women in National Parliaments." IPU Parline, Global Data on National Parliaments. Accessed July 1, 2024. https://data.ipu.org/women-ranking

Isele, C. 1996. "Bedeutung der sozialen Bewegungen in der Schweiz: Entstehungs und Stabilisierungsbedingungen sozialer Bewegungen, und Probleme, die mit der Institutionalisierung einhergehen; erläutert am Beispiel der FraP!" Social Movements, Pressure Groups and Political Parties [Preprint]. Accessed July 30, 2023. http://socio.ch/movpar/t_cisele1.htm.

Issever-Ekinci, E. 2023. "Party Competition and Electoral Reforms." *West European Politics* 47(6): 1363–1391.

IU. 2022. "Plan de Igualdad de Izquierda Unida (2022-2025)." Accessed May 20, 2025. https://izquierdaunida.org/wp-content/uploads/2022/07/Plan_Igualdad_IU_2022-2025.pdf

Jackson, S. 2017. "Green Parties and Gender Politics." In *Routledge Handbook of Gender and Environment*, edited by S. MacGregor, pp. 304–317. London: Routledge.

Jaffrelot, C. 1993. *The Hindu Nationalist Movement in India.* New York: Columbia University Press.

Jaffrelot, C. 2007. *Hindu Nationalism: A Reader.* New Delhi: Permanent Black.

Van Egten, C., Van het Hekke, J., Post, L., De Jong, T., Jansen, A. 2016. *Vrouwenstemmen in de raad.* Amsterdam: Atria, kennisinstituut voor emancipatie en vrouwengeschiedenis.

Janssen, C. 2021. "Ethnicity, Gender, and Intersectionality: How Context Factors Shape the Intersectional (Dis) Advantage Under Proportional Representation Rules." *Politics* 42(3): 289–308.

Janssen, C., S. Erzeel, and K. Celis. 2020. "Intersectional Candidate Nomination: How District and Party Factors Shape the Inclusion of Ethnic Minority Men and Women in Brussels." *Acta Politica* 57: 567–586.

Jansson, M. 2021. "Gender Quotas and Women's Political Agency." Accessed July 1, 2024. https://jean-monnet-saar.eu/?page_id=51375

Janusz, A., S.-N. Barreiro, and E. Cintron. 2022. "Political Parties and Campaign Resource Allocation: Gender Gaps in Brazilian Elections." *Party Politics* 28(5): 854–864.

Johnson, J.E. 2017. *The Gender of Informal Politics: Russia, Iceland and Twenty-First Century Male Dominance.* Basingstoke: Palgrave Macmillan.

Josefsson, C. 2020. "How Candidate Selection Structures and Genders Political Ambition: Illustrations from Uruguay." *European Journal of Politics and Gender* 3(1): 61–78.

Josefsson, C. 2024. *Defending the Status Quo: On Adaptive Resistance to Electoral Gender Quotas.* New York: Oxford University Press.

Joshi, D.K., and M. Och. 2021. "Early Birds, Short Tenures, and the Double Squeeze: How Gender and Age Intersect with Parliamentary Representation." *Politics, Groups, and Identities* 9(3): 629–645.

Kabeer, N. 1999. "Resources, Agency, Achievements: Reflections on the Measurement of Women's Empowerment." *Development and Change* 30: 435–464.

Kaiser, A. 2011. "Lohnunterschiede sind immer noch ein Faktum." Accessed July 1, 2024. http://www.swissinfo.ch/ger/lohnunterschiede-sind-immer-noch-ein-faktum/30455390

Kanter, R.M. 1977. "Some Effects of Proportions on Group Life: Skewed Sex Ratios and Responses to Token Women." *American Journal of Sociology* 82(5): 965–990.

Kanter, R.M. 1993. *Men and Women of the Corporation.* New York: Basic Books.

Kanthak, K., and J. Woon. 2015. "Women Don't Run? Election Aversion and Candidate Entry." *American Journal of Political Science* 59(3): 595–612.

Kantola, J. 2022. "Parliamentary Politics and Polarization Around Gender: The Case of Tackling Gendered Inequalities in Political Groups in the European Parliament." In *European Parliament's Political Groups in Turbulent Times*, edited by P. Ahrens, A. Elomäki, and J. Kantola, pp. 221–243. Basingstoke: Palgrave.

Kantola, J., and C. Miller. 2022. "Gendered Leadership in the European Parliament's Political Groups." In *Women and Leadership in the European Union*, edited by H. Mueller and I. Toemmel, pp. 150–172. Oxford: Oxford University Press.

Kantola, J., A. Elomäki, B. Gaweda, C. Miller, P. Ahrens, and V. Berthet. 2022. "'It's Like Shouting to a Brick Wall': Normative Whiteness and Racism in the European Parliament." *American Political Science Review* 117(1): 184–199.

Kantola, J., A. Elomäki, and P. Ahrens. 2022. "Introduction: European Parliament's Political Groups in Turbulent Times." In *European Parliament's Political Groups in Turbulent Times*, edited by P. Ahrens, A. Elomäki, and J. Kantola, pp. 1–23. Basingstoke: Palgrave.

Kantola, J., and E. Lombardo. 2021a. "Introduction: Populism and Feminist Politics." *International Political Science Review* 42(5): 561–564.

Kantola, J., and E. Lombardo. 2021b. "Challenges to Democratic Practices and Discourses in the European Parliament: Feminist Perspectives on the Politics of Political Groups." *Social Politics* 28(3): 579–603.

Kantola, J., and L. Rolandsen Agustín. 2016. "Gendering Transnational Party Politics: The Case of European Union." *Party Politics* 22(5): 641–651.

Kantola, J., and L. Rolandsen Agustín. 2019. "Gendering the Representative Work of the European Parliament: A Political Analysis of Women MEP's Perceptions of Gender Equality in Party Groups." *Journal of Common Market Studies* 57(4): 768–786.

Karpowitz, C.F., J.Q. Monson, and J.R. Preece. 2017. "How to Elect More Women: Gender and Candidate Success in a Field Experiment." *American Journal of Political Science* 61: 927–943.

Kathlene, L. 1994. "Power and Influence in State Legislative Policymaking: The Interaction of Gender and Position in Committee Hearing Debates." *American Political Science Review* 88(3): 560–576.

Katz, R.S. 2013. "Should We Believe That Improved Intra-Party Democracy Would Arrest Party Decline?" In *The Challenges of Intra-Party Democracy*, edited by W.P. Cross and R.S. Katz, pp. 49–64. Oxford: Oxford University Press.

Katz, R.S., and P. Mair. 1992. "Introduction: The Cross-National Study of Party Organizations." In *Party Organizations: A Data Handbook*, edited by R.S. Katz and P. Mair, pp. 1–15. London: Sage.

Katz, R.S., and P. Mair. 1995. "Changing Models of Party Organization and Party Democracy: The Emergence of the Cartel Party." *Party Politics* 1(1): 5–28.

Keith, D.J., and T. Verge. 2018. "Nonmainstream Left Parties and Women's Representation in Western Europe." *Party Politics* 24(4): 397–409.

Kennedy, R., C. Pierson, and J. Thomson. 2016. "Challenging identity hierarchies: Gender and consociational power-sharing." *The British Journal of Politics and International Relations* 18(3): 618–633.

Kenny, M. 2007. "Gender, Institutions and Power: A Critical Review." *Politics* 27(2): 91–100.

Kenny, M. 2013. *Gender and Political Recruitment: Theorizing Institutional Change.* Basingstoke: Palgrave.

Kenny, M. 2014. "A Feminist Institutionalist Approach." *Politics & Gender* 10(4): 679–684.

Kenny, M., E. Bjarnegård, J. Lovenduski, S. Childs, E. Evans, and T. Verge. 2022. "Reclaiming Party Politics Research." *European Political Science* 20(1): 123–138.

Kenny, M., and T. Verge. 2013. "Decentralization, Political Parties and Women's Representation: Evidence from Spain and Britain." *Publius: The Journal of Federalism* 43(1): 109–128.

Kenny, M., and T. Verge. 2015. "Introduction." *Politics & Gender* 11(4): 746–748.

Kenny, M., and T. Verge. 2016. "Opening Up the Black Box: Gender and Candidate Selection in a New Era." *Government & Opposition* 51(3): 351–369.

Kerevel, Y. 2019. "Empowering Women? Gender Quotas and Women's Political Careers." *Journal of Politics* 81(4): 1167–1180.

Kitschelt, H. 1988. "Left-Libertarian Parties: Explaining Innovation in Competitive Party Systems." *World Politics* 40(2): 194–234.

Kitschelt, H. 1989. *The Logics of Party Formation: Ecological Politics in Belgium and West Germany*. Ithaca: Cornell University Press.

Kittilson, M.C. 2006. *Challenging Parties, Changing Parliaments: Women and Elected Office in Contemporary Western Europe*. Columbus: Ohio State University Press.

Kittilson, M.C. 2013. "Party Politics." In *The Oxford Handbook of Gender and Politics*, edited by G. Waylen, K. Celis, J. Kantola, and S.L. Weldon, pp. 536–553. Oxford: Oxford University Press.

Kjaer, U., and K. Kosiara-Pedersen. 2019. "The Hourglass Pattern of Women's Representation." *Journal of Elections, Public Opinion and Parties* 29(3): 299–317.

Kjerulf Dubrow, J. 2011. "The Importance of Party Ideology: Explaining Parliamentarian Support for Political Party Gender Quotas in Eastern Europe." *Party Politics* 17(5): 561–579.

Kommunernes Landsforening. 2023. "Forebyggelse og håndtering af chikane, trusler, hærværk og vold mod kommunalpolitikere." Accessed February 29, 2024. https://www.kl.dk/media/3ovfc3ry/forebyggelse-og-haandtering-af-chikane-trusler-haervaerk-og-vold-mod-kommunalpolitikere.pdf

Kolltveit, K. 2022. "Gender and Ambitions for Elected and Appointed Political Positions: Insights from Norway." *European Journal of Politics and Gender* 5(1): 109–125.

Kosiara-Pedersen, K. 2024. "Single Ladies and Freedom of Speech: Gendered Explanations and Effects of Violence in Politics." *European Journal of Politics and Gender* 7(2): 221–238.

Krayem, H. 1997. "The Lebanese Civil War and the Taif Agreement." In *Conflict Resolution in the Arab World*, edited by P. Salem, pp. 411–436. Beirut: American University of Beirut.

Kriesi, H. 2018. "The 2017 French and German Elections." *Journal of Common Market Studies* 56: 51–62.

Krook, M.L. 2006. "Reforming Representation: The Diffusion of Gender Quotas Worldwide." *Politics & Gender* 2(3): 303–327.

Krook, M.L. 2009. *Quotas for Women in Politics: Gender and Candidate Selection Reform Worldwide*. New York: Oxford University Press.

Krook, M.L. 2010. "Beyond Supply and Demand: A Feminist-Institutionalist Theory of Candidate Selection." *Political Research Quarterly* 63(4): 707–720.

Krook, M.L. 2016. "Contesting Gender Quotas: Dynamics of Resistance." *Politics, Groups, and Identities* 4(2): 268–283.

Krook, M.L. 2017. "Violence Against Women in Politics." *Journal of Democracy* 28(1): 74–88.

Krook, M.L. 2018. "Westminster Too: On Sexual Harassment in British Politics." *The Political Quarterly* 89(1): 65–72.

Krook, M.L. 2020. *Violence Against Women in Politics.* New York: Oxford University Press.

Krook, M.L., and F. Mackay, eds. 2011. *Gender, Politics and Institutions: Towards a Feminist Institutionalism.* Basingstoke: Palgrave.

Krook, M.L., and J. Restrepo Sanín. 2016. "Violence Against Women in Politics: A Defense of the Concept." *Política y Gobierno* 23(2): 459–490.

Krook, M.L., and J. Restrepo Sanín. 2020. "The Cost of Doing Politics? Analyzing Violence and Harassment Against Female Politicians." *Perspectives on Politics* 18(3): 740–755.

Krook, M.L., and M.K. Nugent. "Intersectional institutions: Representing women and ethnic minorities in the British Labour Party." *Party Politics* 22(5): 620–630.

Krook, M.L., and M.K. Nugent. 2018. "Not Too Young to Run? Age Requirements and Young People in Elected Office." *Intergenerational Justice Review* 4(2): 60–67.

Kröber, C. 2021. "How Parties Led by a Woman Redefine Their Positions: Empirical Evidence for Women's Green, Alternative and Libertarian Agenda." *European Journal of Political Research* 61(1): 175–193.

Krook, M.L., and P. Zetterberg, eds. 2017. *Gender Quotas and Women's Representation: New Directions in Research.* London: Routledge.

Lang, S., P. Meier, and B. Sauer, eds. 2023. *Party Politics and the Implementation of Gender Quotas: Resisting Institutions.* Basingstoke: Palgrave.

Lawless, J.L. 2012. *Becoming a Candidate: Political Ambition and the Decision to Run for Office.* Cambridge: Cambridge University Press.

Lawless, J.L., and R.L. Fox. 2010. *It Still Takes a Candidate: Why Women Don't Run for Office.* Cambridge: Cambridge University Press.

Lawless, J., and S. Theriault. 2005. "Will She Stay or Will She Go? Career Ceilings and Women's Retirement from the U.S. Congress." *Legislative Studies Quarterly* 30(4): 581–596.

Lazarus, J., A. Steigerwalt, and M. Clark. 2022. "Time Spent in the House: Gender and the Political Careers of U.S. House Members." *Politics & Gender* 19(1): 97–132.

Leblanc, L. 1999. *Pretty in Punk: Girls' Gender Resistance in a Boys' Subculture.* Piscataway: Rutgers University Press.

Lefevre, J., A. Tresch, and S. Walgrave. 2015. "Issue Ownership." *West European Politics* 38(4): 755–760.

Lépinard, E. 2018. "The French Parity Reform." In *Transforming Gender Citizenship,* edited by E. Lépinard and R. Rubio-Marín, pp. 62–93. Cambridge: Cambridge University Press.

Levin, L.S. 1999. "Setting the Agenda: The Success of the 1977 Israel Women's Party." *Israel Studies* 4(2): 40–63.

Lewin, L. 1988. *Ideology and Strategy: A Century of Swedish Politics.* Cambridge: Cambridge University Press.

Lindgren, K., S. Oskarsson, and M. Persson. 2019. "Enhancing Electoral Equality: Can Education Compensate for Family Background Differences in Voting Participation?" *The American Political Science Review* 113(1): 108–122.

Lixian, H. 2020. "Rewriting 'The Personal Is Political': Young Women's Digital Activism and New Feminist Politics in China." *Inter-Asia Cultural Studies* 21(3): 337–355.

Lombardo, E., J. Kantola, and R. Rubio-Marín. 2021. "De-Democratization and Opposition to Gender Equality Politics in Europe." *Social Politics* 28(3): 521–531.

Lombardo, E., and L. Mergaert. 2013. "Gender Mainstreaming and Resistance to Gender Training: A Framework for Studying Implementation." *NORA—Nordic Journal of Feminist and Gender Research* 21(4): 296–311.

Lorimer, M., and L.E. Herman. 2023. "The French Elections of 2022: Macron's Half Victory in a Changing Political Landscape." *Journal of Common Market Studies* 61: 80–89.

Lovenduski, J. 2005. *Feminizing Politics*. Cambridge: Polity Press.

Lovenduski, J. 2011. "Foreword." In *Gender, Politics and Institutions: Towards a Feminist Institutionalism*, edited by M.L. Krook and F. Mackay, pp. vii-xi. Basingstoke: Palgrave Macmillan.

Lovenduski, J. 2016. "The Supply and Demand Model of Candidate Selection: Some Reflections." *Government & Opposition* 51(3): 513–528.

Lovenduski, J. 2017. "The Good Parliament and Other Reports." *The Political Quarterly* 88(2): 306–310.

Lovenduski, J. 2019. "Feminist Reflections on Representative Democracy." *The Political Quarterly* 90(1): 18–35.

Lovenduski, J., and P. Norris, eds. 1993. *Gender and Party Politics*. London: Sage.

Lowndes, V. 2014. "How Are Things Done Around Here? Uncovering Institutional Rules and Their Gendered Effects." *Politics & Gender* 10(4): 685–691.

Lowndes, V. 2020. "How Are Political Institutions Gendered?" *Political Studies* 68(3): 543–564.

Lowndes, V., and M. Roberts. 2013. *Why Institutions Matter: The New Institutionalism in Political Science*. London: Red Globe Press.

Lühiste, M., and M. Kenny. 2016. "Pathways to Power: Women's Representation in the 2014 European Parliament Elections." *European Journal of Political Research* 55(3): 626–641.

Lundin, E. 2014. "Feminist Initiative's Poll Success Must Put Pressure on Mainstream Parties." *The Guardian*, 16 September, p. 13.

Mackay, F. 2014. "Nested Newness, Institutional Innovation, and the Gendered Limits of Change." *Politics & Gender* 10(4): 549–571.

Mackay, F. 2021. "Dilemmas of an Academic Feminist as Manager in the Neoliberal Academy: Negotiating Institutional Authority, Oppositional Knowledge and Change." *Political Studies Review* 19(1): 75–95.

Mackay, F., and G. Waylen. 2014. "Introduction: Gendering 'New' Institutions." *Politics & Gender* 10(4): 489–494.

Mackay, F., M. Kenny, and L. Chappell. 2010. "New Institutionalism Through a Gender Lens: Towards a Feminist Institutionalism?" *International Political Science Review* 31(5): 573–588.

Mackay, F., and R.A.W. Rhodes. 2013. "Gender, Greedy Institutions, and the Departmental Court." *Public Administration* 91(3): 582–598.

MacKenzie, C. 2005. *Pro-Family Politics and Fringe Parties in Canada.* Vancouver: University of British Columbia Press.

Madsen, D.H., ed. 2020. *Gendered Institutions and Women's Political Representation in Africa.* London: Zed Books.

Maharat Foundation. 2023. "Shedding Light on Violence Against Women in Politics in Lebanon." Accessed July 1, 2024. https://maharatfoundation.org/media/2561/vawp-final-report-eng.pdf

Mahoney, J., and K. Thelen. 2009. "A Theory of Gradual Institutional Change." In *Explaining Institutional Change: Ambiguity, Agency and Power*, edited by J. Mahoney and K. Thelen, pp. 1–37. Cambridge: Cambridge University Press.

Mair, P. 1998. *Party System Change: Approaches and Interpretations*, Oxford: Oxford University Press.

Mansbridge, J. 2003. "Rethinking Representation." *American Political Science Review* 97(4): 515–528.

Mansbridge, J., and S.L. Shames. 2008. "Toward a Theory of Backlash: Dynamic Resistance and the Central Role of Power." *Politics & Gender* 4(4): 623–634.

Martin, J., ed. 1998. *La parité: Enjeux et mise en oeuvre.* Toulouse: Presses Universitaires du Mirail.

Martin, L.H., H. Gutman, and P.H. Hutton, eds. 1988. *Technologies of the Self: A Seminar with Michel Foucault.* London: Tavistock Publications.

Martínez-Cantó, J., and T. Verge. 2023. "Interpersonal Resources and Insider/Outsider Dynamics in Party Office." *Comparative Political Studies* 56(1): 131–157.

Martinez i Coma, F., and D. McDonnell. 2023. "Australian Parties, Not Voters, Drive Under-Representation of Women." *Parliamentary Affairs* 76(1): 107–124.

Matland, R.E., and D.T. Studlar. 1996. "The Contagion of Women Candidates in Single-Member District and Proportional Representation Systems: Canada and Norway." *Journal of Politics* 58(3): 707–733.

Matland, R.E., and D.T. Studlar. 2004. "Determinants of Legislative Turnover: A Cross-National Analysis." *British Journal of Political Science* 34(1): 87–108.

McCall, L. 2005. "The Complexity of Intersectionality." *Signs* 30(3): 1771–1800.

Meguid, B. 2005. "Competition Between Unequals: The Role of Mainstream Party Strategy in Niche Party Success." *American Political Science Review* 99(3): 347–359.

Meguid, B. 2008. *Party Competition Between Unequals: Strategies and Electoral Fortunes in Western Europe.* Cambridge: Cambridge University Press.

Mendelek, M. 2022. "The Struggle for Women's Rights After the Beirut Blast: A Resurgence of Anti-Feminist Backlash?" *Al-Raida* 46(2): 25–29.

Meyer, T.M., and B. Miller. 2015. "The Niche Party Concept and Its Measurement." *Party Politics* 21(2): 259–271.

Millard, F., M. Popescu, and G. Toka. 2011. "Should Women Push for Fewer Women Candidates? List Preference Voting Systems and Gender Representation." Accessed June 26, 2023. http://energy.ceu.edu/sites/default/files/publications/millardpopescutoka11apsa.pdf

Miller, C. 2021. *Gendering the Everyday in the UK House of Commons.* Basingstoke: Palgrave.

Ministerie van Binnenlandse Zaken en Koninkrijksrelaties. 2022. *Staat van het Bestuur 2022.* The Hague: Ministerie van Binnenlandse Zaken en Koninkrijksrelaties.

Moghadam, V.M. 2010. "Gender, Politics, and Women's Empowerment." In *Handbook of Politics*, edited by K.T. Leicht and J.C. Jenkins, pp. 279–303. Springer.

Morgan, J., and M. Hinojosa. 2018. "Women in Political Parties: Seen But Not Heard." In *Gender and Representation in Latin America*, edited by L.A. Schwindt-Bayer, pp. 74–98. New York: Oxford University Press.

Morlino, L. 1996. "Crisis of Parties and Change of Party System in Italy." *Party Politics* 2(1): 5–30.

Mossuz-Lavau, J. 1998. *Femmes/Hommes pour la parité.* Paris: Presses de Sciences Po.

Mufti, M., and F. Jalalzai. 2021. "The Importance of Gender Quotas in Patriarchal and Clientelistic Polities: The Case of Pakistan." *Journal of Women, Politics & Policy* 42(2): 107–123.

Muriaas, R., and T. Stavenes. 2023. "Gender and Political Seniority: Three Measures." *Politics & Gender*: pp. 1–25. https://doi.org/10.1017/S1743923X23000533

Murray, R. 2004. "Why Didn't Parity Work? A Closer Examination of the 2002 Election Results." *French Politics* 2: 347–362.

Murray, R. 2010. *Parties, Gender Quotas and Candidate Selection in France.* Basingstoke: Palgrave.

Murray, R. 2014. "Quotas for Men: Reframing Gender Quotas as a Means of Improving Representation for All." *American Political Science Review* 108(3): 520–532.

Murray, R. 2015. "What Makes a Good Politician? Reassessing the Criteria Used for Political Recruitment." *Politics & Gender* 11 (4): 770–776.

Murray, R. 2016. "The Political Representation of Ethnic Minority Women in France." *Parliamentary Affairs* 69(3): 586–602.

Murray, R., and E. Bjarnegård. 2023. "Bringing Men and Masculinities into Political Science." *European Journal of Politics and Gender*: 1–18. https://doi.org/10.1332/251510823X16920325768482

Murray, R., M.L. Krook, and K.A.R. Opello. 2012. "Why Are Gender Quotas Adopted? Party Pragmatism and Parity in France." *Political Research Quarterly* 65(3): 529–543.

Mutz, D.C. 2015. *In Your Face Politics: The Consequences of Uncivil Media.* Princeton: Princeton University Press.

Neue Zürcher Zeitung. 1990. "Frauen Macht Politik." 13 February, p. 94.

Nicolau, J. 2006. "O Sistema Eleitoral de Lista-Aberta no Brasil." *DADOS—Revista de Ciências Sociais* 49(4): 689–720.

Nkereuwem, E. 2023. *Why Women Haven't Been Successful in Nigerian Elections.* Washington D.C.: Carnegie Endowment for International Peace.

Norris, P. 1997. *Passages to Power: Legislative Recruitment in Advanced Democracies.* Cambridge: Cambridge University Press.

Norris, P., and J. Lovenduski. 1995. *Political Recruitment: Gender, Race and Class in the British Parliament.* Cambridge: Cambridge University Press.

North, D.C. 1990. *Institutions, Institutional Change and Economic Performance.* Cambridge: Cambridge University Press.

O'Brien, D.Z. 2015. "Rising to the Top: Gender, Political Performance, and Party Leadership in Parliamentary Democracies." *American Journal of Political Science* 59(4): 1022–1039.

O'Brien, D.Z. 2018. "'Righting' Conventional Wisdom: Women and Right Parties in Established Democracies." *Politics & Gender* 14(1): 27–55.

Och, M. 2020. "Political Ambition, Structural Obstacles, and the Fate of Republican Women." In *Good Reasons to Run*, edited by S.L. Shames, R.I. Bernhard, M.R. Holman, and D.L. Teele, pp. 41–55. Philadelphia: Temple University Press.

Omotola, S.J. 2012. "Democratization and Citizenship: The Gender Dimensions of Political Representation in Nigeria." In *Linking Environment, Democracy and Gender*, edited by B. Wejnert, pp. 1–22. Leeds: Emerald Publishing.

Organization for Security and Co-operation in Europe. 2014. "Handbook on Promoting Women's Participation in Political Parties." Accessed July 1, 2024. https://www.osce.org/odihr/120877

Organization for Security and Co-operation in Europe. 2016. *Compendium of Good Practices for Advancing Women's Political Participation in the OSCE Region.* Warsaw: OSCE/ODIHR.

Oskarsson, M., and L. Wängnerud. 1995. Kvinnor som väljare och valda. Lund: Studentlitteratur.

Oskarsson, S., C.T. Dawes, and K.O. Lindgren. 2018. "It Runs in the Family: A Study of Political Candidacy Among Swedish Adoptees." *Political Behavior* 40(4): 883–908.

Osori, A. 2017. *Love Does Not Win Elections.* Lagos: Narrative Landscape Press.

Oyebode, M.O. 2014. "Rethinking Deification, Gerontocracy and Clientelism in Nigerian Political Space." *International Journal of Development and Sustainability* 3(1): 135–149.

Palmieri, S. 2019. "Feminist Institutionalism and Gender-Sensitive Parliaments: Relating Theory and Practice." In *Gender Innovation in Political Science*, edited by M. Sawer and K. Baker, pp. 173-194. Basingstoke: Palgrave.

Panebianco, A. 1988. *Political Parties: Organization and Power.* Cambridge: Cambridge University Press.

De Paola, M., V. Scoppa, and R. Lombardo. 2010. "Can Gender Quotas Break Down Negative Stereotypes? Evidence from Changes in Electoral Rules." *Journal of Public Economics* 94(5–6): 344–353.

Pedersen, M.S. 2020. "Nye Borgerlige deler billede med hænder på lår efter uro hos de Radikale." TV2. Accessed February 29, 2024. https://nyheder.tv2.dk/politik/2020-10-08-nye-borgerlige-deler-billede-med-haender-paa-laar-efter-uro-hos-radikale

Perron, C.F. 2018. Delayed Adulthood: A Critical Analysis of Terminology and the Classification of Young People. PhD Dissertation. Windsor: University of Windsor.

Phillips, A. 1995. *The Politics of Presence.* Oxford: Clarendon Press.

Pierson, P. 2000. "Increasing Returns: Path Dependence and the Study of Politics." *American Political Science Review* 94(2): 251-267.

Pierson, P. 2004. *Politics in Time: History, Institutions and Social Analysis.* Princeton: Princeton University Press.

Pincus, I. 2002. "The Politics of Gender Equality Policy: A Study of Implementation and Non-Implementation in Three Swedish Municipalities." PhD dissertation. Örebro: Örebro University.

Piscopo, J.M. 2016. "When Informality Advantages Women: Quota Networks, Electoral Rules and Candidate Selection in Mexico." *Government and Opposition* 51(3): 487–512.

Piscopo, J.M. 2017. "Leveraging Informality, Rewriting Informal Rules: The Implementation of Gender Parity in Mexico." In *Gender and Informal Institutions*, edited by G. Waylen, pp. 137–160. London: Rowman and Littlefield.

Piscopo, J.M. 2019. "The Limits of Leaning In: Ambition, Recruitment, and Candidate Training in Comparative Perspective." *Politics, Groups, and Identities* 7(4): 817–828.

Piscopo, J.M., and D.M. Walsh. 2020. "Backlash and the Future of Feminism." *Signs: Journal of Women and Culture in Society* 45(2): 267–279.

Piscopo, J.M., and L. Vàzquez Correa. 2024 "From 30 Percent to Gender Parity in Everything: The Steady Route to Raising Women's Political Representation in Mexico." *International Feminist Journal of Politics* 26(1): 54–80.

Piscopo, J.M., and M. Kenny. 2020. "Rethinking the Ambition Gap: Gender and Candidate Emergence in Comparative Perspective." *European Journal of Politics and Gender* 3(1): 3–10.

Pitkin, H.F. 1967. *The Concept of Representation.* Berkeley: University of California Press.

Podemos. 2020a. "Plan de Igualdad." Accessed May 20, 2025. https://podemos.info/wp-content/uploads/2022/05/Plan-de-Igualdad-de-Podemos.pdf

Podemos. 2020b. "A Feminist Transition." Accessed May 20, 2025. https://podemos.info/wp-content/uploads/2020/06/2020_06_Documento_feminismos_Podemos.pdf

Praino, R., and D. Stockemer. 2018. "The Career Length and Service of Female Policymakers in the US House of Representatives." *Government & Opposition* 53(3): 437–460.

Preece, J.R., O.B. Stoddard, and R. Fisher. 2016. "Run, Jane, Run! Gendered Responses to Political Party Recruitment." *Political Behavior* 38: 561–577.

Pruysers, S., and J. Blais. 2017. "Why Won't Lola Run? An Experiment Examining Stereotype Threat and Political Ambition." *Politics & Gender* 13(2): 232–252.

Pruysers, S., and J. Blais. 2019. "Narcissistic Women and Cash-Strapped Men: Who Can Be Encouraged to Consider Running for Political Office, and Who Should Do the Encouraging?" *Political Research Quarterly* 72(1): 229–242.

PSOE-Unidas Podemos. 2019. "Coalición Progresista, Un Nuevo Acuerdo para España." Accessed May 20, 2025. https://www.psoe.es/media-content/2019/12/30122019-Coalici%C3%B3n-progresista.pdf

Puwar, N. 2004. *Space Invaders: Race, Gender and Bodies Out of Place.* London: Berg.

Rahat, G. 2007. "Candidate Selection: The Choice Before the Choice." *Journal of Democracy* 18(1): 157–170.

Rahat, G. 2013. "What Is Democratic Candidate Selection?" In *The Challenges of Intra-Party Democracy*, edited by W. P. Cross and R. S. Katz, pp. 136–149. Oxford: Oxford University Press.

Rais, D., and B.R. Alves Magarian. 2021. "Mandatos Coletivos: Entre a Experiência e o Vácuo Legislativo." Revista Eletrônica de Direito Eleitoral e Sistema Político 5 (1): 87–103. https://bibliotecadigital.tse.jus.br/items/3f25efd1-4c37-4b46-8db2-e7ecbed4d757

Rebughini, P. 2014. "Subject, Subjectivity, Subjectivation." Accessed October 14, 2022. http://cadis.ehess.fr/docannexe/file/2357/rebughini_sociopedia.pdf

Regalia, M. 2018. "Electoral Reform as an Engine of Party System Change in Italy." *Southern European Politics & Society* 23(1): 81–96.

Regalia, M. 2021. *Una democrazia dimezzata: Autoselezione, selezione ed elezione delle donne in Italia*. Milan: Egea Editore.

Rehmert, J. 2022. "Party Elites' Preferences in Candidates: Evidence from a Conjoint Experiment." *Political Behavior* 44: 1149–1173.

Reingold, B., K.L. Haynie, and K. Widner. 2021. *Race, Gender, and Political Representation: Toward a More Intersectional Approach*. Oxford: Oxford University Press.

Remkes, J. 2018. "Lage drempels, hoge dijken: Staatscommissie Parlementair Stelsel." Accessed July 1, 2024. https://www.rijksoverheid.nl/onderwerpen/parlement/staatscommissie.

Rezende de Almeida, D.C. 2024. "Candidaturas Coletivas: Uma Nova Forma de Interação entre Movimentos Sociais e Partidos Políticos." *DADOS—Revista de Ciências Sociais* 67(2): 1–53.

Richardson, D., and C. Rootes, eds. 1995. *The Green Challenge: The Development of Green Parties in Europe*. London: Routledge.

Rolandsen Agustín, L., C. Fiig, and B. Siim 2022. "Practices and Strategies of Gender Representation in Danish Political Parties: Dilemmas of 'Everyday Democracy.'" In *Party Politics and the Implementation of Gender Quotas*, edited by S. Lang, P. Meier, and B. Sauer, pp. 29–50. Basingstoke: Palgrave.

Rosenthal, C.S. 2000. "Gender Styles in State Legislative Committees." *Women & Politics* 21(2): 21–45.

Roth, L., I. Zugasti, and A. de Diego Baciero. 2020. "Feminise Politics Now!" Brussels: Rosa Luxemburg Stiftung. Accessed June 29, 2023. https://www.rosalux.eu/en/article/1586.feminise-politics-now.html

Roy, S. 2014. "Being the Change: The Aam Aadmi Party and the Politics of the Extraordinary in Indian Democracy." *Economic and Political Weekly* XLIX(15): 45–54.

Runderkamp, Z. 2024. "No More Simultaneous Chess: Understanding Dropout of Local-Level Women Politicians in Gendered Institutions." *DiGeSt: Journal of Diversity and Gender Studies* 11(1): 1–14.

Russo, G. 2020. "A explosão de candidaturas coletivas e suas chances eleitorais." São Paulo: Centro de Política e Economia do Setor Público.

Sacchet, T., and K.N. Wylie. 2023. "Advancing and Resisting Inclusion: Electoral Reforms, Political Parties, and Descriptive Representation in Brazil." Presented at the annual conference of the International Political Science Association, Buenos Aires, Argentina, July 15–19.

Samuels, D. 2001. "Does Money Matter? Campaign Finance in Newly Democratic Countries: Theory and Evidence from Brazil." *Comparative Politics* 34: 23–42.

Sanders, A., F. Gains, and C. Annesley. 2021. "What's on Offer: How Do Parties Appeal to Women Voters in Election Manifestos?" *Journal of Elections, Public Opinion and Parties* 31(4): 508–527.

Sarkar, S. 1989. *Modern India: 1885–1947*. London: Palgrave Macmillan.

Sartori, G. 1976. *Parties and Party Systems: A Framework for Analysis*. Cambridge: Cambridge University Press.

Savarkar, V.D. 2003. *Essentials of Hindutva*. New Delhi: Hindi Sahitya Sadan.

Sawyers, T.M., and D.S. Meyer. 1999. "Missed Opportunities: Social Movement Abeyance and Public Policy." *Social Problems* 46(2): 187–206.

Schickler, E. 2001. *Disjointed Pluralism*. Princeton: Princeton University Press.

Schlesinger, J.A. 1966. *Ambition and Politics: Political Careers in the United States*. Chicago: Rand McNally.

Schmidt, V.A. 2010. "Taking Ideas and Discourse Seriously: Explaining Change Through Discursive Institutionalism as the Fourth 'New Institutionalism.'" *European Political Science Review* 2(1): 1–25.

Schneider, M.C, M.R. Holman, A.B. Diekman, and T. McAndrew. 2016. "Power, Conflict, and Community: How Gendered Views of Political Power Influence Women's Political Ambition." *Political Psychology* 37(4): 515–531.

Schneier, E. 1992. "Icelandic Women on the Brink of Power." *Scandinavian Studies* 64(4): 417–438.

Schuster, J. 2013. "Invisible Feminists? Social Media and Young Women's Political Participation." *Political Science* 65(1): 8–24.

Schwarz, S., and A. Coppock. 2022. "What Have We Learned About Gender from Candidate Choice Experiments? A Meta-Analysis of Sixty-Seven Factorial Survey Experiments." *The Journal of Politics* 84(2): 655–668.

Schwindt-Bayer, L.A. 2011. "Women Who Win: Social Backgrounds, Paths to Power, and Political Ambition in Latin American Legislatures." *Politics & Gender* 7(1): 1–33.

Scott, J.C. 1985. *Weapons of the Weak: Everyday Forms of Peasant Resistance*. New Haven: Yale University Press.

Scott, J.W. 1986. "Gender: A Useful Category of Historical Analysis." *The American Historical Review* 91(5): 1053-1075.

Segaard, S.B., and J. Saglie. 2021. "A Gender-Generation Gap in Political Representation? The Contingent Impact of Preference Voting in Norwegian Municipal Elections." *Local Government Studies* 47(1): 145–165.

Sen, A. 2007. *Shiv Sena Women Violence and Communalism in a Bombay Slum*. Bloomington: Indiana University Press.

Sen, D. 2018. *The Decline of the Caste Question: Jogendranath Mandal and the Defeat of Dalit Politics in Bengal*. Cambridge: Cambridge University Press.

Shaffir, W., and S. Kleinknecht. 2005. "Death at the Polls: Experiencing and Coping with Political Defeat." *Journal of Contemporary Ethnography* 34: 707–738.

Shah, P., J. Scott, and E. Gonzalez Juenke. 2019. "Women of Color Candidates: Examining Emergence and Success in State Legislative Elections." *Politics, Groups, and Identities* 7(2): 29–443.

Shames, S.L. 2017. *Out of the Running: Why Millennials Reject Political Careers and Why It Matters.* New York: NYU Press.

Sharma, J. 2003. *Hindutva: Exploring the Idea of Hindu Nationalism.* New Delhi: Penguin Publishers.

Sharrock, D. 1996. "Peace Women Unite at the Ballot Box to Take on Party Dinosaurs." *Daily Mirror*, 29 May, pp. 6–7.

Siavelis, P., and S. Morgenstern, eds. 2008. *Pathways to Power: Political Recruitment and Candidate Selection in Latin America.* University Park: Pennsylvania State University Press.

Da Silva, W.Q., L. Secchi, and R.A. Cavalheiro. 2021. "Mandatos Coletivos e Compartilhados no Brasil: Análise Descritiva de Inovações Democráticas no Poder Legislativo." *Revista Debates* 15(1): 168–190.

Šinko, M. 2022. "Only Stand-Ins? Women's Parliamentary Representation and Quota Implementation in Croatia Since 2011." In *Party Politics and the Implementation of Gender Quotas*, edited by S. Lang, P. Meier, and B. Sauer, pp. 189–210. Basingstoke: Palgrave Macmillan.

Skocpol, T. 1979. *States and Social Revolutions: A Comparative Analysis of France, Russia and China.* Cambridge: Cambridge University Press.

Slegten, C., and B. Heyndels. 2022. "Sex Differences in Incumbents' Turnover Odds: The Role of Preference Vote Performance and the Party Leader's Sex." *Acta Politica* 57(4): 667–686.

De Smedt, N., and A. Vandeleene. 2024. "Young Blood: Needed or Discarded? Untangling Party Strategies for the Selection of Young Candidates." *Politics.* https://doi.org/10.1177/02633957241259091

Smith, D.E. 2005. *Institutional Ethnography: A Sociology for People.* Lanham: Altamira Press.

Smrek, M. 2020. "Do Female Legislators Benefit from Incumbency Advantage? Incumbent Renomination in a Flexible-List PR System." *Electoral Studies* 66: 102–189.

Smrek, M. 2022. "When Is Access to Political Capital Gendered? Lessons from the Czech Parliament." *Parliamentary Affairs* 75(1): 323–336.

Staab, S., and G. Waylen. 2020. "Institutional Change in Constrained Circumstances: Gender, Resistance, and Critical Actors in the Chilean Executive." *Latin American Politics and Society* 62(4): 50–74.

Stauffer, K.E., and D.Z. O'Brien. 2018. "Quantitative Methods and Feminist Political Science." In *Oxford Research Encyclopedia of Politics*, https://doi.org/10.1093/acrefore/9780190228637.013.210

Stephan, R. 2014. "Four Waves of Lebanese Feminism." *E-International Relations.* Accessed July 1, 2024. https://www.e-ir.info/2014/11/07/four-waves-of-lebanese-feminism

Stockemer, D., and A. Sundström. 2019. “Do Young Female Candidates Face Double Barriers or an Outgroup Advantage? The Case of the European Parliament.” *European Journal of Political Research* 58(1): 373–384.

Stockemer, D., and A. Sundström. 2022. *Youth Without Representation: The Absence of Young Adults in Parliaments, Cabinets, and Candidacies.* Ann Arbor: University of Michigan Press.

Stockemer, D., and A. Sundström. 2023. “Age Inequalities in Political Representation: A Review Article.” *Government and Opposition.* https://doi.org/10.1017/gov.2023.11

Stoker, G. 2013. “Designing Politics: A Neglected Justification for Political Science.” *Political Studies Review* 11(2): 174–181.

Strech, M. 1995. “Die Erfahrungen mit getrennten männlichen und weiblichen Listen Repräsentantenhaus Wahl 1991: Frauenförderung oder Frauenverhinderung?” *Tages-Anzeiger*, 1 March.

Streeck, W., and K. Thelen. 2005. “Introduction: Institutional Change in Advanced Political Economies.” In *Beyond Continuity*, edited by W. Streeck and K. Thelen, pp. 1–39. New York: Oxford University Press.

Sundström, A., and D. Stockemer. 2021a. “Conceptualizing, Measuring, and Explaining Youths' Relative Absence in Legislatures.” *PS: Political Science & Politics* 54(2): 195–201.

Sundström, A., and D. Stockemer. 2021b. “Political Party Characteristics and Women's Representation: The Case of the European Parliament.” *Representation* 58(1): 119–137.

Svenska Dagbladet. 2014. “Party Leader Debate in Parliament.” 17 June. Accessed July 1, 2024. https://www.svd.se/partiledardebatten-i-riksdagen

Sweet-Cushman, J. 2020. “Where Does the Pipeline Get Leaky? The Progressive Ambition of School Board Members and Personal and Political Network Recruitment.” *Politics, Groups, and Identities* 8(4): 762–785.

Tarrow, S. 2011. *Power in Movement: Social Movements and Contentious Politics.* 3rd ed. Cambridge: Cambridge University Press.

Tavits, M. 2008. “Party Systems in the Making: The Emergence and Success of New Parties in New Democracies.” *British Journal of Political Science* 38(1): 113–133.

Thelen, K. 2004. *How Institutions Evolve.* Cambridge: Cambridge University Press.

Theriault, S.M. 1998. “Moving Up or Moving Out: Career Ceilings and Congressional Retirement.” *Legislative Studies Quarterly* 23(3): 419–433.

Thomas, S., and C. Wineinger. 2020. “Ambition for Office: Women and Policy-Making.” In *Good Reasons to Run*, edited by S.L. Shames, R.I. Bernhard, M.R. Holman, and D.L. Teele, pp. 75–92. Philadelphia: Temple University Press.

Thomsen, D., and A. King. 2020. “Women's Representation and the Gendered Pipeline to Power.” *American Political Science Review* 114(4): 989–1000.

Thomson, J. 2018. “Resisting Gendered Change: Feminist Institutionalism and Critical Actors.” *International Political Science Review* 39(2): 178–191.

Thomson, J. 2019. “The Women, Peace, and Security Agenda and Feminist Institutionalism: A Research Agenda.” *International Studies Review* 21(4): 598–613.

Tjalma-den Oudsten, H. 2006. *Afgetreden raadsleden: Motieven en ervaringen.* Den Haag: SGBO.

Tremblay, M., and R. Pelletier. 2001. "More Women Constituency Party Presidents: A Strategy for Increasing the Number of Women Candidates in Canada?" *Party Politics* 7(2): 157–190.

TV2. 2020 *Partiernes skjulte overgreb.* Accessed June 13, 2023. https://tv.tv2.dk/partiernes-skjulte-overgreb

United Nations Development Programme & National Democratic Institute for International Affairs. 2012. *Empowering Women for Stronger Political Parties: A Guidebook to Promote Women's Political Participation.* New York: United Nations Development Programme & National Democratic Institute for International Affairs.

Upadhyaya, D.D. 2016. *Integral Humanism: An Analysis of Some Basic Elements.* New Delhi: Prabhat Prakashan.

Vajpayee, A.B. 2000. "Women's Participation in Political Leadership." In *Prime Minister Atal Bihari Vajpayee: Selected Speeches*, vol. 1, pp. 332–336. New Delhi: Ministry of Information and Broadcasting, Government of India.

Valdini, M.E. 2019. *The Inclusion Calculation: Why Men Appropriate Women's Representation.* Oxford: Oxford University Press.

Valentim, V., and E. Dimas. 2024. "Does Party System Fragmentation Affect the Quality of Democracy?" *British Journal of Political Science* 54(1): 152–178.

Vanlangenakker, I., B. Wauters, and B. Maddens. 2013. "Pushed Toward the Exit? How Female MPs Leave Parliament." *Politics & Gender* 9(1): 61–75.

Verge, T. 2012. "Institutionalising Gender Equality in Spain: From Party Quotas to Electoral Gender Quotas." *West European Politics* 35(2): 395–414.

Verge, T. 2015. "The Gender Regime of Political Parties: Feedback Effects Between Supply and Demand." *Politics & Gender* 11(4): 754–759.

Verge, T. 2020. "Political Party Gender Action Plans: Pushing Gender Change Forward Beyond Quotas." *Party Politics* 26(2): 238–248.

Verge, T. 2021. "Legislative Reform in Europe to Fight Violence Against Women in Politics." *European Journal of Politics and Gender* 4(3): 459–461.

Verge, T. 2022. "Too Few, Too Little: Parliaments' Response to Sexism and Sexual Harassment." *Parliamentary Affairs* 75(1): 94–112.

Verge, T. 2023. "'It's the Party, Stupid!': Success of and Resistance to Gender Quotas in Spain." In *Party Politics and the Implementation of Gender Quotas*, edited by S. Lang, P. Meier, and B. Sauer, pp. 341–358. Basingstoke: Palgrave Macmillan.

Verge T. 2024. Feministizising Policymaking in Practice: How Gender and Politics Scholarship Inspires Government Policy, and Vice Versa. *Politics & Gender* 20(4):1015-1021.

Verge, T., and A. Espírito-Santo. 2016. "Interactions Between Party and Legislative Quotas: Candidate Selection and Quota Compliance in Portugal and Spain." *Government & Opposition* 51(3): 416–439.

Verge, T., and E. Lombardo. 2021. "The Contentious Politics of Policy Failure: The Case of Corporate Board Gender Quotas in Spain." *Public Policy and Administration* 36(2): 232–251.

Verge, T., and J. Astudillo. 2019. "The Gender Politics of Executive Candidate Selection and Reselection." *European Journal of Political Research* 58(2): 720–740.

Verge, T., and M. de la Fuente. 2014. "Playing with Different Cards: Party Politics, Gender Quotas and Women's Empowerment." *International Political Science Review* 35(1): 67–79.

Verge, T., and S. Claveria. 2018. "Gendered Political Resources: The Case of Party Office." *Party Politics* 24(5): 536–548.

Verloo, M. 2018. *Varieties of Opposition to Gender Equality in Europe.* London: Routledge.

Vliegenthart, R., S. Walgrave, and C. Meppelink. 2011. "Inter-Party Agenda-Setting in the Belgian Parliament: The Role of Party Characteristics and Competition." *Political Studies* 59: 368–388.

Wäckerle, J. 2022. "Parity or Patriarchy? The Nomination of Female Candidates in British Politics." *Party Politics* 28(1): 10–23.

Wang, V., and R.L. Muriaas. 2019. "Candidate Selection and Informal Soft Quotas for Women: Gender Imbalance in Political Recruitment in Zambia." *Politics, Groups, and Identities* 7(2): 401–411.

Warasin, M., J. Kantola, L. Rolandsen Agustín, and C. Coughlan. 2019. "Politicisation of Gender Equality in the European Parliament: Cohesion and Inter-Group Coalitions in Plenary and Committees." In *Gendering the European Parliament: Structures, Policies, and Practices*, edited by P. Ahrens and L. Rolandsen Agustín, pp. 141–158. London: Rowman and Littlefield.

van de Wardt, M., A. van Witteloostuijn, A. Chambers, and B. Wauters. 2021. "Birds of a Feather Flock Together? The Survival of Underrepresented Groups Within Parliamentary Parties, 1991–2015." *European Journal of Political Research* 60(2): 474–496.

van der Wardt, M. 2015. "Desperate Needs, Desperate Deeds: Why Mainstream Parties Respond to the Issues of Niche Parties." *West European Politics* 38(1): 93–122.

Waylen, G. 2007. *Engendering Transitions: Women's Mobilization, Institutions and Gender Outcomes.* Oxford: Oxford University Press.

Waylen, G. 2014. "Informal Institutions, Institutional Change, and Gender Equality." *Political Research Quarterly* 67(1): 212–223.

Waylen, G., ed. 2017. *Gender and Informal Institutions.* London: Rowman & Littlefield International.

Waylen, G. 2021. "Gendering Political Leadership: Hypermasculine Leadership and Covid-19." *Journal of European Public Policy* 28(8): 1153–1173.

Webb, P., and S. Childs. 2011. "Wets and Dries Resurgent? Intra-Party Alignments Among Contemporary Conservative Party Members." *Parliamentary Affairs* 64(3): 383–402.

Weber, A., M.A. Bodet, F. Gélineau, and A. Blais. 2024. "An Election Too Far: Why Do MPs Leave Politics Before an Election?" *Party Politics* 30(3): 493–504.

Weeks, A.C. 2022. *Making Gender Salient: From Gender Quota Laws to Policy.* Cambridge: Cambridge University Press.

Weeks, A.C., B. Meguid, M. Kittilson, and H. Coffe. 2023. "When Do Männerparteien Elect Women? Radical Right Populist Parties and Strategic Descriptive Representation." *American Political Science Review* 117(2): 421–438.

Weitz, R. 2001. "Women and Their Hair: Seeking Power through Resistance and Accommodation." *Gender and Society* 15(5): 667–686.

Weldon, S.L. 2006. "The Structure of Intersectionality: A Comparative Politics of Gender." *Politics & Gender* 2(2): 235–248.

Weldon, S.L. 2011. *When Protest Makes Policy: How Social Movements Represent Disadvantaged Groups.* Ann Arbor: MI: University of Michigan Press.

Widenstjerna, T. 2020. "Vem väljer vem och varför? Om be tydelsen av homosocialitet och personliga kontakter i partiers nomineringsprocesser." Mid Sweden University. Accessed April 27, 2021. http://urn.kb.se/resolve?urn=urn:nbn:se:miun:diva-37943

Wikstrom, C. 2014. "Sweden Feminists Roar into Political Arena." *Al-Jazeera*, 19 August. https://www.aljazeera.com/features/2014/8/19/sweden-feminists-roar-into-political-arena.

Wiliarty, S.E. 2010. *The CDU and the Politics of Gender in Germany: Bringing Women to the Party.* Cambridge: Cambridge University Press.

Wilson, D.C., L. Branicki, B. Sullivan Taylor, and A.D. Wilson. 2010. "Extreme Events, Organizations and the Politics of Strategic Decision Making." *Accounting, Auditing & Accountability Journal* 23(5): 699–721.

Wolak, J. 2020. "Self-Confidence and Gender Gaps in Political Interest, Attention, and Efficacy." *The Journal of Politics* 82(4): 1490–1501.

Women in the News, "Press release: Limited visibility for women in Lebanese elections coverage," 22 August 2022, available at: https://womeninnews.org/2022/08/press-release-limited-visibility-for-women-in-lebanese-elections-coverage/

World Economic Forum. 2022. "Global Gender Gap Report 2022." Accessed July 1, 2024. https://www.weforum.org/reports/global-gender-gap-report-2022/in-full

Wylie, K.N. 2018. *Party Institutionalization and Women's Representation in Democratic Brazil.* New York: Cambridge University Press.

Wylie, K.N. 2020. "Taking Bread off the Table: Race, Gender, Resources and Political Ambition in Brazil." *European Journal of Politics and Gender* 3(1): 121–142.

Wylie, K.N., P.G. dos Santos, and D. Marcelino. 2019. "Extreme Non-Viable Candidates and Quota Maneuvering in Brazilian Legislative Elections." *Opinião Pública* 25(1): 1–28.

Young, I.M. 2000. *Inclusion and Democracy.* Oxford: Oxford University Press.

Young, L. 2000. *Feminists and Party Politics.* Vancouver: UBC Press.

Yuval-Davis, N. 2006. "Belonging and the Politics of Belonging." *Patterns of Prejudice* 40(3): 197–214.

Yuval-Davis, N. 2007. "Intersectionality, Citizenship and Contemporary Politics of Belonging." *Critical Review of International Social and Political Philosophy* 10(4): 561–574.

Yuval-Davis, N. 2011. *The Politics of Belonging: Intersectional Contestations.* London: Sage Publications.

Yuval-Davis, N., K. Kannabiran, and U. Vieten. 2006. *The Situated Politics of Belonging.* London: Sage Publications.

Zetterberg, P. 2008. "The Downside of Gender Quotas? Institutional Constraints on Women in Mexican State Legislatures." *Parliamentary Affairs* 61(3): 442–460.

Index

For the benefit of digital users, indexed terms that span two pages (e.g., 52–53) may, on occasion, appear on only one of those pages.

The Labors of Resurrection